An Emotional State

Social History, Popular Culture, and Politics in Germany
Kathleen Canning, Series Editor

Recent Titles

Bodies and Ruins: Imagining the Bombing of Germany, 1945 to the Present
    David Crew
The Jazz Republic: Music, Race, and American Culture in Weimar Germany
    Jonathan Wipplinger
The War in Their Minds: German Soldiers and Their Violent Pasts in West Germany
    Svenja Goltermann
Three-Way Street: Jews, Germans, and the Transnational
    Jay Howard Geller and Leslie Morris, Editors
Beyond the Bauhaus: Cultural Modernity in Breslau, 1918–33
    Deborah Ascher Barnstone
Stop Reading! Look! Modern Vision and the Weimar Photographic Book
    Pepper Stetler
*The Corrigible and the Incorrigible: Science, Medicine, and the
    Convict in Twentieth-Century Germany*
    Greg Eghigian
An Emotional State: The Politics of Emotion in Postwar West German Culture
    Anna M. Parkinson
Germany's Wild East: Constructing Poland as Colonial Space
    Kristin Kopp
Beyond Berlin: Twelve German Cities Confront the Nazi Past
    Gavriel D. Rosenfeld and Paul B. Jaskot, Editors
Consumption and Violence: Radical Protest in Cold-War West Germany
    Alexander Sedlmaier
Communism Day-to-Day: State Enterprises in East German Society
    Sandrine Kott
Envisioning Socialism: Television and the Cold War in the German Democratic Republic
    Heather L. Gumbert
The People's Own Landscape: Nature, Tourism, and Dictatorship in East Germany
    Scott Moranda
German Colonialism Revisited: African, Asian, and Oceanic Experiences
    Nina Berman, Klaus Mühlhahn, and Patrice Nganang, Editors
Becoming a Nazi Town: Culture and Politics in Göttingen between the World Wars
    David Imhoof

For a complete list of titles, please see www.press.umich.edu

An Emotional State

*The Politics of Emotion in Postwar
West German Culture*

ANNA M. PARKINSON

UNIVERSITY OF MICHIGAN PRESS
Ann Arbor

First paperback edition 2017
Copyright © 2015 by Anna M. Parkinson

Published in the United States of America by the
University of Michigan Press
Printed and bound by CPI Group (UK) Ltd, Croydon, CR0 4YY

2020   2019   2018   2017   5   4   3   2

A CIP catalog record for this book is available from the British Library.

Library of Congress Cataloging-in-Publication Data

Parkinson, Anna M.
    An emotional state : the politics of emotion in postwar West German culture / Anna M. Parkinson.
        pages   cm. — (Social history, popular culture, and politics in Germany)
        Includes bibliographical references and index.
        ISBN 978-0-472-11968-4 (hardcover : acid-   ISBN 978-0-472-12148-9 (e-book)
        1. Emotions—Political aspects—Germany (West)—History.   2. Emotions—Social aspects—Germany (West)—History.   3. Affect (Psychology)—Germany (West)—History.   4. Social psychology—Germany (West)—History.   5. Germany (West)—Politics and government.   6. Germany (West)—Social conditions.   7. Germany (West)—Intellectual life.   8. Germany (West)—History—Sources.   9. Germany—History—1945–1955.   10. Germany—Social conditions—1945–1955.   I. Title.

    DD258.9.P37   2015
    303.6'60943—dc23

                                                                                    2015014468

    ISBN 978-0-472-03681-3 (pbk. : alk. paper)

Acknowledgments

Although writing is usually a solitary pursuit, the labor of many people, and the residue of different times and places plot a map of gratitude. First of all, I thank Leslie A. Adelson, Dominick LaCapra, Peter Hohendahl, David Bathrick, and Susan Buck-Morss for variously challenging, endorsing, and honing my way of conjuring politics and affect together; it is always a pleasure to think both with and against them. For her unwavering support and intellectual perspicacity, I am indebted to Biddy Martin, who—in spite of her overwhelming commitments—always managed to make time for our discussions. My cohort at Cornell's Society for the Humanities—particularly Jody Blanco, Kim Kono, Joanna Kramer, Catherine Porter, and our indefatigable director, Brett de Bary—gave me a sense of what is meant by intellectual community. In this context, I also thank Helen Petrovsky, intellectual companion extraordinaire and fellow explorer of theories of affect. For their advice, interventions, or just plain good humor at different junctures of the project, I am grateful to my colleagues—many of whom I now count as friends—including Bonnie Buettner, Antke Engel, Ben Frommer, Veronika Fuechtner, Diana Fuss, Gerd Gemünden, Art Gross, Sabine Hark, Bonnie Honig, Irene Kacandes, Tony Kaes, Martina Kerlova, Eric Kligerman, Lutz Koepnick, Alison Lewis, Gunhild Liscke, Franziska Lys, Dan Magilow, Tracie Matysik, David Oels, Georgina Paul, Brad Prager, Karin Remmler, Eric Santner, Helmut Schmitz, Annette Schwarz, Amy Villarejo, Samuel Weber, and Michaela Wünsch.

Northwestern University, now my intellectual home, has been extremely generous in providing me with both the time necessary for the project's completion, as well as financial support through the Dean's Office of the Weinburg College of Arts and Sciences and, most recently and pertinently, by way of a University Research Grant Committee book subvention award. Beyond this, I thank my colleagues in the Department of German for their cordial support and for investing in my research and teaching in and outside of the department. Peter Fenves deserves special mention for his combination of unwavering optimism, timely advice, and intellectual precision; the manuscript workshop he initiated on my behalf provided the critical final impetus for the project's completion. In the context of the workshop I bear a significant debt of gratitude for Rick Rentschler and Johannes von Moltke's canny suggestions and, beyond this, for their ongoing commitment to fostering intellectual exchange; collegiality does not get much better than this. In the Department of German at the University of North Carolina at Chapel Hill, I enjoyed the conviviality of my former colleagues Eric Downing, Jonathan Hess, Alice Kuzniar, Dick Langston, Paul Roberge, Kathryn Starkey, Ruth von Bernuth, and Tin Wegel, as well as generous support for my research from the College of Arts and Sciences and the Provost's Office. To Tina Campt, Emily Cheng, Jay Garcia, Ranjana Khanna, Michelle King, and Mark Sheftall—friends, interlocutors, and fellow travelers in and beyond the walls of North Carolinian institutions of higher education—I value your ongoing presence in my life.

Having a forum for exchange is the essence of academic community. I am appreciative to my colleagues for their invitations to share my work through talks and at conferences at the University of Illinois Urbana Champaign in the Program for Jewish Culture and Society (Michael Rothberg), Indiana University–Bloomington (Claudia Breger and Fritz Breithaupt), Harvard University (Oliver Simmons), Stanford University (Lila Balint), the University of California, Los Angeles (Sam Spinner and Brechtje Beuker), the Boston Psychoanalytic Society and Institute (APsaA), and at Washington University at St. Louis (Ervin Malakaj and the graduate students of the German Department). In Germany, the "History of Emotions" research group at the Max Planck Institute in Berlin provided the testing ground for the dialogue between the history of emotions and affect theory staged in my project. I thank Benno Gammerl, Uffa Jensen, Joachim Haeberlen, and Daniel Wildmann for their conference invitations that facilitated lively intellectual exchange with colleagues specializing in the history of emotion and/or Jewish Studies. Frank Biess, fellow scholar of postwar German emotions, deserves my special thanks for being an advocate of my work and academic endeavors at every turn.

In the German context, my project has benefited significantly from research support in the form of a yearlong postdoctoral fellowship at the Freie Universität Berlin's "Language of Emotions" Excellence Cluster, which gave me invaluable time for writing, an early research grant from the DAAD (Deutscher Akademischer Austausch Dienst) and, more recently, the C.H. Beck Fellowship at the DLA (Deutsches Literaturarchiv Marbach). Closer to home, an academic fellowship at the American Psychoanalytical Association granted me access to national and Chicago-based psychoanalytic forums. Michael Caplan, Kathleen Ross, Charles Amrhein, and Candice Fleishman took extraordinary care with our cohort. It was inspiring to share work across disciplines with fellows from the field of psychiatry; I thank Lisa Madsen, Christina Anston, Emily Gray, and Alexis Armenakis for the pleasure of our punctual conversations. A special thank you is reserved for James M. Herzog for his generous, complex, and moving response to my presentation on German postwar psychoanalysis and affect at the Boston Psychoanalytic Society and Institute.

I thank the DLA in Marbach also for granting me permission to reproduce materials from their collection in my book. I am grateful to the librarians and archivists in Marbach who assisted me with my research, particularly the staff of the Handschriftenabteilung, who were happy to accommodate my archive fever at full pitch. Matthias Mitscherlich kindly gave me permission to cite his father, Alexander Mitscherlich's letters. Likewise, both the Rowohlt Verlag and Harry Rowohlt graciously consented to the reproduction of passages from his father, Ernst Rowohlt's letters. To date all attempts to contact authors of the readers' letters cited in chapter 2 have been unsuccessful.

Working on this book would have been unimaginable without the sustaining camaraderie of friends and family. To my dear friends Chi-ming Yang, Shirin Shenassa, Geoff Winthrop-Young, Sara Wasson, Yasemin Yıldız, Michael Rothberg, Adelheid Voskuhl, Lisa Patti, Sheetal Majithia, Shirleen Robinson, Aaron Moore, Tsitsi Jaji, Doreen Lee, Derek Matson, and Nila Battachartjya—thank you for helping me to keep my balance. For their unfailing ability to make me laugh, my affection and gratitude goes to Susanne Freytag, J-Ho, and Chris Putney. My "alternative family" deserves particular acknowledgment for more reasons than I can list here. Sonja and Emma Boerdner, Torben Lohmüller and Dieter Ingenschay, Sven Brandenburg and family, and Holger Porath and Elke Westermann have my deepest thanks for proving to me, time and again, that Berlin is home. Darcy Buerkle and Yuliya Komska continue to enrich my life with their striking originality, intellectual passion, and sense of the absurd.

My long-distance friends Sven-Erik Rose and Taran Kang I value for being kind, sharp-witted, and immediate. In Chicago, I am fortunate to count among my friends Mimi Brody, Susie Calkins, Jorge Coronado, Scott Curtis, John Alba Cutler, Amy Danzer, Harris Feinsod, Ezra Friedman, Sara Hall, Dacia Harrold, Jana-Maria Hartmann, Kyle Henry, Anna Kornbluh, Andrew Leung, Katharina Loew, Emily Maguire, Cary Nathenson, Cesar Pinto, Alessia Ricciardi, Markus Steinbrecher, Alejandra Uslenghi, Katrin Voelkner, Allen Young, and Shawn Taylor; thank you for keeping me sane. Eric Anderson makes Chicago more than an academic home for me; Sophie and I are affectionately grateful for his presence. I thank Alexander Weheliye, Penny Deutscher, and Nathalie Bouzaglo for their fabulous company. Last, but never least, three cheers to Nick Davis for his Wagnerian efforts at reading many "final" drafts; I treasure him for his thoughtful care, eloquent introductions, and for being in the right place at the right time more than once.

Thank you to my families in Australia, Botswana, and South Africa for their support. In Australia, my sisters Rachael and Bronwen Parkinson, my "bonus" siblings Tanya Shingles, and Tasha and Craig Madden, my mother, Ruth Madden, and my stepfather, James Madden, keep me grounded with their affection, irreverence, and boundless optimism. My deceased father, David Parkinson, my stepmother, Anne Parkinson, my step-brothers Garth and Ross Taylor, and my half-brother Graham Parkinson have been important to me— albeit at a distance. This book is dedicated to my stepfather, Jim, for making sure that important things are said aloud, and equally to my mother, who stayed the distance and showed me how resilience matters.

As a first-time book author, it has been my privilege to work with the wonderful team at the University of Michigan Press. I am grateful to Kevin Rennells for his extraordinary editorial efficiency and warmth. Christopher Dreyer was adept at keeping me in the picture, no matter how much effort was involved. A final, emphatic word of thanks to LeAnn Fields for overseeing the process with great care and an admirable eye for detail, ensuring a smooth passage for the book from beginning to end.

Contents

Introduction: Another Country—Emotions after Freud   I

1   Guilt? Karl Jaspers and the "German Question"   25

2   *Ressentiment:* Democratic Sentiments and the
Affective Structure of Postwar West Germany   67

3   The Inability to Mourn, Terminable and Interminable   113

Conclusion: A Stroll through the Battleground of
Murdered Concepts   147

Notes   169

Index   239

Introduction: Another Country—
Emotions after Freud

> Almost the entire world indicts Germany and the Germans. Our guilt is discussed in terms of outrage, horror, hatred and scorn. Punishment and retribution are desired, not by the victors alone but also by some of the German emigrés and even by citizens of neutral countries. In Germany there are some who admit guilt, including their own, and many who hold themselves guiltless but pronounce others guilty.
>
> —Karl Jaspers, *The Question of German Guilt*

Taken from Karl Jaspers' 1945/46 lectures on the "question of German guilt," the preceding epigraph displays a palette of emotions from the immediate postwar period, including "guilt," "outrage," "hatred," and "scorn." The excerpt suggests that strong and often extremely negative emotions were an integral component of postwar phenomenology, even though they remain the element least thoroughly theorized and most often overlooked in considerations of cultural artifacts from and about this historical period. One intention of this book's concentration on emotions and affect in postwar West German culture is to move our understanding of emotions from the status of descriptors to that of legible social signs in a larger affective structure, with multivalent symptoms, opportunities for creating community or subcultures, and plural sites of political struggle. Episodes from postwar Germany and the fledgling state of the Federal Republic provide the opportunity to "read for emotion" in a vulnerable and volatile ideological landscape. This book's titular phrase "an emotional state" not only refers to the politico-historical specificity of the emergent Federal Republic of Germany in the context of the Cold War but also signals the presence of emotions of historical and ethical significance both preceding and attendant on the founding of the West German state on May 23, 1949.

An Emotional State is a critical endeavor to think through the affective colors and contours of political and psychosocial life in immediate postwar West Germany by deploying the analytical categories of "emotion" and "affective structure." Emotions—their social uses and abuses—supply the lens through which this book views the postwar years from roughly 1945 to 1952, with chapter 3 considering the 1967 text by psychoanalysts Margarete and Alexander Mitscherlich, which has provided a key emotional template for how scholars approach postwar West German culture. I here conceptualize affect and emotion as central sociopolitical forces that both occupy and address the postwar subject in a variety of ways. This book explores a series of vital "scenes" of emotion taken from postwar West German culture under US-Allied control after the official German unconditional surrender on May 8, 1945. In its wider purview, the book analyzes the limits and consequences of the normative role played by emotions in imagining the contours of "reeducated" democratic subjectivity in Allied-occupied postwar West Germany.

Denazification's Primal Scene

Most viewers would have no trouble recognizing Allied journalists' photos of the atrocities in the liberated concentration camps, even if these images address viewers now in a vastly different manner than they did their postwar German counterparts.[1] After the German defeat, the Allies used this constellation of images and documentary footage to stage what I call the primal scene of denazification. Here, Germans came face-to-face, often for the first time, with images of emaciated survivors, serialized corpses, and mass decay from the concentration camps.[2]

Through their wide reproduction and circulation, these images have become what Cornelia Brink terms "icons of extermination."[3] But focusing on these images alone does not tell the full story; indeed, such focus may lead to anachronistic interpretations based more on current norms and values than on the historical context of the images' reception. This scene's insistence on the visual register—a central element of the Freudian primal scene—is doubled by the existence of additional photography and film footage that the Allies took of the German spectators of this material. Thus, for many postwar German viewers, the initial reaction of shock might also have been coupled with an acute awareness of their vulnerability and exposed visibility to an Allied "audience" of reeducators.

In his *Schuldfrage* lectures, Jaspers referred to just such an *Urszene* of photos and captions from the Bergen-Belsen concentration camp, placed on display by the Allied forces in towns and villages across Germany in the summer of 1945. He criticized the US occupation forces for using heavy-handed tactics in accompanying the photos with such text as "Das ist eure Schuld!" (This is your fault! / You are guilty of this!). Disapproving of these shock tactics, he feared that rather than the hoped-for effect of the recognition by German citizens of their guilt and political liability for the Nazi regime, the postings instead solicited a reaction of defensive disavowal. Jaspers' analysis of the "scene" focuses less on the display than on the form of the accusation. In his view, what is uncanny about the posters is their lack of attribution of a source for the postings: "[D]a bemächtigte sich eine Unruhe der Gewissen, da erfaßte ein Entsetzen viele, die das in der Tat nicht gewußt hatten, und da bäumte sich etwas auf: wer klagt mich da an? Keine Unterschrift, keine Behörde, das Plakat kam wie aus dem leeren Raum." ([C]onsciences grew uneasy, horror gripped many who had indeed not known this, and something rebelled: who indicts me there? No signature, no authority—the poster came as though from empty space.)[4] For Jaspers, guilt was a limit state (*Grenzzustand*) that required an addresser and an addressee, even if the subject and the subject's conscience ultimately formed the partnership in this dialogue.

In the most extensive study of the "atrocity films" and their reception to date, Ulrike Weckel examines the documentation of German reactions upon encountering this scene as staged in films screened across Germany, in the Nuremberg trials, and for German prisoners of war interned in Allied camps.[5] Shifting the focus to the German viewer of the images, Weckel calls this score of pictures "shaming images" (beschämende Bilder), arguing for the primary role of shame, rather than guilt, in the visual register of these postwar primal scenes. The staging of this photographic display can be read as an attempt to ignite repulsion for the Nazi dictatorship in German citizens and, simultaneously, as a harsh pedagogical measure fully in line with Allied goals of denazification. A broad spectrum of visible responses was possible, and if spectators did not manifest emotions or gestural responses, it did not necessarily mean that they were left unaffected. Indeed, following shock, the first response was often an involuntary recoiling back on the self that might indicate a defensive posture or be a sign of shame.[6] Reading for emotions in this and similar scenes from the period is further complicated by the multivalence of gestural and verbal articulations.

This is a potent specular scene: the German population is caught looking at images, in turn aware of the critical gaze aimed at them by soldiers of the occupying forces, who have staged the encounter with these images and the accompanying accusatory captions in US-occupied towns across Germany.

The model of the intersubjective response of these spectators captures the dynamics of emotional reflexivity—the way in which certain emotions demand, in turn, an emotional response. As we shall see in the case of postwar Germany, emotional intersubjectivity and emotional reflexivity (or affect responding to affect) become particularly important in situations of crisis that demand an ethical response from an individual. This approach to reading for emotions, without prescribing what we "expect" to see, enables us to glimpse otherwise overlooked affective structures prevalent in postwar West German culture.

Mastering the Past: A Repetition Compulsion?

The focus of *An Emotional State* is not film and photography, nor is it canonical fiction of the postwar era. Rather, to explore the aspect of emotional intersubjectivity, I have chosen three sites, scenes or scenarios that lend themselves to analysis and represent important historical moments in the emotional trajectory of the early Federal Republic of Germany. The "archive of feelings"[7] that gives structure and substance to this book consists of sources ranging across psychoanalytic accounts, philosophical and pedagogical addresses, journal articles, autobiographical narratives, private correspondence, and popular literature of the period. These examples allow me to develop a calibrated analysis of emotions and affective structures across a spectrum of influence in postwar German culture.

Most of these sources are what you might call *Zeitdokumente*, that is, documents contemporary to and often illustrative of their particular time. Except for Ernst von Salomon's autobiographical novel, considered in chapter 2, the sources are concerned less with memory and the past than with the exigencies of their current moment (arguably, von Salomon's book is the most calculatedly aware of the mood of the current moment, even as it is staged as an autobiography). This is not yet another book about *Vergangenheitsbewältigung* and memory, about whether the past has been overcome or mastered and in which way—that is, if the moral balance is just right—although I will critically consider two "classics" from that genre: Jaspers' *Die Schuldfrage* and Alexander and Margarete Mitscherlichs' *Die Unfähigkeit zu trauern* (*The Inability to Mourn*, 1967). This topic has been exhaustively and productively tackled from myriad angles already.[8] Rather, I am interested in the framework established by the discourse of "coming to terms" with the past and its history, inasmuch as this has strongly determined how texts are framed and interpreted in their contemporary context. Each "scene" in my book is an attempt to capture and interpret select elements of a period through examining its affective structure. I consider aspects of the materials that have received less attention, perhaps because they are inarticulate, have been considered less important, or appear to be more ambivalent and thus difficult to weigh on a moral scale.

Norbert Frei argues that German approaches to the National Socialist past are captured through the following periodization: "eine Phase der politischen Säuberung" (a phase of political purging) between 1945 and 1949; "eine Phase der Vergangenheitspolitik" (a phase of politics of the past) from the founding of the Federal Republic up until the late 1950s; "eine lange Phase der Vergangenheitsbewältigung" (a long phase of mastering the past) that concluded at the end of the 1970s; and the phase we have entered since then, "eine Phase der Vergangenheitsbewahrung" (a phase of preserving the past).[9] But historical complexity is less easily captured than Frei's neat and therefore pleasing model would suggest; arguably, the phases Frei designates as that of preserving the past and that of mastering the past share significant overlap. My archive consists of materials from the period of what Frei terms "political cleansing" (re-education and denazification), through the phase of "politics of the past," culminating in the period of "mastering the past," which I consider in an attempt to understand the received image scholars often draw on at this juncture of the first two periods. The immediate postwar years are often characterized as suffering from coldness, or *Gefühlskälte* (Adorno, 1959), and emotional rigidity, or *Gefühlsstarre* (the Mitscherlichs, 1967). Although it is separated from the events of the immediate postwar years by two decades, Alexander and Margarete Mitscherlichs' *Inability to Mourn* is the classic text of this model of frozen affect and emotional "inabilities." With my book, I am interested in "thawing" this emotional landscape by analyzing it on its own terms—that is, putting aside the model of failed melancholia for a reconsideration of emotion and affect—to reveal the dynamics of an intense psychic energy at work in the postwar landscape. Going beyond the guilt paradigm means reading for emotion in the context of affective structures, of which emotion is the legible social aspect. It also means looking for processes of emotional labor that undergird and sometimes even obscure dynamic affective constellations that are ambiguous or difficult to read.

Much earlier on, in a publication from 1946, critical theorist Leo Löwenthal wrote in broad strokes of "the crisis of the individual" through the breakdown of the continuum of the individual's experience in modern society, singling out Germany as a community thoroughly atomized by "terror." He observes of the postwar German population, "They admit the most atrocious crimes, but show not the slightest sense of guilt," and he refers to the response of many Germans toward the Allied occupiers as that of a "continuity of frozen reactions."[10] Significantly, he attributes this frozen quality to the atomizing effects of a political terror structure on individuals in a community. Conjoining a critique of modernity with the structural analysis of recent German history, Löwenthal argues that a terror regime acts on individuals like a series of real or anticipated shocks, curtailing their ability to hope or genuinely feel and reducing members of society to a state of infantile dependency.

Likewise, during a visit to Germany in 1950, Hannah Arendt reflected on this "lack of emotion," "this apparent heartlessness, sometimes covered over with cheap sentimentality": "A lack of response is visible everywhere, and it is difficult to say whether this signifies a half-conscious refusal to yield to grief or a genuine inability to feel."[11] Importantly, Arendt's report manifests an uncertainty at the level of reading emotion—an oscillation before the hermeneutics of emotional intersubjectivity—and thus indicates the complexity and, at times, even opacity of postwar affective structures.

The assumption driving Arendt's and other early accounts about postwar Germany appears to be that if one could read emotions clearly, they might reveal something important about the moral state of German civilians. Reeducation, conceptualized largely as a psychosocial and cultural task, demanded a well-tuned sense of public opinion if democratization were to be successful. This included fostering newspapers and promoting films aimed at the German audience, ostensibly on the basis of their potential to indoctrinate democracy in the population through positive representations of "the American way of life." Jennifer Fay demonstrates, for instance, how the US occupation forces deployed Hollywood film to provide suggestive illustrations of what "fun" democracy could be and the form its performance should take. Fay argues that Hollywood was seen as "a model democratic institution [to be] replicated piecemeal in the American zone." She argues that these films were intended to offer a "mimetic pedagogy" and "to tutor Germans in the gestures, speech, and affect of democratic sociality." Despite the suggestive and creative connections that it enables her to make in her film analyses, Fay's proposed mimetic approach presumes too intimate a link between cause and effect in terms of political and cultural behavior. Further, Fay's account does not pay sufficient attention to mitigating factors impacting on more diffuse affect before it may even be displayed as emotion.[12] It is ultimately unclear how this suggestive course of democratization via mimesis (democratic mimesis?) was intended to take hold of the German population and how (and why) this should occur in a uniform manner.

Postwar accounts seldom neglect to address the emotional disposition of the Germans, either in connection with their mainly miserable living conditions (without food and adequate shelter amid the rubble) or, in a more political vein, as a measure of the country's rue and self-reflexivity. In 1946, Stig Dagerman, a Swedish author assigned to report on postwar life in defeated Germany for the Swedish newspaper *Expressen*, crafted a strikingly perceptive and unusually empathetic account of his firsthand observations, published in his book *Germany in Autumn*. This clear-sighted, sensitive, and sometimes almost tender account gauges personal and political stakes by suspending moral judgment while observing a complex and self-conscious language of affective gestures, as well as acknowledging the suffering of those living among the rubble.

> If any commentary is to be risked on the mood of bitterness towards the Allies, mixed with self-contempt, with apathy, with comparisons to the disadvantage of the present—all of which were certain to strike the visitor that gloomy autumn—it is necessary to keep in mind a whole series of particular occurrences and physical conditions. It is important to remember that statements implying dissatisfaction with or even distrust of the goodwill of the victorious democracies were made not in an airless room or on a theatrical stage echoing with ideological repartee but in all too palpable cellars in Essen, Hamburg or Frankfurt-am-Main. [. . .] People analyse; in fact it is a kind of blackmail to analyse the political leanings of the hungry without at the same time analysing hunger. [. . .] For hunger is a form of unaccountability, not just a physical but also a mental state that leaves minimum space for the leisure of thought. This meant that one naturally heard things which sounded most unattractive but which nevertheless gave one no right to make cocksure prognoses.[13]

Dagerman's account is striking in that it avoids passing moral judgment on the cynicism and apathy he observes among German civilians ("sheer necessity wears down the habit of moralizing on behalf of others").[14] He is invested in understanding the relationship between literature and suffering, although he rewrites the meaning of "poetry" into an ethics of empathy and a hermeneutics of suffering: "Perhaps we can say that simply to suffer with others is a form of poetry, which feels a powerful longing for words. Immediate open suffering distinguishes itself from the indirect kind by, among other things, not longing for words, at least not at the moment at which it occurs. Open suffering is shy, restrained, taciturn."[15] The starkness and honesty of Dagerman's writing convey all the more vividly the complexity of the Germans' emotional state at this bleak historical moment.[16]

American philosopher William Ernest Hocking also understood the complicated semantics of the apparent reluctance among the postwar German population to speak openly about their situation. Of the military defeats and subsequent trials, he writes, "Their total effect, appalling and irresistible, drove the impulse of words, whether for thought or feeling, back into reticence—a reticence which many a dull observer mistook for stolidity or indifference. It was just the reverse."[17] Still, the much-alleged "failure" to exhibit an appropriate measure of the emotion of rue via easily legible signs led to the production of the stereotype of the cold, hard, unfeeling German that we encounter time and again in postwar literature and newspaper reports, such as those cited above. Addressing the obstacles to expressing appropriate emotions in the postwar moment, Hocking questions the desire of the journalistic or reformer's gaze that seeks signs of repentance and of emotional suffering.

> Among the afflictions which the German public had to endure during the first years of recovery was the pest of reportorial investigators seeking "signs of remorse." It is hard to say just what they were expecting to find—whether some modern version of sackcloth and ashes, or at least a prevalent physiognomy of contrition. In any case, not finding it, they raised the question whether Germany was being sufficiently punished. They could not understand that the only "sign" that could concern us was the sign that serious thinking was going on. [. . .] [H]ow else can a deep-going emotional crisis reach its settlement except through long-continued labor of thought?[18]

Hocking, too, recognizes the intertwinement of affect and critical thought, as well as the time necessary for the work of affect and the maturation of thinking. In the wake of the Allied politics of defeat and punishment, he argues, Germans did not evince an inability to feel so much as experience a flood of overwhelming affect to be kept at bay. Thus expressions of discrete emotional signals may have been illegible to the observer or obscured by conflicting emotions.

> It was the free-thinking processes stirred by Defeat and Court—unhurried, unobserved, profoundly passion-filled—that chiefly effected whatever change took place. They were the persistent Backdrop to the stage of our specific activities, of which, on the negative side, denazification was most certainly the most remarkable.[19]

Dagerman and Hocking both argue that emotions may be illegible and remain unarticulated although or even because they are part of a complex affective and even reflective structure. Accounts such as these complicate the ritual condemnation of a postwar German inability to feel or express emotions through appropriate speech, comportment, or gestures.

A contemporary of Dagerman, Morris Janowitz, the founder of military sociology, also had his eye on postwar Germany, particularly on German responses to the revelation of the heinous crimes committed under the Nazi regime. In September 1946, during the period of Dagerman's stay in Germany, Janowitz published an article entitled "German Reactions to Nazi Atrocities,"[20] in which he analyzes the extent of the Germans' awareness of the concentration camps and their function both during wartime and in the postwar period. The resistance with which the population met reports of the Nazi crimes is very much in keeping with the situation Dagerman describes in his series of essays, for Janowitz, too, acknowledges, "The sufferings and the destruction wrought as a result of air warfare were clearly the prime factors in developing this ethical indifference, not so much in the sense that German civilians actually made a practice of equating atrocities in concentration camps with air raids, but rather owing to apathy toward all phenomena outside the immediate personal sphere."[21]

Interestingly, Janowitz is pleasantly surprised to find that this attitude of apathy is replaced by consternation when addressing the persecution of the German Jewish population. In extensive interviews with Janowitz, most Germans remembered "the destruction of Jewish shops and synagogues, the systematic discrimination and final rounding-up and deportation of the Jews from their own community." Although Janowitz was unable to detect a sense of responsibility among those interviewed (it is not clear how he gauged these reactions),[22] he did see demonstrations of shame: "Some Germans were unable to feel any marked hatred against Jews of their own locality. Many deeply religious Germans are now profoundly sensitive in this respect. Some go so far as to lay the blame for the present difficulties of Germany on the mistreatment of the Jews."[23] Janowitz's article, just like the two accounts above, demonstrates how the stated focus on emotion during the years of Allied reeducation intended itself as, in fact, a measure of moral capacity or even a gauge of humanity.

If Dagerman's essays provide explanations for the widespread apathy and indifference among the German population after World War II, Janowitz's brief article returns us to the dilemma of how guilt "should" or even could be expressed in this particularly overdetermined sociohistorical moment. Those interviewed by Janowitz expressed their belief that what might be called the "atrocity campaign" of the US military government proved to be counterproductive in many cases. From their perspective, the link between National Socialism and the abjection of humanity depicted in the photographs from the camps was not made clearly or strongly enough and was delivered solely in punitive terms, with little accompanying analysis. In Janowitz's words, "Our approach, they claimed, was purely negative, since all we attempted to do was to develop a sense of guilt; we offered no means by which the German people could atone for their guilt."[24] Drawing on Weckel's observations of the prevalence of shame rather than guilt in this particular context, I argue that the passage above implicitly expresses shame through the desire for atonement but is also characterized by an easily overlooked tone of anxiety.[25] Further, the emotions considered appropriate to this moment, should they be articulated in the "right way," were no guarantee of critical self-reflection or an ideological change of heart.

Emotion: After Freud

Just how are we to read for emotion in these supposedly monochromatic post-war texts? The working theory of emotions and affect through which I analyze postwar West German culture comes "after Freud."[26] On the one hand, I mean this in the sense of postdating Freud's death in English exile during the Nazi-imposed continental silence on the "Jewish science" of psychoanalysis. On the other hand, I also mean to indicate the project's conceptual debt to Freudian and post-Freudian psychoanalytic accounts of the subject's relation to society's norms. A return to some of Freud's core hermeneutic tools and insights about ambivalence enables a more differentiated reading for emotion in its normative context. Classical Freudian interpretative maneuvers, including symptomatic reading and the interpretation of overdetermination or defense mechanisms, enable a more complex understanding of the vicissitudes of affect and under-score its intersubjective quality. The dynamic aspect of emotional intersubjec-tivity reveals how emotions, rather than being the whole story, form part of larger affective structures.

In the last ten years, there has been a conceptual "emotional" or "affec-tive" turn in fields ranging from media studies to cognitive science; the latter field has been particularly influential in challenging the well-worn binary of reason versus emotion (and similar dichotomies based on this logic, such as male versus female or barbaric versus civilized).[27] Still other theorists use emotion as the critical lens to frame states of feeling in relation to sociopoliti-cal narratives or historical documentation, as in the important recent contribu-tions to the history of emotions by historians William Reddy[28] and Barbara Rosenwein[29] or even earlier, turn-of-the-century sociological accounts by

Georg Simmel that consider emotion as a constitutive element of social bonds within society (*Geselligkeit*).[30] Due to the superabundance of theoretical paradigms in this field, the focus here will be on approaches that engage with cultural-historical aspects of emotion, as well as the nuanced approach to subjectivity at the knot of sociality in (post-)Freudian psychoanalysis. At first blush, this may seem to be an odd coupling, yet it is important to remember that Freud considered the individual subject's fate to be inextricably linked to its conscious and unconscious stance toward the reigning norms of society. Indeed, neurotic symptoms can be read as the stigmata that society unwittingly visits on the individual.

By dint of choosing emotions and affect as the mode of approach to the public culture of the embryonic Federal Republic, the methodological emphasis of this book falls on the "feeling" individual embedded in social structures. In my account, emotions are understood less as expressive outward manifestations of a subject's interiority than as an integral "hinge" or interface between the individual and society. To this end, I make an analytical distinction between "emotion" and "affect," thus departing from orthodox Freudian psychoanalysis. In his annotations to the collected works of Freud, editor James Strachey felt that the confusion caused by the indiscriminate use of the words *Affekt*, *Empfindung*, and *Gefühl* warranted extended commentary.[31] Strachey notes the problems that these terms pose when translated into English: "These three words have different meanings when they are used strictly: 'affect' (not an everyday English word), 'sensation,' and 'feeling' (or 'emotion')." He goes on to say, "The trouble here is that all these words in both languages cover very uncertain ground, and that the meanings of the German and English words do not coincide but overlap."[32] The confusing sensation of standing on uncertain definitional ground is compounded by the fact that, as Strachey states, "Freud himself had flexible views on the use of these words."[33]

Engaging this productive lack of terminological clarity in Freudian psychoanalysis for my definition of the terms *affect* and *emotion*, I suggest qualities that distinguish between the two terms. By doing this, I hope to do justice to Freud's broader insights into sociopsychological processes and formations, while also allowing for the specific historical context of postwar West Germany. My project clearly does not deal with clinical diagnoses of case studies; rather, it employs inference and interpretation to fathom the social implications of emotion and structures of affect in selected West German cultural artifacts and institutions.

Recently deceased French psychoanalyst André Green dedicated most of his career to adumbrating and extending what he saw as the overlooked and simplified reception of the role of affect in and beyond Freudian psychoanalytic theory. In contradistinction to his training analyst Jacques Lacan, who rejected the centrality of affect for psychoanalysis, Green places affect at the center of psychoanalytic practices of interpretation. Green's postwar theories of affect emphasize its dynamic qualities and its "capacity to seep into other domains and inhabit them," where it "transform[s] both itself and the products of the area of the mind which it has occupied."[34] Green also emphasizes the definitional centrality of "force" in the modern usage of the term *affect*, saying, "[force] is essential to affect . . . [and] accounts for the potentially disorganizing aspect of affect whether it appears suddenly, unnoticed, or, as it spreads, accumulates, pervades, and eventually takes hold of vast areas of the mind."[35]

Drawing on Green's clarification and extension of Freud's remarks on the subject, I define affect as a force that structures a subject without necessarily finding resolution in socially recognizable and linguistically legible emotion. There are, of course, moments of overlap between the two terms in this usage, and perhaps emotion might rightly be considered as "congealed" affect, or the form affect takes once it becomes socially and linguistically inhabitable and able to be described as a particular state that the conscious subject experiences. While affect manifests itself in individuals, groups, and institutions, it often distinguishes itself by being in excess of the individual subject or situation; it is not this or that emotion, then, but a process or movement of fluctuating and undifferentiated emotion(s). Affect, inasmuch as it is in excess of the subject, cannot be delimited as an emotion "belonging" to a subject. Thus affective structures are, by definition, difficult to describe, to inhabit, or, by extension, to control.

Although his understanding of feeling is drawn from a cognitive psychological model, William Reddy's concept of an "emotive" goes some way to illustrate the mutability of emotion. Particularly due to his concentration on its expressive and linguistic aspect, Reddy's concept does not map neatly onto the distinction made above between "emotion" and "affect," but it does describe one kind of movement that takes place at the threshold between socially legible expression and the movement of feeling itself. An "emotive" is defined by Reddy as a type of speech act that differs from a constative or performative utterance but nonetheless describes and acts on the world, "because emotional expression has an exploratory and a self-altering effect on the activated thought material of emotion."[36] Put otherwise, for Reddy, an "emotive" would be a speech act at the threshold between socially encoded expressions of emotion and what he calls, in his cognitivist-tinged vocabulary, the more inchoate "material of emotion."[37] The performative valence of Reddy's "emotive" thus comes close to describing the transformative movement between "affective structures" and "emotions," although the purely linguistic nature of an "emotive" does not take into account nonlinguistic signifiers such as gestures, which also beg interpretation.

The distinction I make between "affect" and "emotion" enables questions such as the following: Under which circumstances and how does affect manifest itself? Is it a strong response to a morally circumscribed situation in which certain socially legible emotions are prescribed while others are foreclosed or marked as morally corrupt or suspicious? In other words, what happens when the manifestation or expression of certain emotions become a matter of moral regulation through which certain forms of subjectivity become legible? Under which circumstances may affect be exhibited in an articulate form as emotions—negative or positive—open to moral scrutiny or, its interiorized equivalent, superegoic surveillance?[38] Finally, how are affect and emotion "read" by Germans and the US-Allied military forces in postwar West Germany under the auspices of denazification, reeducation, and democratization? Which emotions are appropriate or even encouraged under these circumstances, and which unwanted emotions might emerge as a response to this historical moment?

In practice, the analytical distinction between "affect" and "emotion" may seem blurred or even nonexistent; in theory—and in examining the sources I have referenced for this book—this distinction is vital for underscoring the normative and social role that emotions play in everyday life, which is even more starkly evident in a state of exception, such as that of postwar Germany in its so-called zero hour.[39] This sometimes inarticulate affective intensity may well be what is encountered after (or even during) seismic events, before a situation has been "put into words" or given structure and direction through its narrative form (the etymological root of narrative is the Latin *gnarus*, which means "to know"). At times, this intense affectivity may elude capture by an emotional descriptor, because the state is so diffuse or perhaps because sensorial and psychological excess works to actively suspend feeling. It is important to keep this distinction in place when analyzing the postwar West German context—and, most likely, any situation that thoroughly undoes a nation or community. Although emotion may not be expressed or otherwise evident in unambiguous, recognizable forms, this does not mean that affect, as such, is absent. Even the feeling of numbness is a sign that affective activity is present yet remains screened.

The term *affect theory* is often used to denote the materialist writings of Deleuzian-Spinozist political philosopher Brian Massumi or, even earlier on, the work of psychologist Silvan S. Tomkins[40] on what Ruth Leys calls the "basic emotion" model.[41] This is precisely the path not taken in this book. Despite what initially appear to be similarities between Massumi's and my own definitions of affect and emotion, the respective accents ultimately fall elsewhere. Potentiality and virtuality of affect as bodily or sensorial intensity is the prime focus of Massumi's work on affect.[42] In his book *Parables for the Virtual*, he defines emotion as "recognized affect" and "the sociolinguistic fixing of the quality of an experience [. . .] into function and meaning"; however, his understanding of emotions as "subjective content" and "personal" reveals how he reads emotions as a paradigm of expressed interiority, and his interest is diverted by affect before he reaches the question of the political and normative dimensions of emotions.[43] Elsewhere in the same book, he defines the divide between affect and emotion in terms of modality: "emotion is contextual," and "affect is *trans-situational*."[44] This distinction illustrates Massumi's concern with tracing an ontology of affect through an examination of the sensorial body. In contradistinction to his focus, my book is concerned with elaborating epistemologies of emotion that enable readers to trace and examine the normative valence of particular emotions in their sociopolitical context.

Emotions are part of a social lifeworld, which means that they are also potentially political. Here, I do not use the term *political* to refer to a literal engagement with traditional political forums, such as party addresses or parliamentary discussions, although affect often plays a significant role in these venues. In this context, *political* is defined in terms of how the norms and mores promulgated by a society impact its community. Norms of conduct or social structures often remain "invisible" to the individual, appearing to the subject as "natural" or "common sense"—two expressions that usually signal the point at which analysis should begin. Forms of behavior seem to be natural or second nature to the subject because the individual has "inhabited" these norms from childhood onward. Again, it is in moments of social crisis—the breakdown of "business as usual"—that norms reveal themselves as social expectations, through the radical reconfiguration or even dissolution of the social environment in which they were rooted. This realization is prompted by a sudden awareness of an uncanny or even traumatic alterity in a familiar environment or situation—an alienation effect, if you will—that displaces the subject's point of view (or makes subjects aware that they occupy a certain attitude toward their world in the first place). Arguably, the defeat of Germany was such a moment of revelatory crisis. Perhaps, solely in this sense, the concept of "zero hour" is entirely applicable to capturing the shriveling of norms and the moral and political vacuum in which the German population found itself, at the very latest, in May 1945.

Emotions are notoriously unstable "objects" of study; they demand creative ways of seeing (or of thinking about) "feeling" in order to be understood as more than a spontaneous subjective phenomenon or a score of hardwired neurological responses. Pierre Bourdieu's concept of "habitus" provides a useful impetus for capturing the feeling subject in its social embeddedness. Sociologist Deborah Gould draws on Bourdieu's term to coin the phrase *emotional habitus*, which describes "a social grouping's collective and only partly conscious emotional disposition" and the "socially constituted prevailing ways of feeling and emoting, as well as the embodied, axiomatic understandings and norms about feelings and their expression."[45] The emphasis on the link between politics, emotions, and normative practice suggested by Gould's refurbishment of Bourdieu's term provides a useful heuristic for examining this juxtaposition of historical snapshots from the postwar West German archive.

In a series of heated debates about "the German question" during the war years, the US-Allied powers were already drafting a much-disputed pedagogy for a new democratic "fantasy of the normal" intended to convert Germany from its fascist fantasies of the past twelve years.[46] The form taken by this "fantasy" depended on your perspective: for the US-Allied forces, it was the educational impetus toward installing a democratic political system along with democratic sentiments and comportment in the inhabitants of the US military zone. The affective norms and investments exhibited through this process of repoliticization, as well as the relationship between ethics and emotion, come under scrutiny in the chapters to follow.

Several conceptual "tools" gleaned from historians of emotion have helped me to think through the nexus between emotion and normativity in this period.[47] William Reddy defines the "emotional regime" constitutive of any political system as "the set of normative emotions and the official rituals, practices, and emotives that express and inculcate them."[48] In the context of postwar West Germany, this entails identifying latent and explicit emotional norms and affective structures taken to indicate the measure of the postwar subject's shifted investment from authoritarian to democratic comportment. Theodor W. Adorno's famous psychosociological investigation of the "authoritarian personality" susceptible to (and structured by) fascist thought, which is based on the premise that particular forms of subjectivity are requisite or even sustained by specific political ideologies, clearly resonates with this prevalent manner of thought.[49] For Reddy, an "emotional refuge" describes forms of comportment or expression coexistent with hegemonic modes and harbors the potential to either support or undermine the "emotional regime."[50] The second chapter in this book will explore the West German "emotional refuge" offered by the "nonpublic" expression of popular *ressentiment* toward the Allied victors—

specifically the American soldiers—which I argue was a significant element of the particular texture of democracy in the wake of the German defeat and occupation.

If reference to an "emotional regime" emphasizes aspects of normativity, power, and the practice of emotional maintenance through the articulation of contextually appropriate emotional styles and speech acts ("emotives") for assessing emotion's role in social formations, medieval historian Barbara Rosenwein's concept of "emotional communities" instead concentrates on how emotions bind people together. Rather than staging a vertical hierarchy, as is suggested by Reddy's model, Rosenwein offers a horizontal model of sometimes overlapping circles to depict the multiplicity of communities bound together by different emotional practices.[51] In my book, then, the concept of "emotional regime" usually references Allied reeducation, whereas the term *community* is used to emphasize the role of empathic identification that fuses a group together in an affective structure.

Analyzing "emotional states" at a particular historical moment warrants careful attention to context and form. To avoid anachronistic semantic pitfalls as much as possible, I have attempted to tease out what is meant by a particular emotion by examining the context from which it arises. Buttressed by archival materials and through close readings of a variety of texts from the period, I have attempted to capture the affective context in thick brushstrokes. Each emotion is taken on its own contextual terms, in an effort to remain faithful to the implied understanding of the emotion in the discourse itself. Each emotion takes place in a "scene" comprised of an important event or series of happenings organized around prominent public figures.

Certain postwar emotional comportments and expressions become legible as this or that particular emotion, be it guilt, grief, resentment, or anxiety, although these emotions describe vastly different states: some take an object, such as guilt, and others take themselves as their primary object, as with *ressentiment*, whereas anxiety is characterized by its lack of a concrete object. Most of the "protagonists" in my book either directly name an emotional state or affective constellation, as with the "inability to mourn" in Alexander and Margarete Mitscherlichs' book, or imply an emotional state, such as with the affective structure of *ressentiment* in Ernst von Salomon's case. Most significant, however, are how an emotion is staged in a text and what effect the emotion has both within and beyond its textual context.

There is a performative aspect to emotion, as I have suggested above in the example of shame, where the performance of the emotion is not meant for the eye of the public yet needs a public (real or imagined) in order to take place at all. The "staged" nature of emotion is indicated by the descriptors used by theoreticians of emotion to capture their socially contoured, repetitive form: *narrative processes*, *emotional scripts*,[52] and *emotives*.[53] Bearing in mind that emotions are never simply expressions of subjective interiority but also may serve a normative function as sociopolitical markers of "community" or a particular "regime" of feeling, this book does not investigate the source or substance of emotions but instead asks after the sociopolitical implications attached to particular emotions in their historical context.

Emotional Stakes

The paradigm of "emotion" was part of the discourse of "coming to terms with the past" from its inception. Ranging from the observations made by Allied soldiers and journalists in the immediate postwar years to the highly charged and almost ritual debates about Germany's relationship to the past (for example, the Goldhagen affair or the *Historikerstreit*), emotion has played a major role, implicitly or explicitly. Two emotional cultures in particular have been central for scholars of postwar German culture: that of guilt and that of an "inability to mourn." The normative aspects of "guilt" and the seeds of the thesis of the "inability to mourn" are touched on in this introduction. The pedigree of both of these models, including their substantial overlap, will be the subject of all three chapters in this book. Chapter 1, on Karl Jaspers' *Schuldfrage* lectures, pays special attention to "guilt," and chapter 3, on the Mitscherlichs' eponymous book, attends especially to "the inability to mourn."

These interpretative paradigms have been extremely productive frameworks for scholarship on Germany after World War II, although they often remain largely unexamined as frameworks.[54] For example, the persistence of the paradigm of a ubiquitous postwar silence has its roots in the aforementioned accounts of German emotionlessness caused by, at best, repression or, at worst, active forgetting[55] of guilt (and other intersubjective emotions that are morally weighted).[56] Robert Moeller and other historians have disproven the hypothesis of a postwar silence about the past, arguing that the past was talked about, though selectively and with the aim of constructing a "useable past."[57] This is not to say that all topics were addressed directly and openly in the postwar period;[58] further, in postwar German scholarship, a shift of analytical perspective was required in order to "hear" previously unacknowledged voices.[59] For instance, the establishment of gender and sexuality as legitimate fields of study opened up many fruitful research vistas, challenging a reticence seemingly intrinsic to the field itself.[60]

By shifting the analytical lens to that of emotion and affect, I ask the reader to reconsider epistemological certainties we associate with postwar Germany. In chapter 3, this takes the form of addressing the second prevalent emotional paradigm in postwar contributions to the field of German studies— that of mourning and melancholia, framed as the notorious German "inability to mourn." The paradigm of mourning and melancholia has become a key interdisciplinary model used to analyze modernity and its discontents.[61] In the field of German studies, this has typically involved thinking in terms of the Mitscherlichian "inability to mourn," which is often read to mean that after World War II, German society's prime emotional habitus was that of blocked mourning. This produces a type of research that I term "melancholic scholarship," which is considered in more detail in the same chapter.[62]

Critiques of the Mitscherlichian paradigm have been rare in the field of German studies; Anke Pinkert's book on postwar East German DEFA (Deutsche Film-Aktiengesellschaft) film is a welcome exception. Pinkert offers valuable insight into cultural production and the working through of postwar loss in the "other" German state, the German Democratic Republic. Analyzing a selection of DEFA films in terms of the complex memory work they perform, Pinkert argues against the premise of the "the inability to mourn" in the East German context. Pointing to the limits of the trauma paradigm,[63] she argues for an analysis of "historically more mute and affectively charged modes of loss."[64] Pinkert makes a case for "reparative" memory work that does not devalue melancholic modes as asocial or abnormal practices. Recognizing the "limited public sphere of death" afforded to the postwar German population, she analyzes the negotiation of a "virtual public sphere" through early DEFA film productions.[65]

I applaud Pinkert's desire to explore "the German experience of war-death and destruction" by drawing on the lesser-examined "archive of feelings" (Cvetkovich, see note 7 above) of postwar DEFA films, and I strongly second her contestation of long-standing taboos associated with postwar memory and mourning. But my approach has a different focus. In this book, I am interested less in specifically recuperating the category of loss or melancholia from the shadow of mourning than with examining the normative valence of emotional states and unacknowledged or overlooked affective structures in the discourses of emotion that make up the fabric of the nascent West German postwar public sphere.

Emotional States: Toward a Politics of Emotion

A number of questions have guided this project and determined the archive I have chosen for it. When reading for emotion in postwar texts, what is the relationship between emotion and affective structures? How does the constellation of emotions and intensities constitutive of affect complicate our understanding of the postwar emotional landscape? What are the normative presuppositions attached to particular emotions such as mourning and guilt in the postwar period? What form does the relationship between emotion, normativity, and moral judgment take in the nascent postwar public sphere? Where and how does a politics of emotion play itself out in postwar West German culture?

My archive is selective, rather than exhaustive. I have chosen three exemplary "scenes" of postwar public debate from the immediate postwar period into the Adenauer era. Each chapter analyzes a specific emotion or affective constellation associated with a public figure who helped to "make emotional history" in postwar West Germany. All three chapters are also organized around exemplary discourses of emotion in circulation at different moments of the postwar years. The chapters could be categorized according to emotions (guilt, *ressentiment*, "inability to mourn"), for the public figures they discuss (philosopher Karl Jaspers, author Ernst von Salomon, psychoanalysts Alexander and Margarete Mitscherlich), or based on the primary texts under analysis (*Die Schuldfrage, Der Fragebogen, Die Unfahigkeit zu trauern*). The scenes under consideration cover social discourses and disciplines, including, respectively, philosophy, fiction and autobiography, and psychoanalysis. More pertinent than these categories is the "event" represented by these texts and their reception; by drawing on archival resources, I have attempted to reconstruct the affective temperature and reigning emotional discourses of each event and to demonstrate their importance for understanding the emotional state of postwar West Germany at the juncture of defeat, during the initial years of the fledgling democratic Federal Republic, and just after the Adenauer era. It is important to keep in mind that each of these "scenes" represents a different historical encounter with emotional norms. Thus each scene calls for a different combination of analytical tools to bring out the specific affective constellations, moral emotions, and aftereffects of each event.

The first scene, already touched on earlier in this introduction, takes us to a crowded lecture hall of the recently reopened Heidelberg University, in which Karl Jaspers gave his postwar lectures on guilt in 1945/46. This scene is exemplary in its display of the navigation of nascent emotional norms and expectations under Allied command. Although references to emotions abound in Jaspers' lectures, they remain secondary to his existential (*existenzphilosophisches*) concept of communication as a potential site of community and open exchange. No friend of psychoanalysis, which he called "totalitarian" despite his early training as a psychiatrist and his emphasis on communication in his philosophy, Jaspers turned to Kantian *Verstand* as a guiding model for his philosophy of communication. His lectures on guilt are characterized by what his former student Dolf Sternberger termed an "erstarrte Unruhe"—his calm yet urgent appeal to critical reason—even as this address is routed through an emotive pedagogical appeal to his audience, many of whom were returned soldiers. Reading for affective tonality in this text entails shifting the focus of interpretation to the perlocutionary function of his delivery, by examining rhetorical gestures in his text alongside several firsthand accounts from members of his audience.

Narrowing the scope of analysis to emotional expressions of "guilt" in Jaspers' lectures overlooks how his rationalism acts as a defense against a complex affective structure of shame, doubt, and, ultimately, frustration. This structure is obscured by his sober analysis of guilt, but it comes to the fore in his correspondence with his former student and then friend and postwar interlocutor Hannah Arendt. Taken in the context of their exchange of letters, parcels, and articles, the lectures on guilt are both an extended dialogue with Arendt about his fears for Germany and a demonstration of his awareness of emotional intersubjectivity—or how affects interact and circulate in public forums. Emotion is not only descriptive but also prescriptive when considering the normative sentiments constitutive of the idealized "reeducated" postwar West German democratic subject. Through an exploration of guilt in Jaspers' lectures and of the underground structure of anxieties and shame that this discourse obscures, chapter 1 demonstrates the limits of emotion understood as a norm, or a legible social text with a prescriptive function. This chapter also makes the argument for an understanding of affective structures in postwar Germany as dynamic and mutable, rather than static and immobile.

The second scene highlighted in this book took place in 1951 among an animated group of people crowded together for an event in a waiting room at the main railway station in Cologne. The occasion was a heated discussion with former conservative revolutionary Ernst von Salomon about his postwar best seller *Der Fragebogen*, one in a series of public lectures and debates at the Kölner Mittwochgespräch. Emotions ran high as participants dismantled the book's ethos of passivity and demanded answers to the question of what the political task of the postwar writer should be. On its release, von Salomon's book, a spirited yet cynical autobiography written under the guise of a series of responses to the 131 questions found in the US-Allied denazification question-naire, became an instant best seller in West Germany and was sought after and translated by international publishers. Although von Salomon and his book have fallen into near oblivion today, the reception of the book by the interna-tional press in the early and middle 1950s generated much excitement, as von Salomon's work was thought of as dangerously explosive and potentially de-stabilizing in the context of the nascent West German democracy.

At the time of the book's release, it was heralded as the first German pub-lication attempting to reckon with the period of Nazi Germany (as well as for revealing terrifying aspects of the German psyche, according to reviewer T. H. Minshall).[66] Historian Hugh R. Trevor-Roper, known at the time for his 1947 book *The Last Days of Hitler*, frames the postwar German politico-cultural environment primarily through emotion in his article "The Germans Reap-praise the War."[67] In addressing the publication of apologia by almost all levels of public figures under Nazism, Roper diagnoses the changes in German soci-ety as "profound emotional alterations" in the period between the German de-feat and the present moment of 1952.[68] He proposes to examine existing publi-cations on Nazi Germany and the postwar period not in terms of their historical veracity but to gauge "the changing political climate of Germany since Hitler's death."[69] Needless to say, this included assessing the affective climate of the German people based on the publications he examined.

The dearth of "objective" scholarly literature on this period, Trevor-Roper argues, has to do not only with an avoidance of the facts but also with the un-availability of the necessary German documents that remained quarantined by the Allied powers, an act that he judges to be shortsighted on their part, as the Germans have instead produced "not objective or expository" accounts of Na-tional Socialism but, rather, texts that are "autobiographical, reminiscent, apol-ogetic."[70] Trevor-Roper maintains that texts like these provide evidence of an-other kind, namely, of "continuous malaise and of clearly discernible shifts."[71] Mood is the guiding thread of interpretation used here for charting the altera-tions in the West Germans' postwar mentality. According to Trevor-Roper, the leading tone of the time is that of "malaise," a general feeling of being uncom-fortable or ill at ease in one's environment. Not an emotion proper, "malaise" is made up of a variety of vague and constantly competing emotions that act to create the discomfort and psychic deracination of the subject.

Why do postwar German citizens express malaise? Trevor-Roper locates the basis of this feeling in their attitude toward Nazism: "At no time since the war have German writers shown themselves comfortable either in support of Nazism or in opposition to it. On the other hand, the mood which they represent has undergone, in seven years, significant change."[72] Trevor-Roper charts this "mood" (his preferred term for affect) in publications throughout 1946–48, arguing that they evinced "revulsion—hatred of Hitler, disillusion with all the broken promises of Nazism, disgust at its suddenly admitted brutality, indignation at its folly and frivolity, repudiation of its works," while simultaneously glorifying the anti-Nazi "resistance" of July 20, 1944. At this time, German books were mostly published abroad and were characterized by "the gloom and nostalgia of German sentiment."[73] This veritable flood of negative emotions demonstrates the complexity of the emotional environment in postwar Germany, which cannot easily be reduced to one particular or even a consistent set of emotions (or, according to the Mitscherlichs, the lack thereof).

Once the German printing houses reopened in 1947, many books by former military officers were published. These books demonstrated a strong leaning toward autobiography and were characterized by nationalist sentiment and an apologetics for militarism. Calling 1949–50 the "years of the generals," Trevor-Roper defines 1951–52 as the "years of the politicians," and he charts a steady reappearance of nationalism, aided by the continuity of anti-Russian sentiment in the West.[74] He finds this turn to nationalism embodied most spectacularly in Ernst von Salomon's *Der Fragebogen*. Trevor-Roper rightly identifies the narcissism supporting this type of literature, which he claims is "not read in Germany for truth, but for comfort."[75] However, more than comfort alone may be obtained by reading von Salomon's text. It offers the opportunity for identification with a wide range of emotions and their attendant political valences, offering up the space for a community of *ressentiment* characterized by the resentment displayed by von Salomon's narrator toward democratic US-Allied forces and totalitarian National Socialists alike.

Trevor-Roper errs about *Der Fragebogen*'s lack of truth. Its reader is exposed to the "truth" of a host of emotional and political attitudes that clearly found strong resonance with some segments of the postwar West German population. To overlook the role played by this constellation of ambivalent, destructive emotions is to underestimate what von Salomon's book and its reception teach us about the politics of emotion and the battles of democratic sentiment in early postwar West Germany. It is to this pedagogical end that I turn to a lesser-known culture of debate in the 1950s in postwar West Germany, using von Salomon's appearance and presentation of his arguments for his book as a kind of litmus test for the struggle of politics with and against emotion in the public sphere at that time.

Complementing a symptomatic reading for emotion in the text with an analysis of the book's reception in its historical context reveals an affectively turbulent image of the first years of the new Federal Republic. In particular, von Salomon's account of his "erroneous imprisonment" by the US-Allied forces demonstrates a deeply ingrained structure of *ressentiment*. The term *ressentiment* has its philosophical roots in the writings of Nietzsche, who used it as a focal point for his inquiry into a constellation of affective intensities, emotions, and comportment. In my redeployment, *ressentiment* arises from a state of disavowed guilt that enables subjects to seek pleasure in what they perversely see as their own suffering at the hands of others. The resentful subject, envious of the victim status of the other, co-opts this position for itself.

In contrast to those contemptuous of von Salomon's novel and wary of its effect in the new democracy, a large group of readers felt vindicated by the book's open expression of otherwise suppressed or disavowed feelings of anger, disappointment, and envy in relation to the German defeat and the "imported" Allied democracy. Letters to von Salomon and his publisher Ernst Rowohlt at the time of the book's publication indicate a deep disaffection with what was perceived as an "emotional regime" of democracy imposed by the Allies. Through strong identification with the experiences of the author/narrator and, at a less conscious level, with structures of *ressentiment* manifest in the book, the correspondents can be seen as members of an emotional subculture: a community of *ressentiment*. I read the discussion and criticism of Ernst von Salomon's book at the Kölner Mittwochgespräch as a test case for democratic processes of debate and tolerance. Once again, affect responds to affect, with *ressentiment* confronting democratic sentiments in a test of the resilience of the nascent public sphere in the recently founded Federal Republic.

The third chapter of this book considers the postwar scene of psychoanalysis in the Federal Republic through a return to psychoanalysts Alexander and Margarete Mitscherlichs' seminal text *Die Unfähigkeit zu trauern* (*The Inability to Mourn*). Published in 1967, the Mitscherlichs' book is an early treatise on postwar emotions and their sociopolitical repercussions. In their account, postwar German culture is depicted as emotionally stagnant, with the citizens of the Federal Republic invested solely in the *Wirtschaftswunder* and the successful economic reconstruction of Germany. The Mitscherlichs' focus on emotional "inabilities" obscures other key emotions and affective structures at work and casts "mourning" as the ideal normative emotional comportment, in this way overlooking or underplaying other structures and dynamics at work, such as those outlined in chapters 1 and 2 of the present study. By imposing a rigid moral code as to what the appropriate emotional comportment for the citizens of postwar West Germany might be, the Mitscherlichs enact their own rage and disappointment with the Federal Republic, while also ignoring the principle of intersubjective empathy on which the psychoanalytic model is based. Focusing on the concept of "inability" and the productive categories of taboo and *ressentiment* expounded in a neglected essay in the Mitscherlichs' multichapter book, I argue for a more subtle and complex exploration of the normative role played by emotions in prescribing "correct" moral comportment in the immediate postwar period in West Germany. Chapter 3 also addresses Alexander Mitscherlich's instrumental role in bringing psychoanalysis back to West Germany and shows how, counter to popular assumptions about psychoanalysis' ahistoricity, the Mitscherlichs' deployment of Freud acts to historicize their project and demonstrates the symbolic capital of the discourse of psychoanalysis at this juncture in time.

The inclusion of a chapter on the Mitscherlichs' book may seem anachronistic at first blush. However, any book attempting to explore the "politics of emotion" in West Germany could not do without an analysis of the longer-term influence of their hypothesis on normative assumptions about emotions and their moral consequences. Their text's publication in 1967 was a foundational event for what I call the "politics of emotion." The habitual referencing of this text as the standard source of knowledge on postwar emotional states, both within and beyond the academy, proves just how political emotions can be. It could be said that this text contributed strongly to normalized thinking about emotions in moral and political terms in the first place.

In my attempt in this book to explore "the fantasy of normalcy"[76] in postwar West German culture, I read for emotions at a number of levels: lexical deployment, representations of "expressed emotion," textual or narrative use of emotion, affective structures inferred and unmasked through symptomatic reading, perlocutionary and phatic affect, and tonalities of emotion. Phrased slightly differently, I ask after the trajectories of certain emotions—specifically guilt, mourning, and *ressentiment*—through a practice of reading for emotion. I consider the intended and actual work performed by these emotions amid their contemporary debates, devoting particular attention to emotion's political and social valence in the postwar public sphere of West Germany. In this endeavor, I will be arguing that to understand what emotions are, we have to comprehend what they do.[77]

CHAPTER 1

Guilt? Karl Jaspers and the "German Question"

> The most extreme slogan which this war has evoked among the Allies, that the only "good German" is a "dead German," has this much basis in fact: the only way in which we can identify an anti-Nazi is when the Nazis have hanged him. There is no other reliable token.
> —Hannah Arendt, "Organized Guilt"

> When Germany attains self-awareness, it will not only be free—at first spiritually and thus then also politically free—it will also be happy.
> —Walter Dirks, "The Path to Freedom: A Contribution to German Self-Awareness"

Perhaps the most volatile and salient public and political feeling in the immediate postwar years in Germany was that of guilt. The feeling was salient because the Allied victors expected this to be the appropriate response in the face of the crimes of the Third Reich; it was volatile because the defeated population was a constituency defined by the heterogeneity of their experiences during the past twelve years, which influenced their affective response to the aftermath of National Socialism in unpredictable ways. Karl Jaspers' 1946 text *Die Schuldfrage* (*The Question of German Guilt*) remains a seminal contribution to the topic of guilt in postwar Germany.[1] In a slender text of just over one hundred pages, Jaspers identifies and analyzes four categories of guilt and formulates his own philosophical response to the "German question." Those four categories of guilt—criminal, political, moral, and metaphysical—are, in part, analytical distinctions made by Jaspers that enable him to differentiate between moral and political dimensions of guilt and liability.[2] In addition to Jaspers' valiant attempt to address the different forms and consequences of guilt accruing to the German population in the wake of the Nazi dictatorship and Jewish genocide, the text, in its context, is a repository for affect. At first blush, both

the analysis of guilt and its delivery in Jaspers' ostensible tone of calm rationality, which is foregrounded in the text, appear unrelated to or uninterested in
the emotional stakes at play in the affective structure of guilt. Indeed, if "guilt"
is to be recognized as a feeling at all in this text, it appears in the guise of an
explicit normative comportment vis-à-vis the crimes of the past and the Allied
present, as part of the "emotional regime" of reeducation.[3] Indeed, the text argues for calm reasoning and rationality and is presented as an objective philosophical analysis of guilt in its various facets.

   This demeanor of rationality and the call for sober assessment certainly
seem to be valid responses in the wake of the overt mobilization of the population's emotions to deadly ends by racist National Socialist ideology. Jaspers'
particular staging of rationality was, no doubt, meant to work as an antidote to
fascist intoxication in the political climate of the Allied occupation. However,
the text resonates with an affective afterlife, which can be excavated by returning *Die Schuldfrage* to its original context of reception in the lecture hall, while
also broadening the context of the book's reception to include Jaspers' personal correspondence in the immediate postwar period—particularly with his
former student and later friend and peer Hannah Arendt. Reading the lectures
in this light suggests that much more was at stake for Jaspers than a philosophical analysis of the question of guilt at this particular historical juncture.
Equally as important as Jaspers' discussion of the question of German guilt is
the historical and interpersonal context in which the lectures took place at Heidelberg University in 1945/46, which reveals a complex structure of affective
response in excess of guilt.

   In the lecture hall before the students, many of whom were returned soldiers, Jaspers dared not endanger his audience's potential for critical engagement with feelings of guilt and political and moral responsibility by allowing
himself to exhibit emotions that might alienate or antagonize his listeners. In
affective terms, this might be thought of as the cultivation and regulation of a
potentially destabilizing affective structure in response to a perceived hegemonic affective repertoire; gesturing toward William Reddy's term *emotional
regime*, I use the term *emotional counterregime* for what I am describing
here.[4] In this context, the charged, anxious, and even unruly affective state of
the postwar German population faced with the accusation of "collective guilt"
before the Allies (and, indeed, the world) might be teased out, to some degree,
from the affective response of the student audience to Jaspers' lectures. Further, excavating Jaspers' own subterranean emotional responses, kept largely
in check in these public lectures, provides a fruitful approach to the stakes of
the less obvious intersubjective emotions and the broader affective structures

at play in the act of delivery itself. This reading demonstrates the unexpected capacity of emotional norms to produce—but also obscure—unanticipated emotions and affective structures in excess of the postwar "emotional habitus." Borrowed from sociologist Deborah Gould, this phrase captures both the normative and habitual aspects of emotion, as well as allowing for the possibility of other coexistent affective structures in excess of legible emotional manifestations.[5]

The conditions under which emotions are recognized and judged as morally appropriate or inappropriate are largely provided by a set of preexisting norms on which any given society relies to interpret and navigate its lived environment. These emotional norms make up our emotional habitus and are negotiated through and regulated by social interactions between individuals, including emotional intersubjectivity, in relation to institutions. Indeed, in order to "reeducate" his students without incurring their *ressentiment* for his own politically and morally untainted status, Jaspers necessarily foreclosed emotion from or unobtrusively ushered it out of his lectures. Jaspers' apparently imperturbable demeanor and coolly rational approach to the question of guilt conceal an affective structure housing shame and grief, which remains latent and contained in the public lecture forum.

Voicing Guilt

For Jaspers, trained psychiatrist turned philosopher, postwar US-Allied reeducation meant more than the strict supervision and control of educational institutions, in his case Heidelberg University. It also meant adherence to the initially harsh original version of Joint Chiefs of Staff Directive 1067, issued by the US military government before the defeat of Germany.[6] The original wording of this infamous Allied directive, in its most punitive incarnation, is said to have contained the phrase "collective guilt," but this was removed from the document within a week of its application, as the phrase was deemed to be detrimental to the process of fostering democratic values in defeated Germany.[7] Indeed, historian Norbert Frei declares the term *Kollektivschuld* to be an invention of the Germans themselves.[8] However, the myth of an international charge of "collective guilt" leveled against the German population in Allied documents took root and spread such that private and public political discussions of postwar Germany leaned—and sometimes continue to lean— heavily on the concept as an organizing principal for their arguments.

Initially, Jaspers had great hopes for genuine change in postwar Germany through a self-critical process of rebuilding its institutions; he strongly believed that the university was the institutional forum par excellence—"eine Instanz der Wahrheit schlechthin" (quite simply, an instance of truth)—through which cultural and moral renewal might be possible.[9] Ideally, this process would have entailed the thorough denazification of the institution, beginning with its personnel and extending to the lingering traces of Nazi ideology. Fortunately for Heidelberg University, this operation was headed by Allied officer Captain Edward Y. Hartshorne, a Harvard sociologist who had conducted extensive research on the German academy in the 1930s and who was favourably disposed, rather than punitively inclined, toward the Germans and German culture. Denazification was the strategic aim and sine qua non of the US military government, although this proved to be more difficult than expected, as members of the Heidelberg University faculty omitted titles of dubious books they had published or gave false information in the obligatory denazification questionnaire (the so-called *Fragebogen*) that the military government required Germans in positions of authority to complete in the immediate postwar years.[10]

Jaspers saw the university as a potential space for existential renewal and the realization of what he termed the "true self" and freedom through communication, as described in his *Existenzphilosophie*. His central concern was of a philosophical and ethical nature: namely, the moral rejuvenation of the German population, starting with the students who attended his lectures on the question of German "collective guilt" in the winter semester of 1945/46. Although Jaspers' approach to *Bildung* was elitist or "aristocratic," as Steven Remy frames it,[11] and even if Jaspers hedged a deep-seated distrust toward democracy, his involvement nonetheless extended to participation in public debate beyond the university on the question of reeducation and the possibility of moral renewal in postdefeat Germany.[12] He initially executed this plan by way of speeches and contributions to newspapers and journals, such as political scientist and chief editor Dolf Sternberger's important postwar journal *Die Wandlung*, for which Jaspers served as a member of the editorial board.[13] However, the university was *the* public forum in which Jaspers expressed his new sense of political responsibility toward the nascent postwar public sphere.[14] Jaspers' often-reserved comportment, bordering on frostiness (in a letter to Hannah Arendt, he self-ironically called himself "the North German block of ice")[15] provided a stark contrast to his new role as public intellectual. This is indeed ironic in the case of a philosopher whose *Existenz* philosophy stresses the pivotal role of communication for the practice of freedom on the way to truth, as well as providing the linchpin of postwar moral and, one might say, spiritual renewal, as rehearsed in his lectures.[16]

The window of opportunity for reeducation was narrow; it lasted approximately three years (1945–48), and its demise was determined as much by external factors as by the psychological work required to engage with the consequences of either fostering or, in other cases, not actively opposing National Socialism. These obstacles, coupled with the fear of confronting one's own immediate past, made Allied and German attempts at denazification an uneven and drawn out process,[17] although more recent scholarship has argued that, in qualitative terms, denazification did not fail completely, making inroads on a political level later on through a broad political and social consensus toward compensation, or *Wiedergutmachung*, for victims of National Socialism.[18] Integral to this intended project of moral renewal, I argue, is what might be termed a "reeducation of the emotions" or a "sentimental reeducation," concerned particularly with the most moral of emotions: namely, that of guilt. This ambivalent emotional habitus, of which Jaspers was well aware, set the affective stage when he took to the podium to deliver his lectures in 1945 and 1946.

Although arguably the most present and multivalenced, Jaspers' voice was one of a chorus in the immediate postwar years. As both Jeffrey Olick and Jennifer Kapczynski have persuasively demonstrated, the lingering assumption that guilt was not a topos of discussion in early postwar Germany, especially in the period between 1945 and 1948, is simply wrong.[19] To the contrary, the much-disputed term *collective guilt* initially provided a point of departure for most postwar discussions about the repercussions of National Socialism and moral renewal.[20] Indeed, in the first few years of the journal *Die Wandlung* (1945–49), the political renewal of Germany and the question of guilt were central reference points of discussion.[21] Writers for the journal included philosopher and political scientist Hannah Arendt, sociologist Alfred Weber, and poet and essayist Marie-Luise Kaschnitz, who, in their contributions, often tackled the thorny relationship between responsibility, guilt, anti-Semitism, and morality after Auschwitz.[22]

Jaspers' initial investment in the restructuring of the university was also partly driven by a residual sense of survivor guilt, what he termed his "schuldvolle Passivität" (the guilt of passivity) as a so-called inner emigrant (to use Thomas Mann's pejorative term) under the National Socialist regime.[23] This residual sense of complicity by dint of his helpless inaction during the Third Reich, common to nonperpetrators who survived this period, left its mark on his postwar work, demonstrated by his new belief in the active role of the philosopher in fostering the public sphere. Of course, Jaspers addressed these matters through the lens of his own philosophy, emphasizing the relationship of the individual *Existenz*, as he termed it, to questions of an ethos of "life conduct"

(*Lebensführung*), the existential philosophical narrative that guided his lectures in 1945/46.

Die Schuldfrage was not Jaspers' first public contribution to discussions about German guilt; he had already addressed the topic directly in his public speech on the occasion of the reopening of Heidelberg University's medical school in August 1945.[24] Parts of the published version of this speech, particularly the section on metaphysical guilt, were reworked in his measured response to an atypically vitriolic letter from Norwegian Nobel Prize-winning author Sigrid Undset. Her letter invoked the charge of German collective guilt and declared the intractability of the Germans and subsequent futility of any attempts at their reeducation due to their essential "national mind-set." She considered the German population to be a lost cause.[25]

In his lectures, Jaspers sought to define the normative contours of "guilt" not as an emotion but, rather, as a form of moral comportment. After dismissing the viability of the concept of "collective guilt," he goes on to offer his student listeners and readers multiple definitions of the term *guilt* in the German context. This approach, which provides a sociopolitical division of labor between different aspects, institutions, and gradients of culpability and responsibility, considers "guilt" in its universal form over and against the particularity of historical figures and the national political body. Although *Die Schuldfrage* can be traced back to Jaspers' lectures, many of the ideas elaborated in the text were also rehearsed in responses to correspondence he received from readers applauding his rebuttal of Undset's claims about the moral intractability of Germans.[26]

Jaspers presented a more complex account than that of Undset; he offered a philosophical and logical template for categorizing guilt in postwar Germany. These lectures break guilt down into distinct categories of judgment, effectively providing a key to his students for interpreting and understanding important differences between some of the multiple discourses on guilt that were in circulation. His lucid awareness of the different audiences he is addressing becomes apparent in his attempts to dispel the students' lingering fears and uncertainties about the role and intentions of the US-Allied forces in Germany, while also alerting the Allied readership to the vicissitudes of some of the German reactions to the occupation. His position as trusted mediator—or, in the less generous words of his colleague Robert Curtius, as "Praeceptor Germaniae"—is perhaps nowhere more evident than in *Die Schuldfrage*, where he attempts to win the students over to an understanding and acceptance of their guilt.[27] The frankness of Jaspers' attempt to grapple with this question and his hope of engaging others in discussion just months after Germany's unconditional surrender to the Allies required a fair amount of courage. In fact, *Die Schuldfrage* indicates the gravity with which Jaspers took up his contention that in the wake of Nazi Germany, philosophy is no longer able to remain the preoccupation of the solitary few at a remove from current realities.[28] Entirely under the sway of his own existence philosophy, however, Jaspers' philosophical response to the exigencies of postwar Germany now seems reductively metaphysical and even naively optimistic.

The State of Guilt

Jaspers' task as teacher and public intellectual was to capture the attention and imagination of his students long enough to convince them to dismantle their ideological bases and defer their suspicions about and alienation from the new political situation of Allied occupation. In other words, Jaspers hoped to encourage his audience to suspend judgment and engage with the substance of the lectures and, in this way, garner the critical tools they would need to analyze Germany's current intellectual, political, and spiritual crisis. To accomplish this task, Jaspers attempted to dispel existing prejudices against the American occupying forces and the Allied-led Nuremberg trials of Nazi leaders, by emphasizing the fairness of the Allies' choice to use due legal process in trying the Nazi leaders for their crimes. By treating only the Nazi leaders as criminally guilty, he argued, the Allies were choosing not to indict the German population as a whole. In support of his argument, Jaspers cited the following statement made by Associate Justice Robert H. Jackson, chief prosecutor for the United States at Nuremberg: "We want to make it clear [. . .] that we do not intend to accuse the whole German people. [. . .] Indeed, the Germans—as much as the outside world—have an account to settle with the defendants."[29]

Drawing on the model of the Nuremberg trials (in fact, citing accounts of the trial from the daily newspaper),[30] Jaspers defines his first category of guilt, "criminal guilt," as a public form of guilt that results in processes of judgment and legal punishment incurred by a person for criminal actions, such that he or she may be held accountable before the law for crimes committed in his or her name. To lay blame at the feet of the Allies for this trial, Jaspers argues, would be to confuse cause and effect, blaming the outcome rather than the source of Germany's current situation.[31] Jaspers' second category of guilt, "political guilt," refers to the political responsibility or liability (*Haftung*) borne by a population for the leaders it elects and the polity under whose rule it lives and acts. Should this authority unexpectedly shift or degenerate into a state of violence (such as war), citizens of the state are to be held accountable for this to all other members of their national community (and external authorities, such as the victors in the case of war). These forms of guilt define political and legal aspects of common participation in national citizenship to which no individual is immune. Criminal and political guilt are accountable to larger agencies or institutions; they entail passing judgment on an individual's or a group's actions (or lack thereof) in terms of their sociopolitical ramifications.[32]

By comparison, Jaspers' third category of guilt, "moral guilt," describes how individuals are ultimately responsible to themselves and their community for their actions, above and beyond the jurisdiction of law and politics. Each individual is answerable only to himself or herself, through what Jaspers terms "conscience" (*Gewissen*), which, in turn, connects each person to a larger moral world.[33] Jaspers' fourth and final category of guilt, "metaphysical guilt," is the most abstract of all the forms. He defines this category of guilt through his existence philosophy as the path to a form of redemption or, to use his preferred term, "purification" (*Reinigung*), which he presents in quasi-theological terms, and to which I will return below. In this instance, the individual's guilt lies in her or his ability to continue to live in the knowledge of active or passive complicity with crimes committed against other human beings; this form of guilt is answerable solely before God.[34] In this way, Jaspers posits moral and metaphysical guilt as categories for which the individual alone bears responsibility and that cannot be imposed by an external instance, be it an institution or an individual.

In theory, these categories are clearly demarcated from one another, and Jaspers goes to some length to chart discrete boundaries among them, particularly through his emphasis on the instance of judgment in each class of guilt. However, the historical particulars and the political demands of defeat in postwar Germany, to which Jaspers often refers in his text, illustrate how the postwar affective climate in Germany was much murkier and more ambivalent in the navigation of everyday life. This was due not least to extensive hardship caused by poverty, hunger, and homelessness among the majority of the population.[35] Correspondence between Hannah Arendt and Karl Jaspers from the immediate postwar years bears witness to these privations. Furthermore, most of their letters between 1945 and 1948—at which point the Jaspers moved to Basel—include inventories of packages containing food and medical supplies sent from Arendt to the Jaspers and Marianne Weber.[36]

General Lucius Clay, military governor of the US zone, understood the toll, both humanitarian and political, that starvation would take on the German people. He focused on securing food for the population of the zone, over all other political agendas.[37] In June 1945, Major General Morrison Stayer, chief medical officer for the US military government, received approval from Clay to conduct a survey of public health and medical care needs for the Germans in the US zone, thus effectively using a "disease and unrest" clause to override the original punitive intentions of the US occupation policy from Joint Chiefs of Staff Directive 1067. Clearly, the expectations on which that directive was based and the actual situation in Germany were incommensurable. Stayer justified his survey by describing the "disorganization, desolation, starvation, and sickness" that he observed, noting an increase in the number of suicides.[38] Under these circumstances, many Germans were thus understandably either incapable of hearing or, on some occasions, outright resistant to even the most benevolent of calls for moral introspection.

Fully cognizant of this situation, Jaspers attempted to ground his philosophical analysis of "the guilt question" by countering the psychological extremes that he imagined his students might withstand as they encountered the uncertainty of occupation and the toll of hunger.[39] His anticipation of a potentially negative reaction to his lectures was palpable even in the lecture's published form; Stephan Hermlin, fully aware of the element of returned soldiers in Jaspers' lecture hall, states in a review of Jaspers' book, "We were unable to ward off the feeling that the ethical implacability of the philosopher Karl Jaspers had yielded to an auditorium that would have been unable to hear anything else."[40] In his introduction to the lectures, Jaspers paints a dark picture indeed of the German population's emotional state; he deploys what might be termed an "emotional thermometer" with which to gauge the type and intensity of emotions exhibited by his fellow citizens. Indeed, extrapolating from Jaspers' cues in the text, the Germans appear to be cold, indignant, consumed by rage, and in an emotional state scarcely conducive to Allied denazification and reeducation, which, at that point, remained the order of the day.

In the introductory section to the lectures proper, Jaspers addresses the students and their current historico-political situation directly, first recognizing the "distrust in all young people" toward the ideological intentions of his lectures and distinguishing between research tainted by National Socialist propaganda and his own pursuit of "truth" (*Wahrheit*) through his *Existenzphilosophie*, where "truth does not exist as merchandise ready-made for delivery; it exists only in methodical movement," and this occurs, for Jaspers, "through the sobriety of rationality."[41] Once again, Jaspers invokes the power of sober rationality, suggesting that he views it as a corrective to irrationality induced by National Socialist ideology and, in particular, to a false sense of community, based ultimately on an unspoken consensus of distrust of the other.[42]

Approaching the substance of his lectures, he signals his awareness of the current affective atmosphere in Germany and his own strong emotional investment in the topic of the lecture, declaring in the foreword to the German version, "Mit allen diesen Erörterungen möchte ich als Deutscher unter Deutschen Klarheit und Einmütigkeit fördern, als Mensch unter Menschen teilnehmen an unserem Mühen um Wahrheit" (With all of these arguments, as a German among Germans, I would like to foster clarity and consentaneity; as a human being among humans I wish to participate in our efforts to attain truth).[43] In addition to the distinction Jaspers unwittingly suggests through the parallelism between "Germans" and "human beings," he describes the tone and impression he wishes to make through his contribution on guilt as one of "clarity" and a "common sentiment." In effect, Jaspers characterizes the voice in which he wishes to speak as one of transparency. Further, he suggests that truth can only be achieved by cultivating a shared emotional inclination. From the very first page, Jaspers' approach to the material is characterized by a heightened awareness of the potential volatility of emotions in this context. He goes on, in surprisingly emotive terms, to warn his students of the potential impact his lectures might have on them: "You will vibrate with me or against me, and I myself will not move without a stirring at the bottom of my thoughts."[44] Of course, Jaspers cannot entirely control (or predict) the emotional state of his audience, but his appeal to clarity and his voice of calm reason indicate that he is at pains to suppress any negative emotions that might be counterproductive to his endeavor.

Jaspers' leading existentialist idiom—his philosophy of *Existenz*—was based on the assumption that on the way to truth, each individual would attain a state of self-illumination through communication, first and foremost with the self and then with others (*ein Miteinanderreden*).[45] Arendt, in an essay on Jaspers' work, argues that he is the legitimate heir of the Kantian Enlightenment, demonstrating the belief "that both politics and philosophy concern everyone."[46] Certainly, Jaspers drew on Enlightenment thinkers Kant and Lessing, prizing *Vernunft* above *Verstand* as a property that enables *Existenz* to fulfill itself through action; for Jaspers, this action is practiced through communication.[47] Jaspers elaborates on the impact that *Existenzphilosophie* has on the individual: "This way of thought does not cognise objects, but elucidates and makes actual the being of the thinker" (Dieses [existence philosophy] erkennt nicht Gegenstände, sondern erhellt und erwirkt in einem das Sein dessen, der so denkt).[48] In other words, Jaspers understands existence philosophy to be an ethical practice over and above a theoretical model or system.

For Arendt—Jaspers' former student and a public intellectual and political theorist in her own right—Jaspers' lectures on guilt provided an example of how, in the face of the German postwar realities of defeat, philosophy—indeed, thinking itself—has, of necessity, become "practical, though not pragmatic."[49] Similarly, Dolf Sternberger, also a former student of Jaspers, recognized this striving for concretion in Jaspers' postwar philosophy as an extension of Jaspers' interwar ideal of communication, which he referred to as "der Weg des liebenden Kampfes" (the path of loving struggle). Sternberger saw Jaspers' philosophical inclination as "eine Ethik der Intimität" (an ethics of intimacy), taking communication beyond the idealized private sphere of marriage, family, and close friends, to include a dimension of what Jaspers calls "Öffentlichkeit" (the public). Ultimately, we find these ideas elaborated much later in the concept of the public sphere in the writings of Jürgen Habermas on intersubjective communication.[50]

Paul Meyer-Gutzwiller, the vice director of Radio Basel, for which Jaspers recorded twelve introductory lectures to philosophy, relates how Jaspers expressed the wish to communicate his philosophy to everyone, not just to the trained intellectual. Jaspers went on to declare that "auch den Chauffeur" (even the chauffeur) should be able to understand his lectures, a strikingly incongruous choice of figure to illustrate what he meant by "the common man."[51] Similarly, in his "Philosophische Autobiographie," he expresses the earnest wish "als Mann auf der Strasse mit dem Mann von der Strasse [zu] sprechen" (to speak with the man from the street as a man on the street). But with his particular abilities and experiences, Jaspers was no ordinary man. Despite his striving to make philosophy accessible to the unschooled mind, his existence philosophy retained a theologico-metaphysical coloring that produced an opaque doctrinal terminology rather than the transparent meaning to which he aspired.[52]

"Germany in the Finest Sense"

Jaspers' *Die Schuldfrage* can be seen as part of an ongoing and parallel discussion about the question of German guilt conducted in his correspondence with Hannah Arendt. This particular conversation on guilt can be dated to when Jaspers read Arendt's prescient and original essay "Organized Guilt and Universal Responsibility," published in the US newspaper *Jewish Frontier* in January 1945, some three months before the Allied forces liberated Heidelberg.[53] Beyond reading Jaspers' text as a response to Arendt's essay—which, on Jaspers' insistence, Arendt published in a reworked German version in *Die Wandlung*[54]—we may also see his lectures as an engagement with these two scholars' rich, frank, and often politically and ethically incisive correspondence, particularly in the period between 1945 and 1949, when Jaspers and Arendt exchanged practicalities and affection, as well as ideas, hopes, and fears about Germany's future in the shadow of National Socialism.

Arendt's argument in "Organized Guilt" concentrates on what she calls "the real political conditions" underlying the accusation of the collective guilt of the German population. She contests the common conflation of Nazis and Germans, stating that it overlooks the cynical Nazi strategies, such as that of the "whisper campaigns" aimed at making the population complicit through their partial and uncertain knowledge of aspects of Nazi-orchestrated violence and criminality.[55] Thus, Arendt claims, everyone from those in positions of power to the "family man"/"philistine" (Spießer), a "new type of functionary" who merely carries out duties to ensure the security of his private sphere, is implicated whether he wishes to be or not. As a consequence, per Arendt, it is virtually impossible to render justice: "[W]here all are guilty, nobody in the last analysis can be judged." This returns us to the epigraph from Arendt with which I opened this chapter. Illuminating truth through her deployment of hyperbole, she claims that the only way to be sure of someone's innocence is when the Nazis have hanged the person.[56] A few pages further on, Arendt modifies this claim by making a distinction between, on the one hand, guilt as a process of consciousness and, on the other, punishment as evidence of criminal guilt.[57] These categories prefigure aspects of the fourfold model of guilt presented by Jaspers to his students.

Writing in her incisive emotive idiom, Arendt's spectacular, passionate insights on the question of German guilt were coined differently from Jaspers' reflections in his lectures.[58] Unlike Jaspers' lectures, Arendt's extraterritorial analysis of the political structure of German guilt was not reined in by caution, nor did it intend to deliver a moral message or issue an appeal for responsibility to university students whose reality for the past twelve years had been dominated by Nazi institutions and propaganda. In a sardonic reference to her essay, Arendt wrote to Jaspers that her contribution was less morally driven or punitive than many of the international German guilt debates raging during the war. She claimed, facetiously, that her essay might act "[a]s a counterweight, as it were—ironically speaking—to the Morgenthau Plan."[59] From her vantage point, Arendt was able to dismiss the myriad punitive suggestions of what should be done with Germany after the war, including the proposal to starve the Germans or, as the Morgenthau Plan proposed, to allow Germany to regress to preindustrial conditions.[60] She argued that such action against the German people "would simply mean that the ideology of the Nazis had won," implying that the Allies would then have carried out the promise of the Nazis by demolishing the population, just as Hitler had threatened to do to save national face should Germany lose the war.

Jaspers obviously saw the value of introducing Arendt's perspective on the topic to a broader German audience and published a translation of her essay in *Die Wandlung*.[61] Members of the reading public in Germany did actually view her text as something akin to a German defense against the Morgenthau plan. Horrified, Arendt wrote in a letter to Jaspers, "I'm not altogether happy about the reactions to my guilt article. I'm getting letters from Germany— these people all feel so well 'understood,' and none seem to have picked up my bias against the 'philistine.' On top of that, the wretched *Hessische Nachrichten* has declared that I am 'Germany in the finest sense.'"[62] The disturbing and inappropriate instrumentalism of this final comment was not lost on Arendt.

Clearly, Jaspers had no prerogative to issue such a frankly critical yet empathic account (much less from a Jewish position) from within the Allied Germany of denazification and reeducation. If Arendt's diagnosis of German guilt was presciently political, Jaspers' response to the "guilt question" was pedagogical and emphatically, almost dogmatically, philosophical—a version of existence philosophy for the uninitiated. Nonetheless, the two contributions sustain an interesting dialogue because of, not despite, their vastly different approaches and positions of address. Further, they share an underlying ethical standpoint from which they launch their argument: namely, the hope for the diminution of the nation-state along with the concurrent establishment of an international community bound together through human solidarity. Taking Arendt's concept of complicity as the pernicious effect of the Nazi strategy to ensnare the population in "organized guilt" through association, Jaspers divides it into the categories of "criminal guilt" and "political guilt" (which, by implication, may include "moral guilt" and "metaphysical guilt"). The former addresses those directly responsible for the atrocities as criminals who must be tried in a court of law, while the latter describes the population's uneasy coexistence with the poisonous knowledge that the form of government they had put in place was a terror organization capable of grotesque mistreatment and murder of human beings it deemed "unworthy of survival."[63]

German Feelings "On Ice"

Postwar Germany was no pantheon of positivity, and Jaspers describes the reigning emotive atmosphere in his lectures using overarching negative terms, detailing defensive emotive responses and the deflection of locating proper objects and grounds for guilt. Jaspers describes the emotional landscape of postwar Germany in critical terms, noting how some individuals are intoxicated ("berauschen") by feelings of pride ("in Gefühlen des Stolzes"); exhibit despair ("Verzweiflung"), outrage ("Empörung"), and defiance ("Trotz"); or express contempt ("Verachtung") and the wish for revenge ("Rache"). Jaspers entreats his audience to do away with these feelings by putting them on ice ("auf Eis legen"),[64] which is no doubt easier said than done. It is as if he believes that by giving contours to emotions, by naming them and exploring the sociopolitical dangers of their existence, he might then be able to induce a process of conscious self-reflection that would dispel the inchoateness of affect, facilitating discussion and providing a common base for normative sociality in postwar occupied Germany.

Jaspers is extremely skeptical of what he calls "unsere dunklen Gefühle" (our dark feelings); in a tone of ethical sobriety and twice in the span of one short paragraph, he warns against trusting them. He qualifies feelings as expressions of a kind, mediated through "inner activities, our thoughts, our knowledge," and he argues that feelings are clarified through thinking ("geklärt in dem Maße als wir denken"). In other words, feelings need thought to be trustworthy. On the one hand, what becomes clear here is Jaspers' Cartesian view of emotions, which separates the act of cognition from that of feeling: "To plead feelings means to evade naively the objectivity of what we know and think."[65] On the other hand, Jaspers specifies that one can come to true feeling ("zum wahren Gefühl") through a process of thinking something through while "constantly surrounded, led and disturbed by feelings." Here, again, emotion (or, in Jaspers' terms, "feeling") becomes the Cartesian handmaiden to reason or critical thought and remains unexplored in its positive sociocultural dimensions, which would have been crucial for Jaspers' politico-existentially informed aims.[66]

Jaspers' awareness of the overcharged affective climate, as well as his specification of particular emotions manifest in Germany, did not lead him to formulate a concise theory of the role of emotion in his analysis of guilt. Emotions are usually described, in negative terms, as something to be overcome on the existential path to truth through existence philosophy and calm reasoning, which is the ultimate teleology of Jaspers' lectures. His emphasis lies on the importance of existence philosophy in the navigation of guilt in his historical moment. In comparison, Arendt is interested primarily in guilt's relationship to the political and moral structures in Germany's idiosyncratic case, without positing a teleological state of grace, such as that of Jaspers' *Reinigung*.

In Arendt's essay on organized guilt and universal responsibility, emotion appears to be the precondition for politics. This becomes particularly clear in her direct reference, in the final section of the essay, to politics in relation to fear and shame. Discussing the necessity for human solidarity in the face of crime, Arendt argues that the motivating force for the individual's participation in political life stems from the "fear," "inescapable guilt of the human race," and subsequent "shame" felt by the human being in the face of crime and "incalculable evil."[67] Her deployment of emotion in this analytical capacity remains suggestive rather than fully developed; thus it seems safe to say that she does not develop a politics of emotion or perhaps even regard emotion as political in this particular essay. Rather, emotion appears to be a necessary but insufficient condition for politics; in other words, emotion is prepolitical. Further, emotion is usually mentioned and then quickly sublated into the structure of the political, as an unnoted prerequisite for political motivation. However, Arendt often mobilizes affect at a rhetorical level in her texts; for instance, in her writing, she practices what Jaspers referred to euphemistically as her "visionary" capacity, evinced through her use of startling metaphors, unexpected analogies, and hyperbole to jolt thought and provoke a response from her readers.

The posture of silent pride—what Jaspers calls a "Maske" (mask)—might initially be an automatic and even necessary (non)emotional comportment behind which to gain distance from events. However, Jaspers cautions against paralysis, which he claims leads to "a mood, that discharges itself in secret, harmless grumbling" and results in heartless coldness ("in herzloser Kälte"), furious indignation ("wütiger Empörtheit"), and, ultimately, a destructive tearing-up of the self ("Selbstverzehrung"). These emotions are hardly conducive to his aim of *Miteinanderreden* (communication), which, throughout the lectures, remains his ideal existence-philosophical condition for any kind of political and moral engagement with guilt.[68] The centrality of the concept of communication is shown when, in his "Philosophische Autobiographie," he defines the event of National Socialism as "the most radical rupture of communication from person to person" (den radikalsten Abbruch der Kommunikation von Mensch zu Mensch), provoking "the end of man being himself" (das Aufhören des Selbstseins des Menschen).[69] Similarly, in his lectures, he describes Nazi Germany as a prison in which "no public discussion was possible for twelve years."[70] Jaspers bites the proverbial bullet when he attempts to offer a point of common identification: that of being a member of the German nation. His own identification with the German nation, as complex and paradoxical as it may be, is what he chooses to share as a common denominator with his audience.

What Is German in the "German Question"?

Jaspers' fraught relationship to German national identity (or, as he phrases it, "die deutsche Seele") is expressed in its full ambivalence in his lectures. For example, he critiques the concept of German collective guilt as logically flawed from the outset, primarily because members of any given nation are never rendered identical through their nationality.

> It is nonsensical, too, to lay moral guilt to a people as a whole. There is no such thing as a national character extending to every single member of a nation. [. . .] Morally one can judge the individual only, never a group. [. . .] One cannot make an individual out of a people. A people cannot perish heroically, cannot be a criminal, cannot act morally or immorally; only its individuals can do so. [. . .] The categorical judgment of a people is always unjust. It presupposes a false substantialization and results in the debasement of the human being as an individual.[71]

Although the concept of collective guilt is deficient because it is dependent on a false essentialization, it follows from Jaspers' argument that the German population, nolens volens, nonetheless forms a collective organized around complicity, for this is the one factor that, in addition to the overarching commonalities of language and citizenship, each German shares.

> Today we Germans may have only negative basic features in common: membership in a nation utterly beaten and at the victors' mercy; lack of a common ground linking us all; dispersal—each one is essentially on his own, and yet each one is individually helpless. Common is the non-community.[72]

Usually, national identity is based on a strong emotional tie to a social and geopolitical identity. However, the emotional responses of Germans to their position as a defeated nation are, unsurprisingly, overwhelmingly negative, including "Entaüschung" (disappointment) and "Kränkung und Würdelosigkeit" (indignity and mortification), reflected in the emotional comportment of "kaltschnäuzige und brüske Ablehnung" (brusque and callous rejection).[73] These emotions do not offer a foundation for any kind of positive feeling of national affiliation. This common negativity—national sentiment based on guilt—comes from a situation in which national feeling and political identity were experienced in radically different ways, depending on the political allegiances and experiences of individual Germans.

At one point, Jaspers employs the term *Mitschuld* (complicity) as the politico-emotive term around which dialogue should take place.

> Thus the German—that is, the German-speaking individual—feels concerned by everything growing from German roots. It is not the liability of a national but the concern of one who shares the life of the German spirit and soul—who is of one tongue, one stock, one fate with all the others— which here comes to cause, not as tangible guilt, but somehow analogous to co-responsibility.[74]

Jaspers is at pains to preserve something like the substance of "Germanness," which he locates in the shared linguistic basis, but which intimates a larger national collective essence at work in the individual. Thus nationalism returns through the back door of the shared identity of the collective: Germany. Just a few paragraphs further on, Jaspers takes up the plea for the particular role accruing to the German collective who "feel" guilt.

> I feel closer to those Germans who feel likewise—without becoming melodramatic about it—and farther from the ones whose soul seems to deny this link. And this proximity means, above all, a common inspiring task—of not being German as we happen to be, but becoming German as we are not yet but ought to be, and as we hear it in the call of our ancestors rather than in the history of national idols. By our feeling of collective guilt we feel the entire task of renewing human existence from its origin— the task which is given to all men on earth but which appears more urgently, more perceptibly, as decisively as all existence, when its own guilt brings a people face to face with nothingness.[75]

Jaspers seeks to mobilize affect through a sense of national complicity that exacerbates a sense of German identity, rather than diminishing it.

In view of his critique of nationalism, it seems counterintuitive that the introductory preamble to Jaspers' analysis of "guilt" emphasizes that his comments are addressed to all Germans, with national identity serving as the appellative, common point of departure for his initial arguments. However, it becomes clear that Jaspers' primary investment in affect is of a perlocutionary nature. His use of the category "German" as *the* point of entry into the guilt question can be interpreted as an act of phatic communion established as a basis or support for what ideally should take the form of a community organized around the recognition of guilt.[76] The *Oxford English Dictionary* defines phatic as "of, designating, or relating to speech, utterances, etc., that serve to establish or maintain social relationships rather than to impart information, communicate ideas."[77] Especially because the substance of his lectures is the sensitive topic of postwar German guilt, Jaspers is highly aware of the importance of building a bridge between himself and his student audience, and he does this partly through phatic communion. Arguably, Jaspers' philosophical concept of "communication" (*Miteinanderreden*) would be impracticable without the establishment of a social relationship and pedagogical bonds between him and his audience, even as he acknowledges the one-sidedness of communication in a university lecture hall.[78]

No mere theory of communicative rationality, Jaspers' *Miteinanderreden* is a process of Enlightenment self-education charged with the existence-philosophical task of moving through truth toward freedom and, ultimately, "purification" (*Reinigung*).[79] The model for this metamorphic process is that of dialogue.

> We want to learn to talk with each other. That is to say, we do not just want to reiterate our opinions but to hear what the other thinks. We do not just want to assert but to reflect connectedly, listen to reasons, remain prepared for a new insight. We want to accept the other, to try to see things from the other's point of view; in fact, we virtually want to seek out opposing views. [. . .] We must restore the readiness to think, against the tendency to have everything prepared in advance and, as it were, placarded in slogans.[80]

According to Jaspers, the goal of speaking with each other requires asking oneself how National Socialism could take root and critically reflecting on one's passive acquiescence or active involvement. It is easy to present critical judgments in an overly affective manner (*affektbetont*); the challenge is to reflect on the situation calmly and see the truth (*das Wahre*) in full knowledge of all that has transpired.

> One requirement is that we do not intoxicate ourselves with feelings of pride, of despair, of indignation, of defiance, of revenge, of scorn, but that we put these feelings on ice and perceive reality. We must suspend such sentiments to see the truth, to be of good will in the world.[81]

Jaspers offers a sobering indictment of potential and existing emotional states in postwar Germany, ending in a plea for love as the correct comportment in light of Germany's recent history; and his own comportment is carefully in keeping with the rationality for which he calls. Moral guilt provides the interface between individual guilt and the reestablishment of a social contract in the community. What is clearly important in this posture is that it be communicated through dialogue—the *Miteinanderreden* that is the aim and purpose of Jaspers' lectures. Furthering collective rehabilitation through processes of *Miteinanderreden* in postwar Germany hinges on people's ability to see themselves in dialectical tension between individual reflection on guilt and collective political responsibility or liability for National Socialism.

Die Schuldfrage aspires to be both equal to the historical situation and pedagogically effective. Its modality of performance, achieved through tone and rhetoric, imbue the document with a provocative interpellative immediacy that deserves closer attention. The phatic or emotionally binding role of Jaspers' series of addresses—rhetorical devices such as inclusive address, emotive interpellation, and conciliatory metaphors—should not be underestimated. For Jaspers, this conflicted population should find a common basis for communication through an affective basis resilient enough to support dialogue between very different partners. Moreover, the performance of Jaspers' lectures— that is, the lectures' time, place, and modality of utterance—warrant as much scrutiny as Jaspers' philosophical and ethical exegesis. He assumes a variety of roles during his lectures: that of the philosopher, the judge, the politician, the survivor of inner emigration, and the defeated German, rendering his lecture series a tentative reterritorialization of the public sphere. His goal—to establish a *Miteinanderreden* in post–National Socialist Germany—overlaps significantly with the phatic and perlocutionary aims of his addresses. Jaspers attempts to make room for dialogue within an affective atmosphere that is threatening to become a space of consensual silence based on *ressentiment* or even revenge, if we take seriously the negative emotions he lists in the previously cited passages.

Emotion, mostly approached by Jaspers with circumspection, is granted the unacknowledged phatic role of engaging his audience and knitting together a community.

> Brainwork [*Arbeit des Verstandes*, "the work of the intellect"] is not all that this requires. The intellect must put the heart to work, arouse it to an inner activity which in turn carries the brainwork. You will vibrate with me or against me, and I myself will not move without a stirring at the bot-

tom of my thoughts. Although in the course of this unilateral exposition we do not actually talk with each other, I cannot help it if one or the other of you feels almost personally touched. I ask you in advance: forgive me, should I offend. I do not want to. But I am determined to dare the most radical thoughts as deliberately as possible.[82]

Aware of the diverse positionings of his student auditors and of their varying degrees of awareness of complicity, Jaspers attempts to build a sense of solidarity among his listeners, seeking to break with the "enforced superficial community" of National Socialist Germany and to expose how "we differ extraordinarily in what we have experienced, felt, wished, cherished and done."[83] For Jaspers, the only possibility of finding a common future in Germany is for individuals to speak openly with one another, as difficult as this task might seem: "Now that we can talk freely again, we seem to each other as if we had come from different worlds. And yet all of us speak the German language, and we were all born in this country and are at home in it. We must not let the divergence faze us, the sense of being worlds apart. We want to find the way to each other, to talk with each other, to try to convince each other."[84]

Jaspers guides his audience through the categories of criminal, political, and moral guilt to that most existential category of metaphysical guilt, which, according to him, defines the existential basis for ethical living that requires constant renewal through acts demonstrating awareness of and responsibility for human solidarity over and against all other identitarian particularities.

Metaphysical guilt is the lack of absolute solidarity with the human being as such—an indelible claim beyond morally meaningful duty. This solidarity is violated by my presence at a wrong or a crime. It is not enough that I cautiously risk my life to prevent it; if it happens, and I was there, and if I survive where the other is killed, I know from a voice within myself: I am guilty of being still alive.[85]

Jaspers' radically humanist understanding of guilt in a theological idiom cuts across all categories of complicity and seems to describe what is known today as survivor's guilt—although on the "other side" of the barbed wire. This category of guilt is absolute in that it cannot be atoned for and demands ongoing acts of reparation or, at the very least, a form of living that demonstrates the awareness of a debt to humanity beyond individual culpability. In a strange combination of the national and the metaphysical, Jaspers describes the aim of metaphysical guilt in existential terms: "What comes out of it has to create the essential basis of what will in future be the German soul."[86] Jaspers once more produces a logical tension by framing existential guilt in national terms, which appear to be at odds with his existential humanism.

"Imagine That I am Germany!"

Later in his autobiographical writings, Jaspers declares a strong attachment to "Sprache, Heimat, Herkunft" (language, homeland, origin).[87] Similarly, in his autobiographical sketch from 1957, Jaspers describes how, during the Nazi dictatorship, he would regularly attempt to redeem the cultural identity "German" for his Jewish wife, Gertrud, by declaring, "Denke, ich sei Deutschland!" (Imagine that I am Germany!). Both Gertrud Jaspers and Hannah Arendt criticized this claim.[88] Arendt wrote to Gertrud Jaspers, "I was very glad you rejected your husband's 'I am Germany.' [. . .] He is not Germany, it seems to me, if for no other reason than that it is much more to be a human being. Germany is no single person. It is either the German people, whatever their qualities may be, or it is a geographical-historical concept."[89] Thus, unlike Thomas Mann, Jaspers assumes there is a "good" Germany that should be kept apart from the violent, chauvinist Germany of the National Socialists.

The women rightly question this troubling collapse of categories. In Gertrud Jaspers' case, she deems his assertion to be "glib," perhaps because it does not acknowledge the gravity of what it meant to be "German" in Nazi Germany, compounded by the fact that as a Jew, she was no longer considered to be a German citizen (or a human being, for that matter). Similarly, Arendt sees a danger in Jaspers making this declaration, particularly because (German) nationalism had resulted in both World War II and what came to be known as the Holocaust, associations with "Germany" that Jaspers surely would not have wished to have ascribed to him. The concept of "Germany," both real and imaginary, remains a complex and ambivalent site of negotiation for Jaspers and his interlocutors.

In Jaspers' lectures, we find a tension between two senses of the pronoun *wir*: that of the German national collective and that of broader humanity (*Menschheit*). The past proud and destructive incarnations of German nationalism are no longer viable or even desirable, Jaspers claims. German national identity is first and foremost a subcategory of humanity and is only thereafter a particularity. Jaspers took exception to Friedrich Meinecke, who turned to Germany's "unblemished" cultural achievements and suggested that Goethe communities be formed as an antidote to National Socialism and a positive basis for postwar Germany identity.[90] Jaspers did not seek to resuscitate Germany's status as *Kulturnation*. Instead, he viewed "Germanness" as a potentiality expressed in the future tense.

> Because in my innermost soul I cannot help feeling collectively, being German is to me—is to everyone—not a condition but a task. This is altogether different from making the nation absolute. I am a human being first of all; in particular I am a Frisian, a professor, a German, linked closely enough for a fusion of souls with other collective groups, and more or less closely with all groups I have come into touch with. For moments this proximity enables me to feel almost like a Jew or Dutchman or Englishman. Throughout it, however, the fact of my being German—that is, essentially, of life in the mother tongue—is so emphatic that in a way which is rationally not conceivable, which is even rationally refutable, I feel coresponsible for what Germans do and have done.[91]

In Jaspers' view, postwar German citizens, conscious of their history of nationalist chauvinism with its recent murderous consequences and open to an uncertain future, should see their national identity as a task (*Aufgabe*) always in the process of becoming, rather than an enduring existence (*Bestand*) or ontological foundation. Telling in the preceding quotation is how Jaspers lists the category "Jew" along with the national categories "English" and "Dutch," as if Jews have no claim to a national identity. In this passage, Jews do not appear to be German, even when they speak German—they appear to belong to an extraterritorial category of their own.

So what kind of a task or process of "becoming" is Jaspers suggesting? How can Germany avoid the fate of a pariah people, or *Pariavolk*, with their national guilt?[92] In his essay on Jaspers, Anson Rabinbach traces the term *Pariavolk* back to its Indian origin, where it is used to describe the caste of the untouchables.[93] It was also used to describe the Jews in terms of what was perceived to be their "foreignness" or outsider status despite their belonging to a national community.[94] In Jaspers' account, the diasporic statelessness of the Jewish people both lends them exceptionality and inspires persecution. The choice of this term to describe the postwar German population's potential rejection by the international community is, at best, thoughtless or, at worst, perverse in the context of Germany's Jewish genocide.[95]

Jaspers was reluctant to retreat entirely from his strong national identification with Germany, even if it did mean quarantining certain aspects of "German" tradition from recent German history. Unlike Thomas Mann, who recognized the utter impossibility—both in cultural and moral terms—of ignoring the intertwinement of that which was "good" and "bad" in German national identity, Jaspers held on to the notion of a "good Germany," as is demonstrated by his valiant attempts to engage with and further reeducation and the restitution of the university infrastructure in the years immediately following the war and up until his departure for a position at the University of Basel. The paradox of this declaration of national identification and restitution is echoed throughout the *Schuldfrage* lectures and sits uneasily with Jaspers' otherwise unrelenting attempts to dispel postwar forms of national chauvinism through his discourse of philosophical sobriety. Further, this torsion of attachment and rejection, constitutive of Jaspers' relationship to Germany, acts as a *Fremdkörper* of sorts in his correspondence with Arendt, as well as prompting negative tirades by Marxist philosopher Heinrich Blücher in his correspondence with Arendt, his wife. Again, we see emotional intersubjectivity at work, with affect reacting to affect, where a strong affective tie to national identity (and the particular imaginary that "being" German represents for Jaspers) encounters a response of anger, disappointment, and disbelief.

Jaspers' attempt to resuscitate a positive point of German identification in his lectures is compounded by his use of metaphysical terminology. Many concepts in *Die Schuldfrage* are coined in a strongly Protestant theological idiom, particularly in the passages where he discusses the category of the individual's "metaphysical guilt," which he defines as the "transformation of human self-consciousness before God."[96] The language in which the sections on metaphysical guilt is written departs noticeably from the dialogue between politics and philosophy. The latter genre of what Jaspers called "a spiritual-political venture," for which he otherwise aims in his lectures, gives way instead to what might be described as a form of existential spirituality, where "[p]hilosophy and theology are called on to illumine the depths of the question of guilt."[97] This tone and choice of words permeates large stretches of the text in which Jaspers describes the quest for truth—the attempt to attain "das Umgreifende" (the all-encompassing) through transcendence—as a form of "purification" (*Reinigung*). This is an odd choice of words in a setting where the population is emerging from over a decade of racist propaganda structured around the dichotomy pure/defiled, which lends anti-Semitism its structural foundation.

Continuing in this idiom, Jaspers argues, along the lines of existence philosophy, for limit situations (*Grenzzustände*) that challenge the individual to "*cleanse one's soul* and to think and do right, so that *in the face of nothingness* we may *grasp life from a new authentic origin*" (italics mine).[98] According to Jaspers, this entails "a *transmutation* of our *being*" that cannot be obtained "without *transillumination* and *transformation of our soul*."[99] The preceding terms in italics all refer to processes of metaphysical guilt and belong to the lexicon of existence philosophy. The sense of obscurity accompanying these terms, even in their very repetition throughout the text, produces the effect of what T. W. Adorno called, in deprecating tones, "the jargon of authenticity," in his eponymous book.[100] To be sure, Adorno's explicit target was Martin Heidegger and, less obviously, Martin Buber,[101] but Karl Jaspers also comes under fire, due to what Adorno sees as the pseudotheological underpinnings of his existence philosophy, falsely conflating the sacred and the secular.[102] In short, for Adorno, all forms of existentialism enact what, in *Minima Moralia*, he calls "business as usual," with existence philosophy being a perfect fit for the secularized serial consumer characteristic of modern capitalist society.

Whether or not Adorno's biting critique of these existentialist thinkers was unbiased (considering the negative pitch of Adorno's tone, one can hardly think so), it does underscore a key weakness in Jaspers' text. Despite Jaspers' desire for a grounded philosophy with concrete practices in postwar Germany, he deploys a technical vocabulary particular to his own existence philosophy. It is questionable whether this language provided a hospitable entry into a world no longer officially defined by fascism. Clearly, Jaspers' lectures are defined by a constitutive tension between the concrete historical specificity of his moment, which he attempts to capture in his lectures, and the metaphysical underpinnings of his philosophical stance.

This language must have been bewildering to a group of students just emerging from years of Nazi indoctrination and propaganda. Besides encouraging direct and honest communication between citizens and providing his audience with an outline and analysis of the state of postwar Germany, Jaspers gives the students little in the way of tools in a common idiom for refashioning a cultural identity beyond that of the nationalist superiority of the *Volk* propagated by Nazi demagogues. In his overly rapid move from a sociopsychological framework of guilt to a theological framework, Jaspers forfeited the very concreteness he sought as the foundation for his postwar philosophy.

In response to this and other idealist tendencies in *Die Schuldfrage*, Arendt's second husband, Heinrich Blücher, penned the following irascibly damning lines in a letter to Arendt:

> Jaspers's guilt-monograph, despite all of its beauty and noble-mindedness, is an anathematized and Hegelianized, Christian/pietistic/hypocritical nationalizing piece of twaddle. [. . .] Jaspers' whole ethical purification-babble leads him to solidarity with the German National Community [. . .]

instead of solidarity with those who have been degraded. [. . .] Wearing the thick spectacles of the Romantic *volk*-concept, he seeks the nature of the true German [. . .] And in order to find this phantom, he accepts a truly Lutheran servitude in a Hegelian way. [. . .] Germany finally has the opportunity to make clear the fronts of the real civil war of our times: republicans against cossacks, in other words the battle of the *Citoyen* against the Barbarian [. . .] Instead, Jaspers is calling for loving understanding and discussion, in order to establish the essence of the *real* German.[103]

In her essays on wartime and postwar Germany, Arendt refused to make a distinction between "*citoyen*" and "barbarian"—or good and bad Germans. She critiqued Jaspers' text for its depoliticization of the question of guilt through his Protestant emphasis on penance and atonement at the metaphysical level. She also felt uneasy with what she saw as a kind of nationalism present in Jaspers' argument.[104] The mutual exclusivity of a form of nationalism based on "the German soul" and a humanist cosmopolitanism through European federation is yet another example of the tensions constitutive of Jaspers' argument. Jaspers himself may even have been aware of this contradiction in his argument and may have tried to temper his entreaties to "the German soul" through his recourse to the ideal of the cosmopolitan citizen, in an attempt to guide students away from the logic of honor and disgrace and toward the democratic teleology of humanist cosmopolitan citizenship, which he describes as "the drive toward world citizenship" (*der Drang zum Weltbürgertum*).[105] Jaspers' own version of a "coming community"[106]—a community yet to form itself through response to questions of culpability and a commitment to truth— would replace what he terms the postwar "membership in a nation utterly beaten" whose members have only their noncommunity in common.[107]

Bringing the political to bear more directly on the philosophical through an existential mode of ethics or life conduct based on communicative reason appears to be the outer limit of Jaspers' vision for a democratic polity. Arendt framed her critique of Jaspers' move toward depoliticization through his existential category of "metaphysical guilt" in a letter in which she first thanks him for clarifying the current psychological situation in Germany. Softening Blücher's irate critique in order to express her own misgivings, Arendt writes, "Monsieur [Blücher], even more than I, insists that assuming responsibility has to consist of more than an acceptance of defeat and the consequences following on that. He has been saying for a long time now that such an assumption of responsibility, which is a precondition for the continuing existence of the German people (not of the nation), has to be accompanied by a positive political statement of intentions addressed to the victims."[108] Thus Arendt ups the political stakes beyond the intentions or purview of *Die Schuldfrage*; a strong political statement of intentions is precisely what is missing from Jaspers' lectures.

Because of the enormity of the Nazi crimes against humanity, Arendt feared that the world was confronted with and confounded by "a guilt beyond crime and an innocence that is beyond goodness or virtue."[109] In other words, she feared that ethical, legal, and political categories had been rendered null and void in the face of systematic genocide. In turn, Jaspers refutes the idea of "guilt beyond crime," opting instead to "see these things in their total banality."[110] For Arendt, "the banality of evil" will become the manner in which heinous crimes can be committed systematically and logically by a "reasonable" person (the "family man," *Spießer*) in such a manner that the deeds are normalized as part of everyday life, bureaucratic tasks, and "business as usual." This rendering everyday of ethically despicable behavior is precisely what is evil. For Jaspers, demonizing the Nazi perpetrators can only serve to make them extraordinary and a site of fascination.[111]

"I Have to Try Again . . ."

In a letter to Arendt in September 1946, Jaspers speaks of his desire to take up the question of Germany once more in his university lectures, despite the indifference he felt that he had encountered at times from the students in the lectures earlier that year: "I have to try again. Philosophy has to be concrete and practical, without forgetting its origins for a minute. Yet my intellectual possibilities are so limited, my knowledge so lacking. I tell myself it's always better to do what you can than to do nothing at all. I have to become more indifferent to the masses. In any case, whatever of importance comes out of Germany now can only originate with individuals and small groups. Chaos grows."[112] Jaspers was unsatisfied with the purely philosophical lectures he had delivered on the tail of his *Schuldfrage* presentations, yet his tone is discouraged and he disparages "the masses," indicating his strong sense that his politico-moral tenets—not to speak of his existence-philosophical positions—were not shared by his students or the population at large. He cryptically refers to his own limitations in the face of this task. It is unclear whether he is referring to a lack of philosophical training, his own sense of ineffectuality in the realm of politics, or his inability to effect change in the public sphere. Jaspers offers his students philosophical rationality as a means to keep negative emotions in check.

According to a handful of eyewitness reports, the response of the student audience to the lectures varied greatly, doubtlessly depending on external factors, the substance of the lectures, and the vantage point of the observers. The latter included German exiles, returned soldiers, Germans who had remained in National Socialist Germany, and the Allied authorities who trained an eagle eye on Heidelberg University—the first university to be reopened after surrender and, thus, a kind of test case. Jaspers was well aware of the importance of tone when composing his lectures, and he often directly addressed his audience. The following statement from near the end of his text indicates that he remained acutely aware of that audience:

> We Germans, no matter how differently or even contrastingly, all ponder our guilt or guiltlessness. All of us do, National-Socialists and the opponents of National-Socialism. By "we" I mean those with whom language, descent, situation, fate, give me a feeling of immediate solidarity. I do not mean to accuse anyone by saying, "We." If other Germans feel guiltless, that is up to them—except in the two points of the punishment of criminals for crimes and of the political liability of all for the acts of the Hitler state.[113]

In the very first sentences of his book, Jaspers addresses potential distrust among the students, as well as the fact that the students may react with cynicism and understand the new political reality of the university in entirely substitutable and superficial terms, where only "the cast has changed," so that "science" and "philosophy" have seamlessly replaced "propaganda" inflected with National Socialism. Germany was under a military government; the German population was not at liberty to participate in "free public discussion of every decisive world-political question" and was best advised to deploy "political tact."[114] Further on in the lectures, Jaspers acknowledges the ambivalent experiences that must have informed some of his students' reactions, particularly those of the returned soldiers. Jaspers walks a tightrope between acknowledging the validity of experiences under the Nazi regime and unsparingly critiquing the "unconditionality of blind nationalism" and the "false conscience" of soldiers who believed that obeying orders exculpated them from guilt. He argues for sober reflection on their culpability, leading to a process of "awakening and self-analysis of this delusion" that turns "idealistic youths into upright, morally reliable, politically lucid German men acquiescing in their lot as now cast."[115]

Jaspers wrote to Arendt that he perceived the lecture hall where he held the *Schuldfrage* lectures to be "peopled by a large, dull mass," and he told her how unsettling he found this "mass," a word loaded with implications of elitism and distain from the cultural pessimism of the Weimar period.[116] In a letter to Arendt six months later, he describes how central his audience was in determining the substance and delivery of his lectures: "It is difficult for me to see hostile faces. I need from my audience, as a minimum, a willing suspension of distrust."[117] Keeping his negative affect in check clearly required constant vigilance and a regulation of the forms taken by emotional intersubjectivity. Again, Jaspers affected a public comportment of calm rationality as he attempted to maintain balance within the postwar affective economy through which he was navigating.

Jaspers was not alone in his sensitivity to the emotional climate in the university aula; several of his colleagues and former students and at least one member of the US military government recorded their impressions. Dolf Sternberger describes Jaspers and his first postwar series of lectures in 1945 as follows:

> With an unforgettably direct boldness, in the first large lecture class after the war—in Winter semester of 1945/46—he took up the topic that was plaguing us all, both young and old. Although the subject addressed in the lectures was, once again, the "spiritual" circumstances (more precisely: the spiritual circumstances in Germany), within this framework he addressed the situation of the occupied country, the possibilities for research and the university in view of the regiment of the Allied Military Government but, above all, National Socialism—the dawning of the era of world history—a German form of taking stock of the situation. One main segment of the lecture dealt with the question of guilt—only this has been published.[118]

Sternberger describes his perception of the students seated in the crowded lecture theater as both expectant and respectfully silent as they absorbed Jaspers' words: "The old lecture hall was full to bursting; not the slightest disturbance could be detected; the clarity and the openness of the lecture created an incomparable sense of authority."[119]

US archival sources documenting the period of the US military government in Germany, particularly reports from the Counter Intelligence Corps (CIC), as well as private correspondence, indicate diverging responses to the lectures. Mark Clark provides a very different perception of the student audience as seen through the eyes of Daniel F. Penham (originally named Siegfried Oppenheimer), a former member of the French Resistance, a Jewish-German emigrant who fled from National Socialism to the United States, and then a CIC special agent in occupied Germany.[120] In a CIC report, he writes of the restless and irreverent expressions of the students who were engaged in "laughing and scraping their feet on the floor at the mention of democracy in connection [with] the spiritual situation of Germany."[121] This behavior might reflect a general impatience toward reeducation and denazification or a sense of *ressentiment* toward the occupation forces.[122] The source is unclear in Penham's description—although he insinuates that the behavior indicated the National Socialist sympathies of the students at Heidelberg, a sentiment for which he had little patience and that he was determined to eradicate. He submitted a memorandum to his superiors, including this description of Jaspers' lecture, which concluded with the recommendation that Heidelberg University be closed. Almost immediately, Penham was relocated by the US military government on the recommendation of Allied university education officer Major Earl Crum, who had been called to Heidelberg to monitor and assuage the general unrest caused by Penham's earnest and zealous attempts to remove the pernicious brown stain from the faculty. Clark does not include Penham's final sentence on Jaspers in his account. Penham's full account describes Jaspers' response to student restlessness at the mention of the word *democracy*. Jaspers "interrupted the lecture and declared that he would not tolerate such a demonstration."[123] Jaspers mediated between Allied and German sentiments, serving as an educator of the emotions; to maintain his authority in the aula, he needed to feel in control of the conditions of reception of his uncomfortable topic.

Jaspers' performance of calm rationality also captured the attention of Shepard Stone, a member of the US military government and a former student of Jaspers. Stone remarks on the aura of gravitas surrounding Jaspers in a *New York Times* article dated January 26, 1947, and titled—most appropriately, in this context—"Report on the Mood of Germany."[124] Having visited a lecture held by Jaspers, Stone comments as follows on what he experienced in the lecture hall:

> At five o'clock these dark winter afternoons, on Monday, Wednesday and Friday, 300 students fill the Old Aula. This is the lecture hour of Professor Karl Jaspers, one of the fathers of Existentialism, more recently author of a four-volume work on logic. During the past year the angular, white-haired Jaspers has been devoting himself to the political education of German youth.
>
> "The German Present and Philosophy" is the title of Professor Jaspers' lecture. The male students—most of them former members of the Wehr-

macht are thin, gray, nondescript; the girls healthier-looking but badly dressed.[125]

The title of the lecture captures its aim of political reeducation and, once again, the tension between the historical and philosophical characteristic of Jaspers' postwar lectures. The lecture covers familiar ground, as it addresses the relation of the Germans to their Allied "liberators" and the necessity for democracy and individual freedom. Rather than offer his own account of the lecture, Stone used the occasion of an interview at Jaspers' home to ask for the professor's opinion on the effect of the lectures, to which Jaspers replied,

> A year ago when I started these lectures there was deep hostility among the students. Even today many students are stubborn chauvinists. But gradually more and more of them are willing to listen. Many come to me, tell me their doubts and problems. Among them are former Nazis. A year ago I felt that the German was the eternal subaltern, beyond the light. Today I have some hope.[126]

In addition to gathering Jaspers' view on the political mood of the students, Stone also met with a group of students to gauge the politico-emotional temperature of the moment. To a question Stone posed about Jaspers, a student responded, "Yes, some of us look up to Jaspers and know he is speaking the truth, but most students here don't give a damn about anything except to get through and find a job. Most of the students are still nationalistic."[127] In the article about his meeting with the students, as in his positive review of the English-language translation of Jaspers' *The Question of German Guilt* in the *New York Times* in 1948, Stone recognizes both the difficult public role of Jaspers and the more personal qualities of "his courage, his honesty, and his aims." He also adds that the publication is a poor substitute for the atmosphere of the actual lecture sessions, stating, "To get the full intellectual and spiritual impact of Jaspers one must hear him in the Aula at Heidelberg."[128]

Similarly, Lieutenant Colonel Saul K. Padover, who worked in the Psychological Warfare Division of the US Army on preparations for the reeducation program in Germany between 1944 and 1945, wrote of his encounter with students studying philosophy at Heidelberg University,

> The students were hard-working, intense, and seemingly eager for some new guiding idea. It is significant that lectures on philosophy are literally mobbed. In Heidelberg they line up by the hundreds and then rush the

doors to hear philosophy. I joined in one of these rushes and it was quite an experience. After the lecture I engaged several students in conversation. One said that while he himself was not a member of the Hitler youth, he believed that "Nazi party members have a right to study as much as anyone else." I brought around the conversation to the subject of democracy, and one young man said firmly, "We have never lived under a democracy. You Americans say it is good. We would like to see it for ourselves. If it is good, we'll adopt it." The others nodded in vigorous assent.[129]

As also substantiated by the comments above from Stone's article, the composition of the political persuasion of the students was mixed. However, Padover's passage suggests that the students were, at base, hungry to learn and open to new ideas.

At the other end of the emotive spectrum, Alexander Mitscherlich, with his characteristic optimism toward his mentors (a role that Jaspers came to fulfill for him during the war years, until they ultimately parted ways over psychoanalysis), waxed rhapsodic about the lectures. He wrote to Jaspers that the first lecture he attended had "so enraptured" him that "he had been unable to sleep."[130] He pronounced in a somber, if not pompous, tone, "That which I have expected of the university and of you has now begun to be fulfilled."[131] Clearly, just as Jaspers had predicted in his introduction to the lectures, the extremely different backgrounds of those attending the lectures very much colored how they experienced the event and determined the emotional temperature of the audience.

The observers' accounts of reactions to Jaspers' lectures are less comprehensive than the written responses to Jaspers' text. The reception of his book spanned a sweep of political and emotional reactions, ranging from unequivocally positive acknowledgment of Jaspers' challenge of self-examination to criticisms, both private and public, of the logic and moral stance of his argument. For Jaspers, however, by far the most disturbing reaction to his book was apathy and general indifference toward the problems discussed. As Clark points out, Jaspers recognized that this response was understandable due to the physical and psychological hardship faced by most of the German population in the immediate postwar years. Jaspers was not yet in a position to fully perceive how the encroaching Cold War would shift the focus from reflecting on the past to planning a new geopolitical future, one in which the "brown past" conveniently could be put aside or disavowed.[132] Ultimately, the fear, sorrow, and even anger that stained the years of the National Socialist era for the Jaspers, emotions he had carefully held at bay for the most part in his public lectures on guilt, made Germany uninhabitable for them.

"Chaos Grows": The Sustenance of Shame

Not many postwar intellectuals had the moral stature of Jaspers, who had remained in Germany during the Nazi era, along with his Jewish wife, Gertrud Jaspers, and had in no way compromised himself.[133] Karl Jaspers' loyalty to Gertrud Jaspers cost them more than his exclusion from the university's administration in 1933,[134] his forced "retirement" from the position of professor in 1937, and a creeping publication ban on his works (although he continued to write prolifically for the "desk drawer" during this period). Throughout the twelve years of Nazi dictatorship, they lived in constant fear, which Jaspers describes in his "Philosophical Autobiography" (1956) as follows: "Inwardly my wife and I experienced this threat to corporeal existence without being able to defend ourselves through long years." He continues, "Outwardly no harm was done to us. We learned [. . .] that it was planned to ship us off on April 14, 1945. [. . .] On April 1, Heidelberg was occupied by the Americans."[135]

The couple's experience of liberation by the Americans no doubt played a major role in Karl Jaspers' attitude toward the occupying forces. This, along with his lifelong faith in the special role of the university as an institution ideally devoted to freedom of research and the search for individual truth, influenced his willingness to participate in the restructuring of Heidelberg University. He joined this initiative despite his bitter disappointment with the Germans who had supported the National Socialists by turning a blind eye to the persecution of their Jewish neighbors and others deemed in Nazi propaganda to be "life unworthy of life."

Although Karl and Gertrud Jaspers emigrated in 1948 to Switzerland, where Karl Jaspers held a chair in philosophy at the University of Basel until his death in 1969, he continued to comment on developments in West and East Germany in numerous articles, book publications, and radio broadcasts and even on television.[136] His popularity "at home" in West Germany rapidly shrank once the university and the city administration of Heidelberg learned of Jaspers' offer from the University of Basel. His subsequent decision to migrate to Switzerland created a great deal of resentment among the Heidelberg academics. Wanting to leave with as little fuss as possible, Jaspers then claimed that the primary reason for his departure was a sense of not being safe in Germany, a sentiment felt acutely by Gertrud Jaspers: "[F]or a Jewish woman, it was very difficult to live here." The situation was exacerbated by feelings of depression at the "apathy expressed toward the Jewish mass murder and, more generally, the 'Jewish question.'" Further and, for Jaspers, most important, he wished for a situation of "peace and freedom" for his work, which he felt was his "sole objective duty." Idealistically (if not in a downright utopian vein, considering the conditions under which most of the German population existed at that time), he declared the following aim: "[t]o work, in the service of truth, toward an occidental, supranational idea of the German-speaking university."[137]

In an essay written twenty years later, in 1967, Jaspers revisited his move from Heidelberg to Basel and complicated what he now termed his "conciliatory approach" from 1948.

> What drove us to leave was clear: the absence of consequences for the mass murder of the Jews—the radical distancing of oneself from the totally criminal state—my isolation in my endeavors at the university—the hostility of the government—excessive strain caused by futile efforts—a reduction in the potency of my philosophical work.[138]

The truncated effect produced by the use of hyphenation in this paragraph suggests an unpleasant flock of memories lurking behind each abbreviated explanation, much as his sober ruminations on guilt had concealed a far more negative complex of affect that came out only in private correspondence and later writings. One such fraught and injurious memory is the example Jaspers gives of his and Gertrud Jaspers' gradual alienation from Heidelberg during the Third Reich. This occurred through a series of events, including the rejection, on racial grounds, of the Jaspers' application to buy a burial plot in the town's *Bergfriedhof*, by the mayor of Heidelberg, a National Socialist functionary (most appropriately named Dr. Neinhaus).[139]

It is difficult to ascertain the veracity of Jaspers' 1967 explanation, published some two decades after his 1948 departure from Heidelberg for Basel and under vastly different historical circumstances, in the now-established Federal Republic of Germany. Nonetheless, there is no mistaking the mood of ambivalence, bordering on hostility, which surrounded Jaspers and the reeducation for which he had come to stand. Even psychoanalyst Alexander Mitscherlich, Jaspers' friend and self-appointed mentee who otherwise addressed Jaspers in a tone of near-worshipful admiration, was unable to suppress the dismay he felt at Jaspers' decision to leave Heidelberg. In a private letter to Jaspers dated March 31, 1948, written in response to Jaspers' farewell address, Mitscherlich pointedly yet euphemistically calls Jaspers' decision to leave a "Fehler" (error), stating,

> If I take your effectuality as an author of our time seriously, then I have to say that I am insulted by your explanation for—and your silence regarding—the most crucial points [about your departure from Heidelberg]. [. . .] This disrespect toward your environment that, until now, has been fatefully given over to you and that you, namely, do not take seriously enough to address candidly, rather treating it diplomatically—that is to say, tactically—will not be so quickly forgiven by your friends in Germany.[140]

In a tone of acute disappointment, Mitscherlich accuses Jaspers of not admitting the truth ("den entscheidenen Punkten" [the most crucial points]; "wahrhaftig anszusprechen" [to address candidly]). Although Mitscherlich gives no further details about what this "truth" might be, the very anti-Semitism and persistence of National Socialist structures and ways of thinking may well be the "crucial points" that he is thinking of as the unspoken, "true" reasons for Jaspers' decision at the time.

Unfortunately, Mitscherlich was, to a large extent, correct about the sense of resentment and insult felt by Jaspers' friends, detractors, and students alike in regard to his decision to leave Germany.[141] In the German press, the response to the news of his decision ranged from disappointment to expressions of barely suppressed animosity. Contemporary articles on the decision often included biting and resentful comments, such as those in a 1948 article in the *Rheinische Merkur*, of which Jaspers kept a clipping: "The philosopher of the tragic-existence-that-fulfills-itself-through-failure has already in the meantime quickly absconded to Switzerland and in this way has taken leave from the misery of the German postwar daily grind." Other articles that Jaspers collected from contemporary newspapers bore headlines such as "Mit schuldigem Respekt gegangen" (Departed with Guilty Respect).[142]

Besides letters such as Mitscherlich's, Jaspers received a number of inimical, often anti-Semitic letters and postcards—what can only be described as "hate mail"—over the years, coming mainly from German addresses, even during his final years in Basel.[143] One such postcard, postmarked "25.3.1948" and bearing the return address "Studentenschaft, Heidelberg Universität" (Heidelberg University Student Body), was sent to Jaspers' home in Heidelberg shortly before his departure for Basel. This hostile missive borrows from classical German literature—no less than Goethe's *Faust*, followed by the lesser-known poem "Der Wilde" by Johann Gottfried Seume—to express the hatred and nationalist sentiment of its anonymous author or authors.

"Die Ratten verlassen das sinkende Schiff."

Original, Fahr' hin in deiner Pracht! —
Wie würden dich die Einsicht kränken:
Wer kann was Dummes, wer was Kluges denken,
Das nicht die Vorwelt schon gedacht? —

["Rats leave the sinking ship."

Go forth in splendor, you primal man!-
How could insight harm you, ever:
Who could think of stupid things or clever,
That past ages didn't, long ago, understand?]

Faust II.2

"Und er schlug sich seitwärts in die Büsche."

[And he disappeared into the bushes.]

Seume[144]

In addition to the blatant frontal assault intended by the opening proverb about "rats leaving a sinking ship," the citation from Goethe's *Faust* represents the voice of Mephisto, who acts subserviently toward his interlocutor yet secretly shares his scorn and disdain of him with the audience. The line taken from Seume's poem has become a saying in and of itself, meaning to secretly leave a place or to extricate oneself from a situation. These passages emote hatred, rage, and scorn and are a far cry from the encouraged stance of cool rationality adopted publically by Jaspers as a philosopher and reeducator during the immediate postwar period. This hate mail also goes some way to explain the anger, disappointment, and sadness Jaspers expressed privately to his confidants and wife.

Whether or not the cause for his departure was as "clear" to Jaspers in 1948 as he states it was in 1967, the explanation he offered in 1967 nonetheless conveys the very real frustration he felt at the stagnation of the initial impetus for change in postwar Germany, a stagnation that dashed his hopes for a new self-reflexivity and cosmopolitan humanism in his home country. Increasingly,

Jaspers felt himself to be cast by others in the role of what he called an "öffentliche Puppe" (puppet of the public).[145] He used this phrase to describe his sense
of instrumentalization at the hands of German politicians and public figures
who sought an exemplar of the "Good German" to ameliorate their dealings
with the Allied occupiers and to make the correct impression on the international press.

From Heidelberg to Basel

It is thus hardly surprising that a darker affective undertow characterized Jaspers' complex relationship to Germany, ultimately finding expression in his
private correspondence, in keeping with his classical cognition/feeling binary
and his division of the private from the public sphere. As discussed above,
Jaspers cultivated a particularly close intellectual and personal relationship
with his former student Hannah Arendt, with whom he shared a melancholic
yet hopeful exchange of letters about their losses, anger, and disappointment,
as well as their doubts and fears about the future. Their frequent correspondence offers a dense affective web through which the reader encounters an
"emotional refuge"—a space allowing for the existence of affective structures
at odds with or differing from the current normative emotions of a society, such
as Jaspers' trademark rational sobriety.[146] Although emotive norms were in
flux and constantly under negotiation in postwar Germany, the emotions expressed and the affect suggested by the correspondence show a different side to
Jaspers than his public countenance of the Cartesian philosopher or "North
German block of ice."

The only emotion explicitly identified by both Arendt and Jaspers as valuable, even as it remains undertheorized, is shame. Jaspers locates shame in relation to metaphysical guilt, where the term remains abstract, bordering on
theological, acting as an emotive signal to individuals that they have failed to
exhibit "die Unbedingtheit" (the unconditioned) toward their fellow human
beings: "There remains shame for something that is always present, that may
be discussed in general terms, if at all, but can never be concretely revealed"
(Es bleibt die Scham eines ständig Gegenwärtigen, konkret nicht Aufzudeck-
enden, allenfalls nur allgemein zu Erörternden).[147] For Jaspers, shame plays
the role of unsettling the individual, but only inasmuch as she or he remains
"vaguely" disturbed, aware of a shortcoming of some kind; it points the individual toward a topic for discussion that "can never be concretely revealed."
Despite the lack of contours Jaspers grants to shame, it would not be an exag-

geration to say that the emotion becomes an existential barometer for measuring the awareness of one's own "bad faith" (to borrow a phrase from Sartre), or one's responsibility in regard to human beings and oneself.

Jaspers' imprecise description of and attempts to intellectualize shame also mark his own ambivalence vis-à-vis this affective structure. He was no stranger to shame, both in terms of the wounds inflicted by his experiences in National Socialist Germany and in light of the comportment of shame he exemplified in his lectures by implicating himself in the same postwar German "we" through which he attempted to interpellate his students. Cultural theorist Sara Ahmed helpfully emphasizes how the structure of shame is characterized by a "double play of concealment and exposure," even at its etymological root.[148] In the context of Jaspers' lectures, shame might be understood as a movement between two affective levels. The first is that of the public performance of exposure in the lecture hall, thus enacting and, indeed, encouraging identification by the listeners with a shame of kinds: namely, the awareness before others of one's complicity. This is accompanied by the unwitting concealment of Jaspers' own sense of shame and conflict in relation to the underlying negative emotions and affective structures concealed and contained by his comportment of extreme rational sobriety. This shame, which threatens to expose the radical difference between Jaspers' experiences and those of the majority of his audience, is precariously held at bay by both his Cartesian comportment and his participation in a broader "German" shame that he addresses in his lectures.

An emotion sustained by intersubjectivity, shame requires a real or imagined audience in order to be "felt" as such. Thus, in his lectures, Jaspers becomes both the object and subject of shame—he who is exposed and he who conceals. A recent object of shame in Nazi society, due to his loyalty to his Jewish wife, Karl Jaspers also occupies a position of the empathic subject of shame, by participating in the guilty "we" that links him to his audience. Jaspers treads a fine line between the exposure and concealment of his own unnamed shame, in his effort to act as the containing witness for his audience as they grapple with their complicity and national shame. Paradoxically, however, as Ahmed observes, the very acknowledgment of national shame can work as a palliative against this shame, thus reestablishing a positive relationship to the nation, or to "the German soul," in this postwar example.[149]

This doubled relationship to shame (as subject and object), which lays bare the emotional intersubjectivity sustaining its affective structure, demands an intense amount of emotional endurance on Jaspers' part and leaves its impression in different ways in his text. In a telling instance, Jaspers' single-minded performance of calm rationality was characterized in 1947 by an anonymous journalist as that of "fanatische Sachlichkeit und heiligen Ernst" (fanatical objectivity and sacred sobriety).[150] In a symptomatic reading, the "fanaticism" and "holy seriousness" noted facetiously by the journalist become indicators of the immense effort required to sustain this performance of rationality. This almost parodic version of "cool conduct" contains an underlying affective structure made up of an admixture of shame, anger, doubt, and despair, which threatens to undo the ethical task of directly addressing Germany's present and past that Jaspers had set for himself. In the aforementioned article, the journalist goes on to describe *Die Schuldfrage* as a text "that with the irresistibility of its objective content puts our fate in correct perspective, with the seminal benignity of the judge who comprehends all possibilities, and that compels us to recognize our own existence."[151] The ungenerous tone of the report, which describes Jaspers' bearing as one of pompous temperance yet simultaneously proclaims him judge and savior of Germany's "fate," strikes precisely at the precariousness of the affective structure housed beneath this pronounced performance of rationality. It is bitter, then, that the ironic edge of this report seems invested in ridiculing, if not directly shaming, Jaspers, even as it is published in response to the announcement of his nomination for the 1947 Goethe Prize.

By comparison, in her essay "Organized Guilt and Universal Responsibility," Arendt shifts focus from her central topic of guilt to a brief discussion of shame in relation to "universal responsibility." For Arendt, shame is linked to a universalizing humanism: "For many years now we have met Germans who declare that they are ashamed of being Germans. I have often felt tempted to answer that I am ashamed of being human."[152] In the next breath, Arendt discusses a shared, transnational "elemental shame," which is all that now remains of "our sense of international solidarity." Arendt argues for the idea of common humanity, "purged of all sentimentality," that ultimately makes all humans responsible, without excluding anyone from guilt for crimes committed. In this sense, Arendt's invocation of "humanity" appears to represent a secular version of Jaspers' "metaphysical guilt." In a final move that makes emotion—in this case, shame—a precondition for the constitution of the political, Arendt states in regard to human solidarity, "Shame at being a human being is the purely individual and still non-political expression of this insight."[153]

For Jaspers and Arendt, shame maintains a complex and potentially productive relationship with guilt, which remains embryonic in their writing. Perhaps Johannes R. Becher, then a recently returned émigré German poet politically active in the Soviet occupation zone, best captured shame's relationship to guilt when he described shame as "ein revolutionäres Gefühl" (a revolutionary feeling) that enabled one to look at oneself from an outside perspective and gain insight into one's guilt.[154] Here, I am in agreement with literary scholar Helmut Peitsch, who, considering the example of Theodor Heuss and others in the immediate postwar period, critiques Aleida Assmann's argument for separate "guilt" and "shame" cultures in this period for being based on insufficient analysis of the language use in that era.[155] Against anthropologist Ruth Benedict's famous claim that Germany represents a guilt culture in contrast to Japan's shame culture, it appears that guilt and shame go hand in hand in many important debates in the postwar period, in both the Soviet and Western Allied occupation zones.[156] Indeed, it might be more useful in this context to make a distinction between emotions based on a spectrum of guilt/shame versus the honor/pride-disgrace ("Ehre/Stolz-Schande") dichotomy, where the latter is clearly a remnant of traditionally conservative forces of militarism and monarchism.[157] These lingering nationalist traditions and their component affective structures are touched on in the next chapter in the context of Ernst von Salomon's 1951 autobiographical novel *Der Fragebogen (The Answers)*.

Although he was still influential as a public intellectual, Jaspers' decision to migrate to Basel in 1947 marks a moment of extreme animosity toward the philosopher (coupled with private and public forms of shaming). He was seen as having deserted Germany in its hour of need. Thus began the gradual yet inexorable neglect of the *Existenz* philosopher's work, particularly in the German university setting, a process accelerated by existentialism's ceding to sociopsychological forms of critique and, finally, neo-Marxism in the 1960s, a historical moment visited in the third chapter of this book.[158] In his metamorphosis from German academic mandarin of the Weimar years[159] to his role as mediator between the Allied occupation powers and the Germans in the initial phase of the restructuring of Heidelberg University, Jaspers had become a strong voice of conscience in the postwar cultural landscape.[160]

Echoing Jaspers' rational and rationalizing approach to the question of Germany's recent past, Theodor Heuss, then cultural minister of Württemberg-Baden, likewise underscored the importance of staving off emotion in order to confront the past with "cool clarity." In his article "Anklageschrift Nürnberg," published just prior to the beginning of the Nuremberg trials, on the front page of the October 24, 1945, issue of the *Rhein-Neckar-Zeitung*, Heuss states, "In the coming days the whole world will eagerly read the indictment, with shock, with hatred, with bitterness, with shame."[161] Here, the international readership is imagined as displaying a spectrum of negative emotions—shock, hatred, and bitterness—toward Germany's National Socialist crimes. Interestingly enough, the readers are also imagined as feeling shame, suggesting the way in which the affective structure of shame is linked to the question of being witness to crime, as well as perhaps also creating the aforementioned sense of human solidarity described by Arendt.

Germany, however, is not invited to participate in these affective responses except, perhaps, in that of shame, as is suggested by Jaspers in his *Schuldfrage* lectures. Shame, it seems, might lead one to accept or even first feel one's belonging to and responsibility toward the human race and might thus allow one to realize one's complicity with crimes committed in one's name. Heuss concludes the article by saying, "It would be good if these accounts could be wrapped up soon—then the air in Germany would be once again able to be free. But before we reach this stage, we must make it through the arguments with cool levelheadedness. Sentimentality is not permitted in this process."[162] In a generous reading, it could be said that Heuss attempts to eschew emotions with his use of strangely neutral and arguably inappropriate euphemisms, such as when he refers to the National Socialist crimes on trial at Nuremberg as "diese Geschichten" (these stories), which he wishes would be "aufgeräumt" (cleaned up / straightened out / put away), or when he invokes the "freie Luft" (free air) that he hopes will soon return to Germany. In his attempt to pit "kühle Klarheit" (cool levelheadedness) against "Sentimentalität" (sentimentality), which is "nicht erlaubt" (not permitted), a structure emerges that is similar to that traced in Jaspers' rational approach to postwar Germany. Again, it is important to note that sentimentality or emotion are not necessarily absent at this historical moment; rather, they are the prerogative of the rest of the world, while Germans receive instructions from public figures and other cultural sources to hide or suppress their emotions, which are considered counterproductive to processes of cognition and reflection. Such suspicion of affect and hyperawareness of the manner in which emotions are expressed or manifested in public extend into the immediate postwar period in Germany. Consider, for example, the epigraph by public figure Walter Dirks with which I opened this chapter; cognition and emotion are there framed as mutually exclusive to one another.

Ultimately, in Jaspers' case, it appears that the emotional labor that undergirded his appeal to reason occurred at a more private—perhaps sometimes even latent—level than might be suggested by an appraisal of the juridical, political, and metaphysical logic of his lectures alone, with their plea for philosophical rationality in the aula of Heidelberg University. In March 1946, Jaspers had already conveyed his doubts to Arendt about pursuing a meaningful life, intellectual or otherwise, in the ruins of postwar Germany: "It is not easy to describe things here. It is a life of irreality. I'm eaten up by day-to-day chores. Reflection withers. [. . .] Things can't go on this way. There seems to be no place at all for real thought."[163] Just a few months later, Jaspers' tone took on even more urgency as he despaired of the hostile emotional climate of his surroundings. In a letter to Arendt, he wrote, "Never before 1937 did I experience so little of a kindly attitude toward me in the auditorium as I do now. Publicly I'm left in peace. But behind my back people slander me: the Communists call me a forward guard of National Socialism; the sullen losers, a traitor to my country. When this kind of thing has been said to my face, I've been able to put out the fires so far with a mild and persuasive response."[164]

Jaspers' reaction to slander reveals precisely and directly how his sober and rational public demeanor covers over inchoate affects that demand the individual's vigilance and a quantum of hope. He continued in his letter to Arendt, "We live in an atmosphere of slander. If a weak point is in fact found, then you are lost. That too is part of the current state of affairs in which, in spite of everything, I hope something vital can flourish."[165] Jaspers initially invested a share of his emotional energy in a project of spiritual renewal of the German youth. Meanwhile, Hannah Arendt, an émigré now living in the United States, identified her sole affective tie to Germany as her mother tongue: "What remains is the language, and how important that is one learns only when, more nolens than volens, one speaks and writes other languages. Isn't that enough?"[166] For Jaspers and Arendt alike, the German language and intellectual traditions alone continued to constitute their affective attachment to a Germany more ideal than actual.

In retrospect, as difficult as the decision had been, Jaspers in no way regretted leaving Germany. In fact, after a visit to Heidelberg in 1950, Jaspers wrote to Arendt, with perhaps just a touch of triumphant self-righteousness, "I feel *no* guilt for leaving this Germany and for *not* yearning to go back.—A small detail: I'm a member of the Heidelberg academy. They happened to have a meeting while I was there. They *forgot* to invite me. A clear sign of how little I mean to those people."[167] Jaspers no longer felt responsible for the question of German guilt, including his own vis-à-vis the land he once idealized; his words are not pervaded by a sense of shame. Just like Arendt before him, Jaspers severed his affective ties to the ideal of a German community that had already ceased to exist.

CHAPTER 2

Ressentiment: Democratic Sentiments and the Affective Structure of Postwar West Germany

> What course political development will take in Germany when a whole
> class of frustrated and starving intellectuals is let loose on an indifferent
> and sullen population is anyone's guess.
> —Hannah Arendt, "The Aftermath of Nazi Rule"

> It was that now the lid was removed and everything could be openly said;
> and not the authorities, but the German public itself, could now settle its
> accounts with them: This was an essential stage on the way to full freedom
> of the press and of public discussion.
> —William Ernest Hocking, *Experiment in Education*

"Frustrated and Starving" Intellectuals: An "Indifferent and Sullen" Population

In a 1944 journal article entitled "The Problem of Germany," Colonel T. H. Minshall of the US Army wrote of his trepidation regarding the establishment of a postwar democracy in Germany.

> It seems to me that the danger of the postwar attitude of democracies is
> that in the early years we shall be all too fierce, all too repressive, all too
> angry, I was almost going to say, all too unfair, too violent anyway. And
> ten years later we shall be all too bored, all too sentimental and all too
> much the other way. Now the ideal attitude to take, which is terribly dif-
> ficult, seems to me to be that of a surgeon who is operating on a wounded
> gangster. The surgeon does not allow his hands or the operation to be af-
> fected either by sympathy for the gangster's wounds or by horror at the
> gangster's criminal record. He just gets on with the job.[1]

Expressing concern about the potential for "unfair" attitudes and "violent" behavior on the part of democratic Allied forces toward the populace of Germany in the initial and later phases of occupation, Minshall frames his misgivings in terms of emotional responses. This implies that where politics and power are at work, emotion is never far behind.

For Minshall, the "ideal attitude" to adopt in the process of instilling democracy is impartial engagement; indeed, he uses the analogy of a surgeon able to operate on a gangster without prejudice or empathy—he "just gets on with the job." Democratization of postwar Germany is conceived of as a delicate and urgent procedure, with Germany in the role of the lacerated "gangster," while the US is the dexterous surgeon dispassionately operating on the villain's wounds. Nonetheless, although Germany is portrayed as both criminal and damaged in this striking scene, it is the Allied soldiers who need to keep their potentially destructive emotions (anger, disgust, despair) in check. Democratization implicitly—and, in this citation, even explicitly—involves instilling in its subjects an idealized form of appropriate attitudes and, by extension, normative nonaggressive or nonvengeful "democratic" comportment.

Integral to this Allied operation of democratization was the extraction of the ideology of National Socialism from the "social body" through the bureaucratic procedure of denazification. The procedure initially involved the screening of all Germans of working age to determine the extent of their involvement in Nazism. Those stained by dint of their involvement with the Nazi Party were to be removed from public positions in the new postwar order. The word *denazification* itself evinces an etymological incision: the addition of the negative prefix *de-* exerts a "privative force"; it "undo[es] the action" or "depriv[es] (anything) of the thing or character therein expressed."[2] In other words, this prefix is performative inasmuch as it actively negates or subtracts from the noun to which it is affixed. The sense of the full force of this negation or "privation" extended from the noun to the German citizen; all German citizens were considered guilty of National Socialist involvement until proven otherwise. Both the function of the negative prefix and Minshall's analogy of a surgical intervention in the body politic imply the removal of a potentially toxic substance. Not surprisingly, the intentions of the American Allies and their intensive implementation of denazification during the initial years of the occupation did not fail to impact the attitudes of the Germans toward the US-Allied forces.

Recent scholarship has argued for the positive long-term effects on German society of the initial processes of denazification in the immediate war years.[3] In contrast, reports from the period paint a less attractive picture. Bureaucratically overambitious and, in the short term, counterproductive in economic terms, the process of denazification was initially curtailed and eventually abandoned.[4] However, the operation of denazification left its mark on the German populace in more than one way. It is precisely such "scars" of denazification that author Ernst von Salomon bares to his reader in his 1951 book *Der Fragebogen* (*The Answers*). His autobiographical account defines German historical and political events in the first half of the long twentieth century, offering the reader detailed insight into the affective scarification von Salomon credits to the US military government's denazification practices and other processes of democratic occupation.

Revisiting this vitriolic yet masterful text offers another window onto the affective structures constitutive of immediate postwar Germany. Indeed, a close reading of von Salomon's lengthy text (over eight hundred pages in its first edition) yields an affective cartography of the postwar subject in terms of what Friedrich Nietzsche called *ressentiment*. This postwar subject is a rancorous figure, taking pleasure in converting his own guilt into what he sees as his suffering at the hands of others, while residing comfortably in the perception that these others are responsible for his suffering. It would be misguided to assume that guilt was not present in postwar West Germany.[5] Guilt was not absent—in some cases, it merely had gone underground to reemerge through the phenomenon of *ressentiment*. This understanding of *ressentiment* as perverted guilt is essential for reading von Salomon's best-selling book as a literary act aimed at the heart of what he perceived to be the sentiments proper to US-Allied democracy.

Reading for Emotion: Feeling Differently

Alongside emotional norms propagated consciously or otherwise through Allied directives and "real, existing" practices of denazification and reeducation, pockets of both passive and aggressive emotional resistance festered in the West German population against the sentiments—the hopes and fears—of this imagined democratic community. The 1949 founding of the Federal Republic of Germany, the advent of the Cold War, and the subsequent loosening of publication bans and Allied media control opened up space in the nascent public sphere for a "counterregime" of kinds, in part reacting to what this community understood to be an "emotional regime" of externally imposed and hypocritical "democratic guilt."[6] Over and against democratic emotional norms propagated under the capacious rubric of "reeducation," a careful reading for emotions of this period reveals a strong nationalist emotional subculture or community of *ressentiment*. Though much literature on postwar Germany assumes a break in nationalism after 1945, the persistence of nationalism in discourses, such as those around Allied policies of denazification and reeducation, suggests a continuity of nationalism under a variety of guises.[7] Counterintuitively, the concept of "collective guilt" calls for precisely such a national form and an investment of pride in nation, as we have seen in chapter 1 with Karl Jaspers' struggles to define "Germanness" without reducing it simply to a community sharing a common spoken language.

Von Salomon's autobiographical novel may be read symptomatically as a text participating in (and enabling) the affective structure of *ressentiment*.[8] To understand the affective charge this book offered to many postwar Germans who identified with von Salomon's experiences and opinions, it is necessary to mine the book through a number of approaches, including examining the textual production of emotions at the level of reader identification (which becomes particularly clear in the book's reception), reading for symptoms of textual repression, and reading for a less definitive affective undercurrent that ultimately manifests itself as the structure of feelings constitutive of *ressentiment*. Nietzsche's understanding of *ressentiment* as a complex of affective interreactions, many of which are not conscious, is crucial for understanding the point of anti-US-Allied identification offered by von Salomon's book. In turn, the "community of *ressentiment*" that formed in response to the affective undertow of the book exemplarizes the space of collision between the fledgling democratic emotional imaginary of West Germany and pockets of a lingering antidemocratic, militant, and nationalist emotional subculture in the founding years of the Federal Republic.

Ressentiment: Implosive Affect

In *The Genealogy of Morals*, Friedrich Nietzsche states of those under the sway of *ressentiment*,

> The suffering are one and all dreadfully eager and inventive in discovering occasions for painful affects; they enjoy being mistrustful and dwelling on nasty deeds and imaginary slights; they scour the entrails of their past and present for obscure and questionable occurrences that offer them the opportunity to revel in tormenting suspicions and to intoxicate themselves with the poison of their own malice: they tear open their oldest wounds, they bleed from long-healed scars.[9]

This citation touches on many important elements of the affective structure constitutive of *ressentiment*. "The suffering"—this is how the subjects of *ressentiment* define themselves in an attempt to escape from guilt—are creative in how they grasp these "painful affects" as raw materials to fuel *ressentiment*. An immense amount of pleasure is garnered by subjects through this resourceful masochistic process of making themselves victims by "dwelling on nasty deeds and imaginary slights" in order to "revel in tormenting suspicions" through which they "intoxicate themselves with the poison of their own malice." Ultimately, the structure of affect proper to *ressentiment* can be traced through the wounds the subject incurs, that is, the wounds that the subject incurs at his or her own hands, by scratching open "long-healed scars." As we shall see in von Salomon's case, the temporality of *ressentiment* is always that of yesterday—focusing on yesterday in order to secure tomorrow's revenge—and the logic of this affective structure is that of reversal for the sake of producing excessive negativity.

The term *ressentiment*, derived from the French word for resentment, is imbued with strong affect and is related directly to the exploration of morality's perversions in the work of philosopher Friedrich Nietzsche. *Ressentiment* describes a cluster or constellation of strong emotions, as well as an unworthy mode of comportment toward others, who are made directly responsible for the suffering of the vengeful subject in this state of being. Nietzsche understands "affect" in strong psychological terms, connecting it directly to morality. This connection makes the concept of *ressentiment* key to understanding the negative "politics of emotion" in the postwar period, of which Ernst von Salomon's autofictitious book is a—if not the—prime example in postwar West German literary culture.

According to Nietzsche, *ressentiment* produces a negative set of "affects" (Nietzsche's umbrella term for what I term "emotions"), such as those of hatred, contempt, and envy, which he describes in *Beyond Good and Evil* as comprising an attitude of "slave morality."[10] These "affects" do not originate from what he terms "the man of *ressentiment*" in *The Genealogy of Morals*; rather, they emerge in a primarily reactionary capacity.[11] This subject is reactionary inasmuch as the stimulus for its affective response always has an external source and entails a turning away from self-reflection: "This *need* to direct one's view outward instead of back to oneself—is the essence of *ressentiment*: in order to exist, slave morality always first needs a hostile external world; it needs, physiologically speaking, external stimuli in order to act at all—its action is fundamentally reaction."[12] Thus a "democratic" notion of honor involves self-reflection, in contrast to the older military code of honor that seeks the source of a breach of honor outside of itself.

Ultimately, the subject of *ressentiment* (re)acts in the external world according to an imaginary inner world of pure affective negativity. The aim of the subject of *ressentiment* is to find relief from its own guilt by making someone else the source of—and thus responsible for—its own "bleeding" from "long-healed scars." However, this inner cartography must remain opaque to the subject of *ressentiment*, lest it realizes that the intense affect it draws on is actually a defense mechanism against guilt from which it suffers. Thus, rather than evincing an "inability to mourn" (Mitscherlichs) in their attempts to ward off the pain of suffering caused by guilt, these subjects inversely exhibit an excess of affect—a "too much" rather than the "too little" affect noted by postwar observers, such as Hannah Arendt.

In the 1912 book *Das Ressentiment im Aufbau der Moralen*, which the author continued to refine and publish in different incarnations up until 1923, philosopher Max Scheler offered a critical elaboration on Nietzsche's writings on *ressentiment*.[13] On the one hand, as a practicing Catholic, Scheler disagreed with Nietzsche's condemnation of Christianity as the main source and enactment of *ressentiment*. Attempting to recuperate religion from Nietzsche's scathing critique, he argued that it was the historical form taken by contemporary religion, rather than religion itself, that lent itself to perversion by *ressentiment*. Scheler approaches *ressentiment* as a "unit of experience"; seeking to differentiate it from revenge and envy, which are aimed at specific objects, he defines it as a "form or structure."[14] At the same time, he uses the metaphor of poison to express the venomous nature of the affect, its contagious potential, and its ability to contaminate a social body.[15]

On the other hand, Scheler vigorously supports Nietzsche's claim for the existence of an "enormous" Jewish *ressentiment*. Scheler argues that this form of *ressentiment* is based on the long-standing disjunction between the "colossal national pride" of being in the position of "the chosen people" and the ubiquitous discrimination encountered by the Jewish people, as well as the discrepancy between a theoretical constitutional equality and actual practices of social prejudice heralded by modernity. Indeed, drawing on an old anti-Semitic stereotype of the acquisitive Jew, Scheler goes so far as to essentialize this quality, attributing this putative Jewish characteristic to *ressentiment* itself in the form of "a deep-rooted disturbance of Jewish self-confidence."[16] I shall return shortly to the complex and intimate relationship between *ressentiment* and anti-Semitism in post-1945 West Germany, where this politically inflammatory affective structure recurs in myriad and often self-contradictory historical guises.

Scheler's emphasis on *ressentiment* as both a "mental attitude" and a "structure of society" underscores how affect may be best imagined as a structure and a set of hierarchical relations, in this way demonstrating the broader insight into political structures gained by reading through emotion.[17] Taking his critique a step further, Scheler advances the paradoxical argument that modern egalitarian societies—those based on the principle of the "universal love of mankind,"[18] what might be called humanism—are a fertile breeding ground for *ressentiment*. Following the perverse logic of *ressentiment*, exactly those societies ostensibly structured by a humanist demand for the equality of humankind create the festering preconditions for the affective structure of *ressentiment*.[19] In somber, even cynical terms, he argues that the humanist model of society is precisely a calculated and reactive response to *ressentiment* and is hence merely its perpetuation in another form.

Echoing the logic of Nietzsche's dichotomy of noble-versus-slave mentality, Scheler declares, "The humanitarian movement is in its essence a *ressentiment* phenomenon, as appears from the very fact that this socio-historical emotion is by no means based on a spontaneous and original *affirmation of a positive value*, but on *a protest, a counter-impulse* (hatred, envy, revenge, etc.) against ruling minorities that are known to be in possession of positive values."[20] Similarly, he argues that, "unable to acquiesce in the sight of higher values," *ressentiment* "conceals its nature in the postulate of 'equality.'"[21] For Scheler, democratic societies provide the perfect preconditions of impotence and powerlessness constitutive of *ressentiment*. He argues that democracy is based on an ethos of equal rights that declares formal equality normative yet, paradoxically, allows ongoing discrepancies in the distribution of power, property, or education of individuals.[22] Of course, this interpretation of *ressentiment* looks different in the historical perspective of post-1945 than it did to Scheler in 1923.

The Answers of Ernst von Salomon: An Antibildungsroman

In 1951, the German publishing house Rowohlt released a book that became the first nonleftist best seller in postwar Germany, Ernst von Salomon's *Der Fragebogen*.[23] The book was rebaptized *The Answers of Ernst von Salomon* in its 1954 English version,[24] circumventing a direct translation of the original German title, "The Questionnaire." Allowing the emphasis to fall on von Salomon's responses rather than the survey provides a clear indication of what lies ahead of the reader in von Salomon's autobiographical digressions and associative minutiae. However, the title of the English version does away with the strong reference to the postwar context signaled by the German version of the title. It also avoids directly naming the US-Allied military government's questionnaire that not only serves synecdochically for the entire apparatus of denazificaton but also provides the narrative framework for the book. The (dis)ingenuous narrative strategy of Ernst von Salomon in *The Answers* is ostensibly just what the title promises: the author's responses to the Allied military government's questionnaire distributed to all German citizens in the American sector, the completion of which was a prerequisite for ongoing employment.

The rubric *Fragebogen* is a synecdoche for the entire bureaucratic and existential phenomenon of denazification. Employing the form of the *Fragebogen*, von Salomon takes hundreds of pages to respond to what was originally a six-page survey to be submitted to the denazification authorities and checked against records for potential Nazi involvement. The conceit of the text is that it supplies honest and detailed answers to all of the 131 questions; the reality of the text is that von Salomon uses the questions to launch his own autobiographical account of his life to date.

Von Salomon's biography is narrated from an ironic and often caustic conservative perspective. Defined by the utter investment in his Prussian identity, von Salomon was a militant conservative revolutionary in the interwar period. Brought up to embrace militarism and Prussian nationalism and having attended several military academies as a cadet, von Salomon was too young to join the army during World War I. After the war, he made up for this missed opportunity by joining the *Freikorps*, volunteer paramilitary organizations that fought both for and against the German state during the Weimar Republic. After the *Freikorps* disbanded, von Salomon joined *Organisation Consul*, an ultranationalist group active in Germany between 1921 and 1922. This organization violently rejected democracy as part of what its members termed the postwar *Erfüllungspolitik* (politics of appeasement), in response to which it murdered over 350 people for "political reasons." In this capacity, von Salomon gained his experience and lingering reputation as a terrorist.

Von Salomon can be counted among the ranks of the conservative revolutionaries, a member of the cohort that Michael Wildt calls "Generation des Unbedingten" (the uncompromising generation), in order to underscore the unbending militant values and fervent nationalistic attitudes of those who came of age in the unstable period after World War I.[25] Such militaristic and nationalistic networks helped precipitate the end of the Weimar Republic and, sometimes unwittingly, but with a fatal blindness, prepared the ground for the National Socialist takeover. In his early twenties, von Salomon was part of the group of conservative revolutionaries gathered around figures such as Ernst Jünger. Von Salomon's fanatical belief in the significance of *die Tat* (the act/

deed) as an existentially definitive moment for the individual led to his involvement at the age of twenty in the murder of Jewish-German foreign minister of the Weimar Republic Walther Rathenau on June 24, 1922. He was convicted as an accessory to the murder—he had procured a car for the assassins—and received a prison sentence of five years, which he duly served.

After his prison term, von Salomon emerged more circumspect about the value of "the act"; he went on to earn his living as a reader for and then an author with the Rowohlt publishing house. According to *The Answers*, the owner and director of the publishing firm, Ernst Rowohlt, became von Salomon's mentor and friend. Rowohlt published von Salomon's postwar reckoning with the American Allies without qualms (and doubtlessly with an eye on his bank account). In the three years leading up to the National Socialist takeover in 1933, von Salomon released four militaristic books with Rowohlt: *Die Geächteten* (*The Outlaws*, 1930), a novel based on his experiences in the *Freikorps*; *Die Stadt* (*It Cannot Be Stormed*, 1932); *Die Kadetten* (The cadets, 1933); and *Putsch* (Coup d'état, 1933). These texts were not an anomaly, being part of a particular literary current—personified by Ernst Jünger—that glorified military experience.[26]

The status of von Salomon's belief in political authoritarianism and his nationalist affinities requires clarification if his position is not to be confused with that of an adherent to National Socialism. Although he admits that the entire nationalist movement, in all of its diverse forms, was anti-Semitic, he declares that this was not the main motivation for Rathenau's assassination, recognizing and simultaneously distancing himself from what he saw as the National Socialist Party's common and vacuous racist doctrines. Rather, von Salomon states that Rathenau was murdered for what young members of the *Organisation Consul* saw as his role as an *Erfüllungspolitiker*, one of the politicians who had "betrayed" the German people by abiding by the terms of the Treaty of Versailles. In *The Answers*, von Salomon even claims to have read all of Rathenau's writings and to have been impressed by him as an individual.[27]

In 1929, after his release from prison, Ernst von Salomon became involved with the *Landvolkbewegung*, a movement of farmers revolting against the steep government taxes in Schleswig-Holstein; he served the movement as fellow agitator and as coeditor, with his brother Bruno von Salomon, of the journal *Das Landvolk*.[28] After his stint with the *Landvolkbewegung*, itself a damaging interwar instance of *Agrarromantik* that helped make the farmers susceptible to National Socialism, von Salomon claimed to have thoroughly disengaged himself from any kind of political activity whatsoever. Instead, he alleges, he placed his energy in the service of writing and publishing, after

Ernst Rowohlt encouraged him to work on a book about his experiences in the *Freikorps*. Von Salomon completed his first book while in prison custody in Moabit for his alleged involvement in laying bombs for the *Landvolkbewegung* in the Reichstag. Released due to insufficient evidence, von Salomon emerged with a completed book, *Die Geächteten*.

In *The Answers*, von Salomon went to some lengths to prove his utter disdain for National Socialism. He was pained when the American Allied officers who arrested him in his home in 1945 called him "a big Nazi," and was insulted when he was detained as a prisoner of war for fifteen months on suspicion of his involvement with Nazism. Although the national chauvinism and the overall tone of arrogance vis-à-vis the United States exhibited throughout von Salomon's book certainly represent an open disdain toward America and the democracy it stands for, this position does not equate him with National Socialism. To the contrary, as Ralf Heyer points out, von Salomon sometimes equates National Socialism with US democracy,[29] which he also disparages: "Die Sadisten nationalsozialistischer Prägung seien Vergangenheit, die Sadisten aus Übersee Realität" (Sadists of a National Socialist inclination belong to the past, sadists from overseas are our reality).[30] Indeed, von Salomon is critical of the National Socialist Party and its plebian nationalism and finds anti-Semitism inexplicable: "The only surprising element was the vehemence with which Hitler plunged into the 'Racial Problem' and its corollary, the fight against the Jews, which he made the centre point of all his speeches and all his views."[31]

Von Salomon's political activism and writings, which may now be considered part of the conservative revolutionary canon, certainly aided and abetted the crisis and subsequent demise of the Weimar Republic. He wrote in the tradition of the right radical conservative; in postwar Germany, however, he remained in a position of *extimité* vis-à-vis the affective and moral quandary of those who supported Hitler. His moral and affective stance is that of cynicism and nihilism. Von Salomon, both the person and the narrator of his fictionalized autobiography, refutes the values of society, refuses maturity, avoids social integration, and makes a virtue of his limits and apathy.

The introduction to von Salomon's book provides the reader with some points of orientation and suggests that this alternatively irascible and stoic antagonist is to be approached with caution. At first glance, the form of the book appears to be dictated by the division of the military government's questionnaire into parts A through I ("Personal," "Secondary and Higher Education," "Professional or Trade Examinations," "Chronological Record of Full Time Employment and Military Service," "Membership in Organizations," "Part

Time Service with Organizations," "Writings and Speeches," "Income and Assets," and "Travel or Residence Abroad"), plus a section at the conclusion of the questionnaire innocently entitled "Remarks." Each section serves a narrative purpose, and each rubric is exploited by von Salomon to stage and perform fictionalized autobiographical episodes. For instance, the "response" narrative itself often undermines the blunt facticity of the survey's questions. At times, the narrator even subverts the rubric in question either by supplying an excess of material only tangentially connected to the query or through the sheer volume of pages dedicated to answering apparently innocuous questions. For example, von Salomon's response to the final category ("Remarks") is a long and cynical account (almost 150 pages) of his cautionary internment as a politically dangerous figure by the US military government.

Categories that appear to be straightforward, such as "Geburtsdatum" (date of birth), elicit a lengthy avalanche of words, including as flippant a response as "Löwe" (astrological sign Leo), accompanied by a detailed and superfluous astrological exploration of the exact coordinates of his birth.[32] Likewise, confronted with the query "Haarfarbe" (hair color), he states that the questionnaire bares its true obsessive nature at this point, that it exhibits what he calls a "manic" property, which he finds characteristic of all surveys. This "manic" attribute, he states, lends the questionnaire the quality of a wanted poster (*Steckbrief*). This category provokes a page-long response, including the author's own manic and irrelevantly detailed observations.

> Nowadays my hair is of an indefinable hue, a sort of dark and dusty color, though each hair when examined individually shows a tendency towards grey. This tendency—as I notice each day with growing dismay—looks as though it will conquer. But the victory, when it comes, seems likely to bring with it the dissolution of that which is conquered. Like all conquest it has a plainly nihilistic side to it.[33]

With this purposeful flippancy—bordering on absurdity—the author distracts the reader from the politico-historical reasons for the questionnaire—as a tool for establishing the degree of complicity of the respondent with National Socialism—by, for example, discussing his hair's graying.[34] To cap it off, he makes a barbed comment about the "nihilistic side" of every conquest, suggesting his critical perspective on the Allied "conquest" of the Germans and its immediate consequences (such as this questionnaire). Thus his text is characterized by constant shifts from an analysis of the collision of history with his past to an anecdotal idiosyncrasy at odds with the aims of the Allied questionnaire. In this way, von Salomon engages acts of verbal wit, laced with cynicism, to deflect from the contemporary political and cultural context. At the same time, the tenor and content of these responses mock the principles and punitive basis of denazification and, by implication, put into question the legitimacy of denazification and the pedagogical efficacy of reeducation.

In a hyperbolic and sarcastic tone, von Salomon claims that his response to the questionnaire demonstrates how he has taken this political instrument more seriously than anyone else: "I can only hope that Military Government will, for its part, [not] deny itself the pleasure of prosecuting and punishing the one person in all the world who has really taken its Fragebogen seriously."[35] Of course, hyperbole serves to undercut the intentions of the questionnaire, by demonstrating its unwieldy scope and ridiculing the threat of disciplinary action for his strict "compliance" with the Allied forces. Taking the challenge of the questionnaire literally—and as an occasion for producing literature—perpetuates the logic of the questionnaire *ad absurdum*, making light of the intention and the act itself and parodying processes of denazification altogether. Even von Salomon's narrative moments of apparent clarity and self-reflection are mere pauses for breath in preparation for his next claim, such as when he declares, "The deeper I plunge into this Fragebogen, the more I find myself compelled, against my will, to make unpleasant confessions."[36]

Due to the wide scope of its distribution in German households, von Salomon's text may be seen as laying an extensive network of potentially explosive emotional mines in an affectively volatile postwar landscape. A strong affective current runs throughout the book, beginning with the disdain, bordering on disgust, implied by its form. The narrator criticizes the minutiae in the first section of the survey, titled "Warnung" (Warning). He begins with a dismissive discussion of the questionnaire by zeroing in on two spelling mistakes in the document. This is clearly intended to be both a critical reflection on the errors endemic to denazification and a pointed reference to the overwhelming paperwork of an understaffed bureaucracy that ultimately tripped the process up. In this context, it is also significant that von Salomon provides his answers in a dialogical manner, eschewing the formal language usually reserved for bureaucratic forms. Instead, he adopts a cheerfully irreverent tone, singed with nihilism according to the degree of stupidity he attributes to each question.

Von Salomon's emotional stakes in the questionnaire become evident early on in the text. The reader receives an inkling of possible negative emotional reactions of the postwar German populace to the occupation when von Salomon writes,

In order to satisfy any doubts on the matter let me say at once that the perusal of all these questionnaires has always produced the same effect upon me: a tumult of sensations is let loose within my breast of which the first and the strongest is that of extreme discomfort. When I try to identify this sensation of discomfort more exactly, it seems to me to be very close to that experienced by a schoolboy caught at some mischief—a very young person, on the threshold of experience, suddenly face to face with an enormous and ominous power which claims for itself all the force of law, custom, order and morality. He cannot yet judge the world's pretension that whatever is is right; at present his conscience is good when he is in harmony with that world, bad when he is not. He cannot yet guess that a happy moment will one day come when he will weigh the world and its institutions in the scales of that still dormant conscience of his, will weigh it and find it wanting and in need of rebuilding from the foundations up.[37]

Here the narrator already demonstrates many of the qualities that come to characterize his stance throughout the book. He casts himself in the position of a young "schoolboy caught at some mischief," not yet fully formed in moral terms and at the whim of "an enormous and ominous power," which he does not understand. At first blush, the "enormous and ominous power" would seem to be the National Socialist dictatorship, until one reminds oneself that von Salomon is addressing his feelings vis-à-vis the Allied questionnaire, making the "force of law, custom, . . . and morality" in question that wielded by the US military government. Purposively eschewing responsibility, von Salomon anticipates the day that this schoolboy will be in a position to judge the world "and find it wanting and in need of rebuilding from the foundations up." This moment has clearly not arrived, for it is framed in the future tense, implying that what will need to be rebuilt and rethought is the democratic order that the Western Allies wish to impose on defeated Germany.

In addition to shirking moral responsibility for the "mischief" that came before the occupation, the narrator's figure of a boy is an intentionally caustic reference to the infantilization associated with the US military government's reeducation program. Former resistance fighter and German-American publicist Norbert Muhlen predicted such an attitude in his article "America and American Occupation in German Eyes" (1952).

Many Germans resent the program. "Education" in a literal translation, the term generally accepted in Germany for speaking of the education

program, is *Erziehung*, which smacks of the three R's—the elementary
schooling given to children, colonial people, and illiterates, with the use
of the rod, while "education" in American usage means many things, including *Bildung* (for which there is no term in English).[38]

The patronizing analogy of the German populace undergoing reeducation with
"children, colonial people, and illiterates" smacks of missionary practices in
which children, colonized people, and the unschooled were all perceived as, at
best, unformed or, at worst, subhuman. Pointing to an incommensurability of
the two cultures, this passage implies that Germany is now a "colonized land"
suffering at the hands of the Allied troops.

It is significant that von Salomon's "schoolboy" is subject to a surge of
affect, which he, in his prelapsarian state, is unable to define in terms other
than as a "tumult of sensations" and a state of "extreme discomfort." This diffuse affect can be differentiated from the codex of morally weighted emotions
(such as guilt or rue), thus freeing the "schoolboy" from the task of self-
reflective ethical obligations. This analogy, taken seriously, has clearly disturbing moral implications, not least because it foreshadows the act of emotive
reversal—the reversal of the categories of victim and perpetrator—proper to
the affect of *ressentiment* lodged at the heart of the book.

At the very least, this passage should be read as a cue to approach the remainder of the book with a healthy dose of skepticism, for the narrator claims
time and again the passive role of the observer in the most precarious of political situations. Despite his declared abhorrence of the Nazis (they did not practice the "right" form of Prussian national statehood), von Salomon avoids spar-
ring with National Socialist tyranny in any form throughout the book,
abandoning any variety of political act and replacing it with an ideology of his
own making, through moral arguments rehearsed in dialogue between characters. This stance and the nihilistic aesthetics of the absurd that shape the tone
and movement of his prose embody von Salomon's response to being "a man
in dark times."[39]

The narrator, acutely aware of the elephant in the room, continues his
apologetics on conscience and truth, all the while questioning both the authority and the validity of the US military government's wielding of what appears
to him to be the weapon of postwar self-reflection.

Now in view of the matters which I have had to discuss in my answer to
Question 19 of this Fragebogen [on religion], I am clearly nowise entitled
to express my opinions on matters of conscience. Nor is it I who wish to

do so. Yet how am I to account for the tone and arrangement of this questionnaire if its general intention is not a new incitement to me to examine this conscience of mine?[40]

Here and throughout the book, von Salomon reduces the question of guilt to a matter for discussion in religious terms, equating it with Catholic confession. In this way, he delimits the full semantic reach of postwar guilt examined by Karl Jaspers. His caustic reference to the mixed self-assurance and naïveté of the Americans indicates his awareness of the broader semantics of guilt. He mockingly recounts the young US military officers' attempts to inculcate conscience in the German populace, suggesting that they are attempting to usurp the institution of the Roman Catholic Church or even the role of God.

> For it is not the Catholic Church that has approached me and requested that I examine my conscience, but another and far less admirable institution, Allied Military Government in Germany. [. . .] It was representatives of A.M.G., men in well-creased uniforms with many brightly colored decorations, who made it unambiguously clear to me that every man worthy to be called a man should study his conscience before deciding whether or not to act in any specific way. They sat in front of me, one after the other, those agreeable and well-groomed young people, and spoke with glibness and self-assurance about so great a matter as a man's conscience. I admired them for their apodictic certainty: I envied them their closed and narrow view of the world.[41]

Once guilt is framed solely in religious terms (in Jaspers' parlance, as "guilt before God"), von Salomon feels free to critique the audacity of the Americans in their assumption of passing judgment, with "glibness and self-assurance," on the question of conscience. Von Salomon resents what he sees as the Allied military government's usurping of God's role, thereby unhelpfully collapsing Jaspers' categories of political liability, existential guilt, and guilt before God (addressed in chapter 1 of the present study). He clearly despises the intrusive tone and aggressive stance of the Allied questionnaire.

> Unlike the priest with the poor sinner remote from the world in the secrecy of the quiet confessional, A.M.G. sends its questionnaire into my home and, like an examining judge with a criminal, barks its one hundred and thirty-one questions at me: it demands, coldly and flatly, nothing less than the truth; it even threatens twice—once at the beginning and once at

the end—to punish me, and the nature and scope of the punishment envisaged I can only too vividly imagine. (See *Remarks*, at the end of this
questionnaire.)[42]

By describing the Allied military government and the questionnaire as agents
of threat and unnecessary aggression—his reference to the "Remarks" section
points toward the violence he will encounter in Allied internment camps—von
Salomon cunningly moves to claim the position of a victim of the new postwar
order.

In the introductory pages of his book, von Salomon not only uses wit and
cynical humor to disarm, convince, and perhaps even comfort and reinforce the
contemporary German postwar reader's attitude toward recent German history; he
also intersperses more serious claims among his anecdotes and critical comments.
Nestled between his humorous episodes and bristling barbs, the following passage
renders the Allied questionnaire a menacing weapon and reduces German defeat
to a bothersome technicality that demands his full nationalist vigilance:

> I can, after searching my now fully aroused conscience, reach only one
> conclusion: I must fear that I am taking part in an act which, in these un-
> controllable circumstances, may result in damage to a country and a na-
> tion to which I unquestionably belong, damage done in the name of for-
> eign powers whose supremacy is based solely on two facts, the military
> collapse of Germany and an agreement made with men who were as-
> sumed by their co-signatories, at the time the agreement was signed, to be
> criminals.[43]

In the English version of the passage above, there are two important omissions
from the translation. First, Fitzgibbon translates the word *Volk* as "nation," thus
eliding von Salomon's conscious use of the emotively imbued National Socialist term used to appellate the German population; the word *Volk* clearly carries
a more loaded, conservative historical and affective resonance. Second, again
skirting von Salomon's overdetermined word choice, Fitzgibbon translates
"die historische Tatsache" with the phrase "two facts." Von Salomon's description of the defeat and occupation of Germany as a "historical circumstance"
veils the dire political situation, the violent regime, and the immense human
suffering put to an end by the Allied defeat of Germany. Von Salomon offers
his reader a version of historical circumstances that appears to be arbitrary and
unmotivated and that can only lead to the shaming of the German people betrayed, once again, by those in power. The best-selling status of his book is a

troubling indication that von Salomon's particular interpretation of the postwar German lot must have held a fascination for many postwar German readers.

Just as von Salomon uses hyperbole to produce excess affect or to extract other emotions from guilt, so too he engages gallows humor when it is a question of his own political engagement in Nazi Germany. Earlier on in the book, in a protracted, arbitrary response to question 25, "List any German University Student Corps to which you have ever belonged," von Salomon blatantly situates himself as forcefully and nihilistically disengaged from the acute sociopolitical crisis of the period. This segment includes a long dialogue with Hans Zehrer about von Salomon's time working with conservative philosopher and economist Othmar Spann in preannexation Austria, as well as an account of his attendance of the Lippoldsberger *Dichtertreffen* at the invitation of Heimat poet Hans Grimm.[44] Von Salomon bares his nihilistic teeth in his response to Grimm and his circle's passionate belief in conservative bourgeois values: "Nothing much glowed in my heart save an intractable desire for life."[45] In the early 1930s, von Salomon had distanced himself not only from his belief in a life-determining, revolutionary "act" but also from any social contracts or moral obligations. Attempting to make a virtue of his vice, he states, "I, I'm not an accepter. I'm a passionately involved observer. That's why I never became a National-Socialist."[46] Fitzgibbon's translation of *Bekenner* as "accepter" elides the aspect of membership involved in the word; the translation "I am not a joiner" might be closer to the spirit of von Salomon's meaning, for he declares himself an adherent to spectatorial disengagement during the Third Reich, no doubt a statement and a position in which many of his postwar readers would have an affective investment.

During the war, von Salomon had earned his living by writing screenplays for UFA (Universum Film AG), the largest film production company in Germany. Despite their abhorrence of the National Socialist Party, he and his partner, Ille Gotthelft, led a comparatively comfortable life—indeed, in a state of gay self-abandonment at times, if his account is to be believed. Unlike von Salomon, many of his friends and acquaintances, including Harro Schulze-Boysen of the Rote Kapelle resistance network and nationalistic anti-Nazi spies planted among the Gestapo, such as Hartmut Plaas, were involved in differing forms of resistance, details that von Salomon shares in his "answers."

Von Salomon revels in his role as a "passionate" passive observer. He claims in response to question 29, which asks after his history of employment and military service from 1931 onward, that UFA was a neutral, apolitical island in Nazi Germany. In a tone smacking of disingenuity, he declares, "The German film world was neutral. It had to be. To sacrifice its neutrality would have meant to sacrifice itself."[47] He goes on to stake an outrageous claim to extraterritoriality for UFA film, quite at odds with the political realities of the day, asserting for himself a position more proper to the condition of exile: "The German film world was neutral territory."[48]

Von Salomon makes a ludicrous argument for separate spheres of art and politics under Nazism:[49] "German cinema could not express political tendencies."[50] Adding insult to injury, von Salomon goes on to imagine himself in an interrogation with the military authorities in which he gleefully shirks responsibility by claiming this space of neutrality.

> After giving the matter careful consideration I have reached the conclusion that, in order to leave out nothing important, I would need the time and the paper to write some two thousand pages—which of course I am ready at any moment to do should I be so instructed. But perhaps it will suffice if this time I depart from the customary procedure of Allied Military Tribunals and hand back the responsibility of producing proof to those gentlemen of Military Government who, armed with the thunderbolts of a strictly examined conscience, tend to ask confidently:
> "What did you do during the nine years from 1936 to 1945?"
> Then, I think I may recall my old master, Rowohlt, and shift my torso from side to side like a polar bear, and reply calmly, with a beaming smile:
> "Ho, ho . . . nothing can happen to me! I was in films!"[51]

I quote this passage in full because it illustrates two tendencies in von Salomon's writing that become exacerbated to the point of recurring symptoms in the final section of the book. First, he seldom misses an opportunity to comment sarcastically on the American military force's superior sense of having a clear conscience—though here he applies sarcasm rather than the affective tow of anger that characterizes his later remarks on the Americans. Second, he literally takes the words out of his former employer Rowohlt's mouth in order to circumvent a direct attribution to himself of this taunt and its irreverent stance toward questions of responsibility during the Third Reich. This tendency takes different forms throughout the book, where von Salomon also uses the conceit of dialogue to stage discussions of difficult and unpleasant topics.

Asked, during an interrogation in the internment camp, why he did not join the NSDAP, he replies, "Well, I became a script-writer instead. As such I earned approximately three times a *Gauleiter*'s salary."[52] He is astounded that the American officer accepts this flagrant claim at face value. This reception renders the comment cynical, rather than merely glib, and indicates the extremely low moral regard in which Germans were held at this point in time.

The narrator describes how, after the surrender of the small Bavarian town in which he was living at the end of the war, two polite yet firm military officers duly came to his home to arrest him, along with his Jewish partner, Ille Gotthelft, whom he had protected during the war. Gotthelft was arrested solely due to her association with von Salomon. Both von Salomon and Gotthelft were interned indefinitely in a camp under US military control in Bavaria. Ostensibly, his arrest was, for him, the final indignity; von Salomon considered himself an avid anti-Nazi, and Ille had been feverishly awaiting the arrival of the Americans. This sparked a vengeful desire to "write back" at the US occupation, as it were, by mercilessly parodying the intent of denazification.

Von Salomon's arrest was based on his inclusion on a list of potentially dangerous Germans that was drawn up by the Counter Intelligence Corps (CIC), the World War II and early Cold War army intelligence division that later became the US Army Intelligence Agency. William Ernest Hocking describes how many politically suspect Germans were arrested and held in detention centers under the control of US soldiers until their interrogation by US military officers could take place.[53] The list of names was also, to some extent, preemptive; that is, some of the people named on the list were former terrorists or agitators from the Weimar period, such as von Salomon. Arrestees were detained not only for their connections to the Nazi Party but also in relation to their pre-Nazi history, in what Hocking called an "anticipatory purge."

> If you will allow the comparison, it was a more humane equivalent of the Hitler process of purge, an anticipatory purge. Only, the purge killed its victims and they made no more trouble. This clean method of slaughter being closed to us, we kept our purged persons, as potential enemies-by-definition, within the community, alive but emasculated.[54]

Using an analogy with an ironic tone comparable to von Salomon's, Hocking described how the Allied forces, for whom this "clean method of slaughter" was unavailable, held their "purged persons" in check, "alive but emasculated," in detainment camps. That von Salomon was considered to be such a "purged person" should come as no surprise. As von Salomon describes it, he was held in various detention camps for a year and a half after the German defeat, despite his declarations that he had never supported the Nazi Party. The lion's share of his fictionalized autobiography is concerned with the injustice of his incarceration by the American military along with members of the SS and top-ranking members of the Nazi military. The text is both a symptom of *ressentiment* and a literary act of revenge aimed at the heart of the new democracy.

The Answer? Explosive Emotions

The narrative voice of the first two-thirds of von Salomon's book adopts a sardonic tone and sometimes employs inappropriate levity in the face of the enormity of National Socialist crimes. The final quarter, ensconced under the seemingly innocuous prompt "Remarks," describes his and Gotthelft's fifteen-month-long "erroneous arrest" in a US internment camp. This section festers with *ressentiment* in the Nietzschean sense; it is galvanized by scarcely veiled contempt, which degenerates at moments into an insulting parody of objectivity and realism.[55] If the US military government intended to impart what I am calling a sentimental (re)education to von Salomon, his rancorous perception of this school of hard knocks instead incited anti-Americanism in him, further exacerbating his preexisting Prussian nationalist and antidemocratic sentiments.

At times, von Salomon's book reads like a veritable who's who of interwar conservative revolutionaries. He lists encounters with Hans Zehrer, Hans Grimm, Ernst Jünger, members of the Salon Salinger, and even Ernst Roehm.[56] In the internment camps, his world shrinks to the company of a motley crew of suspected and actual perpetrators, among whom von Salomon singles out a collection of SS officers and Hanns Ludin, a faithful National Socialist and former ambassador to the Slovak Republic for whom von Salomon serves as a most faithful hagiographer. In this final section, von Salomon alternates between addressing the question of guilt and seething with *ressentiment*.

It is no exaggeration to claim that, on a number of levels, the book cannot make do without affect. First, it is invested in producing certain kinds of strong emotions for purposes of reader identification. Second, it is structured by a less easily defined affective undercurrent that seeks to unmoor certainties and justify the author's/narrator's passivity. In this context, apparently inappropriate textual tones and rhetorical devices (such as sarcasm, displaced attribution, a frivolous or facetious tone, hyperbole, irony, and cynicism) may be read as symptoms marking strong and disturbing emotions that are being disavowed or barely kept at bay by alternative affective structures. Finally, as we shall see in the concluding section of this chapter on the book's reception, its readerships' reactions were defined by a strong positive or negative emotional response to the book. Von Salomon's text is a literary explosive device, planted among the public, set to explode onto the scene of public opinion and eager to go to war with the democratic principles of the Allied occupiers.

Von Salomon claims to have written the book during his time of "erroneous arrest." He even allegedly performed his "answers" as a form of stand-up comedy before other prisoners of war in his camp.

> It became quite a joke. Evening after evening I would go from one barrack room to another and would give a verbal answer to any question they cared to put. On many an evening I spoke for fully three hours. [. . .] It was no great mental effort to fulfil my promise: I simply said whatever came into my head in connection with the question that was put to me, fair or not, simply letting myself ramble on.[57]

By staging a literal performance of the process of responding to the questionnaire and by saying simply "whatever came into [his] head," von Salomon makes a mockery of the process of denazification. His exhibitionistic oral performance, where he "simply let [himself] ramble on," suggests that those answering the Allied questionnaire did so according to their mood and with creative license. However, if these performances did not affect him spiritually, they nonetheless left their mark in other ways.

> But physically it was a considerable strain. For a few days I had been suffering from pains in my throat, and when I endeavoured to raise my voice often nothing would come from my mouth but a gush of warm air. After answering one of the more important questions I would return to my barrack room incredibly exhausted. My whole body would be covered with a disagreeable cold sweat, and I would throw myself on to my bed with a gasp.[58]

The narrator's body feels the strain of answering the questions; he feels "exhausted," his voice reduced to "mere hot air" (my translation). Similarly, he reveals his awareness of the particular past at which the questionnaire is aimed, when he recognizes that there are "more important" questions and when his performative response to these questions literally makes him gasp and renders him in a cold sweat. These rare moments that approach self-reflexivity are almost immediately undercut or neutralized by an ironic phrase or a witty description of an outrageous situation. Inconsistency in tone—and sometimes even in content—is a symptom of conflicting emotional states, which are part of a larger affective structure. Affect feeds affect, both in the book's account of the POWs and in the imaginary relationship between readers and the author, enabling a community of *ressentiment*.

In this community, emotions act as social bonds between otherwise unrelated individuals. Both Barbara Rosenwein's concept of "emotional community" and William Reddy's concept of "emotional suffering" are useful for grasping what is at stake in the emotional bonds formative of community. Rosenwein's concept of "emotional community" suggests that groups are held together not necessarily by physical proximity but by "fundamental assumptions, values, goals, feeling rules, and accepted modes of expression."[59] In the particular case of *ressentiment*, the values and assumptions are undergirded by an oppositional emotional investment in national identity. Rather like Hanns Braun's concept of *Gegengefühle* (counterfeelings, discussed in the conclusion to the present study), these emotional bonds are not dependent on a positive national entity or identity, instead staking their emotional claims via the negation of and in opposition to other national communities. In von Salomon's case, the national countercommunity in question is obviously the United States as represented by the occupying forces and their comportment. Thus readers of *Der Fragebogen* and appreciative letter writers to von Salomon may be considered as bound to one another through their morally driven claim to not be American and, by association, to not behave aggressively or in a morally apprehensive manner.

"Emotional suffering" is one of Reddy's key critical terms, which, in his context, means "an acute form of goal conflict, especially that brought on by emotional thought activations."[60] Eschewing the cognitivist accent Reddy places here, I would like to apply his term to affect as a positive identificatory space. By this I do not mean that emotional suffering is positive per se but, rather, that the thrall of identifying with a position of victimhood and suffering, as outlined by Nietzsche, is one important social bond in this affective community. Emotional suffering, when linked to a national imaginary, thus becomes an emotional comportment including elements of both pride and sorrow. Thus the "community of *ressentiment*" proves to be a nationalist palliative while also serving as a respite from dispossessed feelings of guilt and shame.

Affective Torsions: From Guilt to *Ressentiment*

To understand the structure of *ressentiment* in von Salomon's autobiography, it is necessary to chart the vicissitudes of the emotion of guilt in his text. In his responses to the questionnaire, von Salomon makes no effort to deny Nazi crimes against humanity, including the Jewish genocide. The question of guilt is clearly part of the narrator's world during the years of National Socialist dictatorship and during his internment in Allied POW camps after the German defeat.

The topic of guilt is often circumvented in von Salomon's text by way of literary strategies. For example, approximately halfway through the book, in response to question 40 (regarding the respondent's membership in organizations), von Salomon describes with consternation the events of the Jewish pogrom on the night of November 9, 1938—now known as the Reichskristallnacht (Night of Broken Glass).[61] The narrator's reflections on the event are prompted by the figure of von Salomon's lover, Ille Gotthelft. Portrayed as frustrated and afraid, she demands of von Salomon, "Whose fault is it all?"[62] In a rare (and quickly superseded) moment of sobriety, von Salomon replies that the National Socialists claim that these actions reflect the will of the German people (*Volk*), which, in effect, renders everyone guilty by dint of their being German, thus mirroring the logic of Arendt on "organized guilt." Von Salomon initially goes on to refute his complicity, denying that his activities as a conservative revolutionary in the 1920s had contributed to the destabilization and fall of the Weimar Republic. Changing tack, he then switches to admitting his indirect participation in the events leading up to the pogrom and recognizes the collective responsibility of the German citizens. He does this only to differentiate between those involved in the pogrom and the "good" Germans, including members of the NSDAP, who refused the event by dint of nonparticipation.

> And at this moment how many people do you imagine are sitting, like you and I, in their remotest room behind drawn curtains, talking as we are? And how many Party members do you imagine are doing and saying just this, just like you and I, honourable, decent Party members? Today is one of those days that is never over, that constantly recurs, that lays its claim on history over and over again, that carries with it the curse that can never be forgotten.[63]

This ominous prediction exhibits not only the potential of the eternal return of guilt but also the emotion of shame. Here, shame is directly connected to a lost national and personal honor more proper to a militant and nationalistic Prussian code of conduct—a "cool conduct" (as Helmut Lethen would have it).[64] In this context, the word *cool* indicates not only the distance implied by the genre of New Objectivity (which is Lethen's contention and describes von Salomon's postwar literary style only in part); it also indicates a detached passivity, the illusion of a distance from events that should work to prevent shame or dishonor from tipping over into guilt and culpability. As we have seen in the present study's chapter on Karl Jaspers' postwar lectures, it is not guilt but shame—both personal and public—that is at stake in the postwar German *Gefühlshaushalt*. The connection between shame and guilt in von Salomon's text suggests that although the narrator is not consciously aware of and even argues against feelings of guilt, he is very much susceptible to feeling shame, even if he frames this shame through nationalist discourses related to an ideal of Germany and—above all else—pride in Prussia.

Aleida Assmann's argument for the coexistence of two discrete emotional cultures—that of shame and that of guilt—in postwar West Germany underplays the extensive and complex overlap between the two affective structures. In the postwar context, shame plays a role in relation to both guilt and *ressentiment*. However, in von Salomon's case, Assmann's dichotomy is instructive. For von Salomon, these two cultures cannot coexist, for guilt implies some kind of individual culpability or engagement in a crime, whereas shame is connected to an internal fall from grace in relation to a code of conduct and, by extension, an assumption of noncomplicity due to sheer inactivity or passivity.[65] This is one link in a chain of logic that disavows complicity—and, by association, also guilt—through passivity, while seeking a source outside the self onto which the implicit guilt proper to *ressentiment* might be displaced.[66]

Through the logic of safety in numbers, Von Salomon avoids acknowledging personal complicity or guilt; he even attempts to redeem the "honorable, decent Party members." Interestingly, however, he is unable to deny the larger, historical, and implicitly national shame—even curse—incurred by the Germans on the Night of Broken Glass; it is a day "that constantly recurs, that lays its claim on history over and over again, that carries with it the curse that can never be forgotten." Von Salomon's use of the word *Anspruch* (claim) signals his awareness of the accountability, or debt (*Schuld* and *Schulden*), due to Jewish Germans, even as he denies the claim of guilt.

Similarly, in response to the questionnaire's query about membership in organizations, von Salomon declares, "How could it come about that everyone was guilty, which means of course that no one was guilty? That beneath the slogan of the triumph of the will all will was rotted away?"[67] More important than von Salomon's heavy-handed reference here to Nazi filmmaker Leni Riefenstahl's propaganda film *Triumph of the Will* is the matter of whose atrophied will is in question. This citation, like the passage above, shows von Salomon recognizing his own version of the Arendtian hypothesis of "organized guilt," in this case introducing the term *will*. The choice of this term is odd, considering that the concept implies the firm intention to follow through on a principled decision, which stands in stark contrast to the unwillingness of the protagonist to self-reflectively occupy the category of individual responsibility in these passages.

In another "dialogue" with Gotthelft, about the burning of synagogues, von Salomon goes so far as to note the increasingly deplorable circumstances of the Jews in Nazi Germany.

> I know, of course, what is happening to the Jews. Were I not myself a witness I should still know, for it has been announced often enough what would happen. The burning synagogues simply show that it is happening now. The appalling thing is that nobody can help "the Jews," because any attempt to do so simply increases their peril. The appalling thing is that we cannot help ourselves, and far more is happening to us than to the Jews.[68]

Rather than tarrying with the truly precarious historical situation of the German Jews, von Salomon averts his gaze to the plight of those who, neither Jewish nor National Socialists, become the "true victims." Following the logic of *ressentiment*, where dwelling on one's own guilt is not an option, the resentful subject, thus usurping the position of the persecuted victim, displaces the true sufferer.

Even more aggressively, von Salomon's response to question 119, concerning "Einkommen und Vermögen" (income and assets), evinces the logic of reversal—what could be called the "balancing of the books" in one's favor—that is peculiar to *ressentiment*. Von Salomon describes the good life that he and Gotthelft enjoyed despite the upheavals of the Third Reich: "Oh, we had lived well, there could be no doubt about that! We had lived a bit crazily, but well. We had eaten and drunk like capitalists, but since we spent all our money on eating and drinking, like proletarians, it all came to the same in the long run."[69] Von Salomon continues, candidly yet provocatively,

> I admit that during those years I never once thought of my many contemporaries who were even then locked up in concentration camps: I thought of them as little as they had of me during the years when I was languishing in prison. Axel [von Salomon's friend] preserved his discharge paper from the concentration camp, just as I preserved my discharge from prison. One never knew when the time might come when the rapid production of these documents might not prove invaluable.[70]

Von Salomon's comparison of his incarceration in prison during the Weimar era to his contemporaries' imprisonment in concentration camps by the totalitarian Nazi Party is, in a word, incommensurable; this balancing of books offers a false political and ethical equation. To avoid the sting of conscience, von Salomon implements an opportunistic leveling of difference and reduces all comparisons to prosaic equations: capitalism is to the proletarian as prison under democratic rule is to incarceration in a concentration camp under a totalitarian regime. No matter how one looks at it, this equation does not add up. Further, it introduces an affective edge that replaces guilt with an attitude of flamboyant disregard and contemplation with manic, overcharged affect.

Ressentiment is characterized by helplessness (*Ohnmacht*) and passivity exhibited in all but the subject's affective life. For von Salomon, political participation or civic involvement gives way to smoldering passivity, an insidious cynicism, nefarious identifications, and a will to nihilism. Listening to the speech delivered by Hitler in response to the Röhm Putsch of July 30, 1934, von Salomon considers the extremely limited options that he sees for action of any kind against National Socialism. This situation leaves one "with the foul alternatives of behaving like a fool or like a coward."[71] Trapped in the logic of this specious binary, von Salomon is unable to imagine an alternative: "There must, there must be a third solution. And if there is in fact none, which was preferable: to behave like a fool or to act like a coward?"[72] It is safest and wisest to do nothing, he decides, thus practicing a form of "resistance" that he terms "a sort of Gandhi-ism without Ghandhi."[73] In effect, "Gandhi-ism without Gandhi" amounts to a (non)practice of nonviolent civil (non)resistance without political or ethical aim—in other words, a hollow standpoint devoid of ethical orientation. Once again, the narrator executes a cynical move away from the feeling of guilt, toward an emotional numbing or "coolness" of sorts.

Despite the resentful subject's denial of his or her own complicity, von Salomon and other prisoners repeatedly returned to the topos of guilt—particularly as it pertains to the Jewish genocide. On his way to the internment camp, during a brief stint in prison, von Salomon discusses his exchange with his cellmates about National Socialism and the persecution of the Jews.

> When the soldiers spoke of the war they gave the impression that it had all been great fun, except in Russia. And the civilians seemed to think that National-Socialism had contained a great deal that was good, apart from its essential nature. All, including myself, regarded what had happened to the Jews and in the concentration camps as very filthy; all, including my-

self, swore that though we had had our suspicions we had not known, and that there was nothing we could have done about it.[74]

This "very filthy" business of the persecution of enemies of National Socialism in the concentration camps and the Jewish genocide are not named directly ("eine große Schweinerei"). Nonetheless, in the very same sentence, the speakers disclaim responsibility for these euphemistically addressed events. Von Salomon structures the passage in such a way that it includes him in the broader mass of Germans and allows little room for reflection beyond the clichés expressed by the prisoners. He concludes by summing up the conversation with the sentence "It was not very interesting."[75] This cursory summation underscores his "cool" stance toward the topic of guilt. We encounter this position again during debates between Germans arrested for their potential political danger, as well as Nazi Party members and military officials. "The others," writes von Salomon, "talked from bed to bed, a long, laborious discussion about the concept of 'guilt.' It finally transpired that each one refused to accept himself as having any 'guilt.'"[76]

Discussions about the extermination of the Jewish population in the camp during the Nuremberg trials reveal a collective effort to understand and, ultimately, to deflect the emotion of guilt (the so-called guilty conscience), despite an undeniable sense that the material exposed during the trials "weighed" on the POWs in crucial ways.

> In this camp I had never heard a single cynical remark concerning the atrocious fact of the physical extermination of the Jews—apart from those made by the Americans. At Nuremberg the prosecution was marshalling its documents. They crushed me as much as they did the Nuremberg accused and every inmate of our camp. I had naturally to assume that the accusations would be personally directed at many of my fellow inmates, and it seemed to me logical that they should undergo the same arbitrary fate that they might once have imposed on others; justice, after all, can no more be crystallised from the rapid trials held before the National-Socialist "People's Courts" than from the hundreds of thousands of printed pages produced at Nuremberg. The important thing was not the mass of guilt, the quantity, but the place at which it first came into existence.[77]

In this dense passage, von Salomon recognizes what might be called collective national shame for the atrocities committed under National Socialist rule. However, he goes on to undercut this recognition by returning to his acrimonious double-entry bookkeeping that makes the inappropriate equation of the arbitrary justice meted out by the National Socialist People's Court with that of the trial of the major war criminals before the International Military Tribunal between 1945 and 1946. He moves away from an initial definition of guilt that is close to Jaspers' category of "juridical guilt," only to replace it with a less definitive category that might be said to waver between the categories of "personal guilt" and "metaphysical guilt": "The important thing was not the mass of guilt, the quantity, but the place at which it first came into existence" (518). This distinction between the quantity and quality of guilt indicates the author's awareness, beyond the thesis of "organized guilt," of the moral and affective stakes in postwar Germany. Nonetheless, the cynical anti-Semitism von Salomon attributes to the American soldiers, implying that the American Allies have double standards when it comes to persecution of Jews and non-Jews, can be understood as both a deflection of the question and an expression of von Salomon's growing animosity toward the Americans.[78] This simultaneous association of American soldiers with anti-Semitism and Jewish interests is a recurring topos in postwar German reactions to defeat and occupation and is very much in line with the displacement characteristic of *ressentiment*.[79]

Von Salomon's enigmatic sentence about the importance of the "place" at which guilt came into existence in the individual's life is followed by a qualification.

But this was precisely the point at which the problem collided with individual conscience. This was every individual's experience. No matter what route he might have followed to join the movement he was fully informed in advance concerning the Jewish question. But in almost no case did this question impinge on the realms of his own problems. Only gradually, but steadily, did the Jewish question seep into the individual's own field of activity. And each man was at a given moment faced with this decision—how far did the measures periodically ordered (almost always recognized for what they were, but not as steps in a culminating process) affect the carrying out of what he regarded as his own tasks and duties. I must assume this: that the decision was honestly faced. But even that meant nothing more than the insinuation, into each man's own sphere, of the foulest sort of corruption of which the conscience can perceive, the corruption that compels the individual to choose the lesser of two evils.[80]

In this account, participants in the National Socialist regime at all levels became, at some stage of their involvement, fully cognizant of the genocidal plans to solve the "Jewish question." This being the case, the appropriate question is no longer whether one is guilty but to which degree the individual has been corrupted by the decision to knowingly participate in the Nazi system. Taking the logic of Arendt's hypothesis about "organized guilt" to another level, von Salomon implies that guilt is the wrong emotion or comportment to search for under these circumstances. The only choice is that between "the lesser of two evils." In this way, he shifts the ethical terms of the discussion by exempting the German people from examining their consciences, instead claiming a corrosive corruption—"the foulest sort"—over which they have no control. Following the logic of *ressentiment*, which seeks to evade guilt in order to take up the position of suffering, von Salomon moves from the question of an active awareness of collective guilt to establishing the foundations for a passive community, on which corruption was visited by the Nazis as the people stoically operated in the face of poor choices (in the best case scenario, opting for "the lesser of two evils").

If, as Nietzsche argues, punishment intends to awaken the "feeling of guilt" in a guilty person, while also acting as "the actual *instrumentum* of that psychical reaction called 'bad conscience'" or the "sting of conscience," the subject of *ressentiment* adds another twist to this affective loop by seeking an agent to whom it may attribute this attempt to awaken its "bad conscience."[81] In other words, *ressentiment* is the site from which the subject launches an attack on the potential "feeling of guilt," disavowing the "sting of conscience" by instead submerging the subject in alternative states of feeling, which are also mostly negative and violently self-absorbed. *Ressentiment* might be described as the umbrella term designating this displacement of bad conscience by way of feeling otherwise. This mode of affection perversely finds pleasure in willing displeasure: "We stand before a discord that *wants* to be discordant, that *enjoys* itself in this suffering and even grows more self-confident and triumphant the more its own presupposition, its physiological capacity for life, *decreases*."[82] This triumph in the face of suffering is a marked quality of the hyperbolic and ironic tone Ernst von Salomon deploys in his *Fragebogen*. In effect, these literary strategies act as an affective palliative for a subject in the thrall of *ressentiment*.

In von Salomon's book, Ille Gotthelft often figures as a Socratic interlocutor in a dialogue where one party represents the voice of reason in response to that of *ressentiment*. Von Salomon reacts harshly to Gotthelft's lamenting the constant fear and hatred she suffered under the National Socialist regime: "We've had it lucky, Ille, and we've no cause to be resentful. We belong to the small minority which has no right to squawk. And for just that reason it is our duty from now on to further the cause of commonsense, and nothing but commonsense!"[83] Significantly, this direct reference to Nietzsche's term *ressentiment* is lost in the English translation of the term as simply "resentful." This refusal of the position of *ressentiment* by the narrator appears to be ironic, however, in light of von Salomon's own nihilism and self-righteous hatred for the American Allies.

Later we learn that Gotthelft is Jewish; she has been hiding in plain sight, posing as von Salomon's wife in Germany during the years of National Socialist rule. She declares that fear and hatred determined her comportment during the Third Reich—most likely meaning the fear of being discovered and the hatred she claims to have developed in response to the loss of dignity occasioned by being part of the acquiescent German collective. She describes the self-loathing and, indeed, *ressentiment* produced in response to the heavy cost of remaining passive for her own survival, as did the majority of the German population, under National Socialist rule.

> And for twelve years they've been trying to deprive me of my dignity. What is the meaning of life without love? I wanted to love each day, and the country, and the Germans among whom I lived, and you and me. But I wasn't allowed to. I had to learn to despise everything, the day and the country and the Germans and you and me. How could I love or respect when I was neither loved nor respected? Where there is no dignity there is hatred; I didn't want to hate but I had to learn. I got to know hatred, chiefly hatred of myself—it was myself I hated most. I knew that in the eyes of all other people I had become exactly what all others were all the time in mine.[84]

This outburst occurs after Gotthelft and von Salomon have viewed several of the photographs taken in German concentration camps. These disturbing photographs are never described in the narrative, and this signifying absence in an otherwise loquacious text attests to the sobering horror experienced by the narrator and his partner. Unable to sleep, von Salomon goes to Gotthelft's room. A conversation ensues about the appropriate emotional posture and the individual's relationship to culpability in the aftermath of the revelation that the actual function and operation of the concentration camps far exceeded the limits of their wartime imaginations. "We should never forget," says Gotthelft, "memory must do for us what imagination cannot."[85] What is uncanny about this quotation is that Gotthelft's formulation of the relationship to the recent past is driven by a futurity that promises to erase her present moment of revelation by casting her back into a yet unimagined and unimaginable past. Unable to inhabit her present moment, Gotthelft expresses another emotional aspect of the clusters in the constellation of *ressentiment*: the conglomerate of self-hatred, fear, and guilt feelings. Rather than a sincere attempt to reflect on one's relationship to the past, culpability arises in the text at nodal points, as symptom-like *ressentimental* feelings and an attendant cynical glee.

According to Nietzsche, that to which the subject of *ressentiment* reacts with acute negative affect is also perceived by the subject to be the source of the sense of suffering or persecution.

> For every sufferer instinctively seeks a cause for his suffering; more exactly, an agent; still more specifically, a *guilty* agent who is susceptible to suffering—in short, some living thing upon which he can, on some pretext or other, vent his affects, actually or in effigy: for the venting of affects represents the greatest attempt on the part of the suffering to win relief.[86]

Following Nietzsche further, this "orgy of feeling"[87] paradoxically represents nothing less than an attempt to attain the "narcotic" of *anaesthesia*.

> [The subject of *ressentiment* seeks] to *deaden*, by means of a more violent emotion of any kind, a tormenting, secret pain that is becoming unendurable and to drive it out of consciousness at least for the moment: for that one requires an affect, as savage an affect as possible, and, in order to excite that, any pretext at all.[88]

Expressed in another way, through the "desire to *deaden pain by means of affect*," the subject of *ressentiment* conflates "too little" affect with "too much."[89]

This logic of *ressentiment*, where "too little" becomes synonymous with "too much" (specifically, when guilt is displaced by a surplus of affect or mania), is precisely the logic that von Salomon deploys. He is careful to frame these statements as part of a dialogue; in this way, he avoids gesturing toward interiority, a space that is seldom evoked in his answers to the questions in the main body of the text. Unlike Nietzsche, he rarely psychologizes, unless it is to mock or elevate a person or group. He avoids acknowledging psychological interiority in a variety of ways: through dialogue, by appropriating the victim status, by turning to a sardonic or manic tone, or by making absurd and outrageous claims when reflection threatens to interrupt the ironic tone of his account in the main body of the text. In addition to his liberal use of hyperbole to exhibit the manic triumph in suffering that defines the subject of *ressentiment*, he quite literally outlines, blow by blow, his move from the position of the "guilty" to that of the suffering subject, as well as the jouissance he experiences in this role.

Von Salomon expresses a patent dislike for Americans throughout his book; this expression reaches a climax during his "erroneous" postwar internment. Far from viewing the American Allies as his liberators, von Salomon vents his spleen at their presence, while recognizing the irrationality of his ire: "In fact my anger with the Americans increased daily. I was well aware that this anger was emotional in origin, not intellectual. It was a true German anger at missed opportunities, at the discrepancy between their proclamations and their actual behaviour."[90] By ironically labeling the emotion of anger in nationalistic terms, as "German," von Salomon proposes a community of *ressentiment* that lodged itself in postwar Germany, characterized less by reason than by a virulently nationalized anger at "lost opportunities" and by a sense of being treated in an inconsistent and unfairly persecutory manner.

Before his internment in the POW camp, von Salomon expresses a strong dislike of what he describes as the Americans' "monumental self-righteousness" (*ihre ungeheuerliche Selbstgerechtigkeit*). Gotthelft, in response, gently reminds him that there is a difference "between injustice on the part of the state elevated to the status of a principal and injustice on the part of individuals."[91] Nonetheless, after his and Gotthelft's violent and abusive experiences with the cockily self-proclaimed "Mississippi-boys,"[92] von Salomon's indignation reaches new heights. After losing several teeth during his "induction" to the first camp, von Salomon states,

> I had to a certain extent a feeling of wild triumph, in the first place because it didn't hurt, strike me as they would, it didn't hurt, so what was the point, what was the effect? No. I had this feeling of triumph because it was not I who was doing evil, naturally, that must be it, it was this officer who was so angry, not I.[93]

In the thrall of *ressentiment*, he gains intense pleasure—a wild feeling of triumph—from the punishment meted out by the American GIs. Abuse heightens his sense of the validity of his status as "sufferer": "It is anguish of the soul that deadens the pain of the body, it is not anger but grief. Stop, stop, in that case the sensation of triumph, is the sensation of suffering triumphant . . . dare

I go so far as that, I, I of all people? Suffering is certainly not creative, or is it? [. . .] So suffering exalts?"[94] Anger, a defensive reaction, gives way to the "anguish of the soul," or grief, which, in turn, is displaced by the sense of triumph in one's suffering, defining the structure of *ressentiment*. Von Salomon describes the productive nature of suffering and the metamorphosis of emotions; in this way, he charts the overlapping and volatile nature of affective structures that cannot be reduced to this or that emotion. Navigating the creative force of negativity that makes the sufferer revel in the role, where *ressentiment* makes a blessing out of injury, von Salomon muses, "Perhaps they despised us all the more because of their perpetual inability to realise that in us some remote, strange discernment was at work giving us a sensation almost of bliss at the realization that at last, at last and for once, injustice was not on our side."[95]

Another symptom of the emergence of Nietzschean *ressentiment* is the satisfaction that von Salomon and other camp inmates feel on learning that whisper campaigns beyond the camp equate their suffering with that of the former concentration camps' inmates. "New arrivals told us," he reports, "that, among the population outside, this camp was rumoured to be a 'Starvation and Beating Camp.' So the story had got out, which gave us a certain satisfaction."[96] A triumphant sense of suffering enables von Salomon to attribute guilt to the US-Allied forces, to loosen the hold of any sense of his own culpability, and to turn himself (and other Germans like him) into the suffering party.

Even before his postwar internment by the Allies, von Salomon exhibited a strong tendency toward the extreme outer limit of *ressentiment*, through a darkly nihilistic frame of mind and comportment. There are moments in von Salomon's account when this nihilism is expressed in an unadorned fashion. In the years leading up to the National Socialist regime, von Salomon was, as stated, invited to attend the first Lippoldsberger *Dichtertreffen* (writers' meeting), at the house of the soon-to-be-Nazi poet Hans Grimm. At this meeting, von Salomon realizes that the distance between himself and the other national conservative authors assembled may be measured not so much by his lack of gravitas and tomfoolery (*Clownerei*) as by his abandonment of any values whatsoever—even those of conservative nationalism shared by those around him.

> Nothing much glowed in my heart save an intractable desire for life. That psychological moment had come much later for me; it had occurred neither on the battlefield nor within the framework of a picture that could be said to represent a generation. Perhaps that is why I had so different an attitude to the current events which Hans Grimm deplored in such moving terms. The destruction of those values for which Hans Grimm was fighting so

desperately—tradition, dignity, decency and that curious thing he called the priceless boon of individual freedom—did not fill me, as it did him, with violent rage: but neither was my attitude towards this matter the same as that of the ex-soldiers—I was not simply resigned to it. Rather I was inclined to approve of that destruction in so far as it applied to those circles for which Hans Grimm spoke. This is not because I failed to value such things as tradition, dignity, decency and what for me too was the priceless boon of individual freedom, but because I tended to doubt the real existence of those abstractions or rather to doubt their existence as forces affecting the business of the world around us. It therefore seemed to me more logical to watch the insubstantial shadows vanish than to act in the name of those shadows, better to let a vacuum be created than to shore up an old construction which had shown itself to be a falsehood.[97]

Never a fan of the middle class, von Salomon rejects these humanist values reduced to ineffective and "insubstantial shadows" by the interwar political situation. Finding these values to have been a "falsehood," von Salomon welcomes what he calls "a vacuum." His is a nihilistic stance of absolute passivity vis-à-vis the dangerous ideological vacuum that became apparent during the final years of the discredited Weimar Republic. This provided fertile ground indeed for the seeds of *ressentiment* that blossomed in vivid patches during the postwar years.

In a similarly nihilistic vein, after World War II, von Salomon also dismisses democracy and all it stands for as a political option. In fact, using his faulty logic of equivalences, he goes so far as to argue, "I fear that Hitler's assertion—that his ideological concept was the democratic concept—will prove a hard one to refute."[98] At the very beginning of Hitler's ascendency, von Salomon views the Nazi leader's approach and ideas as "simply an enlarged and exaggerated version of the methods and thought processes employed by liberal-democrats."[99] Von Salomon goes on to say that he himself has only "very rarely" and "with great reluctance" ever used the word *democracy* and that he has yet to find someone who could explain to him what it means.

In addition to his passion for living, his violent aversion to bourgeois values, and his spurious comments about democracy, von Salomon's identification with Prussia serves to quicken his pulse. The mere thought of Prussia arouses emotions of pride and love—this time in the form of excessive national pride for the bygone political entity and authoritarian identity of Prussia. Indeed, Prussia remains more than a politico-historical phenomenon for von Salomon, whose vivid attachment to this (now fantasmatic) political identity borders on—if not crosses over into—fanaticism.[100]

In response to question 16, regarding *Staatsangehörigkeit* (citizenship), von Salomon mournfully traces the demise of Prussia to the rise of the National Socialist regime, with its political *Gleichschaltung* (enforced standardization).[101] He co-opts July 20, 1944, the day on which a resistance group of Prussian military officers and aristocrats planted a bomb that failed to kill Hitler, as the date of Prussia's demise. The outcome of this failed assassination was the execution of those suspected to be involved in the plot: "July 20th, 1944, marked the final collapse not only of the Prussian Army but of the whole educational world of the nineteenth century."[102] Von Salomon sees this as the deathblow to Prussia: "In its true substance Prussia was henceforth no longer a concept, the Prussian being only continued to exist as appearance, the Prussian spirit as a ghost, the Prussian essence as deficit."[103] In the absence of a German sovereign state, Von Salomon, with his manic love for Prussia, ultimately declares, "I am a Prussian and I wish to be a Prussian."[104]

By definition, this identification is (self-)destructive inasmuch as von Salomon's identity is constituted by a fervent identification with Prussia, which is said, not only by the Allied military forces, to no longer exist. Since Prussia no longer can be claimed as a sovereign entity (or even a geographical reality) in postwar Germany, von Salomon is identifying with a political phantom. Thus von Salomon identifies obstinately with a past entity with nonexistent foundations. In turn, this identificatory posture functions through an equation of the self with a defunct entity, whose demise is disavowed in order to gain access to a sense of past national glory. Nihilism's prime emotional comportment is the embrace of *ressentiment* characterized by extreme spitefulness and the overwhelming pathos of self-pity for the ostensibly foundationless, stateless self.

Ressentiment not only provides for a self-destructive and nihilistic comportment; it also effectively recodes any political understanding of emotions and the norms they represent. It does this by only being able to express itself through hyperbolic means, leaving open the question of the sincerity of the emotions expressed through public and social interaction. As a subject of *ressentiment*, von Salomon represents a particular affective attitude and comportment in relation to how emotions not only express but also influence, define, and even produce the public sphere, as concerned Jaspers and also, as we shall see, Alexander and Margarete Mitscherlich. Through its hyperbolic expression and mode of insincerity in this text, *ressentiment* can be seen as a politics of emotion by other means—a negative or void politics of emotions, if you will. This cluster of affects and its attendant social forms of emotion enable the subject to divorce himself from culpability in the very gesture of emotively blaming another, ostensibly stronger party for his own wounds, passivity, and nihilism.

The narrator's parting gift to the reader who has stayed the distance of this text is a final provocative gesture demonstrating how von Salomon's resentful logic of reversal makes heroes from persecutors turned prisoners. The protagonist of von Salomon's parable of martyrdom is foreign diplomat Hanns Ludin, ambassador to the Slovak Republic from 1941 until the end of the war. Von Salomon encounters Ludin in the camp and is greatly taken by his firm belief in National Socialism and his adherence to strong principals of "decency." As German ambassador to the Slovak Republic, Ludin was instrumental in convincing the Slovak government to facilitate and cover up the deportation of Slovakian Jews (although von Salomon insinuates that Ludin did not know where the Jews were being deported to and was horrified once he learned the truth).[105]

The narrator wanted to get to know Ludin, for he found him to be "the best man in the camp" and "the best National-Socialist I had met," thus he developed a respectful and close relationship with him, poignantly casting him in a principal role in a play staged by the POWs.[106] He is shocked when Ludin's written confession of his activities in the Slovak Republic result in him being categorized as a "war criminal"; von Salomon paints Ludin as the self-elected scapegoat for the Slovakian government and a man with immense dignity. Von Salomon's fantasy of Ludin's final words at his execution serve as the closing words of the book. The writer's hagiographic and pathos-laden conclusion imagines Hanns Ludin's execution through death by strangling as a noble, patriotic event, leaving the reader with one further ambivalent gesture.

Hanns Ludin, horribly emaciated in the grey flannel suit that was far too big for him, suffered the cord to be put around his throat. The executioner slowly tightened it. Hanns Ludin was dying [suffered] for twenty minutes. His last words were a message to his wife and his son, Tille, and the cry:

Long Live Germany![107]

Through this flagrant conflation of Hanns Ludin, "the best man," with this imagined last patriotic cry for Germany, the figure of a misguided martyr for the cause of a greater Germany is created. Ludin's figure provides the ultimate metonymic slippage from a figure responsible for suffering to one of patriotic sacrifice—the necessary suffering attendant on the subject of *ressentiment*. Thus Ludin is stylized to provide a conduit for immense sympathy and to give a specifically nationalist meaning to suffering. In von Salomon's cynical reversal, Ludin remains exempt of guilt and provides an idealized model for noble suffering on behalf of a "greater" Germany.[108] Cynicism in the text is usually a signal that a defense mechanism is at work under the sign of *ressentiment* and against the feeling of guilt—in this case, through the social bonds of imagined national pride and loyalty.

Using excessive affect as a means of deadening the "sting of bad conscience," the subjects of Nietzsche's *ressentiment* are firmly in the grip of negative emotions such as revenge and hatred: "how ready they themselves are at bottom to *make* one pay; how they crave to be *hangmen*."[109] In vitriolic terms, Nietzsche underscores the affective lot of these subjects, describing their state of being as "a whole tremulous realm of subterranean revenge, inexhaustible and insatiable in outbursts against the fortunate and happy and in masquerades of revenge and pretexts for revenge: when would they achieve the ultimate, subtlest, sublimest triumph of revenge?"[110] Arguably, for von Salomon, the act of writing *Der Fragebogen* under the pretext of merely answering the Allied denazification questionnaire, followed by the successful publication and reception of his best seller, constituted the "sublimest triumph of revenge," a sort of poison injected into the context of the newly founded Federal Republic of Germany in its nascent democratic state.

Reception: Demanding Questions for *The Answers*

The national and international reception of von Salomon's book suggests that it was extraordinary in more than one sense. Indeed, as right-wing writer Armin Mohler announced in *Merkur*, *Der Fragebogen* "was unquestionably West Germany's best seller for 1951."[111] Published after the lifting of bizonal Allied censorship laws, the first 10,000 copies of von Salomon's book were sold out on the day of their release; the number of preorders for the second edition (11,000–20,000) was high enough that the second run was sold out before it was even released;[112] 200,000 copies were sold in the first year alone, and over 236,000 copies had been sold by the beginning of 1953, with a steady stream of approximately 5,000 books purchased per month.[113] The book was translated into several languages and released in 1953 by Gallimard in France (reissued in 1981) and in 1954 by Putnam in the United Kingdom and Double-day in the USA.[114] We can gauge the immense popular response to the book by the flood of correspondence and invitations to readings, lectures, and discussions (let alone the adulating offers of friendship) received by von Salomon in the wake of the book's publication.

Garnering attention for von Salomon's text were not only its intensely subjective rendering of the history of the first half of the twentieth century and its excessively nationalist tenor but also its skillful use of language and cutting deployment of irony, delivered in a tone Derek van Abbé quite rightly describes as "disarmingly nonchalant."[115] At the same time, von Salomon's strident apologetics and his anger at the occupying forces reverberate throughout his book, turning it into not so much a "Vergangenheitsschelte" (a chastisement of the past) as an "Umerziehungsschelte" (a berating of reeducation), as Norbert Frei frames it.[116]

"This Will Anger You"

In his 1955 review in the *Chicago Daily Tribune*, Hans J. Morgenthau (the name already bodes ill for von Salomon in this context) concisely and appropriately defines von Salomon's book as "part autobiografy [*sic*], part fiction, part a political tract for our times."[117] In 1956, the *Journal of Modern History* shelved the book under the category of "political autobiography."[118] The reviewer for *Time* called von Salomon "passionately passive," with "a rotten radiance about his cynicism"; he said the text was "a well-written but viciously anti-American autobiography of a convicted murderer" and a "monstrous clever book"; and warned its readers that they would be "shocked" but also "fascinated."[119] Orville Prescott of the *New York Times* oscillated between admiration and condemnation: calling the book "detestable," "clever and witty," and "gruesomely interesting," he said of von Salomon, "However deplorable his character and infamous his politics, this man can write."[120] On its English-language release, this book clearly aroused emotions in its international readership, but of what kind?

For *Observer* reviewer Harold Nicolson, the book was "distasteful" and "unbearable, but important." He admirably captured the affective tone in which it was written, describing it as one of "*Hohngelächter*, namely a compound of scorn and rancour, far more vindictive than our own mild phrase 'derisive laughter.'"[121] The *Daily Boston Globe* ran a review of the book with the heading "This Will Anger You," stating, "Resentment, anger, revulsion, even fear and a painful twinge of conscience will be aroused in the American reader."[122]

Distaste, scorn, and rancour are emotions stirred up in some readers, while others might feel resentful, angry, afraid, or even guilty. This is not a book that left its international readers cold; but what about the reception closer to home, in West Germany?

"Ein literarischer Remer" for a Community of Ressentiment

On May 19, 1951, respected journalist and critic Friedrich Luft published a damning review of Ernst von Salomon's book in the chief newspaper of the American zone, *Die neue Zeitung*, with the title "Ein literarischer Remer."[123] Referring to Otto-Ernst Remer, the Nazi military officer who was pivotal in undermining the military takeover attempt by generals on July 20, 1944, in a plot against Hitler, Luft draws an unflattering parallel between the destructive behavior of this Nazi puppet and von Salomon's own politico-literary blow aimed at democracy in postwar West Germany. Luft's reaction not only pinpoints the literary aspirations of von Salomon's text ("feuilletonistische Eleganz") but also underscores the danger of publishing such an "evil" (böse) book at this uncertain historical junction ("dieser unsicheren Jahre"). Von Salomon's book, he believes, will be embraced as a justification for the resurgence of negative feelings and regressive ideas, as indicated by Luft's phrase "hämische neu-nazistische Lust" (malicious new-Nazi notions).

This contemporary review offers a diagnosis of the extant state of affective attachment to former political ideals and norms in postwar West Germany. It also represents one of two typical responses to von Salomon's book: a critique of the cynicism that drives the book and a condemnation of the antidemocratic political provocation it launches. The second type of response captures different aspects of what I am calling a "community of *ressentiment*"—those who are invested in feeling differently, in investing in *ressentiment* as a possibility for enabling affective structures very similar to those of anti-Semitism, but this time with the object of the US-Allied occupiers as the "cause" of hypocrisy and misery.

Von Salomon received a multitude of positive and admiring letters from prominent and unknown members of his readership (apparently he did not keep critical responses to his book, as his collected correspondence consists of only like-minded responses). People from all walks of life wrote to express their approval: two young women wrote in glowing terms and thanked von Salomon for filling them in on pre-Nazi history and for his "fair and unresentful accounts" (fairen und ressentimentlosen Berichte);[124] a twenty-five-year-old man worryingly asserts that many young people have understood the book very well, perhaps meaning that he and his cohort embraced the affective nihilism offered by the book, as evidenced when the man writes that "the sole implication recognizable in this [book] is the capriciousness of existence" (die Inkonsequenz des Daseins als die einzigste Konsequenz in diesem zu erkennen).[125]

Ressentiment is often mentioned in the correspondence in order to be immediately negated as that which von Salomon does not represent. A peer of former left-wing Nazi Otto Strasser writes a lengthy letter of praise (including a request for help in placing a book by Strasser), in which he states,

> For as long as the Western occupation powers do not make reparations, at least as far as it is materially possible, for the misdeeds and crimes committed at the time of the cease-fire (just as during the period of the "peaceful occupation"), we will reject any association with the West. This is not *ressentiment*, but rather a self-evident demand for international justice.[126]

It is remarkable how this letter writer has utterly co-opted the language of victimhood, staking claims in terms of *Wiedergutmachung* and demanding the right to use international law, all terms and processes that are associated more with the victims of National Socialism. Another correspondent acknowledges that this historical moment is one characterized by *ressentiment*: "In an era of *ressentiment*, where everything is politically distorted, your book has a particularly beneficial effect. At heart it speaks of a true and warm humanity." (In einer Zeit des Ressentiments, wo alles politisch verzerrt wird, ist Ihr Buch in seiner Wirkung besonders wohltuend. Aus ihm spricht im Grunde eine echte und warme Menschlichkeit.)[127] Clearly, the writer displaces the *ressentiment* manifested in the book onto the *Zeitgeist*, indicating that von Salomon's book does not take part in this spirit and is characterized instead by "humanity." Again, when we read for emotion, it is significant that *ressentiment* is mentioned time and again in connection with von Salomon's book, only to then be denied. This repetition only serves to underscore the haunting presence of *ressentiment* that characterizes the tone and structures the content of his book.

Some correspondents even appear to know that the emotions this book propagates go against the new emotional norms of democratic sentiment. They enjoy the feeling of communal transgression that reading and approving of the book appear to represent; for example, a woman writes to von Salomon, "That many people do not understand it [the book], had to be the case. At all events I feel as if it has been written from the soul." (Daß es viele Menschen nicht verstehen, muß wohl sein. Mir ist es jedenfalls aus der Seele geschrieben.)[128] In addition to signaling her strong emotional investment in the text and the stance

of transgressive bravado for which it stands, the writer indicates her willingness to become a member of the community of experience represented by von
Salomon's book. Despite all of the diverse physical locations of the
correspondents—coming from all regions of Germany and as far afield as a
prison in Denmark and a business in Turkey—they all explicitly deny the cynicism of the book while embracing the sense of a binding communal expression of their shared experience of *ressentiment*.

Talk of the Town: The Kölner Mittwochgespräche

Finally, in the context of its reception, von Salomon's book may be read as a
test instance of open discussion of divergent emotional norms and political
opinions in postwar West Germany. Phrased differently, the book and its reception beg the question, how much *resentiment* can a newly formed democracy
tolerate?

Depicted in a black-and-white image from 1951 is a corpulent man
dressed in suit pants and a crisply pressed white shirt, wearing highly shined
shoes and sporting a dark tie. His mouth torn open and his eyes narrowed by
emotion, he gesticulates wildly, pointing a finger accusatorily at someone beyond the photograph's frame, while his other hand is bunched up in a fist. Ernst
von Salomon sits, Humpty Dumpty–like, above the heads of the two other men
in the image, on what appears to be the ornate metal casing of a radiator. A pile
of coats and hats beside him, von Salomon silently bellows into the unseen
crowd in the large waiting hall at Cologne's main railway station. This space
had been reserved solely for the weekly gatherings of the exceptionally popular Mittwochgespräche that took place frequently in Cologne between 1950
and 1956; the photo of Ernst von Salomon described here forms part of the
modest documentation of these events.

Railway station bookseller Gerhard Ludwig and Rheinish author Jakob
Kneip developed the idea for the events; they would take place between December 1950 and July 1956, on 260 occasions.[129] The discussion of von Salomon's book in the author's presence was the forty-fourth session of the
Mittwochgespräch. These open public forums, conducted on diverse sociocultural, existential, and political topics, included "Muß die junge Generation
beiseite stehen?" (Must the young generation step back?), led by author Nikolaus Schücking in June 1950; "Die Situation des deutschen Nachkriegsfilms"
(The state of German postwar film), introduced by actor and returned Jewish
émigré Peter Lorre and Dr. Hannes Schmidt in September 1951; "Warum
Trümmerliteratur?" (Why 'rubble' literature?), facilitated by *Kahlschlag* au

thors Heinrich Böll and Paul Schallück in July 1952; "Adolf Hitler—Schicksal, Dämon oder Verhängnis?" (Adolf Hitler—destiny, demon, or fate?), facilitated by journalist and author Walter Görlitz in June 1953; and "Todesstrafe—ja oder nein?" (Yes or no to the death penalty?), opened by academic and social democratic politician Carlo Schmid in March 1955.

The "Wednesday conversation" (Mittwochgespräch) was greeted with monumental enthusiasm from its inception: forty-two attendees, instead of the tentatively envisaged five, appeared at the first event. The inaugural public debate, on December 6, 1950, was led by one of the meeting's two initiators, author Jakob Kneip, along with two further authors, Josef Winckler and Edzard Schaper, on the theme "Die Aufgabe des Dichters in unserer Zeit" (The task of the poet/writer in our times).[130] During the first few events, Ludwig noticed that those in attendance were more invested in public discussions of the questions raised by the lecture than in the lecture itself. Public participation and the open voicing of divergent opinions was clearly experiencing a renaissance after twelve years of Nazi dictatorship, and those who attended were keen to cut their discursive teeth in public, given the right setting.

> Precisely after 1945 the public sphere was understood as a newly reclaimed space in which one could intervene in social discourse freely and without fear of denunciation. It manifested itself originally—controlled more or less by the British military government—by way of media such as the radio and newspaper. A short time later this was complemented by public discussion groups and conversation and literary evenings.[131]

As many as eight hundred attendees, hungry for a forum in which to encounter and express shared values and differing opinions, could be expected at any given meeting, although the hall only allowed for a crowd of three hundred participants at full capacity (an overflow room was set up on such occasions). The attendees helped foster what might be called the emergence of a culture of "engagierte Streitgespräche" (engaged disputations),[132] public exchange that requires participation and performance if it is to become part and parcel of an individual's and a society's sociopolitical habitus.

It is important to keep the significance of the form and process of the Mittwochgespräch in mind, for in this period of postwar history, this open forum for debate was just as meaningful as the content of the discussions. One could say that the content of Ernst von Salomon's *Der Fragebogen* pales beside the attentive and equivocal reception accorded to the text at the time of its publication—a fact that is difficult to grasp now, considering how this politically ambivalent book has been consigned largely to the unexamined debris of post-war history.[133] The reception of *Der Fragebogen* includes von Salomon's provocative performance and the ensuing debate at the Kölner Mittwochgespräch on October 17, 1951. For this reason, the event itself, of which at least part exists today as a recording, deserves more than passing attention in the present attempt to fathom affective cultures spawned in postwar West Germany.

Ernst von Salomon's appearance at the Kölner Mittwochgespräch was heralded under the title "Die Aufgabe des Schriftstellers in unserer Zeit" (The task of the author in our times), a theme that he had chosen in a self-proclaimed ironic vein and that may indeed be a parodic reference to the title of the first Mittwochgespräch, "Die Aufgabe des Dichters in unserer Zeit." As was customary, von Salomon delivered his lecture in fifteen to twenty minutes (the event's host, Ludwig, strictly regulated time); then discussion was opened up to the floor. An extremely lively argument ensued between the author and many members of the audience; the event was covered by journalists from all over Germany and was summed up appropriately by Ludwig with the word *sensationell*.[134] The remaining fragments of the discussion, which were recorded by Ludwig in his first taping session of the Mittwochgespräche, bear witness to both the boisterousness of von Salomon and the spleen of the participants during the discussion.[135] On this particular evening, in arguments around the bluntly forthright yet politically loaded and cynical book by von Salomon, the Cologne weekly meetings became a space for unlicensed discussion of some of the most difficult questions of the contemporary period—among which were those related to the affective constellation of guilt and *ressentiment*.[136]

During the course of the discussion, which took the form of a heated and defensive question-and-answer debate, von Salomon was called on to explain his political stance and rationale for publishing such an explosive book. Some members of the public accused him of being cynical and of demonstrating apathy toward questions of war guilt ("Kriegsschuldfragen"), while one man, who had been stationed in Poland during the war, expressed his anger at von Salomon's equating the treatment of a defeated population by the Americans with that of the Germans' actions in occupied countries during the war. Von Salomon insists, somewhat disingenuously, that he wrote the responses to the *Fragebogen* in the camp, with "no political and no literary intentions" (keine politische Absicht und keine literarische Absicht).

An enraged member of the audience declares not only that von Salomon got off lightly during the Nazi period but also that his book contributes to an active forgetting of the fact that six million Jews had been murdered in Poland and elsewhere. The audience applauds this speaker's contribution, and he continues, "As a German I have seen the chimneys of Auschwitz smoking." He concludes by calling von Salomon's book "a catastrophe" (ein Unglück) demonstrating "the wrong psychological attitude" (die psychologisch falsche Einstellung) and an opportunity for "old German cavaliers" ("alte deutsche Kavaliere") to discredit the new democracy. Other audience members call the book "barbarous" (unmenschlich) and criticize von Salomon for remaining unaffected ("unbetroffen") by events and of financial opportunism and acting as the "prototype of the cynic" ("der Prototyp des Zynikers"). One audience member goes so far as to wish that both von Salomon and Ernst Jünger would make a declaration apologizing for leading young people astray with their writings.

Von Salomon declares his book to be an act demonstrating just how much these events affected him ("Ich bin betroffen!"), as well as an attempt on his part not only to destroy the template ("Schablonen") of the Allied questionnaire but also to ironize his own templates. At some point, his publisher, Ernst Rowohlt, one of the two other men depicted in the photograph of the event, intervenes, defending his choice to publish von Salomon's book, by pointing out the international interest shown in the text as well as the immense number of copies sold in Germany. In response to the request for an apology, Rowohlt replies, "If the German democracy and the youth are unable to stomach this book, then I feel sorry for democracy and the youth" (Wenn die deutsche Demokratie und die Jugend dieses Buch nicht verdauern können, dann tut mir die Demokratie und die Jugend leid).

Although Rowohlt's comment is sarcastic, it directly addresses the uneasiness produced by von Salomon's book and its reception: what kind of influence could a contentious, politically explosive book exert in the tentative West German public sphere?[137] I argue that one could view the publication and reception of *Der Fragebogen* as a test case for the new confidence in public debate and the ability to tolerate difference in the fragile West German democracy. Following the Derridean understanding of *pharmakon* as both poison and remedy, it would seem that rather than realizing the fear that von Salomon's book might poison and destroy the politico-affective system of the body politic of the new Federal Republic, it instead serves as an instance that confirms the developing fortitude of new democratic sentiments under negotiation in West Germany.

Taking it one step further, this episode suggests that some form of *ressentiment* is perhaps constitutive—a necessary precondition and by-product—of democracy, against which democratic sentiments are able to perform and reinstate their durability. The publication and reception of *Der*

Fragebogen represent a significant event in early postwar West German culture because they demonstrate the emergence of a new democratic public sphere and its ability to tolerate a discussion of and reflection on less honorable German politico-affective traditions and the casualties of the country's recent past.

Reading for emotions in this instance of a counternormative community of *ressentiment* over and against the new "emotional regime" of democratic sentiment is instructive. In hindsight, what might be considered counternormative feelings or competing normative regimes appear to be constituent of democracy. Precarious events such as this tested the mettle of the new political hegemony of democracy in West Germany and demonstrated its capacity to accommodate toxic political emotions through the public acknowledgment of their existence and in open public exchanges. Instead of destabilizing the new democratic basis, these debates allowed for an exploration of difference and negativity, as well as a negotiation of democratic practices.

My interpretation of this episode as an example of postwar politics of emotion that demonstrates how, ideally, a healthy democracy can tolerate difference without being thrown into crisis resembles political theorist Chantal Mouffe's model of agonistic politics. Mouffe argues, "Too much emphasis on consensus, together with aversion toward confrontations, leads to apathy and to a disaffection with political participation."[138] Contrasting and competing regimes of emotion are constitutive of self-declared democratic societies, particularly at the level of process and of making sense of alternative emotional repertoires and their potential to challenge or strengthen hegemonic affective structures. In terms of reading for emotions, "feeling differently," such as with *ressentiment* in this case, is constitutive of the horizon of potential political futures. Some futures may be realized; others may be contested in order to address or negotiate the boundaries of a political habitus: this is the politics of emotion *in actu*.

CHAPTER 3

The Inability to Mourn, Terminable and Interminable

And with regard to any therapeutic application of our knowledge, what would be the use of the most acute analysis of social neuroses, since no one possesses power to compel the community to adopt the therapy? In spite of all these difficulties, we may expect that one day someone will venture upon this research into the pathology of civilized communities.
—Sigmund Freud

In a 1993 article on the attitudes of West and East Germans toward their past, published in the psychoanalytical journal *Psyche*, German psychoanalyst Margarete Mitscherlich argued that although, by and large, the hypothesis of a specifically German "inability to mourn" still holds, there are signs that this is beginning to change.[1] Her examination of German national identity in relation to its National Socialist past certainly is not unusual; remarkable, however, is how she frames the hypothesis of "the inability to mourn." Rather than returning to the linchpin of the argument she put forward with her husband, Alexander Mitscherlich, in their 1967 text *The Inability to Mourn*—namely, that Hitler was the unmourned object creating an affective blockage in the postwar German population—Margarete Mitscherlich uses "the inability to mourn" to refer to the lack of empathy with the victims of National Socialism. This displacement seems fully in line, however, with the manner in which the Mitscherlichs' text has become a reified paradigm within discourses on German memory and the Holocaust. Margarete Mitscherlich does not comment on this slippage, which suggests that she herself is now replicating one of the main "misreadings" of her original text in its reception and afterlife: namely, that the process of mourning in question was for the victims of the Nazi regime and not for Adolf Hitler, which was the premise of the Mitscherlichs' original argument.

Perhaps the most well-known point of critical reference in the accounts of postwar (West) Germany based in literary theory and cultural studies, Alexander and Margarete Mitscherlichs' *Die Unfähigkeit zu trauern* (*The Inability to Mourn*) has enjoyed unrivaled popularity in the canon of discourses on West German *Vergangenheitsbewältigung*; the book has not been out of print since its initial publication run in 1967. Apparently, no analysis of postwar German culture is complete without reference to this psychosocial evergreen, although, like many field-defining works, it is largely overcited and underread.[2] As psychoanalyst Christian Schneider observed, the Mitscherlichs' text has become a political rallying point or "parole" (slogan) rather than the "diagnosis" it ostensibly set out to perform.[3] In literary and cultural studies, responses to the hypothesis of a postwar West German "inability to mourn" have often produced scholarly accounts that infer a moral assessment, which sometimes overwhelms accompanying aesthetic or sociohistorical analyses of books, films, or events. The heritage of this line of thought in the field of German studies is a critical genealogy of "good" versus "bad" postwar objects of study, with "good" objects either performing or enabling mourning, as in the *Holocaust* television series broadcast in West Germany in 1979 or any number of antifascist works by members of the so-called Gruppe 47.[4] "Bad" objects tend to induce anxiety and discomfort, often due to moral ambivalence. This, in turn, may lead to critical neglect, as in the case of Ernst von Salomon's writing and, on the other side of the moral divide, Jewish-German survivor Hans Keilson's darkly humorous novels.[5] In demarcations of "good" and "bad" objects of postwar study, moral judgment may foreclose the analysis of equivocal objects or ambivalent or less readily legible affective structures, as demonstrated in the previous two chapters. As argued in the introduction, by the standards of this discourse, artifacts attain merit in direct proportion to their demonstrated impulse to "mourn" (or induce mourning); they are combed by scholars searching for expressions of regret, rue, or—even better—guilt.

In short, critical accounts that diagnose the postwar German collective as at least disturbed, if not outright pathological, often unwittingly appropriate the Mitscherlichian concept to propose a set of normative emotions proper to "correct" mourning and contrition. In this way, I argue, a sociopsychological version of psychoanalysis has become central to cultural analyses or diagnoses of the West German "case." This chapter revisits the Mitscherlichs' hypothesis in its historical context to examine the discursive conditions that produced and propagated their claim. In turn, this discursive excavation prompts us to ask whether this affective hermeneutic paradigm, which effectively narrowed the breadth of analysis of emotions at the same time in which a new bourgeois democracy was being established in West Germany, has outlived its usefulness. How might we begin to reconceptualize our approach to the affective landscape of postwar German culture? Further, how might we read the text as an expression of the authors' own disappointment at or mourning of what they see as the inability of the West German population to live up to a libidinally charged national ego ideal of the Mitscherlichs' design?

As addressed in the introduction, much recent scholarship in the ever-expanding field of the study of emotions,[6] more popularly known by the short-hand of "the emotional turn,"[7] concentrates on delineating historical genealogies of particular emotions as they emerge in society. This chapter is concerned with the relationship between "emotions" (which I define as socially articulated expressions of feeling open to normative judgment) and the more ambiguous territory of "affect" (a diffuse, not yet legible, and often morally ambivalent manifestation of feeling). As demonstrated in the preceding chapters, affect often appears to be less socially adaptable (or "useful" or appropriate in its particular historical context) and is recognizable, more often than not, as a structure or constellation, rather than defined as a single, particular emotion. In other words, in this chapter, reading for emotion takes the form of asking which normative emotions are present in postwar German society and which affective structures are overlooked or even obscured through a concentration on morally correct emotional comportment. As argued in the previous two chapters, the postwar affective structure cannot be captured adequately through the paradigm of an "ability" or "inability" to manifest "correct" moral emotions; rather, the emotional landscape consists of a complex reaction of affect to affect that requires a careful practice of reading of emotional intersubjectivity between these two postwar moments (post-1945 and pre-1968).

The initial focus of this chapter is an analysis of Alexander and Margarete Mitscherlichs' seminal tome, in which they make the case in psychoanalytical terms for what they diagnose as the postwar German population's apparent "inability to mourn." My contention is that this morally driven postwar classic unquestionably not only hit the nerve of gathering second-generational unrest on the eve of the 1968 student rebellion but, in its role as a touchstone for analyses of postwar Germany, also continues to generate an opus of what I termed, in the introduction to this book, postwar "melancholic scholarship." Rereading the Mitscherlichs' text, it is difficult to overlook the disappointment and even anger that sets the tenor of the book, indications of the authors' own frustration with the sociopolitical comportment of the West German population.

As stated, scholars of postwar melancholia base their analysis of literature and film on a largely uncritical acceptance of the argument made by the Mitscherlichs about a German "inability to mourn." Consequently, scholars analyzing German culture's "ability" to demonstrate *Vergangenheitsbewälti-*

gung (overcoming of the past) in a morally appropriate way often embrace the imperative driving their claims, overlooking the psychoanalytic inaccuracies of the Mitscherlichs' argument.[8] Whereas the Mitscherlichs' text may be characterized by an undertow of anger, disapproval, and a stark tone of disappointment, the work of melancholic scholarship sometimes evinces the wish for reparation of a "unusable past" or exhibits an elegiac attempt to undo or at least understand this history within the parameters of loss.[9]

The second part of this chapter analyzes the politico-historical context from which the "postwar" Alexander Mitscherlich emerged in order to better understand the network of discourses in which the concept of "the inability to mourn" was incubated. This also entails revisiting the historical (self-)representation of Alexander Mitscherlich and the arguments he and Margarete Mitscherlich make in their text, particularly in the wake of three recently published German biographies about Alexander Mitscherlich's life and work. It is productive that a revisitation of this sustained textual act of moral pedagogy aimed at German restoration is carried out in light of the tension that emerges between Alexander Mitscherlich's postwar adaptation to traditions of liberal democracy and his allegiance to psychoanalysis. Mitscherlich's later postwar commitment to democracy as a form of governance was not entered into without hesitation and, interestingly enough, contrasts sharply with his earlier political loyalties toward and participation in factions of the Conservative Revolution, from the interwar years through to the early period of National Socialism.

The third section of this chapter places Freud's reflections on taboo in his text *Totem and Taboo* in dialogue with the premises of the Mitscherlichs' arguments on the absence of processes of mourning in postwar West Germany. The Mitscherlichs' text will be read against the grain in relation to the taboos it established in postwar West Germany and its particular relationship to emotional ambivalence. My aim is not to detract from the invaluable enabling role that Alexander Mitscherlich inarguably played in his relentless interrogation of the sincerity of the new democratic sentiment in postwar West Germany, to which contemporary newspaper articles and interviews bear witness. These reports refer to Mitscherlich's postwar West German public persona as the "Seelenarzt der Deutschen" (the psychoanalyst/"soul doctor" of the Germans),[10] "Sigmund-Freud-Anhänger" (Sigmund Freud devotee),[11] "Aufklärer" (enlightener), "Emanzipator,"[12] and "Praeceptor republicae,"[13] as well as describing how "eine gewiße politische Angriffslust" (a certain political aggressiveness) made him "zu einer streitbaren und unbequemen Persönlichkeit" (into a controversial and uncomfortable figure).[14]

This critique is not meant to play down Mitscherlich's pivotal mediating role in reintroducing Freudian psychoanalysis into postwar West Germany. Rather, I seek to contextualize the author based on his particular history, which he sometimes refashioned and from which he omitted less favorable details that nonetheless help to explain his approach to psychoanalysis. This also serves to contextualize the emergence of his and Margarete Mitscherlich's best-selling *The Inability to Mourn*, with the cluster of emotions it houses and the readings it continues to encourage. In this way, we may gain a better understanding of the taboos and blind spots that arise from the tenacious textual hagiography of the Mitscherlichs' thesis, and examine how the "return" of Freudian psychoanalysis to Germany does not necessarily imply continuity or repetition but, rather, rupture and reinvention.

The Inability to Mourn, One More Time

In his 1933 introductory lectures to psychoanalysis, Sigmund Freud boldly stated, "Where the id was, there ego shall be."[15] Almost fifty years later, journalist and writer Wolfgang Ignée adjusted the terms to fit a new historical and sociopolitical state: "Where the id was, there we shall be."[16] Between Freud's 1933 lectures on psychoanalysis and writer Ignée's 1978 German newspaper article in the *Stuttgarter Zeitung* about Alexander Mitscherlich's work, there is an explicit shift from the individual "ego" to a collective "we." With this shift, Ignée underscores the way in which the Mitscherlichs' particular brand of psychoanalysis extends Freud's readings from the individual subject to a collective ("we"). Ironically, the implicit effect of this slippage is to remove from the equation altogether the "ego"—the individual subject's conscious and social interface—and thus also the source of possible self-reflexive agency. Understanding this shift necessitates a return to Alexander and Margarete Mitscherlichs' *Inability to Mourn* (1967), their exemplary instantiation of the collective "we" that develops an unorthodox and ultimately untenable conflation of the anthropological and psychoanalytic currents in Freud.

The Mitscherlichs' narrative about the emotional state of the immediate postwar years in West Germany runs as follows: Confronted with the loss of self-worth occasioned by absolute defeat and the occupation by the Allied powers in 1945, the German population was not able to digest its difficult past. This process, according to the Mitscherlichs, should have begun with mourning the loss of their "Führer," Adolf Hitler, in whom the German population had invested an enormous sum of narcissistic affect. The subsequent loss of their ego ideal[17] through Hitler's death, which ended the Nazi party's grandiose plans for world domination, should have resulted, they argue, in a depletion of narcissism. This deflated sense of self-worth that results from the narcissistic injury sustained by the subject who has lost a loved or idealized person usually, according to Freud, results in processes of mourning. However, the Mitscherlichs contend that this process of confrontation with loss and the accompanying passage of mourning did not occur in the Federal Republic. Indeed, their argument implies that the Germans were not even capable of melancholia, which, based on Freud's scant yet suggestive writings on the topic, has, in a process of categorical reduction, most often been understood to be the dark twin or failed process of mourning. Making a critical link between the psychic household and the socioeconomic situation of Germany, the Mitscherlichs argue that had the Germans been beset even by melancholia, they would not have been able to produce the activity and psychic energy with which they ignited the *Wirtschaftswunder* (postwar economic miracle) and ultimately rebuilt their shattered country.[18]

Returning to the immediate postwar moment of defeat, in the face of the 1945–46 Allied campaigns to make the extent of the Nazi crimes public, those Germans who had professed ignorance could no longer do so. The Allies deployed widely disseminated information at the outset of the occupation, as a form of anti-Nazi propaganda.[19] According to the Mitscherlichs, the "normal" response of the German population in the face of this awful truth should have been the emotion of guilt, which is constitutive of the affective topography of loss and reparation in mourning.

> What should a collective do when it finds itself exposed to the naked realization that in its name six million people have been murdered for no reason other than to satisfy its own aggressive urges? It has hardly any choice but to continue to deny its motives or else to *retreat into depression*.[20]

In other words, the German population not only avoided feeling guilt but was incapable (*unfähig*) of even feeling melancholia, of which, according to Freud's account, depression is a symptom. The Mitscherlichs' use of the rather pessimistic substantive *Unfähigkeit* (inability) in their book's title is significant, for it implies either an ontological shortcoming or an equally problematic conscious decision not to mourn on the part of the German population.

Further, as suggested above, it is technically incoherent to expand the analysis of select individuals (namely, three case histories) to a national collective. In one of his most anthropological texts, *Civilization and Its Discontents*, on which the Mitscherlichs appear to have drawn strongly in their writing,

Freud cautions against extending the principals of individual psychoanalysis to "civilized societies."

> I would not say that such an attempt to apply psycho-analysis to civilized society would be fanciful or doomed to fruitlessness. But it behoves us to be very careful, not to forget that after all we are dealing only with analogies, and that it is dangerous, not only with men but also with concepts, to drag them out of the region where they originated and have matured. [. . .] And with regard to any therapeutic application of our knowledge, what would be the use of the most acute analysis of social neuroses, since no one possesses power to compel the community to adopt the therapy? In spite of all these difficulties, we may expect that one day someone will venture upon this research into the pathology of civilized communities.[21]

Thus, despite Freud's misgivings, the Mitscherlichs ventured onto this "dangerous" path, dragging concepts from their familiar regions into their analysis of "the pathology of [a] civilized communit[y]."

The Mitscherlichs' assessment implies (if it does not directly suggest) that the emotional comportment of postwar Germans was, for the most part, a conscious, calculatedly recalcitrant, and perhaps even malicious response. This is clearly a provocative gesture on the part of the authors, one not at all in keeping with the premise of the Freudian analyst-analysand relationship, where an empathic environment is a key precondition for psychoanalytic therapy.[22] Instead, the Mitscherlichs argue that the German population engaged in "Derealisation"[23] or a "manische Ungeschehenmachen"[24] (processes of "making unreal" or a "manic undoing of the past") in order to conserve affective energy and fend off the narcissistic wound of their thwarted investment in Hitler and National Socialism. They continue,

> If Germans had to live with the unvarnished memory of their Nazi past— even if their personal share in that past was merely in being obedient, fatalistic, or enthusiastically passive—their ego could not easily integrate it with their present way of life.[25]

The authors' deployment of the first-person plural *wir* (we), which Jaspers employed in his lectures on guilt to the same end, invites readers to identify with the Mitscherlichs' argument and intentionally levels different degrees of culpability.[26]

Following a parallel line of inquiry, it is pertinent to ask after the status of this authorial collective "we" in relation to the two authors' respective contributions to the text. In a 1968 interview published in *Die Zeit*,[27] Alexander Mitscherlich answers this question by saying, "Meine Frau ist mir intellektuell überlegen, ich hingegen kann Erkenntnisse aus einem intellektuellen Kampf immer zu Papier bringen. Zahlreiche Ideen zu dem Buch stammen von meiner Frau. Wir haben sie dann gemeinsam entwickelt." (My wife is intellectually superior to me; on the other hand, I can always express in writing insights resulting from an intellectual struggle. Numerous ideas for the book originated with my wife. We then went on to develop these together.) Although Margarete Mitscherlich-Nielsen (then Margarete Mitscherlich) is listed as coauthor of the book, recent research indicates that her contribution consisted of the three clinical case studies cited, on which the first essay's argument is based, while Alexander Mitscherlich wrote the remainder of the book alone.[28] It is interesting (but perhaps not surprising, considering Alexander Mitscherlich's talent as a polemicist) that Margarete Mitscherlich is never present—or cited—in interviews or newspaper reviews from this period.

The above excerpt from *The Inability to Mourn* suggests that should the Germans have taken their Nazi past seriously, they would have found it difficult to "survive" (or flourish economically, it is implied) in the manner in which they did during the postwar *Wirtschaftswunder* (economic miracle). Similarly, the Mitscherlichs find no trace of appropriate moral emotions in the postwar German populace.

> Where there is guilt, we expect remorse and the need to make amends. Where loss has been suffered, mourning follows, and where an ideal has been tarnished, where face has been lost, the natural consequence is shame. But the process of denial extended in the same way to the occasions for guilt, mourning, and shame.[29]

The term *politische Affekte* (political affects) is mentioned in passing earlier on in the essay by the Mitscherlichs, but they neither define nor return to it.[30] It is an apt term to use for describing the charged climate of popular political debate unleashed by the book's publication. This response is constitutive of the fabric of the West German "politics of emotion" and demonstrates how certain emotions receive social approval while others are repudiated, and hence, how emotions accrue a moral valence. Emotions, acknowledged and morally evaluated, form part of less clearly defined affective structures that may defy categorization due to their complexity. In other words, when communicated (or capable of expression) in legible form, emotions (both public and private) are open to social scrutiny and may even be seen as representing the expressive subject's ethical stance toward a situation or event.

In the citation above, a triumvirate of moral emotions is listed—guilt, mourning, and shame—which might be seen as constituting a genus of politicized emotions in the postwar West German context. For obvious reasons, the emotion of guilt took precedence as the focal point for the immediate postwar period. Shame, part of an affective structure that is notoriously difficult to pin down due to the shamed subject's desire to remain unseen, is important yet often overlooked, as we have seen in the first chapter on Jaspers' postwar shame.[31] Shame is, by and large, a nonpublic emotion that often remains invisible to the observer, being an emotion that does not want to be shared, but it is also constitutive of the transgression of socially held norms.[32] The emotive foci through which a society is viewed shift over time, and after the publication of the Mitscherlichs' book in 1967, mourning arguably becomes the fulcrum and mainstay of attention in terms of emotions sought after in analyses of the postwar political and psychological landscape.[33]

In their text, the Mitscherlichs declare that the most appropriate emotional response to a past ruptured by crimes of this magnitude should rightly have been feelings of *Mitgefühl* (compassion), although it remains unclear precisely for whom this compassion should be felt. Per the Mitscherlichs' diagnosis, failing this appropriate emotive response of mourning, the German population should then have fallen into a state of melancholia, but it did not.

> The Federal Republic did not succumb to melancholia; instead, as a group, those who had lost their "ideal leader," the representative of a commonly shared ego-ideal, managed to avoid self-devaluation by breaking all affective bridges to the immediate past. This withdrawal of affective cathecting energy, of interest, should not be regarded as a decision, as a conscious, deliberate act; it was an unconscious process, with only minimal guidance from the conscious ego.[34]

This passage delivers the main hypothesis of the Mitscherlichs' account, namely, that a radically enacted break with—a "derealization" of—the Nazi past allowed the West German population to continue with "business as usual" after the catastrophic events of the Nazi years. This achievement was enabled, the Mitscherlichs argue, by a reorganization of libidinal economy, in which libidinal energy is decathected from the past. With this libidinal "economic gain," the German population reinvested instead in "monomaniacal" efforts of "the restoration of what had been destroyed," what came to be known as the German *Wiederaufbau* or *Wirtschaftswunder*.[35]

The heart of the Mitscherlichs' argument is that this affective state of affairs impeded the capacity of the population to respond positively with what might be called correct "democratic comportment." Instead, citizens of the Federal Republic demonstrated an "autistic attitude" that equated democracy with little more than the postwar (capitalist) economic system.[36] Indeed, the Mitscherlichs diagnose the population's emotive posture as "eine auffallende Gefühlsstarre" (a striking emotional rigidity), an unreflected identification with the victors, and "das manische Ungeschehenmachen" (the manic derealization) of the collective efforts invested in the West German *Wiederaufbau* (reconstruction).[37] In other words, the Federal Republic is characterized by the absence or inadequate expression of moral emotions befitting democracy, such as empathy, guilt, and, in their argument, mourning. However, after the Nazis' skillful channeling of intense affect for propaganda purposes in Hitler Germany, strong emotions were viewed with circumspection and even led to the conclusion that public expression of overly emotive reactions was largely incompatible with democracy in the Federal Republic.[38]

More problematically, within the parameters of their selective use and understanding of Freudian psychoanalysis, the authors oscillate between assigning the affective life of West Germans to either partially conscious or solely unconscious structures.[39] Shortly after explaining the Germans' affective withdrawal from their recent past as an unconscious process ("ein unbewußt verlaufendes Geschehen"), they not only describe the populace's reaction as one of "Verleugnungsarbeit" (the work of disavowal) but also demote their important technical explanation of the difference between "Verleugnung" (disavowal, a partially conscious process) and "Verdrängung" (repression, an unconscious process) to a footnote.[40] This easily overlooked semantic slippage surely has the potential for provoking significantly different moral responses in the lay reader: while repression is an unconscious process, or a struggle between the id and the ego in which the ego has no direct or conscious access to the repressed material, disavowal is a partially conscious process of the splitting of the ego.[41] In other words, because disavowal may also occur at a consciously registered level and hence is open to amendment, it may possibly be seen to be morally reprehensible behavior, whereas repression, as unpleasant as its results may be, remains a process largely beyond the control of the conscious subject/ego and hence deserving of a different ethical response than that of disavowal.[42] This blurring of categories induces a slippage from self-proclaimed technical psychoanalytic interpretation to a moral framework.

The Mitscherlichs' text oscillates between a critique of a lack of emotion and a description of affect in excess of an appropriate emotional response. In other words, they charge the citizens of the Federal Republic not so much with a lack of feeling as with either a lack of emotion or inappropriate emotions expressed unexpectedly in relation to objects or situations. They describe this affective and cognitive disjuncture as a form of "social immobilism and provincialism [. . .] and the stubbornly maintained rejection of memories, in particular the blocking of any sense of involvement in the events of the Nazi past that are now being so strenuously denied."[43] In fact, they go so far as to draw attention to a lack of friendliness in their fellow citizens, lamenting the minority status in the Federal Republic of what they call "den freundlichen Deutschen" (the friendly German).[44] In addition to the fuzzy logic of this statement, it is clearly a reductive formulation that perpetuates the logic of prejudice and national stereotyping.

This state of social immobility and provincialism might have been avoided, the Mitscherlichs argue, if, instead of responding to their defeat and confrontation with the crimes of the Nazi regime with derealization, the West German population had, based on their admission of guilt, allowed the process of mourning to take its course: "Without a working-through of guilt, however belated, there could be no work of mourning."[45] It remains unclear precisely why an admission of guilt should lead to mourning and not to the state of "Gefühlsstarre" (emotional rigidity) attributed to a disgraced, displaced, and hungry population. What does become clear is the normative status of the emotive expectations held by the Mitscherlichs.

Ultimately, the Mitscherlichs impose on the population what William Reddy terms a national "regime of emotions." Although Reddy does not distinguish between affect and emotions, his insights into the normative role of emotions are useful. Defining an "emotional regime" as "the set of normative emotions and the official rituals, practices, and emotives that express and inculcate them," he points out that all political systems are necessarily underpinned by such a regime. Further, Reddy convincingly argues that within "emotional regimes," the "ritual" practice of emotions through their repeated expression is politically central to the direction and maintenance of an ethos of social unity, whereby communities may view emotion as a vital sphere of effort to be managed and negotiated. Reddy maintains that our task as scholars interested in a society's politics of emotion is to excavate and critique these regimes and their practices.[46] In the particular case of the Federal Republic of Germany, we do not have to dig too deep to unearth the relationship between emotion and politics, largely because the diagnosis of the "emotional regime" of West Germany in the Mitscherlichs' book deploys, in the language of psychoanalysis, a tradition of thought deeply indebted to an attentiveness to both emotions and affect.

The Mitscherlichs' template for the Federal Republic's "emotional regime" is a diagnosis of the population as pathological or psychically damaged and, more important, as morally compromised because of its inappropriate (or nonnormative) emotional comportment. In other words, in the eyes of the Mitscherlichs, the citizens of West Germany have mostly failed to adhere to the new "emotional regime" proper to democracy. Despite the effort to include themselves in the capacious deployment of "we" throughout their book, when taking up a moral position vis-à-vis their "patient" (the Federal Republic), the Mitscherlichs tend to distance themselves from the very psychoanalysis that they intend to defend and support in the postwar German context.

The Mitscherlichs' moral reprehension sits awkwardly with the role of the empathic and open listening position ideally expected from the Freudian psychoanalyst; their assumption of the position of moral arbitrator renders them closer to the role of the judging superego and implies an immense emotive investment in a largely unexamined countertransferential position from which they form their diagnosis in relationship to their "patient." They appear to be aware of the danger of confusing the message with the messenger, when they write, "The affects it [psychoanalysis] may invoke in some readers should, however, be directed at the authors and not at psychoanalysis, the most precious tool we possess for gaining an understanding of man."[47] Indeed, with their diagnosis of the postwar times, the Mitscherlichs obviously intend to position themselves directly in the tradition of Freudian analysis, the "Jewish science" that they wish to shield from anti-Semitic attacks in the context of post–National Socialist West Germany.[48]

"Eine Art Shibboleth": From Psychoanalytical Diagnosis to Popular Slogan

Since its publication in 1967, the Mitscherlichian diagnosis has retained a public status in one way or another, extending from its prominence among participants in the 1968 student rebellion[49] to its longevity as one of a handful of foundational popular social texts of the democratized Federal Republic.[50] It appears to have held an inviolable status in psychoanalytic circles, which may be measured by the astounding lack of any form of sustained scholarly critique of the text's argument. The first psychoanalytic contribution critiquing the Mitscherlichs' book was published in the early nineties, some twenty-five years after its 1967 publication.[51] This critique, psychoanalyst Tilmann Moser's 1992 essay "Die Unfähigkeit zu trauern—eine taugliche Diagnose?" (The inability to mourn—a suitable diagnosis?), initially appeared in *Psyche*, a journal cofounded by Alexander Mitscherlich in 1947 and coedited by him almost until his death in 1982.[52] The establishment of the journal as a German forum for psychoanalytic and psychological debate was part of Mitscherlich's tireless efforts to reorganize and strengthen psychoanalysis in postwar West Germany.

The conciliatory and cautious tone of Moser's critique indicates that he was well aware that his criticism was aimed at a sacred cow of postwar leftist cultural politics.[53] He was also sensitive to the possibility of his critique being misconstrued as a patricidal, oedipal gesture, for Moser had received his training in classical Freudian psychoanalysis in the 1960s at the Sigmund Freud Institute in Frankfurt am Main, under the direction of Mitscherlich. His initial (unvoiced) criticism of the Mitscherlichs' book dates back to his initial reading of the text, most likely shortly after its publication in 1967, as evinced by his discovery of earlier scribbled objections in the margins of his copy. This marginalia attests to his sensitivity toward what he describes as an admixture of psychoanalysis and accusatory morality, captured, for example, in the following note from his 1967 copy of the text: "psychoanalytische Bußpredigt, Daueranklage und diffamierende Entlarvung der Deutschen" (psychoanalytic penitential sermon, unrelenting indictment, and defamatory unmasking of the Germans).[54] This is scarcely a resounding endorsement of the book.

Moser's criticism was directed principally toward what he saw as flaws in the practice of the Mitscherlichs' psychoanalytical approach, with his strongest criticism aimed at an improper and potentially damaging admixture of psychoanalysis and unremitting moralizing. He observed of the book, "It reads like a catalog of insults rather than a document expressing the desire to understand. [. . .] Empathy is scarcely discernable."[55] As an analyst, Moser knows that within the psychoanalytical setting one cannot expect to effect change or self-reflection in a patient without therapeutic detachment guided by empathy. In fact, he argues that moralizing is more likely to result in a sense of persecution and a hardening of the analysand's pathology rather than in heightened self-awareness or change in the analysand. Of course, that a collective and not an individual is at stake makes this approach even more questionable.

Cognizant of the danger that his critique might be taken as an apologetics,

Moser nonetheless makes a plea for recognizing the traumatization of many postwar German citizens in the aftermath of defeat. He argues that, for many Germans, this may have led to an unconscious equation of their defeat and occupation with an "archaic punishment" of some kind, an aspect that is absent in the Mitscherlichs' analysis.[56] As problematic as an uncritical identification with the victim position may be, Moser clearly is correct in his argument that stern moralizing, a lack of empathy, and disappointment about the emotional states exhibited by their patients are not the most enabling correctives to an unconscious persecutory complex and are less than likely to induce self-reflection and an acknowledgment of guilt (let alone expressions of mourning).[57]

From Moser's assessment of the emotion of rage ("Wut") as the ground tenor of the Mitscherlichs' text, it is possible to extrapolate that the desired posture of mourning might indeed have less to do with the German population and instead express the affective structures defining the Mitscherlichs' sociopolitical milieu of antifascist, left-liberal intellectuals. Indeed, their text could be read as an extended expression of disappointment at postwar West Germany's inability to strive toward idealized emotional postures and forms of memory work, which they frame here in terms of mourning. Extending Moser's insights, I argue that the Mitscherlichs' position in the text, which exhibits typical manifestations of rage, moralizing, and disappointment associated with frustrated mourning or melancholia, appears to be a sustained enactment of the authors' own ongoing mourning of the unattained (nationalized) emotive ego ideal that they have postulated for the postwar West German population. My interpretation, although carefully avoided by Moser, is supported by his suggestion that it is not surprising that the population exhibited other, less "appropriate" emotional reactions in the face of the numbing aftermath of National Socialism. Moser thus shifts the focus of attention from mourning to the emotions of shame, despair, and rue, which would be some of the necessary emotional precursors of mourning were it to eventuate.[58]

In response to Moser's essay, Christian Schneider, a former student of Oskar Negt who went on to train in psychoanalysis at the Sigmund Freud Institute after the death of Alexander Mitscherlich, initially defended the Mitscherlichs' position. A 1993 issue of the journal *Psyche*, appositely entitled "Psychoanalyse und Moral," contained several responses to Moser's critique. This included an essay by Margarete Mitscherlich, in which she not only defends the diagnosis of "an inability to mourn" but goes on to extend it to both the East and West in recently unified Germany, a peculiar gesture, considering the discrete histories of the two former states.[59] Although Schneider's initial response was to refute Moser's critique of the Mitscherlichs' work, he has offered more differentiated perspectives in subsequent contributions. Nonetheless, Schneider's initial rapid assumption of a defensive posture indicates that more is at stake in the debate of the Mitscherlichs' book than a disagreement about psychoanalytic technique.

Both Moser and Schneider recognize the problematic transformation of the Mitscherlichs' methodologically flawed psychoanalytical diagnosis into a moral imperative. Likewise, both are critical of this move, with Schneider taking his lead from Moser by proposing that the hypothesis of a German "inability to mourn" was the latter-day psychological correlation to the much-discussed postwar "collective guilt" hypothesis and "thereby at the same time the ticket to raising oneself as part of the former moral elite over and against the mass of the guilty."[60] If the situation is as Schneider suggests, the affective constellation of mourning, characterized here in negative terms through its absence, came to displace guilt as the prime emotional and moral desideratum in postwar West German society. In other words, in another instance of affect responding to affect, postwar Germany's emotional state is structured less by the emotional desideratum of guilt than by an affective response to the angry imperative to feel guilt and remorse.

Even in his first essay on the topic, Schneider admits that when reading the book for the first time, he too had recoiled at its moralizing. "Privatsprachlich" (in private language)—that is, for himself alone—he defined this strident moral underpinning as a "kategorischen Imperativ der Einfühlung" (categorical imperative of empathy).[61] Two things are striking in his admission. First, his choice of words indicates that this response was not an opinion he felt comfortable airing publically at the time, attesting to the inhibition or taboo attached to criticizing this postwar classic. Second, with his reference to Kant's "categorical imperative," Schneider suggests that the Mitscherlichs have confused a psychoanalytic diagnosis (of the Federal Republic) with an idealized philosophical and moral category that neither leads to the wished-for posture of mourning nor, more important for Schneider, can supply the basis for political action.

Schneider's subsequent writings on the Mitscherlichs' book are characterized by greater clarity, not least because he largely ceases to read it as a psychoanalytic diagnosis.[62] He criticizes the psychoanalytical ideal of mourning set out by the Mitscherlichs as thoroughly unrealistic in the aftermath of the wartime experiences and losses of the majority of Germans. For him, the German population's tendency to deny their emotional participation in National Socialism and their (unconscious) restriction of their processes of mourning to their own immediate losses comprise an emotionally reduced but psychologically understandable response to the experience of war and capitulation.[63] Further, Schneider notes that mourning is a process unavailable to moral postulating; rather, it is an affectively spontaneous or creaturely ("kreatürlich") act that cannot be manufactured or reconstructed on demand.[64]

Although Schneider may quibble with the diagnostic aspects of the Mitscherlichs' text, he nonetheless acknowledges the historical and sociopolitical importance of the application of their diagnosis as a "parole," which he describes as "eine Art Shibboleth" for those committed to a critical working through of the Nazi past, even if they have never read the Mitscherlichs' book[65] and are unsure what form this coming-to-terms might take.[66] Thus, through a process of metaphorization, "the inability to mourn" shifts from a diagnosis to a slogan or catchphrase. In the course of the text's reception, what was intended as a psychosocial diagnosis has been converted into a "thick" metaphor to capture a sense of the social malaise experienced and observed by the Mitscherlichs in the postwar (West) Germany of the early 1960s.[67]

Despite the tenacious cultural and political afterlife of the Mitscherlichs' diagnosis and the existence of a compendious Alexander Mitscherlich archive in Frankfurt, the lack of published biographical information available about Mitscherlich beyond his expansive yet most selective memoir marked an equally aggressive disinterest in the source of the diagnosis turned parole.[68] The following ambivalent comments about Mitscherlich from the *Frankfurter Rundschau* are symptomatic of this attitude: "Mitscherlich hat sich niemals als Praeceptor Germaniae gefühlt, aber für einige Zeit war er, nicht ohne seine Mitwirkung, aber doch ohne seine Absicht, eine Art Praeceptor republicae. Davon ist heute keine Rede mehr." (Mitscherlich never felt himself to be the Praeceptor Germaniae, but, for a span of time—not lacking his involvement, but certainly without it being his intention—he was a kind of Praeceptor republicae. Today there is no mention of this.)[69] The article featuring these comments was published on the occasion of Mitscherlich's sixty-fifth birthday, only six years after the appearance of his book and four years after he received the Peace Prize of the German Book Trade (Friedenspreis des Deutschen Buchhandels).

Over time, a lack of contextualization of the diagnosis lent the slogan a spectral politico-poetic malleability—a politico-cultural afterlife all its own. Hans-Martin Lohmann, whose slim biography from 1987 represented the sole Mitscherlich biography until recently, aptly stated, "Alexander Mitscherlich war noch nicht tot, da war er in der alten Bundesrepublik schon so gut wie vergessen" (Alexander Mitscherlich was not yet dead when he was already as good as forgotten in the old Federal Republic).[70] Lohmann's biography was based largely on Alexander Mitscherlich's memoir, which meant that the self-propagated image of Mitscherlich remained largely intact after his death. Ironically, whereas Mitscherlich's person attracted little attention in the immediate aftermath of his death, his name became known in German households through the title of his book, in the manner of a minor, nationally specific Freudian popularization.

Alexander Mitscherlich and *The Inability to Mourn* in Context

Not until 2008, on the occasion of the centenary of his birth, was sustained attention devoted to Alexander Mitscherlich's biography and work in historical context.[71] A flurry of biographical publications examined the complex and conflicting image of Mitscherlich that emerged from the archives, filling in striking omissions from his own account of his life. Three meticulously researched biographies frame Mitscherlich's life in productively different ways.[72] They clearly enjoy the advantage of having emerged in a politico-historical climate in Germany that, after the tumultuous unification of the two Germanies and the foundation of the Berlin Republic, is marked by a new German self-confidence in regard to its past.[73]

Significantly, these new biographies emphasize Mitscherlich's earlier, as well as his later, intellectual and political influences, which would ultimately lead to a broader reevaluation of his work and legacy in the Federal Republic.[74] They also help to contextualize the history and reception of *The Inability to Mourn* and to indicate how Mitscherlich arrived at the particular emotional politics at work in the book. Earlier accounts of Alexander Mitscherlich portray him as one of the founding public intellectuals of democracy in the Federal Republic, as well as a tireless champion for the reestablishment of Freudian psychoanalysis in West Germany after its exile under the National Socialist regime. Despite a period of incarceration in 1937 by the National Socialists due to his publication and support of works by Ernst Niekisch, an anti-Nazi, National Bolshevist thinker, and agitator for the Conservative Revolution, Mitscherlich remained in National Socialist Germany. He trained in neurology at Heidelberg University with physician Viktor von Weizsäcker and then worked as his assistant until 1945. During his time in Heidelberg, he moved in circles where he met intellectuals such as Karl Jaspers, whose work and person he lionized for some time.

Due to his poor standing with the National Socialist Party, Mitscherlich was viewed in positive political and moral terms by the US-Allied occupying forces in Heidelberg, where he enjoyed a privileged status and held key positions in the new postwar political order, including a brief stint as a civilian political administrator.[75] In 1946, he was asked to document the Nuremberg doctors' trial, which indicated his high standing with the new powers, even as it made his professional life in medicine increasingly difficult. His colleagues viewed his candid assessment of the inhumanity of the medical profession under National Socialism as an act of national, professional, and personal treachery, and as a result, he often met with resistance in the medical profession thereafter.[76]

There is no question that Mitscherlich's postwar political and intellectual engagement increasingly coincided with the Allied democratization efforts, inasmuch as he became a leading voice for political and social enlightenment. Although he was originally skeptical about democracy, by the time he wrote *Inability to Mourn*, he critiqued the (West) Germans for failing to establish an emotional regime conducive to democracy and instead fostering a libidinal connection to pride in their work (this, of course, also suggests, although Mitscherlich does not elaborate on this point, that capitalism and democracy may well have emotional regimes entirely at odds with one another).[77] His politics of emotion were, indeed, in line with the emotional regime of democracy, with his writings offering a sustained critique of the hatred attendant on structures of prejudice, political apathy, and the lack of empathy caused by defense mechanisms, such as nationalistic pride, against guilt feelings about the Nazi past. Indeed, from the 1970s onward, Mitscherlich appeared sporadically as a colorful presence in the media, where he is referred to, on the one hand, as a "Moralist"[78] and "Nestbeschmutzer"[79] (a then-popular term for a national traitor) and, on the other, as the "Psychoanalytiker der Nation"[80] (psychoanalyst of the nation) and a "bundesdeutsche Institution"[81] (West German institution). These titles illustrate how his proselytizing ambitions often took precedence over a coherent systematic approach to his particular brand of psychoanalysis, which, on closer examination, is more akin to the line of thought of anthropology or sociopsychology, for which he mined Freud's oeuvre.[82] Nonetheless, Mitscherlich's attitude toward the (in)capacity of postwar Germans to embrace the new democratic political system and emotional regime was significantly more complex than both the received image of his person and *The Inability to Mourn* might suggest. By revisiting Mitscherlich's formative interwar influences and examining several of his contributions to postwar debates on guilt, reeducation, and amnesty, we gain a more nuanced understanding of the influences beyond psychoanalysis that inform the line of argument in *The Inability to Mourn*.

Mitscherlich's political orientation and intellectual development is pithily described by historian and biographer Martin Dehli as a passage from the tradition of cultural pessimism of the ilk of Oswald Spengler's *The Decline of the West* to the more complex psychoanthropology of Sigmund Freud's *Civilization and Its Discontents*—although, on reading Mitscherlich's postwar psychoanalytic and social diagnoses, the question arises whether he ever truly left Spenglerian pessimism behind.[83] Dehli and other biographers describe Mitscherlich's youthful idealization of Ernst Jünger, whom he heard speak at a reading in Munich on September 29, 1930. After a drunken night of revelry with Jünger and his acolytes, Mitscherlich followed him to Berlin,[84] where he intially embraced Jünger's circle of conservative revolutionaries. With the benefit of postwar hindsight, Mitscherlich describes this chain of events as follows: "A number of bizarre figures kept company at the Jüngers' house, principally right-leaning conspirative types [. . .]: Schauwecker, Salomon, Roßbach, and whatever the others' names were."[85] It is interesting to note that, for a short time, Mitscherlich and Ernst von Salomon moved in the same national conservative circles.

In oscillations from the radical right to the radical left, Mitscherlich became an admiring member of Niekisch's Berlin *Widerstandskreis* (circle of resisters) a few years later, transferring his attachment from the rather indifferent Jünger to the more receptive Niekisch. He provided financial support and publicity for Niekisch's publications in the early 1930s through a bookshop he managed in Dahlem. Niekisch's writings were both communist and ultranationalist, directed against the Weimar Republic and Hitler alike, whom Niekisch eschewed as a mere distraction hindering the overthrow of democracy.[86] His support of Niekisch brought the SA (Nazi storm troopers) to Mitscherlich and his bookshop, where he had placed Niekisch's publications in the display window. On March 22, 1937, the National Socialists arrested Niekisch and fifty-seven of his followers; Mitscherlich narrowly avoided this fate, only because he was in Zurich at the time, where he remained and began studying medicine.[87]

Mitscherlich unwisely visited Germany briefly in December 1937 and was promptly arrested by the Gestapo. He remained in prison for three months, although he was prone, in later accounts of his life, to extend the length of his imprisonment to eight months.[88] After May 1945, the Allies registered Mitscherlich under the category of those politically persecuted by the National Socialist regime (*Verfolgte*), a social category in postwar Germany that carried significant symbolic capital for the designee, particularly because of the scarcity of those warranting inclusion in this category. This is not to make light of Mitscherlich's experience of persecution but, rather, to put it in context, a practice toward which Mitscherlich himself sometimes exhibited a rather elastic approach.

It is very likely that Mitscherlich's encounters in the 1920s with members of what Michael Wildt has termed a "Generation des Unbedingten" (unconditional generation)[89] contributed toward the cultural pessimism that lingered in his writings and *Weltanschauung* after World War II. These individuals born between 1900 and 1910 responded to their experiences of financial and sociopolitical instability, violence, and chaos with a radical antiliberal critique of the middle class and with animosity toward the parliamentary democracy represented by the Weimar Republic. Dehli argues that Mitscherlich's familiarity with this tradition of thought is key to understanding his attraction to and interpretation of Freud's differently accented, but equally pessimistic, cultural anthropological writings. However, the difference between these forms of cultural pessimism is that Freud coins the development of culture as a struggle between instincts and social demands and as an "anthropological constant," rather than as a sign of Western decadence and decline, as in the Spenglerian tradition.[90] Even if Mitscherlich later underplayed the significance of these interwar encounters, depoliticizing them as oedipal dramas, his texts, including the *Inability to Mourn*, still bear traces of this earlier political and cultural pessimism.[91] There is no doubt that these earlier connections would have been looked on with pointed concern by the Allied occupiers, who harbored great suspicion toward German traditions evincing national chauvinism of any stripe. Indeed, Mitscherlich most likely would not have enjoyed the same extensive privileges he was granted in postwar Heidelberg by the Allies, let alone the fleeting admiration of the generation of 1968 some twenty years later, had he revealed these earlier loyalties.[92] This may explain, in part, why an account of the complex inheritance of his thought was left to a later generation of biographers.

In the immediate postwar years, the Mitscherlich associated with *The Inability to Mourn* had not yet taken form, and his political emotional attachments were unclear. In the wake of the Nuremberg doctors' trials in 1947 and his courageous publication of *Diktat der Menschenverachtung* (*Doctors of Infamy*), Mitscherlich seldom spoke about Germany's catastrophic past. Similarly, few references to the National Socialist past are found in Mitscherlich's publications from the 1950s.[93] When they occur, they are often written in a startlingly different tenor than that associated with the strident moralizing anger and disappointment characteristic of his and Margarete Mitscherlich's magnum opus. Clearly, Mitscherlich was still searching for appropriate tools of analysis for articulating the relationship between emotion and politics in the newly established Federal Republic. Further, the lack of resonance and the repulsion and animosity that his book on the Nuremberg doctors' trial met with no doubt also indicated to Mitscherlich the unreceptive climate for critiques of this nature in Adenauer's Germany.[94]

In a 1946 essay, "Die schwerste Stunde" (The darkest hour), published in the short-lived postwar literary journal *Die Fähre* (1946–47), Mitscherlich argued that the German population was able to deal with little more than day-to-day survival:"It must also be taken into account that reflection/contemplation has become extremely burdensome for the individual, because this process necessarily occurs in an existential atmosphere of misery and niggardliness; of hunger, homelessness, turmoil, resentment, denunciation; of narrowness, joylessness and desperation."[95] This essay was Mitscherlich's contribution to the critique of denazification, particularly the deployment of the *Fragebogen* (questionnaire), which was originally intended as the prelude to reeducation.

> However, this year [1946] those few clear-sighted individuals could not fail to see that the German environment threatened to fall victim to unbridled feelings. No other place discriminated to a greater degree between German and German, between believers in dictatorship and violence and believers in the fundamental ethical obligations of human beings, in a manner of speaking, between evil and "less evil" Germans. The hate word of condemnation presides equally over everyone. A consequence of this is that like all other aspects of our existence en masse, even morality is defined in bureaucratic terms. This is the principal dubiousness of the questionnaire that should not be confused in any way with the necessity of asking questions. But even he who has a clean questionnaire looks hopelessly like a henchman, a vocation that is not to the liking of many of those who defended themselves for a long time and with great sacrifice against the collective terror and those who now consequently withdraw once again into their now-habitual isolation.[96]

Mitscherlich connects excessive affect ("unkontrolliertes Gefühl") with the bureaucracy-induced morality ("Sittlichkeit von der Bürokratie") effected by practices of denazification (and potentially, by extension, also reeducation). He identifies the artificially induced norms of emotional comportment measured in terms of one's morality ("zwischen bösen und 'weniger bösen' Deutschen" [between evil and "less evil" Germans]) and critiques this morally reductive practice. This essay offers another example of the emotional intersubjectivity, or emotional responses to expressed emotions, that we saw with the "primal scene" of the German reactions to photographs from the concentration camps, discussed in the present study's introduction. The perceived or actual "Haß-wort der Ächtung" (hate word of condemnation) of the Allies (and perhaps even the international community) provokes the threat of "unkontolliertes Ge-fühl" from the German population. Between two emotional regimes—that of the recently defeated Nazi regime and the Allied plans for reeducation—it is unclear just what these emotions may be. What is clear, however, is the poten-tial threat and unpredictability they may represent in this prolonged state of exception of occupied Germany.

In a similar vein, three years later, in an article provocatively titled "Am-nestie statt Umerziehung" (Amnesty, not reeducation) and published in the *Frankfurter Hefte* (a politico-cultural journal founded in 1946 by leftist Catho-lics Eugen Kogon and Walter Dirks), Mitscherlich seems even less optimistic about reeducation and entirely pessimistic about human beings: "Unfortu-nately, we must start out from the pessimistic-sounding assumption that most people are unable to change their political outlook. They neither learn anything further, nor do they forget anything. Their political opinions are linked to their 'honor'; in this context, discussion could be seen as a sign of feebleness."[97] It is striking that, in 1949, Mitscherlich uses the word *unfähig* to describe a cer-tain rigidity associated with affect—he says that humans are "unable" (*un-fähig*) to change their political beliefs due to the fear of showing one's weak-ness, which would wound one's sense of pride, or *Ehre* (honor). In addition to addressing Germany's long history of militarism and chauvinism attached to the term *Ehre*, this sentence signals a lingering pessimism, with the term *un-fähig* appearing to belong more to the heritage of dystopian Weimar culture, such as the legacy of the conservative revolutionaries, than to the culture of democratization, with its tenet of the multiple "abilities" conveyed through the trope of reeducation. Of course, it is necessary to make a distinction between an inability to alter a cathexis to a political idea and the inability to acknowl-edge the existence of that cathexis in the first place.

Mitscherlich goes on to argue that in the absence of a genuine popular revolution against Nazism, "an administrative paper movement" (eine admin-istrative Papierbewegung) will do little to neutralize the affects still bound up with Nazism. He judges attempts at political reeducation to be "a morally grat-ifying, yet politically ineffectual pipe dream" (ein moralisch erfreulicher, aber politisch wirkungsloser Wunschtraum).[98] He argues that without the participa-tion of all German citizens in the new democracy, there is no hope for democ-ratization, declaring, "In the spirit of fair play, we therefore must give former Nazis the opportunity to participate in the consolidation of German relations by granting them amnesty (of course, with the exclusion of those who are charged with crimes against humanity)."[99] In the refrain of his article's title, Mitscherlich argues for an amnesty for those from the broad middle class, who, he claims, should be able to provide the foundation for intelligent leadership. This article presents a politically resigned, pragmatic Alexander Mitscherlich, who differs from the politicized, polemical figure that has come to be associated with his writings by the 1960s and the emotional regime of democracy.

The radical shift in Mitscherlich's position, from a proponent of interwar cultural pessimism to a sociopsychological enlightener struggling toward a popular confrontation with the recent Nazi past, can be explained partly through his increasing investment in psychoanalysis in the 1950s. In his memoirs and the selective version of his biography in circulation, psychoanalysis appears as his guiding critical approach from the beginning. The misleading title of his 1980 memoir, *Ein Leben für die Psychoanalyse* (A life for psychoanalysis), certainly contributed to the legend of the longevity of his involvement with psychoanalysis. But perhaps life truly began for Mitscherlich at age fifty, in 1958/59, when, under much pressure from the Deutsche Psychoanalytische Vereinigung (German Psychoanalytical Association), he finally completed, in London with Paula Heimann, the requisite analytical training in psychoanalysis officially qualifying him as a psychoanalyst,[100] although he had been practicing and teaching analysis long before this.[101]

His interest in psychoanalysis remained principally theoretical—or, even more precisely, phenomenological and anthropological—rather than clinical, with his scholarly work limited to a few contributions, mainly on psychosomatics and the introduction of psychology and psychoanalytical thought into sociology.[102] Mitscherlich's strength, as is attested to in all three biographies, lay more in his controversial ability to mobilize public attention, at times through a virulent friend-foe logic that cost him many friendships and alliances. Indeed, it is symptomatic that a newspaper article on Mitscherlich's nomination for the Peace Prize of the German Book Trade bears the subtitle "Ein Mann mit vielen Feinden: Der Friedenspreisträger" (A man with many enemies: the winner of the peace prize) and then goes on to provide a long list of such enemies.[103]

In the latter part of his career, Mitscherlich dedicated himself to the role of *Wissenschaftspolitiker* (politician on behalf of research), with the express aim of creating and facilitating an institutional home for the psychoanalysis that he was instrumental in reimporting from abroad. Even if members of the Frankfurt School privately harbored a lack of respect for his comparatively limited philosophical agility and eclectic theoretical systematism, they were wise enough to respect his ability to forge and sustain institutional relationships abroad with the aim of resurrecting psychoanalysis as an active field of thought and practice in the Federal Republic.[104] Above all else, the 1950s constituted a time of increasing engagement with psychoanalysis for Mitscherlich, initially through a fellowship he received from the Rockefeller Institute in 1951, giving him access to forms of psychoanalysis integrated into psychiatry in the American context.[105] Contact with psychoanalysts, including Jewish émigrés from Germany and Austria through whom psychoanalysis was, ironically, to return to Germany largely altered by American ego psychology, strengthened Mitscherlich's determination to find an institutional home for psychoanalysis in postwar Germany. In this sense, then, psychoanalysis became one kind of emotional regime that Mitscherlich was eager to consolidate, even if this meant, in part, distilling his interpretation of Freud through a form of political popularization.[106]

In this spirit, he founded the Department for Psychosomatic Medicine at Heidelberg University in 1949, despite his increasingly strained relationship with the medical faculty in Heidelberg, primarily due to his commentary on the Nuremberg doctors' trials in 1947. His initial efforts to incorporate psychoanalysis into the clinic at Heidelberg met with resistance, not least from the head of the Department of Psychiatry, Dr. Kurt Schneider,[107] whose dislike of both psychoanalysis and any form of challenge to his psychiatric institution led him to write a formal statement against Mitscherlich's proposal for the establishment of an Institute of Psychotherapy, addressed to his colleague Karl Jaspers (copied to Mitscherlich). Schneider wrote, "I would therefore only be able to agree to the foundation of an institute for psychoanalysis if [the institution] were limited to the counseling and treatment of non-psychiatric conditions and would not accept psychogenic conditions for treatment (often incorrectly called 'neuroses'). Also, its appellation would have to be different and may in no way be associated with the syllable 'psych.'"[108] Nonetheless, Mitscherlich continued his valiant struggle to retain the syllable "psych" in his form of analysis, and a decade later, in 1956, he organized a series of psychoanalytical lectures at the University of Heidelberg in commemoration of Freud's one-hundredth birthday, with the support of the Frankfurt Institute for Social Research. Invited speakers included Michael Balint, E. H. Erikson, and Herbert Marcuse. The success of this psychoanalytic lecture series was repeated in a second series of lectures in Frankfurt and Heidelberg in 1961/62, which included talks by international figures in psychoanalysis such as Jeanne Lampl-de Groot and Paula Heimann.[109]

This critical engagement with psychoanalysis certainly determined Mitscherlich's writings from the 1960s onward, as did a second strong influence, the sociology of the Frankfurt School, whose various affiliates also shared stronger or weaker ties with psychoanalytical thought. Frustrated in his attempts to introduce psychoanalysis into his field of psychosomatics at Heidelberg University, Mitscherlich ultimately relocated to Frankfurt am Main and, in 1960, became the first director of the Institut und Ausbildungszentrum für Psychoanalyse und Psychosomatik (Institute and Training Center for Psychoanalysis and Psychosomatics), which had been founded on the political initiative of Max Horkheimer, Theodor W. Adorno, and Georg August Zinn, the current minister of Hessen, in 1959. In 1964, the institution was renamed the Sigmund-Freud-Institut.[110]

Further, the growing social unrest of the student generation in the middle to late 1960s led to a new emphasis on the individual, with a critique of the psychological costs, as well as the structural problems, of modern societies. In addition to sociology, which had been imported into West Germany in the 1950s from the United States and was intimately associated with both the study and application of democratic social structures, psychological paradigms increasingly gained in popularity as an approach for analyzing the significant ills of modern Western society.[111] This, in turn, promoted a broader receptivity toward politicized psychoanalytic models of critique in West Germany. With their emphasis on emotion and expressivity, Herbert Marcuse, Wilhelm Reich, and, at least initially, Alexander Mitscherlich appeared to embody this ideological orientation both biographically and intellectually.[112] Among other publications, Mitscherlich's 1963 book *Auf dem Weg zur vaterlosen Gesellschaft* (*Society without the Father*), which, in some ways, anticipates the diagnosis of the collective West German emotional state in *The Inability to Mourn*, had established him as a leading left-Freudian figure in the eyes of the antiauthoritarian student movement.[113] Thus the so-called psychological turn[114] of the 1960s meant that the Mitscherlichs' diagnosis of the West German "malady" of an "inability to mourn" and a refusal to face the Nazi past fell on fertile ground, even if Mitscherlich's popularity with the student left was not to last.[115]

The seeds of the central ideas expressed in *The Inability to Mourn* were already present in the Roberts Memorial Lecture that Alexander Mitscherlich delivered at Yale University in the summer of 1963, titled "A Defence against Mourning: A Contribution to the Study of Psychological Processes in Groups."[116] Emigrant psychoanalyst Henry Lowenfeld and other analysts at the lecture responded positively to the talk, although Lowenfeld, quite presciently, warned against Mitscherlich's concentration on missed mourning at the expense of repressed guilt feelings, as well as critiquing the paucity of the case studies (a total of three analyses conducted by Margarete Mitscherlich) on which the Mitscherlichs based the group diagnosis. Both points of criticism would be left unaddressed in the published version.[117]

Mitscherlich was curious about the effect that his speculative thesis might have in the potentially less-receptive West German context. He took advantage of an invitation from the Studium Generale in 1964 to present a slightly revised version of his Yale lecture before a large audience of students in Freiburg, this time with the title "Die Unfähigkeit zu trauern: Ein deutsches Phänomen psychoanalytisch betrachtet" (The inability to mourn: a German phenomenon considered through psychoanalysis). Mitscherlich biographer Timo Hoyer describes the extremely positive reception of Mitscherlich's talk by an absorbed audience of more than twelve hundred people, mainly students, who devoured his hypothesis.[118] Despite the overwhelmingly positive reaction to his address, the rewriting and reconceptualizing of the material into publishable form was to take a further three years and an immense amount of effort.

Although the book was written principally by Alexander Mitscherlich, Margarete Mitscherlich provided the three case analyses on which their thesis was based, as well as critical theoretical and analytical responses to the eponymous first chapter of the loosely linked collection of essays of which the book is composed.[119] In addition to Margarete Mitscherlich's contribution, Hoyer describes the enormous amount of editorial work contributed by Piper editors Walter Hinderer and Hermann Schulz (whom Mitscherlich thanks in the foreword to the book), not only in refining the structure of the text, but also in providing a substantive critique of the book's psychoanalytical theories.[120] The book's main title was chosen precisely because of its "gentle belletristic impact" (leise "belletristische" Einschlag),[121] a calculation that proved to be immensely successful; the ongoing resonance of the title phrase in scholarly research confirms the title's appeal and tenacity. At the last moment, the editors were forced to engage in an acrobatic feat of diplomatic persuasion when, in a characteristically choleric fit of pique, Mitscherlich decided that he no longer wanted to publish his book with Piper. Apparently his colleague (and former mentor) Karl Jaspers, who also published with Piper, had made a disparaging remark about psychoanalysis. Jaspers, underscoring his well-known scorn for psychoanalysis in an interview in the *Münchener Merkur*, called psychoanalysis quackery, "a fake in scientific terms" (im wissenschaftlichen Sinne ein Schwindel), a comment that Mitscherlich characteristically took to be directed at his own person.[122] Nonetheless, the text was published with Piper and went on to become a German classic. With publication figures for the book amounting to seventy-six thousand copies sold in its first two-and-a-half years[123] and over one hundred thousand in the first three years, the book marks a rare occurrence—a psychoanalytic best seller.[124]

Productive Inabilities: From Melancholia to Taboo

The tools enabling the critical deconstruction of the eponymous first chapter's moral imperative can be found in a subsequent chapter of the Mitscherlichs' book. Awaiting excavation under this tombstone erected to a German "inability to mourn," the Mitscherlichs' analysis of the coupling of taboo and *ressentiment* offers a fruitful approach to understanding particular emotional responses to Allied occupation among the German postwar population. As argued in chapter 2 of the present study, I contend that an exploration of the structure of affect represented by *ressentiment* best captures the complex and common emotional response of pockets of the German population to the perceived or real demand by occupation forces for a sincere posture of remorse in response to the atrocities of the Third Reich. The remainder of this chapter analyzes how normative emotions produced and sustained through taboos are productive of affective structures in excess of those emotional norms. In other words, in which ways did the Mitscherlichs' chief complaint about what they saw as the West Germans' inability to establish a democratic emotional regime actually work to produce taboos that hindered, rather than fostered, a democratic emotional regime?

The chapters following *The Inability to Mourn*'s titular essay, which usually remain unread, turn to a more complex array of emotions and affective clusters than the morally polarized binary of remembering/feeling versus derealization and "Gefühlsstarre" (rigidity of feeling) established in the opening essay, even if the authors do not follow through on these observations. The second chapter in their book is titled "Variationen des Themas" (Variations on the theme), and a subsection of this chapter, entitled "Tabu-Ressentiment-Rückständigkeit demonstriert an geschichtlichen Entscheidungen" (Taboo, ressentiment, and backwardness, as demonstrated by historical decisions), unwittingly describes the very structure of taboo and moralization that the book itself performs and instigates and that is persistently staged in readings of the affective climate in the immediate postwar era and beyond.[125]

According to Freud, neuroses act on the neurotic subject in such a way that he or she unwittingly engages in a divisive psychic battle where repressed, unconscious wishes, manifesting themselves in symptom formations and unexpected affect, struggle for expression over and against socially mandated contours of the ego (or conscious subject) and the monitoring instance of the superego (or conscience). This pattern of ambivalent movement between conscious social norms and prohibited unconscious desires produces the torsion characteristic of the divided subject of psychoanalysis. Likewise, it structures the logic of taboo, which is also organized around the conflict between prohibited and socially prescribed behavior.[126] This means that, by definition, emotions and affective structures can remain hidden and unavailable to consciousness, knowledge, and comprehension.

In social situations in which taboos are established, a high level of emotional ambivalence exists, and unconscious wishes emerge in displaced and unexpected affective forms that vie with prohibition. Subsequently, these wishes may be channeled into forms of comportment unconsciously organized to deflect the content of the wish. This enables the unconscious desire to persist as ambivalent emotion despite and perhaps also because of the prohibition that has prevented it from becoming conscious. Freud addresses the strength of these competing unconscious and conscious claims on the subject.

> As a result of the repression which has been enforced and which involves a loss of memory—an amnesia—the motives for the prohibition (which is conscious) remain unknown; and all attempts of disposing of it by intellectual process must fail, since they cannot find any base of attack. The prohibition owes its strength and its obsessive character precisely to its unconscious opponent, the concealed and undiminished desire—that is to say, to an internal necessity inaccessible to conscious inspection.[127]

In other words, whatever is condemned by prohibition may undergo a process of erasure from consciousness—a "loss of memory"—but nonetheless continues to determine the affective life of the individual, without being available for intellectual analysis. Freud continues,

> The instinctual desire is constantly shifting in order to escape from the *impasse* and endeavors to find substitutes—substitute objects and substitute acts—in place of the prohibited ones. In consequence of this, the prohibition itself shifts about as well, and extends to any new aims which the forbidden impulse may adopt. Any fresh advance made by the repressed libido is answered by a fresh sharpening of the prohibition. The mutual inhibition of the two conflicting forces produces a need for dis-

charge, for reducing the prevailing tension; and to this may be attributed the reason for the performance of obsessive acts.[128]

The adherence to the law of prohibition put in place by a taboo, on the one hand, and the unconscious desire that consistently attempts, nonetheless, to manifest itself as affect, on the other, compete for preeminence in the individual. As a result of this tension, affect is produced, which subsequently undergoes a complex process of distortion and often also displacement. Freud argues that the "emotional ambivalence" manifested in the subject's behavior remains difficult for her or him (or an outside observer) to explain in rational terms.

Transferring Freud's insights into the structure of taboo to the context of post-1945 West Germany helps us to understand how taboo acts as a productive unconscious force, rather than solely in terms of absence and rigid inactivity, which is implied by the word *inability*. Even if the subject's actions and the accompanying affective charge remain inscrutable due to their unconscious nature, Freud's account nonetheless offers an interpretation of the subject's emotional response that helps to illuminate some of the strange affective responses attributed to Germans in the years following their defeat at the end of World War II. Indeed, the strange affective responses (or even the absence of feeling) may represent what Freud calls "compromise actions" that emerged under the pressure of the prolonged state of exception in occupied Germany. On the topic of compromise actions, Freud writes,

> In the case of a neurosis these are clearly compromise actions: from one point of view they are evidences of remorse, efforts at expiation, and so on, while on the other hand they are at the same time substitutive acts to compensate the instinct for what has been prohibited.[129]

The subject's behavior, which appears counterintuitive, may itself be interpreted as an expression of the struggle between tabooed behavior and an unconscious affective declaration of remorse or rue for the very attachment to the prohibited object or behavior in the first place.

According to Freud, remorse of this nature will not be expressed as a conscious admission of guilt; instead, it manifests itself as an uneasy sense of shame. The subject may seek a logical explanation for this sense of uneasiness, but due to the prohibition on the object or acts that initiated the attachment, these feelings and their preconditions cannot be consciously articulated.[130] In the context of post–World War II Germany, this sense of remorse may arise where the prohibiting instance attempts to maintain a taboo through emotional rewards or punishment cast in a pedagogical frame (as with the US occupying forces' concept of "reeducation" of the German population toward democratic autonomy). If an environment lacks the psychological resources, desire, and time to interpret latent as well as manifest affective reactions, individuals subject to prohibitions will appear to have an emotional comportment at odds with expected responses. Characterized by affective ambivalence pulling in conflicting directions, the subject's behavior may appear alienating and uncanny, even to the subject herself or himself.

Most interestingly in the context of the Mitscherlichs' argument, Freud's privileged example in his examination of the structure of prohibition and remorse in taboo is the relation of the living to the dead. Pace Freud, the emotional ambivalence occasioned by the death of a known person awakens both sorrowful and hostile feelings in the living, and the process of mourning attempts to contain this complex of competing feelings. Freud argues that mourning's purpose is "to detach the survivors' memories and hopes from the dead." When successful, the process of mourning diminishes pain over time, and the sense of remorse and self-reproach the survivor feels toward the dead similarly recedes. According to Freud, a set of taboos and ceremonies existed in premodern societies to contain the conflict of positive and hostile emotions aroused in those who survived the dead person. Modern society, mostly lacking in such rituals, labels as "neurotic" those who express self-reproach and remorse as a means to circumvent the hostility and ambivalence they feel toward the dead. In other words, according to Freud's model, the melancholic represents an anachronistic remnant of the emotional ambivalence occasioned by death that once was allowed fuller expression.

> Where, in earlier times, satisfied hatred and pained affection fought each
> other, we now find that a kind of scar has been formed in the shape of
> piety, which declares "*de mortuis nil nisi bonum.*" It is only neurotics
> whose mourning for the loss of those dear to them is still troubled by obsessive self-reproaches—the secret of which is revealed by psychoanalysis as the old emotional ambivalence.[131]

Thus those untouched by modernity's scar of piety, the melancholics among us, reveal the ambivalence that always already lay at the base of the subject's response to death. Freud's observations about the remorse felt by these subjects also grounds his approach to the formation of conscience, which he defines as "the internal perception of the rejection of a particular wish operating within us." This leads him to define the consciousness of guilt as "the perception of the internal condemnation of an act by which we have carried out a particular wish."[132] In short, the logic that inspires a sense of consciousness of guilt is identical to the structure of emotional ambivalence produced by a taboo, linking the emotion of guilt to a larger, more ambivalent affective complex and suggesting that guilt itself is an affective complex well in excess of the normative contours granted to this socially salient emotion.

In both cases, what is of central importance is that there is a dual current of opposing feelings, one of which remains unconscious and is kept under repression by a dominant emotion.[133] Freud compares the structure of what he calls "a sense of guilt" with the affective complex of anxiety. This "dread of conscience" points toward the continuing presence of an opposing feeling despite its repression: "And this reminds us that there is something unknown and unconscious in connection with the sense of guilt, namely the reasons for the act of repudiation."[134] What, then, is the relationship between moral prohibitions and taboo and the complex of "ambivalent emotions" that Freud traces to both? Freud responds, "the neuroses are [a]social structures; they endeavor to achieve by private means what is effected in society by collective effort."[135] In Freud's terms, the attempt to transpose the diagnosis of neurosis of the mourning or melancholic individual to an entire society only results in a confusion of analytical categories.

Juxtaposing Freud's text against that of the Mitscherlichs, it becomes clear that emotion may be seen as the winning strategy over the complex affective dynamics of the tripartite Freudian topology of the id, ego, and superego. Emotion appears to involve fewer variables and obscured aspects, lending itself to an easier process of interpretation and categorization, hence the common insistence on emotions as a "unit" of measurement in considering moral norms. Reading for emotion thus involves taking into consideration the legible status of emotion and the possibility that the emotion expressed (or, for that matter, repressed or apparently absent) might be the tip of a far more complex affective structure evading normative (or even conscious) judgment. In reading Freud against the Mitscherlichs, we see how key concepts of psychoanalysis, such as affect and a differentiated focus on the affective productivity of tabooed (unconscious) wishes, are not deployed to their full explanatory potential in the Mitscherlichs' text. Reading for emotion and identifying affective structures bring these blind spots into focus and show how the Mitscherlichs' text produces, rather than illuminates, foreclosures on what counts as emotion in the postwar context.

Raising Emotion: Affective Pedagogies?

Despite their dependence on—in fact, their attempt to recuperate—Freudian psychoanalysis in postwar West Germany, the Mitscherlichs evince strong suspicion, bordering on adversity, toward all structures of affect or emotion expressed in post-1945 West Germany. This manifests itself in their oft-repeated dichotomizing gesture of understanding reality as a condition attained only through a process of searching for critical insight (or reason) beyond the distorting lens of affect.

As was the case with Karl Jaspers' Cartesian "great divide" between intellect and emotion (discussed in the first chapter of the present study), the Mitscherlichs land securely on the side of critical insight in the binary they establish between reason and affect. For example, they state, "Insight is a function of the ego, which is periodically able, by reflecting and examining, to loosen its tie to drive-promoted desires. The ego is then in a position to apprehend its own and the common reality of all men, without the crude colorings and distortions imparted by our affects."[136] References like these abound in the book, such as the equation of primary processes with affect: "The more passionately the individual is concerned and rationally involved, the less he is emotionally manipulable by appeals to his primary-process-type fantasies."[137] In another segment of the book, the Mitscherlichs equate the manifestations of emotion described as prevalent in West Germany with behaviors associated with preconscious or unconscious emotions usually overcome through emotional development and maturation.

> Order, as achieved by the critical ego, whether represented by the individual or through society, is unstable; it is acquired by learning processes in the face of emotional tendencies (instinctual appetites, anxiety, and the like) by which it can be easily overridden; this was shown by the fascination which the mythicizing, confused doctrines of Nazism exercised over millions of people.[138]

Assessments such as the above lend the Mitscherlichs' work a highly moralizing tone in synch with that of an educator of childlike and stunted individuals who, if the logic is followed through to its ironic conclusion, appear largely unaccountable for their underdeveloped behavior and the instability of their moral comportment. In fact, in their book, rational, critical insight is opposed to what they describe as "Ressentiments," the presence of which, they rightly argue, leads to the elimination of "critical ego work" (incorrectly translated as "intelligence" in the English translation).[139] In this way, they overlook the manner in which critical thought and emotion work hand in hand, and they neglect the central Freudian achievement of alerting us to how a subject's unconscious is unwittingly at work in what appears to be utterly conscious behavior. By drawing on a Cartesian logic, they stop short of examining how *ressentiment*, as an affective structure, draws on its own rationalizing logic that bears further examination as a structure, rather than a binary, as I hope is demonstrated in the present study's second chapter (on Ernst von Salomon's novel *Der Fragebogen*) and conclusion.

However, as we know, at least since Nietzsche, that which is set under erasure by a taboo does not necessarily cease to exist. To the contrary, the prohibitive power of proscription enables a perverse productivity fueled by the pleasure of perceived rebellion against the prohibitive stance of such pedagogy.[140] Similarly, Freudian psychoanalysis demonstrates the recalcitrance of tabooed emotions and sexual inclinations, as well as the way in which they flourish and gain a secret or unconscious life of their own over and against societal prohibitions that supposedly do away with them in the first place.

By failing to acknowledge the normative dimensions of remembering and mourning promoted by their pedagogically driven diagnosis of post-1945 West Germany, the Mitscherlichs ran the risk of establishing taboos and affective prohibitions. Like Hannah Arendt and others before them, they also misread the ambivalence of affect as emotional rigidity and stasis. In their attempt to establish the priority of an "Erziehung" (education) of the emotions, they create an artificial binary pitting critical thought over and against affect, overlooking their critical interdependence.

Just as one is unable to remember and mourn the past on command, so too one is unable to determine the morally "correct" emotional comportment through pedagogical measures and stringent moral judgments alone. Recalcitrant affect and its less savory moral manifestations might be one necessary starting point for societies grappling with violent pasts and the attendant disturbing blurring of moral categories of agency. A high tolerance of ambivalence is a necessary precondition for critical self-reflection. An inability to think through affective structures resulting from disturbing histories may promote zones of taboo that conserve, rather than elucidate, affect's moral intractability. Reading for emotion in this context means understanding the productive affective structure promoted by taboo and recognizing the complex intersubjectivity of emotional responses. Despite the great differences between them, Karl Jaspers and Alexander Mitscherlich ultimately appear to support a similar emotional regime, one dividing critical thought from emotion only to privilege reason.

Conclusion: "A Stroll through the Battleground of Murdered Concepts"

> But there are no longer any anti-Semites. The last of them were liberals who wanted to express their antiliberal opinions.
> —Max Horkheimer and T. W. Adorno, *Dialectic of Enlightenment*

> If it is held against you all the time, a certain instinct for self-preservation comes about emotionally.
> —"Z," group discussant, Institute for Social Research, *Guilt and Defense*

This book has offered an extended argument for the salience of examining postwar Germany's emotions and affective structures, demonstrating the way in which these are a vital component of how sociopolitical collective entities are imagined and inhabited. Moving away from the model of postwar "melancholic scholarship" and its prescriptive diagnosis of a nation "unable to mourn," I have argued for an affective cartography of exemplary scenes from immediate postwar West German culture, ranging from Karl Jaspers' 1945 lectures on guilt at Heidelberg University to Ernst von Salomon's turbulent appearance at the *Mittwochgespräch* in the waiting room of Cologne's central railway station in 1951. I have examined such scenes through the lens of socially codified emotions and have identified processes of emotional intersubjectivity in them that responded to actual and imagined emotional regimes during the period of Allied victory and occupation. Likewise, my book illustrates the symbolic gain of tarrying with less readily legible and often unruly affective structures, particularly as they manifest themselves in constellations of affective communities that are less public but no less cathected. Emotions and undergirding affective structures clearly play a vital role in our understanding of the politics at work in both the public and private sphere. With his term *imaginary community*, Benedict Anderson captured the fantasmatic investment of citizens in the ideal of a nation, suggesting the central role of affect in the libidinal cathexis formative of (national) community.[1] In this sense, affect is constitutive of politics or, alternatively, is part of a "politics of emotion." A principal aim of this book has been to indicate emotion's centrality to conceptions of the political, broadly writ; the state of a nation cannot be properly understood without reading for emotion.

In my analysis, in chapter 2, of the reception of von Salomon's *Der Fragebogen*, I underscored the importance of less obvious yet paradigmatic postwar affective communities that coexisted with more codified emotions and comportment. The affective constellation of *ressentiment* sustaining nationalist subcultures in the early years of the Federal Republic constitutes a particularly resilient and adaptable structure. *Ressentiment* is, despite Nietzsche's importance in our understanding of this term, not an entirely German invention.[2] Having considered, in chapter 2, the moral and psychological contours of the term in Nietzsche's writing, I here return to this affective structure in order to emphasize its resonance and significance in and beyond Germany, "after Auschwitz" and well into the twenty-first century.

References to *ressentiment* abound in press and journal publications well into the postwar period. For example, in newspaper clippings from the 1950s in Karl Jaspers' estate, the word appears frequently. In an article on the front page of *Die Zeit* from early in that decade, chief editor Ernst Friedlaender criticized a general climate of *ressentiment* that he believed was bedeviling the political and affective climate of West Germany.

> The common denominator of all such utterances is *ressentiment*. And who today in Germany can count themselves above this? Who stands above their own tale of suffering; above the grudges against all who are doing better, or once did better, than they are doing now? In the period immediately after 1945 the *ressentiment* of the "anti-fascists" was dominant. [. . .] Today we are contending with counter-*ressentiment* among "Nazis" toward "anti-fascists" and the Allied powers; among soldiers toward members of the resistance; among displaced people toward local inhabitants; among the younger toward the older generation.[3]

The following passage from the same article has been underlined, presumably by Jaspers, who clearly was no stranger to *ressentiment* himself:

> We must try, once and for all, to break free from collective judgment and *ressentiment*. [. . .] the *ressentiment* of the genuine resistance fighter to-

ward all those who did not share his common cause, and that of everyday ("normal") Germans, who, in many instances, were Party members and, in still more cases, against the resistance.[4]

Surely Jaspers shared these sentiments, which are very close to those expressed in *Die Schuldfrage*.

Newspaper reviews of von Salomon's *Der Fragebogen* in Karl Jaspers' estate also demonstrate critical attention to emotions and politics.

> Reading the literary 'Questionnaire' [. . .] provokes a series of feelings [. . .] Clearly, he believed that with his questionnaire he would most likely comply with public feeling; but with his *ressentiments* and hubris, he made a mockery not only of the Americans' questions, but also of his own literary experiment. [. . .] But for all that, this will not do.[5]

This article deploys a strong rhetoric of negative affect to critique the perceived politico-emotional danger of the *ressentiment* manifest in von Salomon's book. Other reviews also speak to an awareness of an undercurrent of *ressentiment* in the political culture of West Germany, partly motivated by the anxiety about the affective structure's potential consequences for the new democracy.

In 1968, some two decades after the Cold War had crystallized alliances, a publication coauthored by Dolf Sternberger and titled *Aus dem Wörterbuch des Unmenschen* (From the Lexicon of the Inhuman) included *ressentiment* in a list of "inhuman" or "barbarous" words.[6] Based on earlier contributions by editor Sternberger to *Die Wandlung* (1945–49), this is the third (and last) edition of the text, following its prior release in 1945 and again in 1957. Each new edition had been revised and amended, and in the final edition, Sternberger concludes with a medley of essays on then-current debates about "Sprachkritik." In his preliminary notes, he emphasizes that the entries not only represent the ideological abuse and pernicious misuse of language during the Third Reich but also offer contemporary exemplars of ideologically stained or compromised language.[7] The word *ressentiment* is one of six new entries in the 1968 edition, suggesting that the term must still have had sufficient currency to be familiar to contemporary readers.

Sternberger's 1968 entry charts the word's logical and moral contortions in its contemporary incarnation. As we have already seen in the reception of von Salomon's *Der Fragebogen*, when the word *ressentiment* is used, it usually serves to decry the presence of the affective structure, which is viewed unfavorably as an "Untugend" (vice).[8] Following Sternberger's explanation, when a German describes a person as without *ressentiment*, it generally indicates a perceived absence of resentment against the German qua German in the specific historical context of postwar Europe. However, Sternberger argues that this is not the correct use of the term; in fact, the entry in the *Sprach-Brockhaus* defines *ressentiment* as "Groll, lange und oft unbewußt gehegter Haß oder Neid" (Grudge, a longstanding and often unconsciously fostered hatred or envy).[9] Sternberger imagines the potential German response to this strongly negative definition as a protest: this cannot be what the German speaker meant by the term, since the origin of the *ressentiment*—namely, the German's presence—would have to be quite clear and conscious to the person who encounters him or her.

Turning to Dornseiff's *Deutschen Wortschatz*, Sternberger finds the definition of "Neid" (envy) and also stronger negative emotions, such as "Übelwollen" (to wish someone ill), "Tücke" (perfidy), and "Schadenfreude" (gloating/malicious joy). Average Germans, Sternberger surmises, would deny that they ascribe such negative emotions to those who had been exposed to German occupation and National Socialist crimes. In fact, the Germans praise the absence of *ressentiment* in former enemies or even victims. Yet their positive impression of their interlocutors' lack of *ressentiment* toward them suggests that the Germans unconsciously anticipate precisely such negativity as a possible response to their "Germanness." As we can see, by focusing on the negative feelings of the other, the German avoids reflecting on his or her own postwar *ressentiment*, thus eliding the grounds for its existence in the first place. This negation of a negative affect indicates the complexity and moral ambiguity of *ressentiment*, as well as its strong affective undertow.

Returning the reader to the father of the moral psychology of *ressentiment*, Sternberger argues somewhat reductively that Nietzsche deems the affect to be less a response to experience than a psychological tendency of an individual. In doing so, Sternberger overlooks the social vulnerability, often caused by a historical shift in power relations, that is the catalyst for *ressentiment*. Nietzsche identifies anti-Semites and Jews alike as susceptible to *ressentiment*. Thus the term's German usage that Sternberger focuses on in 1968 corresponds to neither its dictionary definition nor its philosophical genealogy. Sternberger interprets this ominously as an indication of "welche dunklen Wünsche ihnen durch die Seele ziehen" (which dark wishes move through their souls).[10] By projecting the affective tonalities of *ressentiment* onto others (even if only to indicate the affect's apparent absence in the other), "the German" deflects attention from the legitimate anger or hatred potentially felt by a victim in response to actual historical wrongdoing and suffering at the hands of the Nazi regime.[11] Sternberger states, "On the contrary, one can dispute the right of feeling 'ressentiment'; there is—according to its popular conscious or unconscious German usage—no reason for it. No reasons, but only abysses."[12] The force of negativity conveyed by the term *Abgründe* (abysses) is a measure of the vehemence of the affective structure in question.

A connection between *ressentiment* and anti-Semitism is suggested in the next breath, with Sternberger's example of a Jewish emigrant as the non-German at the heart of the structure of avoidance captured by the "German" usage of the word: "Why don't they say, 'That Jewish emigrant doesn't feel any hatred, any hatred of the Germans, any Germanophobia'?"[13] Clearly, *ressentiment* signals the presence of a complex, strongly negative affective response—or defense mechanism—with distinctly moral contours. It is a structure of affect working obstinately to produce and then counter a display of affect, namely, the sociohistorical affective coordinates between Jewish Germans and non-Jewish Germans, with the murderous anti-Semitism of the Jewish genocide as the unmentioned ch(i)asmic backdrop.[14] In other words, the potential display of residual negative affects toward Jewish Germans is preempted or even repressed by the attribution of affective agency to the Jewish German and not the non-Jewish German, who effectively circumvents the development of negative affect or its expression through an insistence on *ressentiment*'s absence (with its accompanying spectrum of hatred and rage).

In this usage, the term itself signals the presence of disavowed wishes and unconscious libidinal cathexes. Furthermore, the ascription of *ressentiment* (or the absence thereof) to another may be read as the enunciation of a power relationship (real or fantasized)—as one facet of the postwar politics of emotion. Counterintuitively, *ressentiment* is invoked precisely when the German subject wishes to say to his or her interlocutor, "There is no reason for this feeling, since I am not guilty of a thing."

Sternberger recognizes the political and moral dimensions of this usage from a slightly different perspective when he explains, "Ultimately, the "wrong" usage of the term arises from the need to escape from the reasons [for *ressentiment*], to have them be forgotten, to forget them oneself, even at the cost of those who have reason [to feel this way]."[15] According to this logic, *ressentiment* applies to those with good reason to complain only insofar as they refrain from complaining, thus preserving the German's sense of innocence or noncomplicity. This popular use of the term reveals the contortion or reversal of moral and power relations, whereby the nonvictims are ultimately felt to be entirely at the mercy of the victims' judgment. Likewise, as we have seen, by conflating the Allies with the victims of National Socialist brutality, the Germans are able to resent both the conquerors and the victims as oppressors.

It is similarly important to emphasize *ressentiment*'s strong link not just to national identity but also to a libidinally charged German nationalism. A 1949 contribution to Sternberger's *Die Wandlung* by author and theater critic Hanns Braun is paradigmatic in this regard. Titled "Die Studenten und die nationalen Ressentiments," the essay was originally delivered by Braun as a lecture at a political colloquium in November 1948, at the invitation of the Allgemeinen Studenten-Ausschusses der Technischen Hochschule München.[16] In addition to signaling the close relationship between nationalism and *ressentiment*, the talk's title also conveys the atmosphere in which national pride struggled against national shame in the German lecture halls replete with former soldiers, no doubt similar to those encountered by Karl Jaspers in the winter of 1945/46.

Presumably due to the volatile topic proposed to him by the students, Braun states that he was originally reluctant to give the talk. He describes the term *ressentiment* as "kitzlig" (ticklish), due to what he sees as its contagiousness, whereby one cannot speak about *ressentiment* without producing *ressentiment*, specifically the "das antideutsche Gegengefühl" (anti-German counterfeeling) and "die Gegengefühle dieses Gegengefühls" (counterfeeling of this counterfeeling). In the unsteady politico-emotional climate of 1948–49, at a time of "Not und Bedrängnis" (misery and hardship), Braun expressly states that he does not intend to produce "strammer und zeitgemäßer Gegengefühle" (stalwart and timely counterfeelings) with his paper. Like Jaspers in his *Schuldfrage* lectures, Braun cautions against destructive emotional comportment based on "Mißgunst, Neidhaß und schleichender Groll in all seinen Unarten" (distrust, envy-hatred, and stealthy rancor), warning that the air Germans breathe is "auf besondre Weise ressentimentvergiftet" (especially poisoned with *ressentiment*).[17] In the contemporary moment, Braun argues, *ressentiment* is stoked by a national self-righteousness directed at the Allied forces. He states,

> National *ressentiment* drew a great deal of its power from nothing more than the opposition between the victors' moral demands, which were expressed through tribunals and a large number of defamatory lawsuits, and practical experiences. The latter amounted to the age-old recognition that we humans are no angels, and thus there is little cause to consider oneself better than the 'other.' But what conclusions have we drawn so far from this rectifying insight? You can hear it on every street corner. All varia-

tions add up to the same thing: as the others who said that they were better than us have turned out not to be so, that which they blamed us for was therefore also no longer bad; rather, it was just the thing that 'everyone does'—the normal, quite simply, the usual.[18]

The structure of *ressentiment* captured here by Braun attests to the pernicious afterlife of nationalist sentiments in the postwar German emotional landscape, as well as to their perceived political volatility.

Beyond the postwar German landscape, *ressentiment* has played out its affective politics in many different contexts and times. In his wide-ranging book *Resentment in History*, philosopher Marc Ferro illustrates the term's extensive historical purchase.[19] Ferro explores the long and industrious career of resentment in the contexts of slavery, religion (Christianity and Judaism), revolution (French and Russian), national memory (Poland and Austria), postcolonialism (Algeria/France), and communalism (the Black Power movement). *Ressentiment's* temporal longevity is matched by its extensive geopolitical sweep. For example, sociologist Jeffrey Olick sees resentment as a key factor in his approach to analyzing what he calls "the politics of regret" in a transnational setting.[20] Similarly, in his book on ethnic violence in twentieth-century Eastern Europe, political scientist Roger Petersen deploys a cognitive approach, using "resentment" to help understand the pervasiveness of ethnic violence and genocide in the Baltic States.[21] Unsurprisingly, in recent years, resentment has become a frequent category of analysis in the international field of transitional justice.

Ferro concludes his expansive study by noting six characteristic qualities of *ressentiment*. First, it arises from an inferiority complex produced by real or imagined trauma or humiliation. Second, it has its roots in the context of a sense of impotence—the unconscious sense of aggravation increases in proportion to the level of perceived helplessness. Third, "resentment is reciprocal," meaning that it is not peculiar to those occupying the victim status, that it may emerge in multiple parties simultaneously or alternate between interacting or diverse groups, and that it is often to be found in situations where a sudden reversal of power relations has occurred. Fourth, *ressentiment* is characterized by its longevity and is thus often part of various communities of memory. Fifth, resentment distorts or manipulates the sense of history as chronological time, through the subject's conscious or unconscious fixation on the perceived or real injury received. Finally, resentment can compel a group to revalorize their identity, which may culminate in identity claims constructed out of the "woundedness" particular to *ressentiment*.[22]

The characteristics of *ressentiment* thus include real or imagined humiliation, a sense of impotence, and a sudden reversal of power structures. The very possibility for reciprocity and reversibility is taken up passionately in an important essay titled "Ressentiments" in a volume published in 1966 by Jewish-Austrian author, former resistance fighter, political prisoner, and survivor Jean Améry (originally called Hans Mayer).[23] Améry's affective stance toward the structure of *ressentiment* could not be further removed from that of von Salomon. Améry criticizes what he sees as overhasty postwar overtures of appeasement—"trembling with the pathos of forgiveness and reconciliation"—expressed by Jewish public figures in Germany.[24] He feels equally compelled and repulsed by the reversal of political and moral power that symbolically accompanies the shift in his position from victim of the Nazi regime to survivor and witness of Germany's defeat. With his statement "I speak as a victim and examine my resentments," Améry eschews any easy form of reconciliation. Instead, in an attempt both to elucidate and to release himself from his sense of powerlessness and solitude vis-à-vis his former persecutors, Améry claims the fantasmatic position of the individual who resents the German collective's unwillingness to acknowledge and take responsibility for Nazi crimes.[25] In this way, he exposes and disrupts the logic of reversal targeted in Sternberger's examination of the defensive displacement at work in the German usage of the term.

Améry represents precisely that spectral figure or revenant of guilt that the German usage of *ressentiment* tries to elide or erase. Refusing to read his stance of *ressentiment* in either moral or pathological terms, Améry practices a politics of emotion that provides an ethical challenge, as well as a critical sociopolitical response.[26] When one considers the widespread presence and awareness of *ressentiment*, Améry's example is uncannily similar to Sternberger's description of the German understanding of the term, but from a diametrically opposed position. Améry writes,

Conversations like the one I had in 1958 with a South German businessman over breakfast in the hotel were enough. Not without first politely inquiring whether I was an Israelite, the man tried to convince me that there was no longer any race hatred in his country. The German people bear no grudge against the Jewish people, he said. As proof he cited his government's magnanimous policy of reparations, which was, incidentally, well appreciated by the young state of Israel. In the presence of this man, whose mind was so at ease, I felt miserable: Shylock, demanding his pound of flesh.[27]

Améry drives home the perverse emotional politics at work in *ressentimental* logic, stating sardonically, "The Germans no longer had any hard feelings towards the resistance fighters and the Jews. How could they still demand atonement?"[28] The tone of bitterness does not override Améry's despair at what he sees as the Germans' assumption and grandiloquent renunciation of the territory of *ressentiment*. In Aleida Assmann's words, Améry "aims at presenting resentment in a new light and to present it as a paradigm of moral feeling."[29] Not only denying the Germans' spurious claim to this political emotion, he goes on to lay claim to *ressentiment* as a driving moral emotion, such that his claim cannot be read as anything other than a political and ethical challenge extended to his German readers. He confronts them with the enduring wounds of National Socialism's victims, attempting to gain the Germans' ethical recognition (in contradistinction to *Wiedergutmachung*, or financial compensation).

In Améry's understanding of the temporal dimensions of *ressentiment*, the flow of what he calls biological or social time has abruptly halted for the victims and becomes, instead, moral or achronological time; while biological time heals all wounds, moral time annuls time altogether for the victim.[30] Unlike von Salomon, who perversely denies harboring any *ressentiment* whatsoever, Améry both actively claims the affect of *ressentiment* and recognizes the emotional politics that come with it: "We victims of persecution, the high-soaring man says, ought to internalize our past suffering and bear it in emotional asceticism, as our torturers should do with their guilt."[31] For the victim, it seems, emotional asceticism would entail divorcing oneself from a moral perspective on the past and the political possibilities held out by this affective structure.

Describing the hoped-for outcome of his politics of emotion, Améry maintains that only by directly facing their past as their "own negative possession" could Germans hope for reconciliation with the victims of Nazism. If this were to happen, he writes, "on the field of history there would occur what I hypothetically described earlier for the limited, individual circle: two groups of people, the overpowered and those who overpowered them, would be joined in the desire that time be turned back and, with it, history would become moral. If this demand were raised by the German people, who as a matter of fact have been victorious and already rehabilitated by time, it would have tremendous weight, even so that by this alone it would already be fulfilled."[32] But Améry's challenge went unrecognized, and the loneliness and abandonment he expressed persisted unacknowledged. The difficult—perhaps even utopian— encounter he had hoped for did not take place in his lifetime. For von Salomon and Améry alike, but for vastly different reasons, the politics of emotion proffered by *ressentiment* failed to bear fruit. Recognizing this failed encounter, Améry reflects,

> There I am with my resentments, in Frankfurt, Stuttgart, Cologne, and Munich. If you wish, I bear my grudge for reasons of personal salvation. Certainly. On the other hand, however, it is also for the good of the German people. But no one wants to relieve me of it, except the organs of public opinion-making, which buy it. What dehumanized me has become a commodity, which I offer for sale.[33]

Améry's essay remained a monologue in his lifetime, perhaps because his potential interlocutors resented (or simply ignored) his expressions of emotional suffering. His readers appeared ill prepared—or even unwilling—to question the emotional refuge *ressentiment* offered them in the 1960s.

The "organs of public opinion-making" invoked by Améry provide a final suggestive scene. Embedded in this scene are members of the Frankfurt Institute for Social Research, who, in their analyses of anti-Semitism, applied transatlantic sociological "tools" garnered in the 1930s and 1940s in the United States to their analysis of residual fascism in "nonpublic opinion" in the Federal Republic of the 1950s and 1960s. Their project of critical social analysis underscores the continuity of a libidinal investment in certain affective structures in postwar West German culture.

The Same Difference? *Ressentiment* and the Structure of Anti-Semitism

In 1947, four years before Rowohlt released von Salomon's *Der Fragebogen*, the Querido publishing house in Amsterdam released a book of philosophical fragments, titled *Dialektik der Aufklärung* (*Dialectic of Enlightenment*), by critical theorists Max Horkheimer and Theodor Adorno. Written during their wartime exile in the United States, this much-discussed book is a critique of the broken promises of Enlightenment reason from Homer to Hitler; it offers a diagnosis of how modern society's "progress" is actually a dialectic between barbarism and enlightenment, rather than a teleological path to the good life. The text houses a nested fragment titled "Elemente des Antisemitismus: Grenzen der Aufklärung," which describes anti-Semitism's psychological structure as the prejudiced subject's inversion of his or her relationship to the surrounding environment.

Startling in Horkheimer and Adorno's account of anti-Semitism is how much it bears in common with the structure of *ressentiment*. In fact, von Salomon's sense of victimization by the US-Allied forces mirrors to a tee the logic of reversal and projection described by Horkheimer and Adorno. This striking parallel suggests that what von Salomon and other like-minded Germans in postwar Germany failed to come to terms with bears a strong structural resemblance to the affective structure of anti-Semitism. Von Salomon's text could be read as a damning illustration of how, rather than reflecting on the logic and deadly consequences of anti-Semitism qua affective structure, one might merely reverse the psychological perspective by taking up residence in this affective structure as the victim of the American "oppressors."

The extreme motility of *ressentiment*, where perpetrators may unconsciously usurp the position of victims as a defensive mechanism of displacement against unconscious envy and guilt, can also be seen in Horkheimer and Adorno's description of the dialectical reversal constitutive of anti-Semitism: "Rage is vented on those who are both conspicuous and unprotected. And just as, depending on the constellation, the victims are interchangeable: vagrants, Jews, Protestants, Catholics, so each of them can replace the murderer, in the same blind lust for killing, as soon as he feels the power of representing the norm."[34] In the postwar context, the sudden shift in power relations meant that although "the Germans" occupied the position of the perpetrators in the eyes of the world, German individuals facing privation, loss, and the contempt of the international community perceived themselves as disempowered victims (*ohnmächtig*) vis-à-vis the occupying forces. This emotional dialectic clearly has broader political ramifications, inasmuch as it is founded on shifting power relations and hierarchies with definitive socioeconomic and moral consequences.

Horkheimer and Adorno's analysis of the anti-Semite's relationship to the outer world captures the complex reciprocity and perverse emotional intersubjectivity characteristic of both anti-Semitism and *ressentiment*.

Anti-Semitism is based on false projection. It is the reverse of genuine mimesis and has deep affinities to the repressed; in fact, it may itself be the pathic character trait in which the latter is precipitated. If mimesis makes itself resemble its surroundings, false projection makes its surroundings resemble itself. If, for the former, the outward becomes the model to which the inward clings, so that the alien becomes the intimately known, the latter displaces the volatile inward into the outer world, branding the intimate friend as foe. Impulses which are not acknowledged by the subject and yet are his, are attributed to the object: the prospective victim. [. . .] Those impelled by blind murderous lust have always seen in the victim the pursuer who has driven them to desperate self-defense, and the mightiest of the rich have experienced their weakest neighbor as an intolerable threat before falling upon him.[35]

Projection of repressed impulses onto the outer world and a paranoid sense of being persecuted by the potential victim—in short, the logic of reversal—are the structuring mechanisms of anti-Semitism in Adorno and Horkheimer's account. These displacements enable the potential persecutor to justify his or her violent actions as a function of the self-ascribed victim status. As the authors note, what is disturbing about anti-Semitism is not so much the projective behavior in and of itself but, rather, the absence of any kind of critical reflection on the part of the anti-Semitic subject: "Instead of the voice of conscience, it hears voices; instead of inwardly examining itself in order to draw up a protocol of its own lust for power, it attributes to others the Protocol of the Elders of Zion."[36] *Ressentiment* is a politics of privation by other (psychological) means, as empty as it is opaque to the subject: "It is not just the anti-Semitic ticket which is anti-Semitic, but the ticket mentality itself. The rage against difference which is teleologically inherent in that mentality as the rancor of the dominated subjects of the domination of nature is always ready to attack the natural minority, even though it is the social minority which those subjects primarily threaten."[37]

After his 1949 return to the reestablished Institute for Social Research in Frankfurt, Adorno continued to analyze and write about "anti-Semitism."[38] As a social critic and member of what would become known as the Frankfurt School, Adorno was committed to evaluating and critiquing the socio-emotional climate of West Germany vis-à-vis the recent past. A perennial critic of society's failure to lead "the right life" ("Wrong life cannot be lived rightly" ["Es gibt kein richtiges Leben im Falschen"]),[39] many of Adorno's postwar writings and radio broadcasts embody what could be called a practice of writing "after Auschwitz." In other words, his thinking and writing were, unsurprisingly, characterized by a perpetual critical wariness toward and an awareness of the negative traces that the Nazi past and the Jewish genocide left in all facets of the new Federal Republic.

Adorno's sociological writings and radio addresses, albeit less well known, remain invaluable resources.[40] In particular, two pieces from the 1950s demonstrate his keen awareness of the postwar emotional state of West Germany. "Was bedeutet: Aufarbeitung der Vergangenheit?" ("What Does Coming to Terms with the Past Mean?") is perhaps Adorno's most well-known critical contribution to the so-called discourse of *Vergangenheitsbewältigung*. As is clearly apparent in the counterterm *Aufarbeitung*, Adorno purposively eschewed the popular phrase as "höchst verdächtig" (highly suspect), due to its implied eagerness to take leave of the past.[41] This piece directly addressing the lingering effects of *ressentiment* enjoyed incarnations first as a radio broadcast (1960), then as a public lecture (1962), and finally as an essay (1963). A wave of anti-Semitic aggression in West Germany in 1959 and 1960, specifically the desecration of Jewish synagogues and cemeteries after he had delivered the talk for the first time, confirmed the validity of Adorno's critique. As he would state in regard to his 1962 lecture, "the filthy wave of anti-Semitism lent it a sad topicality," whereby his "sociological theory to a certain extent had preceded empirical reality and been confirmed by it."[42]

The West German populace's reluctant relationship to the Nazi past, argued Adorno, is the source of *ressentiment*. Similar to Améry, Adorno defines the reigning attitude as one that believes "it would be proper for everything to be forgiven and forgotten by those who were wronged."[43] This stance is assumed precisely by those who are least in a position to make this demand morally, namely, "the party that committed the injustice."[44] Adorno recalls a Spanish proverb attributed to Cervantes, "In the house of the hanged one should not speak of the noose"; to describe the postwar West German attitude toward Nazi crimes, Adorno reformulates the aphorism so that it reads, "In the hangman's house one shouldn't speak of the noose, otherwise you wind up with ressentiment."[45] In the wake of German crimes, it is the victims of National Socialism to whom one might attribute *ressentiment* as an understandable affective reaction, yet Germans who were not directly targeted or persecuted under National Socialism are those with the greater potential to harbor *ressentiments*.

Although he does not characterize it directly as *ressentiment*, Adorno goes on to describe the logic of moral attribution, writing about the Germans' defensive readiness to meet (often unvoiced and merely presumed) accusations with counteraccusations: "Such things, so a lazy consciousness comforts itself, could not have occurred if the victims had not presented some kind of provocation; and this vague 'some kind of' can then flourish wildly."[46] These acts of moral misapprehension are characteristic of projection, with its malleable spectrum of implication that can metamorphose bystanders and perpetrators into victims—and vice versa. Adorno recognizes the effects of affective distortion and displacement, stating, "Now it is indisputable that, in relation to the past, there is much that is neurotic: defensive gestures when one isn't attacked; massive affect in situations that do not fully warrant it; and often simply a repression of what was known or half-known."[47] Again, we see that affect is not absent in the postwar German context; rather, its manifestations appear inappropriate or out of proportion.

Adorno's critical observations in his 1963 essay recall an earlier project on public opinion in West Germany launched by the newly reopened Institute for Social Research in Frankfurt.[48] Based on surveys conducted in West German cities between 1950 and 1951, *Gruppenexperiment* (*Group Experiment*), published in 1955, is a sociological analysis of the topics of guilt and defense that offers a glimpse into the contemporary affective climate and the mentality of an—albeit limited—cross section of the West German population.[49] This text, translated in 2010, joins the body of the Frankfurt School's lesser-known sociological research that is now available in English translation and increasingly becoming the focus of broader critical attention.[50]

Adorno's 1960 text on working through the past draws heavily on his critique in *Gruppenexperiment*, in which he provides a qualitative analysis to supplement quantitative data evaluation. The "group experiment" was driven by empirical sociological research methods adapted from those encountered by members of the Frankfurt School during their time in the United States (particularly by Adorno, through his exposure to sociological research for Paul Lazarsfeld's Princeton Radio Project and, later, in a Berkeley group study).[51] Drawing on public opinion surveys and discussion groups, this method of empirical research was accompanied by the group's customarily more speculative critical analysis, thus granting the sociological approach of the Frankfurt School its own particular analytical edge in evaluating emerging social structures.[52] Relying on Freudian psychoanalysis, *Group Experiment* was a continuation of the type of "democratic" sociological analysis favored by Adorno, characteristic of his contribution to *The Authoritarian Personality* (1950). This earlier book documents the results of a Berkeley-based empirical sociological group study that attempted to measure the susceptibility of individuals to authoritarianism using the so-called F-scale (fascism scale) designed by Adorno.[53] In *Group Experiment*, as in *The Authoritarian Personality*, the authors were confronted with the dilemma of how to extend their analysis beyond the manifest opinions of the discussants to excavate latent attitudes and beliefs. In his foreword to *Group Experiment*, politician and economist Franz Böhm coined the term *nonpublic opinion* to describe the concealment and revelation of socially tabooed topics, describing the difference between public and nonpublic opinion as that of "the sum of opinions we wish people believed we had as our real opinion" versus "the sum of opinion that we truly have."[54]

Most likely drawing on the premises of "indirect research" conceptualized for an unrealized experimental Hollywood film project from the 1940s on anti-Semitic prejudice, the discussion environment for the "Gruppenexperiment" project was meant to be as "natural" or unconstrained as possible.[55] Horkheimer likened it to a train compartment, underscoring the atmosphere of intimacy and confidence the group hoped to attain so that participants might feel comfortable enough to reveal their true opinions, even those diverging from reigning public opinion.[56] Similarly, the group conceptualized opinion research as a dialectical process rather than a static and subjective response to a fixed survey. Their so-called basic stimulus for prompting discussion among the group members was the "Colburn Letter," an apocryphal missive ostensibly written by a US Army officer stationed in Germany, to a newspaper "back in the US." This fictional text was presented to 137 different groups of Germans by a researcher, who subsequently moderated the group discussion.[57] The fictive officer's letter conveyed the "average" GI's impression of the German population in a representative yet unexaggerated manner. Sergeant Colburn—the letter's putative author—was presented as American to those discussants in the US-occupied zone and as English to those in the British-occupied zone, thus playing expressly on experiences of the defeated German population with the occupying forces in their zone.

"Colburn" claims that he has gotten to know "average Germans and their opinions first-hand, and especially how ordinary people feel."[58] His account purports to address what the sergeant has learned about the German population—in other words, he offers the reader a brief sketch of the everyday politics of emotion under reeducation. "A lot of nonsense" has been written about Germany, argues Colburn, such as the attribution of a collective German guilt or the allegation that all Germans were Nazis. He contends that such opinions are doubtless intended to allay routine anxieties. The letter presents Colburn as a sympathetic and judicious figure; he describes himself as a "sober GI" who "doesn't let anyone pull the wool over his eyes" but who is also not vengeful.[59] Clearly, the sentiment expressed in these passages aimed at quelling potential defensive reactions in the discussion groups.

The remainder of the letter strikes a balance between listing positive qualities and perceived flaws of the occupied population. Germans are described as clean, hardworking, not often insubordinate, intelligent, and orderly; they demonstrate no outright brutality or crudeness and are good-natured, kind, and friendly. The letter goes on to rehearse perceived shortcomings of the Germans, many of which had been explored earlier by Jaspers and Arendt: namely, they have not "taken to heart what was done to people under Hitler," nor do they appear capable of considering the suffering of others. To be sure, the fictive author mentions the Germans' own vicissitudes during the war as a possible source for their apparent lack of empathy. Colburn also criticizes the Germans for their arrogance and attitude of superiority in relation to Americans.[60]

Most telling, however, are the central passages of the letter that turn to the scorebook mentality regarding suffering and guilt. Colburn writes,

> They [the Germans] apparently have the feeling that the world did the greatest injustice to them. Whenever something goes badly with us, they become indignant. When we are in a difficult situation, as in Korea, one sometimes gets the impression that they are secretly glad about it and do not think about the fact that we alone protect them from the Russians. Admitting the mistakes of one's own country and talking openly about them appears to be a weakness to them. They are still hostile towards the Jews and use the DPs [displaced persons] in particular as a pretense for one-sided judgments.[61]

This paragraph enacts the motility of *ressentiment*, with its shifting identifications, dissociations, distortions, and acts of defensive projection. Colburn describes the German response to racial persecution in the United States as equally disturbing: "They [Germans] act especially strangely when there is talk about racial persecution in America. As soon as they hear that a Negro was lynched in the South, they rub their hands together [as if relishing the inconvenient parallel]."[62] This reaction recalls von Salomon's perverse glee after being beaten up by officers at the internment camp which he attributed to his sense of finally not being the party in the wrong.

There are striking structural similarities between my reading of von Salomon's text as symptomatic of a postwar politics of *ressentiment* and Adorno's analysis of anti-Semitism in the psychological defense mechanisms at work in the discussions documented in *Group Experiment. Der Fragebogen*, one might argue, provided an unrepentant "literary" voicing of what Böhm called "nonpublic opinion." In his contribution to the *Group Experiment*, Adorno cites von Salomon's book as an example of the prevalent tendency in West German society to claim the status of victim when faced with the Nazi past: "It is easy to put oneself in the right and to make yesterday's persecutor today's victim, as for instance is practiced in *The Questionnaire* of Mr. [Ernst] von Salomon."[63] Clearly von Salomon's book struck a nerve with more than one affective community.

In *Group Experiment*, Adorno's chapter "Guilt and Defense" portrayed the central role played by displaced guilt for the subjects of the study; a perhaps even more apposite chapter title might have been "German *Ressentiment*."

Such a title would have also expressed the resentfulness and hostility that Horkheimer feared would be the reaction to *Group Experiment*. The members of the Institute for Social Research navigated between criticism and political alliances in their analysis of residual fascism and their representation, just short of caricature, of Allied opinions in the Colburn stimulus letter.[64] Such caution was not unwarranted, as the negative reception of the book indicates.

Just as *ressentiment* functions in *Der Fragebogen* as a symptomatic display and a communal propensity, Adorno defines defensiveness as an unacknowledged awareness of—and a refusal to be held accountable for—injustice.

> When one fends off guilt feelings and responsibility for what the Nazis did, that does not only mean that one wants to exculpate oneself but just as much that one did in fact regard what was done as unjust and for that reason refuses to accept responsibility. Were that not the case, the eagerness for dissociation would not be necessary.[65]

In *ressentiment*, knowledge and guilt negate each other. In the words of Adorno, "One transforms one's own guilt into the guilt of others by taking the mistakes these others have made or are supposed to have made as the cause of what one has done oneself."[66] The defense mechanism of projection acts as an artificial moral salve for an otherwise ethically intolerable situation. By attributing one's own disowned or disavowed urges to an other, "one thus lives up to the expectations of one's superego, and at the same time has the opportunity to release one's own aggressive inclination under the heading of legitimate punishment."[67] In this way, Adorno employs *ressentiment* to explain the structure of anti-Semitism, both in the *Dialektik der Aufklärung* and in the prejudice studies, first in the United States and later in the Federal Republic of Germany.

Like von Salomon, discussants in *Group Experiment* display their susceptibility to the ideal of a nationalist "imaginary community." They are prone to "keeping score" of guilt in national terms—what Adorno terms "the balancing out of suffering"—where, for example, America's complicity in the knowledge of the Nazi atrocities before and during the war is cited with the aim of relativizing Germany's responsibility for Nazi crimes.[68] This nationalist displacement of guilt with honor is captured in the recurring figure of speech of "the bird who befouls his own nest" (*Nestbeschmutzer*)—the German who criticizes and thus besmirches "his own" people—a colorful and derogatory expression also used to describe Jaspers and Mitscherlich and with which Adorno and other returned émigrés were all too familiar.[69]

In this vein, conservative Austrian social psychologist and former Wehrmacht psychologist Peter R. Hofstätter wrote a starkly negative review of *Group Experiment* in the flagship German sociological journal.[70] He critiques both the book's methodology and its premise of tracing residual attachment to National Socialism. He castigates the authors for presuming the "truth content" of opinions uttered in the affective state of ire or wrath. Drawing on the pejorative expression *in vino veritas*, he criticizes their modus operandi as one of *"in ira veritas,"* claiming that the study falsely assumes that once group discussants are brought to a high enough affective pitch, they will articulate otherwise suppressed or inappropriate (i.e., nonpublic) opinions.[71] Ignoring the coauthors' carefully explained resolves, he states, "[I]t seems justified to ask whether the letter from a fictitious soldier of the occupation army, which is in part and intentionally vexatious, provides a suitable framework for addressing the question of guilt, which is laden with despair. Put differently, where in anger does truth begin and where does the group arrangement impede personal introspection?"[72] Questioning the use of psychoanalysis in general as an analytic tool, Hofstätter levels specific criticism at Adorno's contribution, arguing that rather than providing a neutral assessment of the discussants' opinions, the analysis offers a sustained "accusation" or "a summons for genuine psychic contrition."[73] This mischaracterization of the group study's method and aim is, ironically enough, more in line with the approach the Mitscherlichs introduced a decade later to scrutinize the emotional state of the nation's *Gefühlshaushalt*.

In his invective, Hofstätter unwittingly invokes the specter of the postwar German "primal scene" of the Allied concentration camp photography. In response to this assumed accusation by the coauthors, he declares,

> The nation could (and perhaps should) try to exorcise this horror in a ritual of penitence; however, since this has not happened so far, it is not surprising that single individuals from all strata of the population avoid the topic of guilt or assess their own personal guilt as minimally (subjectively) as possible.[74]

Anticipating later discourses of *Vergangenheitsbewältigung*, this passage underscores the centrality of tropes of emotion in negotiating the vexed terrain of the West German public sphere. Moving between the dichotomies public/private and national/individual, Hofstätter invokes the central yet ambiguous role played by emotion, concluding that "there is simply no individual feeling that could satisfactorily correspond to constantly considering the annihilation of a million people."[75] This begs the question of just what the alternative to this "individual feeling" might be if not collective feeling (which he discounts from the outset). Is Hofstätter proposing a politics of emotion whereby appropriate feeling (which he rules out in advance as an option) would be an adequate or "satisfactory" response to genocide? Or is he simply reiterating a refusal to take responsibility for the crimes of the National Socialists? And who precisely are the unnamed "million people" who have been murdered? This tactic of recognizing National Socialist atrocities ("annihilation") in nationalist terms while defensively retracting both political and moral responsibility recurs throughout the postwar period.

Unsurprisingly, Hofstätter's review prompted Adorno's indignation, culminating in an impassioned and rigorous critique that, among other things, accused Hofstätter of denying fascism's ideological residue in the sociopolitical fabric of the new Federal Republic.[76] Taking up the affective gauntlet cast at his feet by Hofstätter, Adorno accuses him, in turn, of not writing from a position entirely "*sine ira et studio*" (without hate and zealousness).[77] Adorno points out that the "ideological potential" of West German society, rather than actual behavior, past or present, is the object of analysis in the group project. Further, he disagrees that *Gruppenexperiment* is a "summons for genuine psychic contrition," as Hofstätter phrases it. Instead, drawing attention to the nondialectical logic underpinning Hofstätter's argument, Adorno decries the binary simplicity of Hofstätter's model as a "kind of counter-enlightenment best translated as black and white (*Clair-Obskurantismus* [i.e., Chiaroscuro in painting])."[78] Most significantly, in response to Hofstätter's claim about the impossibility of shouldering the burden of Auschwitz, Adorno deftly isolates and critiques what I have called the reverse logic of *ressentiment* in face of the question of culpability.

> It is [however] the victims of Auschwitz who had to take its horrors upon themselves, not those who, to their own disgrace and that of their nation, prefer not to admit it. The "question of guilt" was "laden with despair" for the *victims*, not for the *survivors*, and it takes some doing to have blurred this distinction with the existential category of despair, which is not without reason a popular one.[79]

It comes as no surprise that Adorno repeatedly returns to the topic of anti-Semitism throughout the 1960s. He continues to draw implicitly on the structural similarities between *ressentiment* and anti-Semitism, elaborating his own unacknowledged and undertheorized politics of emotion. For instance, in his essay "Zur Bekämpfung des Antisemitismus heute" (1964),[80] Adorno traces critical reflection on anti-Semitism back to his and Horkheimer's critique of the structure of prejudice in *Dialectic of the Enlightenment*, from 1944.[81] Locating anti-Semitism as part of an overarching mentality of prejudice and as a structural problem inherent in particular social and political formations allows Adorno to criticize broader sociopolitical phenomena without repeating the gesture of exclusion by isolating "Jewishness" as the source and cause of anti-Semitism. While attending to the specificity of anti-Semitism in Germany by flagging the contemporary dangers of what he terms "Krypto-Antisemitismus" (anti-Semitism that proliferates at the level of nonpublic opinion due to official taboos) and "sekundären Antisemitismus"[82] (fascist anti-Semitism "inherited" by children of parents who were eager adherents to National Socialism), Adorno also specifies the structural particularities—or "basic subterfuges"—of anti-Semitism (the "wesentlichen Tricks von Antisemitismus").[83] Significantly, Adorno links acute contemporary anti-Semitism and the "antiamerikanischen Affekt."[84] This brings us full circle and back to the connection between *ressentiment*, anti-Semitism, and anti-Americanism explored in the 1951 reception of von Salomon's *Der Fragebogen*, demonstrating the persistence of an emotional politics located not so much at the level of repression and silence, as rather in loquacious moral reversals and a plethora of tenacious negative feelings.[85]

A Postwar West German Politics of Emotion?
The Afterlives of *Ressentiment*

What has happened to the political emotions and the affective structures that Adorno and Horkheimer, among others, were at pains to reveal and critique? *Ressentiment* certainly had a long afterlife in postwar Germany, flaring up sporadically, as in author Martin Walser's notorious 1998 speech at the Paulskirche in Frankfurt. As the recipient of the Peace Prize of the German Book Trade (Friedenspreis des Deutschen Buchhandels), Walser delivered an address titled "Experiences When Writing a Soap-Box Oratory," which stirred up political emotions directly related to the question of German guilt once again and was framed by Walser as a strong rejection of the guilt and burden of Auschwitz.[86] Walser claimed that intellectuals continued to employ Germany's Nazi past as what he termed a "moral cudgel" on the German population. Stating that it was not appropriate to use Auschwitz as a form of routine threat ("Drohroutine"), he called for an end to the moralizing genuflection and a moratorium on discussions of national shame.

If Walser's speech was not troubling enough, argues historian Dirk Moses, the subsequent debate he conducted with German Jewish leaders Salomon

Korn and Ignatz Bubis manifested disturbing forms of exacerbated emotion and fantasy. Walser's responses constituted an overt "secondary anti-Semitism," indicating the perverse circular logic of blaming the Jews for having stigmatized the German nation through the Holocaust.[87] Similar expressions of defensive emotions can be found in film director Hans Jürgen Syberberg's publications *Die freudlose Gesellschaft* (1981) and *Vom Unglück und Glück in der Kunst in Deutschland nach dem letzten Kriege* (1990). Other, perhaps even more unsettling instances of *ressentiment* continue to make themselves manifest through persistent xenophobia. After the fall of the Berlin Wall in 1989, this took the form of fatal attacks on migrants, exemplified by the murderous and tragic neo-Nazi arson attacks on families of Turkish origin in the cities Solingen and Mölln. In perhaps the latest incarnation of nationalist *ressentiment*, Theo Sarrazin binds a stalwart nationalism with racism when he argues for the intellectual inferiority of immigrants of Turkish and Arabic background in his 2010 book, with the controversial title *Germany Abolishes Itself*.[88] Although the cast of characters has shifted from Germans versus Jews to Germans versus immigrants of Turkish or Arabic background, the driving logic of negative feeling and exclusion, plus the artificial reversal of the sociopolitical hierarchy, such that Germans once again become self-defensive victims of foreign forces outside of themselves, remains the same.

The model of *ressentiment* that I have developed is not offered in lieu of the Mitscherlichian paradigm of failed mourning. I do not want merely to replace one affective structure with another without attending to either historical and cultural contexts or the propensity to use emotions to facilitate moral judgment or even moralizing—precisely what my book set out to critique. Instead, this study of *ressentiment* suggests the complex coexistence of multiple emotive regimes and overlapping affective communities with equally elaborate political potentialities, agendas, and pitfalls. Reading for emotion opens up alternative ways of seeing cultural histories and shifts our relations to the historical narratives and hegemonic hermeneutic models that organize the world.

Likewise, emotional intersubjectivity—the affective response to real or perceived emotional expectations and reactions—suggests that emotional regimes are never imposed unilaterally but instead take place between multiple subjects in relation to one another. The Mitscherlichs' provocative castigation of West German society explicitly passes moral judgment on the collective's failure to incorporate the (vaguely defined) norms of the ideal democratic emotional regime. However, as we have seen in the case of Jaspers, the disjuncture between public and private emotions and broader affective structures sometimes requires reading at an oblique angle to hegemonic political emotions. On the other hand, the community of nationalist *ressentiment* performed and enabled by von Salomon's book offers an example of how what we understand as the political and the public spheres are multiple, malleable, yet resilient social constructs constantly under revision and renegotiation. Neither located entirely in a political regime nor found exclusively in affective communities, the politics of emotion exists in the tension between what a society is, what it could be, and what it might possibly become. Reading for emotion holds out the promise of deciphering the ambiguous, even ambivalent emotional politics of texts and their contexts, so as to better understand the stakes—and consequences—of affective structures constitutive of contemporary emotional states.

Notes

INTRODUCTION

The opening epigraph is from Karl Jaspers, *The Question of German Guilt*, trans. E. B. Ashton (New York: Capricorn Books, 1961), 27. The German original reads, "Fast die gesamte Welt erhebt Anklage gegen Deutschland und gegen die Deutschen. Unsere Schuld wird erörtert mit Empörung, mit Grauen, mit Haß, mit Verachtung. Man will Strafe und Vergeltung. Nicht nur die Sieger, auch einige unter den deutschen Emigranten, sogar Angehörige neutraler Staaten beteiligen sich daran. In Deutschland gibt es Menschen, welche Schuld, sich selber einschließend, bekennen, gibt es viele, die sich für schuldfrei halten, aber andere für schuldig erklären." Karl Jaspers, *Die Schuldfrage* (Heidelberg: Lambert Schneider, 1946), 29.

1. For a thorough and engaging analysis of the role of shame in the German reaction to the Allied documentary films about the liberated concentration camps, see Ulrike Weckel, *Beschämende Bilder: Deutsche Reaktionen auf alliierte Dokumentarfilme über befreite Konzentrationslager* (Stuttgart: Franz Steiner, 2012). Cornelia Brink wrote one of the first books to extensively analyze these images, *Ikonen der Vernichtung: Öffentlicher Gebrauch von Fotographien aus nationalsozialistischen Konzentrationslagern nach 1945* (Berlin: Akademie, 1998).

2. Sociologist Morris Janowitz writes that it was the intention of the Allied powers to show the pictures of the atrocities widely and to as many German citizens as possible: "Disrupted communications did not prevent widespread dissemination of information about atrocities. Within four weeks after V-E Day, almost every German had had direct and repeated contact with our campaign to present the facts." Morris Janowitz, "German Reactions to Nazi Atrocities," *American Journal of Sociology* 52.2 (September 1946): 141–46. Janovitz's article was based on interviews conducted in Germany after these campaigns; some interviewees expressed their doubts about the efficacy of the campaigns, due to their concentration only on the negative (read "punitive") aspects without making clear enough the critical connection between National Socialism and the atrocities.

3. See particularly Brink's chapter on these images in precisely this context, "Bilder vom Feind—Das Scheitern der optischen Entnazifizierung 1945," in *Ikonen der Vernichtung*, 23–99.

4. Quotes in this paragraph are from Jaspers, *Die Schuldfrage*, 44; Jaspers, *German Guilt*, 47.

5. Weckel analyzes the response of German spectators who watched the so-called atrocity films based on a variety of (mostly American) Allied surveys, recordings, and memoirs. These sources indicate that the world was indeed watching Germany and the Germans to see how they reacted to these crimes of humanity. Weckel, *Beschämende Bilder*, 200–246, 278–328, 390–417, 418–97.

6. In her analysis of the relationship between shame and guilt in the postwar German context, Aleida Assmann underscores how shame represents the emotion experienced in a process of the subject recoiling upon itself as it experiences itself as the object of another person's gaze. Assmann writes, "Scham ist die Umkehrung des imperialen und perspektivischen Blicks; es geht stets darum, daß man sich selbst als Wahrnehmungsobjekt eines anderen Blicks erfährt." ("Shame is the reversal of the imperial and perspectival gaze; it is always a matter of experiencing oneself as the object of perception of another's gaze.") Translations throughout the book are mine unless otherwise specified. Aleida Assmann and Ute Frevert, *Geschichtsvergessenheit/Geschichtsversessenheit: Vom Umgang mit deutschen Vergangenheiten nach 1945* (Stuttgart: Deutsche Verlags-Anstalt, 1999), 87. Taking issue with the paucity of historical evidence on which Assmann's claims are based, Weckel uses the occasion to problematize the methodology and premises of "memory studies," particularly the concept of "collective memory." Weckel, *Beschämende Bilder*, 16, 35–38.

7. This evocative turn of phrase is from Ann Cvetkovich, a scholar of feminist and queer cultural studies, who describes "an archive of feelings" as "an exploration of cultural texts as repositories of feelings and emotions, which are encoded not only in the context of the texts themselves but in the practices that surround their production and reception." Ann Cvetkovich, *An Archive of Feelings: Trauma, Sexuality, and Lesbian Public Cultures* (Durham: Duke University Press, 2003), 7.

8. My work draws on important insights from many of the following recent sources, which offer a slight cross section of the literature on *Vergangenheitsbewältigung* in the fields of history, literary studies, sociology, media studies, and cultural studies: Konrad Jarausch, *After Hitler: Recivilizing Germans, 1945–1995* (Oxford: Oxford University Press, 2006); Jeffrey K. Olick, *The Politics of Regret: On Collective Memory and Historical Responsibility* (New York: Routledge, 2007); Harald Welzer, *Täter: Wie aus ganz normalen Menschen Massenmörder werden* (Frankfurt am Main: Fischer, 2005); Harald Welzer, *Das kommunikative Gedächtnis: Eine Theorie der Erinnerung* (Munich: C. H. Beck, 2002); Harald Welzer, Sabine Moller, and Karoline Tschuggnall, eds., *"Opa war kein Nazi": Nationalsozialismus und Holocaust im Familiengedächtnis* (Frankfurt am Main: Fischer, 2002); Moische Postone and Eric Santner, eds., *Catastrophe and Meaning: The Holocaust and the Twentieth Century* (Chicago: University of Chicago Press, 2003); Avishai Margalit, *The Ethics of Memory* (Cambridge, MA: Harvard University Press, 2002); Gesine Schwan, *Politik und Schuld: Die zerstörerische Macht des Schweigens* (Frankfurt am Main: Fischer, 1997); Norbert Frei, *1945 und wir: Das Dritte Reich im Bewußtsein der Deutschen* (Munich: Deutscher Taschenbuch, 2009); Nancy Wood, *Vectors of Memory: Legacies of Trauma in Postwar Europe* (Oxford: Berg, 1999); Anne Fuchs, *After the Dresden Bombing: Pathways of Memory, 1945 to the Present* (New York: Palgrave Macmillan, 2012); Friederike Eigler and Jens Kugele, eds., *Heimat: At the Intersection of Memory and Space* (Berlin: De Gruyter, 2012); Aleida Assmann and Linda Shortt, eds., *Memory and Political Change*

(New York: Palgrave Macmillan, 2012); Francis Guerin, *Through Amateur Eyes: Film and Photography in Nazi Germany* (Minneapolis: University of Minnesota Press, 2012); Caroline Sharples, *West Germany and the Nazi Legacy* (New York: Routledge, 2012); Jörg Arnold, *Allied Air War and Urban Memory: The Legacy of Strategic Bombing in Germany* (Cambridge: Cambridge University Press, 2011); Gavriel David Rosenfeld, *Building after Auschwitz: Jewish Architecture and Memory of the Holocaust* (New Haven: Yale University Press, 2011); Marianne Hirsch, *The Generation of Postmemory: Writing and Visual Culture after the Holocaust* (New York: Columbia University Press, 2012); Bill Niven and Chloe Paver, eds., *Memorialization in Germany since 1945* (New York: Palgrave Macmillan, 2010); Anke Pinkert, *Film and Memory in East Germany* (Bloomington: Indiana University Press, 2008); David Bathrick, Brad Prager, and Mike Richardson, eds., *Visualizing the Holocaust: Documents, Aesthetics, Memory* (Rochester: Camden House, 2008); Bill Niven, ed., *Germans as Victims: Remembering the Past in Contemporary Germany* (New York: Palgrave Macmillan, 2006); Susan Rubin Suleiman, *Crises of Memory and the Second World War* (Cambridge, MA: Harvard University Press, 2006); Anne Fuchs, Mary Cosgrove, and Georg Grote, eds., *German Memory Contests: The Quest for Identity in Literature, Film, and Discourse since 1990* (Rochester: Camden House, 2006); Wulf Kansteiner, *In Pursuit of German Memory: History, Television, and Politics after Auschwitz* (Athens: Ohio University Press, 2006); Dagmar Herzog, *Sex after Fascism: Memory and Morality in Twentieth-Century Germany* (Princeton: Princeton University Press, 2005); Jeffrey K. Olick, *In the House of the Hangman: The Agonies of German Defeat, 1943–1949* (Chicago: University of Chicago Press, 2005); Klaus Naumann, ed., *Nachkrieg in Deutschland* (Hamburg: Hamburger Edition, 2001); Dan Diner, *Beyond the Conceivable: Studies in Germany, Nazism, and the Holocaust* (Berkeley: University of California Press, 2000); Michael Rothberg, *Traumatic Realism: The Demands of Holocaust Representation* (Minneapolis: University of Minnesota Press, 2000); Frank Schirrmacher, ed., *Die Walser-Bubis-Debatte: Eine Dokumentation* (Frankfurt am Main: Suhrkamp, 1999); Helmut Dubiel, *Niemand ist frei von der Geschichte: Die nationalsozialistische Herrschaft in den Debatten des Deutschen Bundestages* (Munich: Carl Hanser, 1999); Assmann and Frevert, *Geschichtsvergessenheit/Geschichtsversessenheit*; Susan Linville, *Feminism, Film, Fascism: Women's Auto/biographical Film in Postwar Germany* (Austin: University of Texas Press, 1998); Dominick LaCapra, *History and Memory after Auschwitz* (Ithaca: Cornell University Press, 1998); Anson Rabinbach, *In the Shadow of Catastrophe: German Intellectuals between Apocalypse and Enlightenment* (Berkeley: University of California Press, 1997); Marianne Hirsch, *Family Frames: Photography, Narrative, and Postmemory* (Cambridge, MA: Harvard University Press, 1997); Dagmar Barnouw, *Germany 1945: Views of War and Violence* (Bloomington: Indiana University Press, 1996); Heide Fehrenbach, *Cinema in Democratizing Germany: Reconstructing National Identity after Hitler* (Chapel Hill: University of North Carolina Press, 1995); Andreas Huyssen, *Twilight Memories: Marking Time in a Culture of Amnesia* (New York: Routledge, 1995); Ian Buruma, *The Wages of Guilt: Memories of War in Germany and Japan* (New York: Farrar, Straus and Giroux, 1994); Manfred Kittel, *Die Legende von der "Zweiten Schuld": Vergangenheitsbewältigung in der Ära Adenauer* (Berlin: Ullstein, 1993); Saul Friedlander, *Memory, History, and the Extermination of the Jews of Europe* (Bloomington: Indiana University Press: 1993); Saul Friedlander, ed., *Prob-*

ing the Limits of Representation: Nazism and the "Final Solution" (Cambridge, MA: Harvard University Press, 1992); Eric L. Santner, *Stranded Objects: Mourning, Memory, and Film in Postwar Germany* (Ithaca: Cornell University Press, 1990); Hans Jürgen Syberberg, *Vom Unglück und Glück der Kunst in Deutschland nach dem letzten Kriege* (Munich: Matthes and Seitz, 1990); Peter Baldwin, ed., *Reworking the Past: Hitler, the Holocaust, and the Historians' Debate* (Boston: Beacon, 1990); Martin Broszat, ed., *Zäsuren nach 1945: Essays zur Periodisierung der deutschen Nachkriegsgeschichte* (Munich: Oldenbourg, 1990); Anton Kaes, *From Hitler to Heimat: The Return of History as Film* (Cambridge, MA: Harvard University Press, 1989); Charles S. Maier, *The Unmasterable Past: History, Holocaust, and German National Identity* (Cambridge, MA: Harvard University Press, 1988); Anson Rabinbach, "The Jewish Question in the German Question," *New German Critique* 4 (1988): 159–92; Ralph Giordano, *Die zweite Schuld oder von der Last ein Deutscher zu sein* (Munich: Knaur, 1987); Rudolf Augstein et al., *"Historikerstreit": Die Dokumentation der Kontroverse um die Einzigartigkeit der nationalsozialistischen Judenvernichtung* (Munich: Piper, 1987); Barbro Eberan, *Luther? Friedrich "der Grosse?" Wagner? Nietzsche? Wer war an Hitler Schuld? Die Debatte um die Schuldfrage, 1945–49* (Munich: Minerva, 1983); Lutz Niethammer, *Die Mitläuferfabrik: Die Entnazifizierung am Beispiel Bayerns* (Berlin: Dietz, 1982); Hans Jürgen Syberberg, *Die freudlose Gesellschaft: Notizen aus den letzten Jahren* (Frankfurt am Main: Ullstein, 1981); Caspar von Schrenck-Notzing, *Charakterwäsche: Die Politik der Amerikanischer Umerziehung in Deutschland* (Stuttgart: Seewald, 1965); Armin Mohler, *Vergangenheitsbewältigung: Von der Läuterung zur Manipulation* (Stuttgart: Seewald, 1968). For a historical overview of the different debates and discursive turns, one can now consult an encyclopedia for "Vergangenheitsbewältigung": Torben Fischer and Matthias N. Lorenz, eds., *Lexikon der "Vergangenheitsbewältigung" in Deutschland: Debatten- und Diskursgeschichte des Nationalsozialismus nach 1945* (Bielefeld: transcript, 2007).

9. Frei, *1945 und wir*, 41–55.

10. Leo Löwenthal, "Terror's Atomization of Man," *Commentary* 1.3 (1946): 1–8. I thank Johannes von Moltke for pointing me to this reference.

11. Hannah Arendt, "The Aftermath of Nazi Rule: Report from Germany," *Commentary* 10.4 (1950), reprinted in *Essays in Understanding, 1930–1954*, ed. Jerome Kohn (New York: Harcourt Brace, 1994), 248–69, here 249.

12. In other words, I find Fay's argument monocausal in this respect. However, her differentiated argument in which she compares reeducation in some aspects to processes of assimilation and demonstrates how the films and their proponents are oblivious to their obvious racism and anti-Semitism is original and convincing. Jennifer Fay, *Theaters of Occupation: Hollywood and the Reeducation of Postwar Germany* (Minneapolis: University of Minnesota Press, 2008): see particularly the introduction, "Theaters of Occupation" (ix–xxx, xii, and xv–xvii); chapter 2, "Hollywood's Democratic Unconscious" (39–82).

13. Stig Dagerman, *German Autumn*, trans. Robin Fulton Macpherson (Minneapolis: University of Minnesota Press, 2001), 9–10, 11, 14. Dagerman's book was originally published in Swedish in 1947.

14. Ibid., 45.

15. Ibid., 111.

16. Graham Greene's customarily brief response to Dagerman's book admires the powerful emotional tow of his prose: "Stig Dagerman wrote with beautiful objectivity. Instead of emotive phrases, he uses a choice of facts, like bricks, to construct an emotion." Ibid., back cover. Considering the tight economy of Greene's own sharply objective prose, this is high praise indeed. Further, it also demonstrates that emotion can be written into and contained in many different representational forms and tonalities, even when its presence is perhaps not immediately obvious.

17. William Ernest Hocking, *Experiment in Education: What We Can Learn from Teaching Germany* (Chicago: Henry Regnery, 1954), 39.

18. Ibid., 52.

19. Ibid., 62.

20. Morris Janowitz, "German Reactions to Nazi Atrocities," *American Journal of Sociology* 52.2 (September 1946): 141–46.

21. Ibid., 145.

22. There was also a widespread practice of blaming the Jews for Germany's "misfortunes" during the final stages of the war and extending into the postwar period. Often this process of blaming included an erasure of boundaries between identities, such that the Jews were, perversely enough, seen as standing behind all of the Allied powers simultaneously. For example, an internal memo to the NSDAP "Kreisleitung" from the "Gauleitung" of a region in Weißenberg o.D., dated "21.6–20.8.1943" and bearing the title "*Judenfrage, Bolschewismus*," reads, "Eines stimmt: Es ist gleich, ob England, USA oder UdSSR die Macht in Europa antritt, den hinter diesen 3 Mächtegruppen steht der Jude. [. . .] Das Volk muß erkennen, daß e skein zweites 1918 mehr geben wird und geben darf. Der Jude würde dann für immer die Herrschaft über die Welt antreten." Otto Dov Kulka, Eberhard Jäckel, et al., eds., *Die Juden in den geheimen NS-Stimmungsberichten 1933–1945* (Düsseldorf: Droste, 2004), 530. See also Dov Kulka, "Die Kriegsjahre (1939–1945)," in ibid., 406–547, especially 535, 537, 543, 545.

23. Janowitz, "German Reactions to Nazi Atrocities," 145.

24. Ibid., 146.

25. Weckel argues that the only response to the atrocity films that could be read in a completely unambiguous manner would be that of the immunity to shaming ("Immunität gegen Beschämung"). However, even demonstrative shamelessness could be seen as a defense mechanism against other emotional responses, especially in these precarious, emotionally intersubjective encounters. Weckel also notes perspicaciously that signs of shame (or, I would argue, remorse) do not automatically lead to a self-reflective critic. Weckel, *Beschämende Bilder*, 532–34.

26. The modest objective of this book is to study the politics of emotion in postwar West German culture; that and the tyranny of brevity dictate bracketing, for now, the more philosophical debates in emotion studies around such putative binaries as cognitivism versus anticognitivism, materialism versus abstraction, or neurosciences versus cultural criticism. A recent interview with Ruth Leys offers an interesting account of the cognitivist versus anticognitivist debate, although Leys tends to shore up, rather than deconstruct, binary thinking in discussions of affect. Ruth Leys and Marlene Goldman, "Navigating the Genealogies of Trauma, Guilt, and Affect: An Interview," *University of Toronto Quarterly* 79.2 (2010): 656–79. Historian Robert A. Kaster attempts to bring together multiple approaches to emotion when he writes of emotional expression as

follows: "Think of all such talk as just the end product of a process that engages body and mind together: any emotion term is just the lexicalized residue of what happens when the data of life are processed in a particular way—through a sequence of perception (sensing, imaging), evaluation (believing, judging, desiring), and response (bodily, affective, pragmatic, expressive)—to produce a particular kind of emotionalized consciousness, a particular set of thoughts and feelings." Robert A. Kaster, *Emotion, Restraint, and Community in Ancient Rome* (Oxford: Oxford University Press, 2005), 8.

27. Much recent work on the study of emotion emerges from the fields of cognitive psychology and neuroscience rather than psychoanalysis. A major contribution of this work is its emphasis on the cognitive aspect of emotion, which challenges and recalibrates the Cartesian division between "reason" and "emotion." For an influential account of the role of emotion in thought (especially judgment), see Martha C. Nussbaum, *Upheavals of Thought: The Intelligence of Emotions* (Cambridge: Cambridge University Press, 2001).

28. William Reddy's approach to the "history of emotions" combines cultural anthropological and cognitive psychological approaches, while harshly (and routinely) critiquing poststructuralism for having done away with subjectivity and discourses of liberation, for framing social inquiry as spurious, and for ultimately practicing a form of metaphysics. Needless to say, poststructuralism functions as a type of straw man against which Reddy establishes his theory of emotions. It seems to me that Reddy's theoretical approach is robust enough to do without this hackneyed invective against poststructuralism. He aims at an anti-Cartesian understanding of subjectivity, instead envisaging emotional subjectivity as a rich site at which "thought material" is organized by way of "attention." He further draws on cognitive approaches to emotion in the emancipatory attempt to construct "a notion of emotional liberty as a political ideal that can be used to make judgments about emotional regimes both Western and non-Western." William M. Reddy, *The Navigation of Feeling: A Framework for the History of Emotions* (Cambridge: Cambridge University Press, 2001), 111. Reddy's work resonates strongly with my own inasmuch as emotions are considered highly significant in political terms. But his desire to recuperate liberation as a politico-historical possibility leads him to polarized normative judgments about emotion that associate nonhegemonic emotions with liberty and "emotional regimes" with oppression. For a recent article that draws on neuroscience and practice theory to critique what Reddy sees as Foucault's Saussurian-inflected understanding of language, see William M. Reddy, "Saying Something New: Practice Theory and Cognitive Neuroscience," *Arcadia: International Journal for Literary Studies* 44.1 (August 2009): 8–23.

29. Barbara Rosenwein declares that she has written a book on "the history of emotions" that will act as a corrective to past histories on the topic, in order to force historians to take emotions seriously. Rosenwein is interested in marrying a Foucauldian-inflected notion of "discourse" with the Bourdieuian concept of "habitus" in her analysis of "emotional communities" (specifically those of the early Middle Ages). Rosenwein eschews psychoanalysis as an instance of the hydraulic model of feelings, opting instead for a variant of cognitive theory that allows her recourse to a social constructivist understanding of emotions as normative and socially determined. Barbara H. Rosenwein, *Emotional Communities in the Early Middle Ages* (Ithaca: Cornell University Press, 2006), 1–31.

30. See, for instance, Georg Simmel, "Soziologie der Geselligkeit" (1910), reprinted in *Georg Simmel, Gesamtausgabe*, vol. 12, ed. Otthein Rammstedt (Frankfurt am Main: Suhrkamp, 2001), 177–93.

31. James Strachey, "Notes on Some Technical Terms Whose Translation Calls for Comment," in *The Complete Psychological Works of Sigmund Freud*, vol. 1, *Pre-psycho-analytic Publications and Unpublished Drafts (1886–99)*, ed. James Strachey (London: Hogarth and Institute of Psychoanalysis, 1981), xxiii–xxvi.

32. Ibid., xxiii.

33. Ibid.

34. André Green, "Postscript 2: The Representation of Affects (and Their Consequences for Our Understanding of What We Call Psychical)," in *The Fabric of Affect in the Psychoanalytic Discourse*, trans. Alan Sheridan (New York: Routledge, 1999), 275–94, here 285. Green's book was originally published in French as *Le Discours Vivant* (Paris: Presses universitaires de France, 1973).

35. Ibid., 286.

36. Reddy, *Navigation of Feeling*, 128.

37. Similarly, Reddy redefines the Freudian unconscious, in his cognitivist terms, as signals "that are inadvertent, deriving from effects of activated thought that 'short circuit' attention." Ibid., 106. Here the word *attention* describes cognitive or conscious signals.

38. My line of thought here is indebted to Judith Butler's Foucauldian and Freudian model of subjectivity, which she details as a site of both subjection and subjectivization (or becoming socially legible as subject). See Judith Butler, *The Psychic Life of Power: Theories on Subjection* (Stanford: Stanford University Press, 1997). For a discussion of the logic and political ramifications of a contemporary politics of victimization and reparation critiquing the structure of "left melancholia," see Wendy Brown's *States of Injury: Power and Freedom in Late Modernity* (Princeton: Princeton University Press, 1995) and *Politics Out of History* (Princeton: Princeton University Press, 2001).

39. For an interesting collection of essays on the concept of *Stunde Null* (zero hour) in Germany, see Geoffrey J. Giles, ed., *Stunde Null: The Ending and the Beginning Fifty Years Ago* (Washington, DC: German Historical Institute, 1997). For a critical exploration of the claim to a literary and cultural *Stunde Null*, see Stephen Brockmann, *German Literary Culture at the Zero Hour* (Rochester: Camden House, 2004).

40. Tomkin's affect theory was introduced into literary theoretical circles primarily through Eve Kosofsky Sedgwick's work on the affect of "shame." For Tomkins, affect is biologically determinate and operates on the model of a fixed and limited spectrum of responses felt by the sentient being. In her elegant writings on Tomkin's affect theory, Sedgwick performs her customarily incisive act of the "anti-axiomatic"; that is, Sedgwick uses the biological focus in Tomkin's work to unsettle what she sees as problematic "truisms" of contemporary theory, such as the maligning of the biological as the enemy of culture. See Sedgwick's "Shame in the Cybernetic Fold: Reading Silvan Tompkins (Written with Adam Frank)," in *Touching Feeling: Affect, Pedagogy, Performativity* (Durham: Duke University Press, 2003), 93–121. My thought has benefited greatly from deconstructive approaches to affect in the work of feminist and queer theorists. However, this project does not intend to take up the ongoing constructivist nature-versus-culture debate that occupies feminist projects and emotion theoreticians alike.

Obviously, this is not the driving question of my inquiry into postwar West German emotional culture. For those interested in pursuing this line of argument, a good place to begin is with the contributions from sociology and anthropology, which have long demonstrated that human conduct is as much a product of the social environment as it is a function of biology. For a feminist anthropological approach to emotion, see Catherine Lutz, *Unnatural Emotions: Everyday Sentiments on a Micronesian Atoll and Their Challenge to Western Theory* (Chicago: University of Chicago Press, 1988); Lutz and Lila Abu-Lughod, eds., *Language and the Politics of Emotion* (Cambridge: Cambridge University Press, 1990); Rom Harré, *The Social Construction of Emotions* (Oxford: Blackwell, 1986); Arlie Russell Hochschild, *The Managed Heart: Commercialization of Human Feeling* (Berkeley: University of California Press, 1983).

41. The "basic emotion" paradigm, stemming from the work of Charles Darwin and flowing through the theory of Silvan Tomkins to that of Paul Ekman, proposes that emotions are noncognitive, nonintentional, pre-ideological, and rooted in the intensities of the body. These theorists also believe that there is a basic palette of emotions (such as fear, anger, and joy) that are expressed by the body and can be identified and categorized. For a detailed account of the "basic emotion" model proposed by Leys, see Ruth Leys, "The Turn to Affect: A Critique," *Critical Inquiry* 37 (Spring 2011): 434–72. See also Ruth Leys, *From Guilt to Shame: Auschwitz and After* (Princeton: Princeton University Press, 2007), 133–50.

42. For Ruth Leys' critique of what she sees as the antirepresentationalism, Cartesianism, involantarism, and materialism in the work of Brian Massumi and William Connolly, see Leys, "Turn to Affect."

43. Brian Massumi, *Parables for the Virtual: Movement, Affect, Sensation* (Durham: Duke University Press, 2002), 35, 61.

44. Ibid., 217.

45. Gould's attraction to Bourdieu's theory is based partly on his inclusion of sensorial and bodily practices in the term *habitus*, which is central to her analysis of the emotional practices and politics of the activist organization ACT UP Chicago (of which she was a founding member) during the AIDS crisis in the 1980s and 1990s: Deborah Gould, *Moving Politics: Emotion and Act Up's Fight against AIDS* (Chicago: University of Chicago Press, 2009), 32, 10. Of course, the period I examine is a continent apart and temporally distant from today's experiential horizon, not to mention politically incommensurable. In her book, Gould makes a distinction between emotion and affect in terms very similar to my own, with the caveat that her distinction is taken directly from Massumi and is thus, as in Massumi's case, also invested in what she terms "affective ontologies." Ibid., 19–23.

46. For debates around the trope of "the German patient" and Germany's rehabilitation, see Jennifer M. Kapczynski, *The German Patient: Crisis and Recovery in Postwar Culture* (Ann Arbor: University of Michigan Press, 2008); for a study of the work performed by the figure of "youth" in postwar West Germany, see Jaimey Fisher, *Disciplining Germany: Youth, Reeducation and Reconstruction after the Second World War* (Detroit: Wayne State University Press, 2007); for an overview on some of the potential American "fantasies of normalcy" for postwar Germany, see Anton Kaes, "What to Do with Germany? American Debates about the Future of Germany," *German Politics and Society* 13.3 (Fall 1995): 130–41. See also the episodic and rather anecdotal book by

Saul K. Padover describing his time on the field in Germany from 1944 through 1945: *Experiment in Germany: The Story of an American Intelligence Officer* (New York: Duell, Sloan and Pearce, 1946).

47. Study of the history of emotion is experiencing a boom in Germany. For an excellent overview of many of the debates about that history in both Germany and the United States, see Bettina Hitzer, "Emotionsgeschichte—ein Anfang mit Folgen," November 13, 2011, http://hsozkult.geschichte.hu-berlin.de/forum/2011-11-001.pdf. Jan Plamper, a former scholar of the Max Planck "History of Emotions" research group led by historian Ute Frevert, has written an excellent historical and theoretical overview of emotion studies: Jan Plamper, *Geschichte und Gefühl: Grundlagen der Emotionsgeschichte* (Munich: Siedler, 2012). For an overview of theoretical debates that have been central to "the historical studies of emotion," see the "virtual roundtable" led by Frank Biess, with participants Alono Confino, Ute Frevert, Uffa Jensen, Lyndal Roper, and Daniela Saxer, in "Forum: History of Emotions," *German History* 28.1 (2010): 67–80. See also the conversation between Nicole Eustace, Eugenia Lean, Julie Livingston, Jan Plamper, William M. Reddy, and Barbara H. Rosenwein in "American Historical Review Conversation: The Historical Study of Emotions," *American Historical Review* (2012): 1487–1531.

48. Reddy, *Navigation of Feeling*, 129.

49. Theodor W. Adorno et al., *The Authoritarian Personality* (New York: Harper, 1950).

50. Reddy, *Navigation of Feeling*, 129.

51. Rosenwein, *Emotional Communities*, 1–31, especially 24–25. Rosenwein defines "emotional communities" as "groups in which people adhere to the same norms of emotional expression and value—or devalue—the same or related emotions." Ibid., 2.

52. Robert Kastner discusses the manifestation of emotions in terms of "narrative processes or scripts," where an "emotional script" is defined as "the little scenarios that we play out—as sequences of cause and effect, of perception, evaluation, and response—when we experience any emotion." Kastner, *Emotion*, 29. In a recent interview, Barbara Rosenwein also referred to the performance of emotions with the term *scripts*. Rosenwein et al., "American Historical Review Conversation," 1516.

53. The term *emotives*, which differs from the previous terms in that it recognizes both the creative potential of emotion and a cognitive approach to emotion, is defined by William Reddy as follows: "A type of speech act different from both performative and constative utterances, which both describes (like constative utterances) and changes (like performatives) the world, because emotional expression has an exploratory and a self-altering effect on the activated thought material of emotion." Reddy, *Navigating Feeling*, 128.

54. Belonging properly to the genre of books analyzing, rather than participating in, discourses of "mastering the past," Karyn Ball's incisive book examining the suppositions behind "proper" approaches to the Holocaust in intellectual history demonstrates why it is important to examine the (moral) assumptions grounding a field of study and the ends to which they may be deployed. Karyn Ball, *Disciplining the Holocaust* (Albany: State University of New York Press, 2009). Another scholar, the German historian Anthony D. Kauders, has likewise noted that "references to repression after 1945 conflate affective disorders ("repression") with ethical judgment (the need for shame),

thereby prescribing correct behavior rather than explaining West German society after 1945." Anthony D. Kauders, "History as Censure: 'Repression' and 'Philo-Semitism' in Postwar Germany," *History and Memory* 15.1 (2003): 97–122, here 97.

55. The locus classicus for this interpretation, which includes a critique of capitalism as democracy's helping hand to amnesia, is Theodor W. Adorno's essay "Was bedeutet: Aufarbeitung der Vergangenheit?" from 1959, to which I shall return in due course.

56. This exceedingly popular interpretation, which will be the object of analysis in chapter 3, took on definitive form (and a mythical life of its own) in 1967, with the Mitscherlichs' publication of their eponymous book, *Die Unfähigkeit zu trauern: Grundlagen kollektiven Verhaltens* (Munich: Piper, 1967). It is important to note here, as I do in chapter 1, that other critical observers of the period made similar prognoses in the immediate postwar period, such as Hannah Arendt in her essay (written for the American Jewish Committee) "The Aftermath of Nazi Rule: Report from Germany," *Commentary* 10.4 (1950): 342–53.

57. Robert G. Moeller, *War Stories: The Search for a Usable Past in the Federal Republic of Germany* (Berkeley: University of California Press, 2001), 14. See also "Introduction: Writing the History of West Germany," in *West Germany under Construction: Politics, Society, and Culture in the Adenauer Era*, ed. Robert G. Moeller (Ann Arbor: University of Michigan Press), 1–30. For a detailed history of the discourses both by and about returning POWs, see Frank Biess, *Homecomings: Returning POWs and the Legacy of Defeat in Postwar Germany* (Princeton: Princeton University Press, 2006). See also the invaluable collection of essays in Hanna Schissler, ed., *The Miracle Years: A Cultural History of West Germany, 1949–1968* (Princeton: Princeton University Press, 2001). For an analysis of postwar history in terms of continuity rather than rupture, see Wolfgang Schivelbusch, *In a Cold Crater: Cultural and Intellectual Life in Berlin, 1945–1948*, trans. Kelly Barry (Berkeley: University of California Press, 1998), 1–38. Jeffrey Herf offers an ambitious overview of German memory culture and history from the 1930s through the 1990s, arguing that the repressive frame of reference "capture[s] only part of the postwar politics of memory" in the postwar period of 1945–60. Jeffrey Herf, *Divided Memory: The Nazi Past in the Two Germanys* (Cambridge, MA: Harvard University Press, 1997), 334.

58. Further, this does not mean that disturbing sociopolitical tendencies were not present—even overwhelmingly so at times—in immediate postwar and Adenauer Germany. On the contrary, in the "phase of the politics of the past" (Norbert Frei) in the 1950s, German newspapers were rife with stories indicating that something was rotten in the new state, such as the Hans Globke affair during the 1950s, which illustrated the return of former National Socialists to positions of power during the Adenauer administration. Even after his emigration to Basel, Switzerland, in 1948, Karl Jaspers continued to collect newspaper articles from Germany covering irruptions of the Nazi past in the present. For instance, he kept an article titled "Dokumentation über die Mitschuld" that he had cut out from the *Israelitisches Wochenblatt* (undated, but most likely published around 1961). This cutting is a review of a new publication of documents pertaining to Hans Globke: Reinhard M. Strecker, *Dr. Hans Globke, Aktenauszüge, Dokumente* (Hamburg: Rütten und Löning, 1961). These documents can be found in box 42: Politik/Zeitgeschichte: Israel, in Karl Jaspers' literary estate at the Deutschen Literaturar-

chiv, Marbach. For more detail on continuities of administrative and bureaucratic personnel, public servants, and bureaucrats between the Nazi and the Adenauer eras, including a brief survey of Globke's activities, see Curt Garner, "Public Service Personnel in West Germany in the 1950s: Controversial Policy Decisions and Their Effect on Social Composition, Gender Structure, and the Role of Former Nazis," in Moeller, *West Germany under Construction*, 135–95. For an exhaustive analysis of this "phase of a politics of the past" in juridico-political terms, see Norbert Frei, *Vergangenheitspolitik: Die Anfänge der Bundesrepublik und die NS-Vergangenheit* (Munich: C. H. Beck, 1997), trans. Joel Golb as *Adenauer's Germany and the Nazi Past: The Politics of Amnesty and Integration* (New York: Columbia University Press, 2002).

59. For a summary of the coverage of the topics of persecution and guilt in the Berlin newspapers in postwar Germany, see Ursula Heukenkamp, "Schuld und Verfolgung in den Berliner Zeitschriften der Nachkriegszeit," in *Der 8. Mai 1945 als historische Zäsur: Strukturen, Erfahrungen, Deutungen*, ed. Arnd Bauerkämper, Christoph Kleßmann, and Hans Misselwitz (Potsdam: Brandenburgische Landeszentrale für politische Bildung, 1995), 218–31.

60. Not all topics were raised with equal volume in either the immediate or even the recent postwar period. For example, the overwhelming silence in the immediate postwar and the Adenauer years in West Germany shrouding the topic of rape was not broken until recently (1990s). The gendered silence of shame over German women's rape by occupation soldiers received long-overdue scholarly attention in the pathbreaking work of Norman M. Naimark and Atina Grossmann: Norman M. Naimark, *The Russians in Germany: A History of the Soviet Zone of Occupation, 1945–1949* (Cambridge, MA: Belknap Press of Harvard University Press, 1995); Atina Grossmann, "A Question of Silence: The Rape of German Women by Occupation Soldiers," in Moeller, *West Germany under Construction*, 33–52. Work in the field of gender and sexuality in German cultural studies has refined our understanding of the powerful norms at work shaping female subjectivity in the postwar German period. For research on the drastic shifts in social structures at the end of the war, including the influx of returning POWs and refugees from the East and the emergence of "Fräuleins" and "Veronikas" (women who fraternized with the Allied occupation soldiers, sometimes for pleasure and often for material benefit in a time of scarcity, and who coexisted alongside the mythologized "rubble women"), see Maria Höhn, *GIs and Fräuleins: The German-American Encounter in 1950s West Germany* (Chapel Hill: University of North Carolina Press, 2002); Petra Goedde, *GIs and Germans: Culture, Gender, and Foreign Relations, 1945–1949* (New Haven: Yale University Press, 2003). For an examination of cultures established around American culture in postwar Germany in terms of gender and sexuality, see Uta G. Poiger, *Jazz, Rock, and Rebels: Cold War Politics and American Culture in a Divided Germany* (Berkeley: University of California Press, 2000). For a provocative Foucauldian analysis of the role of sexuality in postwar Germany, see Dagmar Herzog, *Sex after Fascism: Memory and Morality in Twentieth-Century Germany* (Princeton: Princeton University Press, 2005). For other books on postwar West Germany that are informed by an analytics of gender, see Elizabeth D. Heineman, *What Difference Does a Husband Make? Women and Marital Status in Nazi and Postwar Germany* (Berkeley: University of California Press, 1999); Erica Carter, *How German Is She? Postwar West German Reconstruction and the Consuming Woman* (Ann Arbor: University of Michi-

gan Press, 1997), an original study of women and the consumption of popular culture in postwar Germany. Heide Fehrenbach's seminal book *Cinema in Democratizing Germany* laid the substantive groundwork for ensuing sociocultural and aesthetic explorations of this period of occupation history through the apparatus, milieu, and medium of film. Johannes von Moltke picks up on Fehrenbach's observations about the marked excessiveness of the genre of postwar *Heimatfilme* and, performing a genealogy of the concept of *Heimat* alongside close readings of these films, reveals the uncanny charms of the critically neglected genre of *Heimatfilme* as a depository of postwar anxieties and fantasies. Johannes von Moltke, *No Place Like Home: Locations of Heimat in German Cinema* (Berkeley: University of California Press, 2005); for an analysis of the traditional status of *Heimatfilme* as a "bad object" of film studies, see 21–69. Focusing on the "bad object" of the screen Nazi in 1950s film, Sabine Hake explores the ongoing fascination with the fascist imaginary. Hake analyzes films from the postwar through the post–Berlin Wall periods in terms of cinematic affect, spectatorship, and the "floating signifier" of democracy. Sabine Hake, *Screen Nazis: Cinema, History, and Democracy* (Madison: University of Wisconsin Press, 2012).

61. This paradigm has enjoyed much scholarly attention from the 1990s onward. One influential version was Judith Butler's deployment of the model to theorize a constitutive "heterosexual melancholia," with drag as a performative enactment of this melancholia. See Judith Butler, *Bodies That Matter: On the Discursive Limits of "Sex"* (New York: Routledge, 1993). In gender studies and queer theory, see also Douglas Crimp, *Melancholia and Moralism: Essays on AIDS and Queer Politics* (Cambridge, MA: MIT Press, 2002); David Eng and David Kazanjian, eds., *Loss: The Politics of Mourning*, with an afterword by Judith Butler (Berkeley: University of California Press, 2003). In postcolonial studies, see Ranjana Khanna, *Dark Continents: Psychoanalysis and Colonialism* (Durham: Duke University Press, 2003); Paul Gilroy, *Postcolonial Melancholia* (New York: Columbia University Press, 2005); Anne Anlin Cheng, *The Melancholy of Race* (Oxford: Oxford University Press, 2001). In the field of literary studies, see Sanja Bahun, *Modernism and Melancholia: Writing as Countermourning* (New York: Oxford, 2014); Neil Brooks and Josh Toth, eds., *The Mourning After: Attending the Wake of Postmodernism* (New York: Rodopi, 2007); Jonathan Flatley, *Affective Mapping: Melancholia and the Politics of Modernism* (Cambridge, MA: Harvard University Press, 2008); Thomas Pfau, *Romantic Moods: Paranoia, Trauma, and Melancholy, 1790–1840* (Baltimore: Johns Hopkins University Press, 2005); Vivasvan Soni, *Mourning Happiness: Narrative and the Politics of Modernity* (Ithaca: Cornell University Press, 2010). In the field of literary and film studies, see Alessia Ricciardi, *The Ends of Mourning: Psychoanalysis, Literature, Film* (Stanford: Stanford University Press, 2003). In the field of philosophy, see Gillian Rose, *Mourning Becomes the Law: Philosophy and Representation* (Cambridge: Cambridge University Press, 1996); Max Pensky, *Melancholy Dialectics: Walter Benjamin and the Play of Mourning* (Amherst: University of Massachusetts Press, 1993).

62. In her article on W. G. Sebald's reading of Günter Grass and Wolfgang Hildesheimer, Mary Cosgrove argues that Sebald pits the two authors against one another in order to "test the authenticity of the 1960s discourse on 'Trauer.'" Cosgrove concludes that in relation to the Jewish genocide, Sebald ultimately understands *Trauer* (mourning) as a form of terminal melancholia. In this sense, Cosgrove has located Se-

bald and his work along the spectrum of what I am calling postwar "melancholic scholarship," which she frames as "melancholy competitions." Mary Cosgrove, "Melancholic Competitions: W. G. Sebald Reads Günter Grass and Wolfgang Hildesheimer," *German Life and Letters* 59.2 (2006): 217–32. Similarly, Anne Fuchs critiques what she calls "memory contests" or "retrospective imaginings that simultaneously articulate, question and investigate the normative self-image of previous generations." These intergenerational contests operate within a paradigm of memory still dominated by the "psychoanalytic narrative of the drama of repression, acting out, and repetition compulsion," along with the narrative that "restores the Enlightenment paradigm through the story of its critical engagement with the past." Anne Fuchs, "From 'Vergangenheitsbewältigung' to Generational Memory Contests in Günter Grass, Monika Maron, and Uwe Timm," *German Life and Letters* 59.2 (2006): 169–86.

63. For an overview of the different uses and abuses of trauma, see Dominick LaCapra's *Writing History, Writing Trauma* (Baltimore: Johns Hopkins University Press, 2001) and *History and Memory after Auschwitz* (Ithaca: Cornell University Press, 1998). For other key texts in the debates about memory and trauma, see Cathy Caruth, *Unclaimed Experience : Trauma, Narrative, and History* (Baltimore: Johns Hopkins University Press, 1996); Ruth Leys, *Trauma: A Genealogy* (Chicago: University of Chicago Press, 2000). For a recent study of psychological and other theories of trauma as they manifest themselves in postwar German literature about the bombing of Germany during World War II, see Susanne Vees-Gulani, *Trauma and Guilt: Literature of Wartime Bombing in Germany* (Berlin: De Gruyter, 2003). For a historical account of the connection between World War I, trauma, and the history of psychiatry, see Paul Lerner, *Hysterical Men: War, Psychiatry, and the Politics of Trauma in Germany, 1890–1930* (Ithaca: Cornell University Press, 2003).

64. Anke Pinkert, *Film and Memory in East Germany* (Bloomington: Indiana University Press, 2008), 6–8.

65. Ibid., 3.

66. Thomas H. Minshall, "Review: The Answers of Ernst von Salomon to the 131 Questions in the Allied Military Government 'Fragebogen' by Constantine Fitzgibbon," *International Affairs* 31.1 (1955): 106–7.

67. H. R. Trevor-Roper, "The Germans Reappraise the War," *Foreign Affairs* 31 (1952–53): 225–37.

68. Ibid., 225.

69. Ibid.

70. Trevor-Roper notes, "As it is, inaccessibility of sources prevents them from even trying, and the consequent ignorance among Germans, of their own true history, may well prove politically unfortunate in coming years." Ibid., 226.

71. Ibid.

72. Ibid., 226–27.

73. Ibid.

74. Ibid., 230–35.

75. Ibid., 237.

76. Always a canny critic of contemporary practices of normativity, Lauren Berlant emphasizes the role of affect as the connecting tissue between norms and the establishment and perpetuation of community through what she terms (in her intricate study of

femininity, sentimentality, and the American public sphere) "the affective fantasy of the normal." She maintains that this fantasy of normalcy, with its attendant social privileges, keeps the motor of normativity purring. In the context of the acute political and humanitarian crisis in the aftermath of the Nazi dictatorship and World War II, the "fantasy of the normal" would certainly have been in dire need of radical revision and most likely also beyond the imaginative powers, material and social resources, and even concern of German citizens concentrating on the task of feeding and housing themselves. Lauren Berlant, *The Female Complaint: The Unfinished Business of Sentimentality in American Culture* (Durham: Duke University Press, 2008), 1–31, here 9.

77. Here I draw on Sara Ahmed's book in which she investigates forms of emotional attachment in contemporary Western neoliberal political culture through what might loosely be called a Marxist-inflected model of object relations. Sara Ahmed, *The Cultural Politics of Emotion* (New York: Routledge, 2004), 4, 8, 13, 15.

CHAPTER 1

The opening epigraphs are from Hannah Arendt, "Organized Guilt and Universal Responsibility," *Jewish Frontier* 12 (January 1945), reprinted in *The Portable Hannah Arendt*, ed. Peter Baehr (New York: Penguin, 2003), 146–56, here 148; and Walter Dirks, "Der Weg zur Freiheit: Ein Beitrag zur deutschen Selbsterkenntnis," *Frankfurter Hefte* 1.4 (1946): 50–60, here 60. Dirk's original German reads, "Wenn Deutschland sich selbst erkennt, so wird es nicht nur frei werden, zunächst geistig und dann und deshalb auch politisch frei, es wird auch glücklich werden."

1. I will be referring to the first German edition: Karl Jaspers, *Die Schuldfrage* (Heidelberg: Lambert Schneider, 1946). English citations are taken from Karl Jaspers, *The Question of German Guilt*, trans. E. B. Ashton (1947; reprint, New York: Capricorn Books, 1961).

2. Jaspers, *German Guilt*, 31–36.

3. William Reddy defines an "emotional regime" as "[t]he set of normative emotions and the official rituals, practices, and emotions that express and inculcate them; a necessary underpinning of any political regime." Reddy, *Navigation of Feeling*, 129. See the discussion of Reddy in the present study's introduction.

4. Reddy, *Navigation of Feeling*, 129.

5. Deborah Gould, *Moving Politics*, 19–23. This term is also discussed in the introduction.

6. Other specifications of JCS 1067 included demilitarization; denazification, achieved through the dissolution of Nazi organizations and the screening and exclusion of former Nazis from public life and influential positions; a ban on fraternization with the Germans; and control of the economic life of German citizens in the American occupation zone, such that they were permitted a basic livelihood, with their standard of living not exceeding that of neighboring countries. "Directive to the Commander in Chief of the US Occupation Forces (JCS 1067)," accessed June 6, 2012, http://germanhistorydocs.ghi-dc.org/sub_document.cfm?document_id =2297.

7. Aleida Assmann notes this and cites the original version of this passage in the directive, in which the phrase *collective guilt* appears in the same sentence as the terms

war guilt, crimes, and *concentration camps.* She concludes that contrary to popular belief in postwar Germany, the term *Kollektivschuld* was not a term used in any official documents by the Allied forces. Assmann and Frevert, *Geschichtsvergessenheit Geschichtsversessenheit,* 124.

8. Frei rightly interprets this response of the Germans as a psychological anticipation of a widespread feeling of personal implication. See Norbert Frei, "Von deutscher Erfindungskraft; oder: Die Kollektivschuldthese in der Nachkriegszeit," in *1945 und wir: Das Dritte Reich im Bewußtsein der Deutschen* (Munich: Deutscher Taschenbuch, 2009), 159–69.

9. Evidence of Karl Jaspers' passionate commitment to an ideal of the university as "eine Instanz der Wahrheit schlechthin" (quite simply, an instance of truth) and "die übernationale abendländische Idee" (the supranational, occidental idea) dates back to at least 1923, when Jaspers published a book on the importance of the university as an ideologically free space in which individuals could encounter and pursue ideas and even truth. Karl Jaspers, *Die Idee der Universität* (Berlin: Springer, 1923). Jaspers published a new draft of the book with the same title in 1946. In 1961, Jaspers, together with Kurt Rossmann, published a new edition of the book, also with the same title. All three versions of the book were published by Springer. See Jaimey Fisher, *Disciplining Germany: Youth, Reeducation, and Reconstruction after the Second World War* (Detroit: Wayne State University Press, 2007), 129–74.

10. For a thorough account of Hartshorne's involvement in the 1945 reopening of Heidelberg University, see James F. Tent, "Edward Yarnall Hartshorne and the Reopening of the Ruprecht-Karls-Universität in Heidelberg, 1945: His Personal Account," in *Heidelberg 1945,* ed. Jürgen C. Heß, Hartmut Lehmann, and Volker Sellin (Stuttgart: Franz Steiner, 1996). See also Steven P. Remy, "Constructing the Myth," in *The Heidelberg Myth: The Nazification and Denazification of a German University* (Cambridge, MA: Harvard University Press, 2002). My next chapter will provide a more detailed contextual analysis of the denazification questionnaire.

11. Remy documents the "aristocratic" approach to *Bildung* manifest among the older professors returning to reform Heidelberg University after the German defeat. Jaspers' approach to democracy was characterized by suspicion after his experiences with the Weimar Republic. Remy, "Constructing the Myth," 116–46.

12. For a brief summary of Jaspers' various engagements in the public sphere in print medium between 1945 and 1948, see Mark W. Clark, "A Prophet without Honor: Karl Jaspers in Germany 1945–48," *Journal of Contemporary History* 37.2 (2002): 197–222, here 208–13. See also Suzanne Kirkbright, *Karl Jaspers: A Biography; Navigations in Truth* (New Haven: Yale University Press, 2004), 187–98. For Jaspers' own account, see Karl Jaspers, "Philosophical Autobiography," in *The Philosophy of Karl Jaspers,* ed. Paul Arthur Schilpp (New York: Tudor, 1957), 5–94.

13. After a short time, Jaspers found that the weight of the journal, which originally drew on politics, critique of language, philosophy, sociology, and literature, shifted significantly toward a literary focus—what Jaspers calls "eine Literalisierung der Politik." Karl Jaspers, "Von Heidelberg nach Basel (1967)," in *Schicksal und Wille: Autobiographische Schriften,* ed. Hans Saner (Munich: Piper, 1967), 147. It is an ironic coincidence that the demise of the journal was synchronous with the founding of the Federal Republic of Germany in 1949.

14. As Jaimey Fisher elaborates in his analysis of Jaspers' relationship to the university in postwar Germany, the university might be seen as a symbol of the "most complex, often contradictory aspects" of Jaspers' understanding of education and politics—and, I would add, of the application of his existence philosophy. See Fisher, *Disciplining Germany*, 133.

15. Karl Jaspers to Hannah Arendt, August 29, 1954, in Hannah Arendt and Karl Jaspers, *Correspondence, 1926–1969*, ed. Lotte Kohler and Hans Saner, trans. Robert Kimber and Rita Kimber (New York: Harcourt Brace and Company, 1992), 245.

16. For an illuminating analysis of the place of the university and the figure of "the student" in Jaspers' postwar writings and speeches, see Jaimey Fisher, *Disciplining Germany*, especially chapter 4, "Modernity's Better Others: Youth in Jaspers's Postwar University and Wiechart's Reconstructive Agenda," particularly 129–55.

17. A plethora of different primary and secondary sources attest that in comparison to their French and British counterparts, the US military government sorely lacked a solid and well-organized plan in preparation for "reeducation" and "denazification" for their US-Allied forces in the European theater. In part, this is because those forces had reckoned with a speedy withdrawal of their troops from Europe, which was not to be the case. Many of the officers had little or no cultural exposure to Germany and the German language and people, and they were not always positively disposed toward them, especially in light of the camp atrocities that some of them had witnessed during liberation. The officers were also constantly relocated, so very few of them had an overview of the situation in any one region—let alone the entirety—of the zone for which they were responsible. In addition to this, after liberation, the US military government was confronted with significant portions of the German civilian population, especially in those cities that had been bombed, which were starving, homeless, and lacking access to basic services, such as electricity and water. There are many interesting firsthand accounts of the US military government's ill-fated "reeducation" and "denazification" programs. See, in particular, Lucius D. Clay, *Decision in Germany* (New York: Doubleday, 1950). Clay was US deputy governor in Germany in 1946 and became known as "the father of the Berlin airlift" during his tenure as military governor of the US zone between 1947 and 1949. For a detailed and fascinating account of the American reeducation and denazification based on interviews of veterans of the occupation as well as examination of declassified documents from the era, see James F. Tent, *Mission on the Rhine: Reeducation and Denazification in American-Occupied Germany* (Chicago: University of Chicago Press, 1982). For a thorough and compelling exploration of the years of US occupation, see Jeffrey K. Olick, *In the House of the Hangman: The Agonies of German Defeat, 1943–1949* (Chicago: University of Chicago Press, 2005).

18. Cornelia Rauh-Kühne, "Die Entnazifizierung und die deutsche Gesellschaft," *Archiv für Sozialgeschichte* 35 (1995): 35–70. As examples of this reevaluation of the effects of Allied denazification, Rauh-Kühne cites the following publications: Clemens Vollnhals, ed., *Entnazifizierung: Politische Säuberung und Rehabilitierung in den vier Besatzungszonen 1945–1949* (Munich: Deutscher Taschenbuch, 1991); Klaus-Dietmar Henke and Hans Woller, eds., *Politische Säuberung in Europa: Die Abrechnung mit Faschismus und Kollaboration nach dem Zweiten Weltkrieg* (Munich: Deutscher Taschenbuch, 1991). For more recent literature that evaluates democratization in a positive light, see Konrad H. Jarausch, *Die Umkehr: Deutsche Wandlung 1945–1995* (Mu-

nich: Deutsche Verlags-Anstalt, 2004); Konrad Jarausch, "Amerikanische Einflüsse und deutsche Einsichten: Kulturelle Aspekte der Demokratisierung Westdeutschlands," in *Demokratiewunder: Transatlantische Mittler und die kulturelle Öffnung Westdeutschlands 1945–1970*, ed. Arnd Bauerkämper, Konrad H. Jarausch, and Marcus M. Payk (Göttingen: Vandenhoeck und Ruprecht, 2005), 57–81. See also *Demokratie im Schatten der Gewalt: Geschichten des Privaten im deutschen Nachkrieg*, ed. Daniel Fulda, Dagmar Herzog, Stephan Ludwig Hoffmann, and Til van Rahden (Göttingen: Wallstein, 2010).

19. See especially the introduction and the first chapter ("Sick of Guilt") in Kapczynski, *The German Patient*, 1–25, 26–74; Olick, *House of the Hangman*, 139–56, 180–202, 270–96.

20. Many postwar intellectuals, authors, psychoanalysts, politicians, and members of the clergy of different dominations discussed the question of responsibility and faced the issue of guilt with varying degrees of candor in debates about the German population's purported collective guilt. Although I will not be able to address most contributions in any depth in this chapter, a brief sample of the "guilt debates" includes contributions as varied as Hannah Arendt's perceptive essay on "organized guilt" (originally published in the United States in January 1945), and Erich Kästner's "Die Schuld und die Schulden" (1945), which constitutes the irate response of Kästner—a popular Weimar children's book author, novelist, and editor of *Die Neue Zeitung* in Allied-occupied Germany—to psychoanalyst C. G. Jung's postwar essay in support of German psychological collective guilt (Jung is often credited with coining the term). Hannah Arendt, "Organized Guilt and Universal Responsibility," in *The Portable Hannah Arendt*, ed. Peter Baehr (New York: Penguin, 2003), 146–56; Erich Kästner, "Die Schuld und die Schulden," in *Erich Kästner Werke*, vol. 5, *Splitter und Balken*, ed. Hans Sarkovicz, Franz Joseph Görtz, and Anna Johann (Munich: Carl Hanser, 2004), 500–505. See C. G. Jung, "Nach der Katastrophe 1945," in *Aufsätze zur Zeitgeschichte* (Zurich: Rascher, 1946), 73–116. Other contributions to the debate include the (presumably staged) "letter to an anonymous American," addressing the finer distinctions between criminal and moral guilt, published at the conclusion of neo-Kantian philosopher Julius Ebbinghaus' book *Zu Deutschlands Schicksalswende* (1945); the "Gericht und Gewissen" of Eugen Kogon, concentration camp survivor and Catholic intellectual and journalist (1946); a statement recognizing responsibility and guilt on the part of the Protestant Church, known as the *Stuttgarter Erklärung* (Stuttgart declaration of guilt, 1945); and the debates about the virtues of inner versus outer emigration pursued in a heated exchange of letters between Thomas Mann, Walter von Molo, and, later on, Frank Thieß (1945). Julius Ebbinghaus, "Brief an einen Amerikaner über die Schuldfrage," in *Zu Deutschlands Schicksalswende* (Frankfurt am Main: Klostermann, 1947), 155–64; Eugen Kogon, "Gericht und Gewissen," *Frankfurter Hefte* 1.1 (1946): 25–37, reprinted in *Die unvollendete Erneuerung: Deutschland im Kräftefeld 1945–1963; Politische und gesellschaftliche Aufsätze aus zwei Jahrzenten* (Frankfurt am Main: Europäische Verlagsanstalt, 1964), 7–22; Martin Niemöller et al., "Die Stuttgarter Erklärung," in *Martin Niemöller: Reden 1945–1954* (Darmstadt: Stimme, 1958), 322; "Die Auseinandersetzung mit der 'Inneren Emigration,'" in Thomas Mann, *Fragile Republik: Thomas Mann und Nachkriegsdeutschland*, ed. Stephan Stachorski (Frankfurt am Main: Fischer, 2005), 23–46. For a discussion of the Mann–von Molo exchange, see Kapczynski, *Ger-*

man Patient, 138–47. See Olick's valuable and extensively researched discussion of the guilt discourses in currency during the immediate postwar period, in *House of the Hangman*, 180–202, 270–96. For the literary angle, see Stephen Brockmann, "The Consciousness of German Guilt," in *German Literary Culture*, 21–70. See also Ursula Heukenkamp, "Schuld und Verfolgung in den Berliner Zeitschriften der Nachkriegszeit," in *Der 8. Mai 1945 als historische Zäsur: Strukturen, Erfahrungen, Deutungen*, ed. Arnd Bauerkämper, Christoph Kleßmann, and Hans Misselwitz (Potsdam: Brandenburgische Landeszentrale für politische Bildung, 1995), 218–31.

21. *Die Wandlung*, vols. 1–4.

22. The designation "after Auschwitz" is best known in the context of philosopher Theodor W. Adorno's writings about culture in the context of National Socialism and genocide. Adorno was one of the most insistent and complex critical thinkers, philosophers, and sociocultural theorists to wrestle directly with the legacy of "Auschwitz," which he did while in exile in the United States in the early 1940s and then back in Frankfurt throughout Germany's Adenauer era. It is interesting to note that Adorno returned to Frankfurt from Los Angeles in 1949 and that Jaspers left Heidelberg to emigrate to Basel in 1948, shortly before the reinstitution of the Frankfurt Institute for Social Research in Frankfurt under Max Horkheimer's leadership.

23. Richard Wolin reads Jaspers' *Die Schuldfrage* as a belated admission of his guilt vis-à-vis his lack of public opposition to the Nazis, as well as what Wolin sees as a continuation of a mandarin "inwardness" demonstrated by his withdrawal from the public eye during the Nazi years. Richard Wolin, *The Frankfurt School Revisited, and Other Essays on Politics and Society* (New York: Routledge, 2006), 141. While this criticism may hold true for Jaspers' elitist worldview and deprecation of "the masses," politics, and democracy during the last gasps of the Weimar Republic, this claim conflates Jaspers' willed pre–National Socialist political ignorance with his attempt to remain socially invisible during the National Socialist dictatorship in order to protect his Jewish wife Gertrud Jaspers from further persecution.

24. Jaspers' speech, "Die Erneuerung der Universität," was published in *Die Wandlung* 1.1 (1945): 66–74. See also Kirkbright, *Karl Jaspers*, 192–93.

25. Undset's letter, "Die Umerziehung der Deutschen," appeared in October 1945 in *Die Neue Zeitung*. Jaspers' response, "Antwort an Sigrid Undset," was published in the same newspaper in November 1945. Undset's and Jaspers' letters and two articles by Jaspers, including his speech "The Rejuvenation of the University," were published in book form in 1947. Karl Jaspers, *Die Antwort an Sigrid Undset mit Beiträgen über die Wissenschaft im Hitlerstaat und den neuen Geist der Universität von Karl Jaspers; Im Anhang: "Die Umerziehung der Deutschen" von Sigrid Undset* (Konstanz: Südverlag, 1947).

26. Passages from several letters written by Karl Jaspers to readers who had written to him in the aftermath of Undset's attack concerning the question of German "collective guilt" are later reproduced almost verbatim in the *Schuldfrage* publication. See, for example, Jaspers' response in the form of marginalia written in the borders of a twelve-page manuscript titled "Antwort an Karl Jaspers (Sigrid Undset und die deutsche Schuld)," which Jaspers received from Dieter Bischoff on October 28, 1945, after the publication of his response to Undset. Jaspers enters into a virtual dialogue (no actual further correspondence between the men is present after Jaspers receives the letter),

replying in the margins of Bischoff's letter to statements made by Bischoff, such as "Sie verlangt die Unerbittlichkeit gegen uns selber, dass wir jedes Schicksal, dass die alliierten Mächte uns jetzt auferlegen mögen, ruhig auf uns nehmen, und sie verbietet jeden Zorn und jede Entrüstung über das Tun der Anderen, auch bei offenbarem Unrecht. Sie verlangt das tiefe Zurückgehen in uns selber auf die letzten Quellen unseres Seins und Tuns als so gewordene Menschen." (It makes the inexorable demand on us to accept calmly any fate that the Allied powers wish to force on us, and forbids all anger and any outrage over the acts of the others, even when these are obviously unjust. It demands going deeply into ourselves to the ultimate sources of our being and actions that have made us the humans we are today.) Jaspers' response in the margins is "Das habe ich nicht gesagt. Aber in der Tat mir ist in solchen Wahrheit." (I did not say that. Though, truly, I find truth in this.) Similarly, a passage from a letter of November 8, 1945, addressed to Jaspers from the SPD politician Dr. Franz Josef Huber from Donauwörth, in reaction to the Undset response, is taken up directly in Jaspers' text (although he does not extend the logic to the ridiculous lengths exhibited in this excerpt), showing the extent to which his everyday life was determined by the question of German guilt after this publication, which was only to escalate after the publication of *Die Schuldfrage* in 1946. The passage from Huber's letter reads, "Wenn Frau S. Undset also sagt, die Deutschen sind Nazis, so hat sie schon mit dem ersten Wort unrecht: wenn man 'die' sagt, ist man schon auf dem falschen Wege. Es gibt nicht 'die' Engländer, oder 'die' Franzosen, auch nicht 'die' Deutschen nicht einmal 'die' Menschen, ja wahrscheinlich— nur hier kommen wir nicht ganz dahinter—nicht einmal 'die' Pferde, oder 'die' Hunde." (When Mrs. S. Undset says that the Germans are Nazis, she is in the wrong with her very first word: by saying the word "the," one already is on the wrong track. There are no "the" English, "the" French, "the" Germans, most likely not even "the" people—and here we can't quite get to the bottom of it—not even "the" horses or "the" dogs.) Dieter Bischoff to Karl Jaspers, October 28, 1945, letter accompanied by a twelve-page manuscript titled "Antwort an Karl Jaspers (Sigrid Undset und die deutsche Schuld)," box 26: Bundestagsdebatte über Verjährung, folder titled Schuldfrage; Briefe zu Undset; Zeitspannsschnitte u.a., Jaspers Estate, Deutsches Literaturarchiv, Marbach.

27. In his belated indictment in 1949 of Jaspers' 1947 Goethe Prize address, titled "Our Future and Goethe," Ernst Robert Curtius scathingly commented on what he saw as Jaspers' ambition to become "Praeceptor Germaniae" of postwar Germany. For an account of the so-called Curtius affair and its effect on Jaspers, see Kirkbright, *Karl Jaspers*, 218–20; Stephen Brockmann, *German Literary Culture*, 127–32.

28. Anson Rabinbach writes that although Jaspers and Heidegger saw themselves before 1933 as a "*Kampfgemeinschaft*, a kind of philosophical duo resolutely struggling together against the official Kantianism of the day," Jaspers, who was greatly disappointed by Heidegger's original support of the Nazi revolution, was instrumental in the imposition of a teaching ban imposed on Heidegger in January 1946 at the University of Freiburg. See Anson Rabinbach, *In the Shadow of Catastrophe: German Intellectuals between Apocalypse and Enlightenment* (Berkeley: University of California Press, 2000), 129–33.

29. Robert H. Jackson cited in Jaspers, *German Guilt*, 52.

30. Jaspers cites directly from a statement made at the first Nuremberg trials in November 1945 by Robert H. Jackson, which Jaspers had underlined in a newspaper

article by Dr. Franz C. Heidelberg, "Vor dem Nürnberger Gerichtshof: Randbemerkungen," in the section "Aus der Rede des Hauptanklägers der USA," *Rhein-Neckar-Zeitung*, November 28, 1945, 4, box 26, Jaspers Estate, Deutsches Literaturarchiv, Marbach. Jaspers cites only the first few sentences of Jackson's address in his lectures, although his underlining in this section is extensive.

31. Jaspers, *Schuldfrage*, 50; *German Guilt*, 51–52.

32. Jaspers, *Schuldfrage*, 47–57; *German Guilt*, 51–60, 61–63.

33. Jaspers, *Schuldfrage*, 57–63; *German Guilt*, 63–70.

34. Jaspers, *Schuldfrage*, 63–65; *German Guilt*, 71–73.

35. The German officials originally set the early ration quotas at a level below subsistence, ranging from nine to eleven hundred calories per day, although the figure differed from one occupation zone to the next. Displaced persons were given two thousand calories per day. The situation was so dire, especially in the urban areas, that four hundred thousand tons of Army supplies were brought in during the summer of 1945 for the displaced persons, so that the local population would not starve. Thus the potential for a breakout of diseases related to malnutrition was high. See Harold Zink, *American Military Government in Germany* (New York: MacMillan, 1947), 111–13. For a thorough quantitative and qualitative analysis of the malnutrition and undernourishment prevalent in Germany in the immediate postwar period, see Jörg Echternkamp, "Nachkriegskrise: Kriegsfolgen, Alltagsnot und Abgrenzung," *Nach dem Krieg: Alltagsnot, Neuorientierung und die Last der Vergangenheit 1945–1949* (Zurich: Penda, 2003), 15–73. For an interesting historical account of scarcity, consumption, and politics in the shadow of the Cold War, through a case study of Berlin, see Paul Steege, *Black Market, Cold War: Everyday Life in Berlin, 1946–1949* (Cambridge: Cambridge University Press, 2007).

36. Arendt and Jaspers, *Correspondence*, 21–101 (October 28, 1945–January 30, 1948).

37. In his memoir, General Clay documents the dire situation of hunger in which many Germans found themselves: "For three years the problem of food was to color every administrative action, and to keep the German people alive and able to work was our main concern. From the first I begged and argued for food because I did not believe that the American people wanted starvation and misery to accompany occupation, and I was certain that we could not arouse political interest for a democratic government in a hungry, apathetic population." Lucius D. Clay, "Food and Health for the German People," chapter 14 in *Decision in Germany*, 263–80, here 263.

38. This information, as well as the citation from Stayer, are taken from James Tent, "E. Y. Hartshorne and the Reopening of the Heidelberg University," in *Mission on the Rhine*, 58–59.

39. Jaspers and Arendt often discuss the deteriorating situation of food availability in their correspondence between 1945 and 1948. During the so-called Hunger Winter of 1946/47, Jaspers addresses the desolate material and psychological state of the Germans in a letter to Arendt: "Our questions and concerns become insignificant in light of the misery most people are experiencing. It becomes meaningless to speak as I have been speaking—not ultimately, but in view of present conditions. When basic needs are paramount, that's all anyone will care about. One finds little response if one says: The defeated could have been dealt with far more harshly. The response is: It's just a matter

of method. The way things are going now, half of the population will perish, and the rest can then eke out a minimal existence on the land." Jaspers to Arendt, January 1, 1947, in *Correspondence*, 72. This response resonates with the population's fear of the US implementation of the Morgenthau plan.

40. Stephan Hermlin, "Karl Jaspers, 'Die Schuldfrage,'" in Stephan Hermlin and Hans Mayer, *Ansichten: Über einige neue Schriftsteller und Bücher* (Wiesbaden: Limes-Verlag, 1947), 130–35, here 132. "Wir können uns des Gefühls nicht erwehren, daß die ethische Unerbittlichkeit des Philosophen Karl Jaspers hier einem Auditorium nachgegeben hat, das etwas anderes nicht hätte hören können."

41. Jaspers, *Schuldfrage*, 11–13; *German Guilt*, 7–9.

42. Frank Biess terms this kind of approach to rationality versus perceived National Socialist irrationality a practice of "emotional control" or "emotional demobilization." For an analysis of how rationality was used to counter the perceived irrationalism of National Socialism, see Frank Biess, "Feeling in the Aftermath: Toward a History of Postwar Emotions," in *Histories of the Aftermath: The Legacies of the Second World War in Europe*, ed. Frank Biess and Robert G. Moeller (Oxford: Berghahn Books, 2010), 30–48.

43. Jaspers, *Schuldfrage*, n.p. This statement is not included in the English translation of the lectures.

44. Jaspers, *German Guilt*, 16."Sie werden mitschwingen oder gegen mich fühlen, und ich selber werde nicht ohne Erregung im Grunde meines Denkens mich bewegen." Jaspers, *Schuldfrage*, 18.

45. Thus Hannah Arendt, in an essay on Karl Jaspers' work, claims that for Jaspers, "[t]ruth itself is communicative, it disappears and cannot be conceived outside communication; within the 'existential' realm, truth and communication are the same." Hannah Arendt, "Karl Jaspers: Citizen of the World?" (1957), reprinted in *Men in Dark Times* (London: Jonathan Cape, 1970), 85.

46. Arendt, "Karl Jaspers: A Laudatio," in *Dark Times*, 74. Arendt delivered this essay as an address when the German Peace Prize was awarded to Karl Jaspers in 1958.

47. Karl Jaspers, "Philosophische Autobiographie," in *Karl Jaspers*, ed. Paul Schilpp (Stuttgart: Kohlhammer, 1957), 1–79, see 57–62 and 72–79; Karl Jaspers, "Philosophical Autobiography," in *The Philosophy of Karl Jaspers*, ed. Paul Schilpp (New York: Tudor, 1957), 5–94, see 70–75 and 87.

48. Jaspers, "Philosophical Autobiography," 40; Jaspers, "Philosophische Autobiographie," 29.

49. Arendt, "Karl Jaspers: Citizen of the World?" in *Dark Times*, 86.

50. Dolf Sternberger, "Jaspers und der Staat," in *Karl Jaspers, Werk und Wirkung*, ed. Klaus Piper (Munich: Piper, 1963), 133–41, 134. On his concept of communication as the political foundation of the public sphere, Jaspers writes, "Echte Politik ist aber nur möglich, wenn eine Wirkung durch Überzeugung des Anderen in Rede und Gegenrede stattfindet, in der die Erziehung eines öffentlichen Bewußtseins durch freien Kampf der Geister sich vollzieht." Jaspers, "Philosophische Autobiographie," 45. ("The end of genuine politics suspends the interest for politics; but real politics is possible only if the result is effectuated through the persuasion of others by discourse pro and con, in which the education of public consciousness takes place by means of a free combat of minds.") Jaspers, "Philosophical Autobiography," 57.

51. In 1948, Jaspers broadcast a series of twelve introductory lectures to philosophy, titled "Die kleine Schule des philosophischen Denkens." Paul Meyer-Gutzwiller, "Karl Jaspers und der Rundfunk," in Piper, *Karl Jaspers*, 169–71, here 170. Meyer-Gutzwiller praises Jaspers for consciously avoiding using "Fach- und Fremdwörter" in his radio broadcasts. This position shows just how diametrically opposed Jaspers was to Theodor W. Adorno, who saw in Jaspers' and Heidegger's existential philosophy the pinnacle of obfuscating jargon and metaphysical hogwash. Similarly, for Adorno, "Fremdwörter" held an important conceptual valence as regards their extraterritorial relationship to the language that labels them as such. This sentiment is captured in his aphorism "Fremdwörter sind die Juden der Sprache." Theodor W. Adorno, *Minima Moralia: Reflexionen aus dem beschädigten Leben* (1951; reprint, Frankfurt am Main: Suhrkamp, 2001), 200. ("German words of foreign derivation are the Jews of language.") Theodor W. Adorno, trans. E. F. N. Jephcott (Brooklyn, NY: Verso, 2006), 110.

52. Examples of terminology taken from Jaspers' existential philosophical framework in *Die Schuldfrage* include formulations of metaphysical guilt in terms of a relationship to the encompassing ("das Umgreifende"), and diagnosing a limit situation ("Grenzzustand") that requires illumination ("Erhellung") and purification ("Reinigung") in order to be equal to its claim to truth ("Wahrheitsanspruch"). Jaspers deploys this terminology in long passages in *Die Schuldfrage* when describing the way to truth and freedom through facing one's metaphysical guilt before God. These terms also furnish the idiom in which his "Philosophische Autobiographie" is written.

53. Hannah Arendt, "Organized Guilt and Universal Responsibility," *Jewish Frontier* 12 (January 1945): 19–23. The version I cite here was reprinted in *The Portable Hannah Arendt*, ed. Peter Baehr (New York: Penguin, 2003), 146–56.

54. Hannah Arendt, "Organisierte Schuld," *Die Wandlung* 1.4 (April 1946): 333–44.

55. Arendt, "Organized Guilt," 146–51.

56. Ibid., 146, 148–51.

57. Ibid., 150–51.

58. In a letter to Arendt in 1946, Jaspers marks this difference in style and approach when he gently criticizes other essays by Arendt: "Would it be possible to articulate the connections more cautiously and therefore more powerfully—that is, to present them in a historically more correct and less visionary way?"; "in this vision, too, there is much that is correct, but at the same time it is a vast 'exaggeration.'" Jaspers to Arendt, June 27, 1946, in *Correspondence*, 45–46.

59. Arendt, "Organized Guilt," 150–51.

60. Wartime US treasurer Henry Morgenthau Jr. (1934–45) formed a Treasury committee to draw up a plan titled "Program to Prevent Germany from Starting a World War III," which recommended a harsh approach to the Germans and Germany on their defeat. The program is included in the book *Germany Is Our Problem*, published in 1945. In short, the program proposed that Germany be completely demilitarized and that the armament industry be destroyed, that new boundaries reducing the current size of Germany be imposed (France would receive the Saar and the Rhineland territories, Poland would receive East Prussia, and an international zone would be created to contain the Ruhr and surrounding industrial areas), and that Germany be partitioned into two states. According to the program, restitution and reparation were to take shape via the transfer of German resources and territories, using forced German labor outside of Germany,

and the confiscation of all German foreign assets. All schools and universities were to be closed and reorganized, German media were to be placed under Allied control, and a process of political decentralization was to be implemented. Henry Morgenthau Jr., *Germany Is Our Problem* (New York: Harper and Brothers, 1945). As the Reich minister for propaganda in Nazi Germany, Joseph Goebbels put rumors about Morgenthau's harsh plan for defeated Germany to good use for the Nazis, inflaming anti-Semitic hatred toward the Jewish Morgenthau and the United States and sowing the seeds of fear and uncertainty that characterized the attitude toward the Allies in the immediate postwar period. "Morgenthau" thus became a symbol for the Germans' fear of the vengeful and punitive future awaiting them should Germany be defeated. For a thorough and engaging account on the history and political uses and abuses of the Morgenthau Plan, see Olick, *House of the Hangman*, 73–94.

61. Arendt to Jaspers, January 29, 1946, in *Correspondence*, 28–33.

62. Arendt to Jaspers, August 17, 1946, in *Correspondence*, 56.

63. Arendt, "Organized Guilt," 146–47.

64. Jaspers, *Schuldfrage*, 15; *German Guilt*, 12.

65. *German Guilt*, 29. "Sich auf Gefühle zu berufen ist die Naivität, die der Objektivität des Wißbaren und Denkbaren ausweicht." Jaspers, *Schuldfrage,* 30.

66. Ibid.

67. Arendt, "Organized Guilt," 156.

68. Jaspers, *Schuldfrage*, 19; *German Guilt*, 17.

69. Jaspers, "Philosophical Autobiography," 82; Jaspers, "Philosophische Autobiographie," 68.

70. Jaspers, *Schuldfrage*, 20; *German Guilt*, 18.

71. Jaspers, *German Guilt*, 40–41. "Es ist auch sinnwidrig, ein Volk als Ganzes moralisch anzuklagen. Es gibt keinen Charakter eines Volkes derart, daß jeder einzelne der Volkszugehörigen diesen Charakter hätte. . . . Moralisch kann immer nur der einzelne, nie ein Kollektiv beureilt werden. . . . Ein Volk kann nicht zu einem Individuum gemacht werden. Ein Volk kann nicht heroisch untergehen, nicht Verbrecher sein, nicht sittlich oder unsittlich handeln, sondern immer nur die einzelnen aus ihm. . . . Die kategoriale Beurteilung als Volk ist immer eine Ungerechtigkeit; sie setzt voraus eine falsche Substanzialisierung,—sie hat eine Entwürdigung des Menschen als einzelnen zur Folge." Jaspers, *Schuldfrage*, 38–39. Only the question of political guilt pertains to a sense of collectivity, Jaspers argues, as a people elect those who govern their country: "Aber die politische Haftung trifft sie mit, weil sie auch ihr Leben durch die Ordnung des Staates haben. Es gibt kein außerhalb in modernen Staaten." Jaspers, *Schuldfrage*, 57. "Yet they [the nonpolitical persons], too, are included among the politically liable, because they, too, live by the order of the state. There is no such aloofness in modern states." Jaspers, *German Guilt*, 62.

72. Jaspers, *German Guilt*, 18. "In Grundzügen gemeinsam ist uns Deutschen heute vielleicht nur Negatives: die Zugehörigkeit zu einem restlos besiegten Staatsvolk, ausgeliefert der Gnade oder Ungnade der Sieger; der Mangel eines gemeinsamen uns alle verbindenden Bodens; die Zerstreutheit: jeder ist im wesentlichen auf sich gestellt, und doch ist jeder als einzelner hilflos. Gemeinsam ist die Nichtgemeinsamkeit." Jaspers, *Schuldfrage*, 20.

73. Jaspers, *Schuldfrage*, 20, 52, 105; *German Guilt,* 18, 48, 91.

74. Jaspers, *German Guilt*, 79. "So fühlt der Deutsche—d.h. der deutsch sprech-

ende Mensch—sich mitbetroffen von allem, was aus dem Deutschen erwächst. Nicht die Haftung des Staatsangehörigen, sondern die Mitbetroffenheit als zum deutschen geistigen und seelischen Leben gehörender Mensch, der ich mit den andern gleicher Sprache, gleicher Herkunft, gleichen Schicksals bin, wird hier Grund nicht einer greifbaren Schuld, aber eines Analogons von Mitschuld." Jaspers, *Schuldfrage*, 70–71.

75. Jaspers, *German Guilt*, 80–81. "Ich fühle mich näher den Deutschen, die auch so fühlen—ohne daraus eine Pathetik zu machen—und fühle mich ferner denen, deren Seele diesen Zusammenhang zu verleugnen scheint. Und diese Nähe bedeutet vor allem die gemeinsame, beschwingende Aufgabe, nicht Deutsch zu sein, wie man nun einmal ist, sondern Deutsch zu werden, wie man es noch nicht ist, aber sein soll, und wie man es hört aus dem Anruf unserer hohen Ahnen, nicht aus der Geschichte der nationalen Idole. Weil wir die Kollektivschuld fühlen, fühlen wir die ganze Aufgabe der Wiedererneuerung des Menschseins aus dem Ursprung—die Aufgabe, die alle Menschen auf der Erde haben, die aber dringender, fühlbarer, wie alles Sein entscheidend, dort auftritt, wo ein Volk durch eigene Schuld vor dem Nichts steht." Jaspers, *Schuldfrage*, 72.

76. Drawing on the Foucauldian discussion of "common discourse" and Bourdieu's concept of "habitus," medieval historian Barbara Rosenwein has coined the evocative phrase *emotional community* to describe social groups where the primary bond between the members is that of a constellation of shared emotional norms. She defines these communities as "groups in which people adhere to the same norms of emotional expression and value—or devalue—the same or related emotions." Rosenwein, *Emotional Communities*, 2, 25–26.

77. *OED Online*, http://www.oed.com/, accessed May 22, 2012.

78. Jaspers, *German Guilt*, 16.

79. In theologically saturated terms, Jaspers describes the process as one of self-insight ("Selbstdurchhellung": literally, an illumination of the self), where truth must shine through ("durchleuchten") in order to attain a state of awakening ("Erwachen"), purgation ("Reinigung"), and a "purity of soul" ("Reinheit der Seele"). Jaspers, *Schuldfrage*, 45, 60, 89–102, 17. It is perhaps not surprising that Jaspers' two favorite books were the Bible and Kant's writings. See Kirkbright, *Karl Jaspers*.

80. Jaspers, *German Guilt*, 11–12. "Wir wollen lernen, miteinander zu reden. Das heißt, wir wollen nicht nur unsere Meinung wiederholen, sondern hören, was der andere denkt. Wir wollen nicht nur behaupten, sondern im Zusammenhang nachdenken, auf Gründe hören, bereit bleiben, zu neuer Einsicht zu kommen. Wir wollen den anderen gelten lassen, uns innerlich versuchsweise auf den Standpunkt des andern stellen. . . . Wir müssen die Bereitschaft zum Nachdenken wiederherstellen gegen die Neigung, alles gleichsam in Schlagzeilen plakatiert schon fertig zu haben." Jaspers, *Schuldfrage*, 14–15.

81. Jaspers, *German Guilt*, 12. "Dazu gehört, daß wir uns nicht berauschen in Gefühlen des Stolzes, der Verzweiflung, der Empörung, des Trotzes, der Rache, der Verachtung, sondern daß wir diese Gefühle auf Eis legen und sehen, was wirklich ist. Wir müssen solche Gefühle suspendieren, um das Wahre zu erblicken, um liebend in der Welt zu sein." Jaspers, *Schuldfrage*, 15.

82. Jaspers, *German Guilt*, 16. "Dazu gehört nicht nur Arbeit des Verstandes, sondern durch ihn veranlaßt eine Arbeit des Herzens. Diese Arbeit inneren Handelns trägt die Verstandesarbeit und wird von ihr wiederum erregt. Sie warden mitschwingen

oder gegen mich fühlen, und ich selber werde nicht ohne Erregung im Grunde meines Denkens mich bewegen. Wenn wir auch bei den einseitigen Vortrag nicht faktisch miteinander sprechen, so kann ich nicht vermeiden, daß mancher sich fast persönlich getroffen fühlt. Von vornherein bitte ich: Verzeihen Sie mir, wenn ich beleidige. Ich will es nicht. Aber ich bin entschlossen, die radikalsten Gedanken in möglichster Besonnenheit zu wagen." Jaspers, *Schuldfrage*, 18.

83. Jaspers, *German Guilt*, 17. "Unter der Decke einer erzwungenen, äußerlichen Gemeinschaft"; "weil wir unter uns in dem, was wir erlebt, gefühlt, gewünscht, geschätzt, getan haben, außerordentlich verschieden sind." Jaspers, *Schuldfrage*, 19.

84. Jaspers, *German Guilt*, 19. "Nun wir heute wieder frei reden können, finden wir uns so, als ob wir aus verschiedenen Welten kämen. Und doch sprechen wir alle die deutsche Sprache und sind alle in diesem Lande geboren und haben hier unsere Heimat. Die Verschiedenheit, ja Weltenferne darf uns nicht verdrießen. Wir wollen zueinander finden, miteinander reden, uns zu überzeugen suchen." Jaspers, *Schuldfrage*, 21.

85. Jaspers, *German Guilt*, 71. "Metaphysische Schuld ist der Mangel an der absoluten Solidarität mit dem Menschen als Menschen. Sie bleibt noch ein unauslöschlicher Anspruch, wo die moralisch sinnvolle Forderung schon aufgehört hat. Diese Solidarität ist verletzt, wenn ich dabei bin, wo Unrecht und Verbrechen geschehen. Es genügt nicht, daß ich mein Leben mit Vorsicht wage, um es zu verhindern. Wenn es geschieht, und wenn ich dabei war, und wenn ich überlebe, wo der andere getötet wird, so ist in mir eine Stimme, durch die ich weiß: daß ich noch lebe, ist meine Schuld." Jaspers, *Schuldfrage*, 64.

86. Jaspers, *German Guilt*, 74. "Was daraus erwächst, das muß die wesentliche Grundlage dessen schaffen, was in Zukunft deutsche Seele sein wird." Jaspers, *Schuldfrage*, 66.

87. Jaspers, "Philosophische Autobiographie," 50. In response to his own question "Was heißt es, ein Deutscher zu sein?" Jaspers responds, "Das natürliche, fraglose Deutschsein, worin ich lebte, war Sprache, Heimat, Herkunft, war die große geistige Überlieferung, an der ich von früh an teilgewann" (The natural unquestioned being-German, in which I lived, was language, home, heritage; was the great intellectual tradition in which I participated from an early age).

88. Gertrud Jaspers wrote to Arendt, "My husband often said to me after '33: ''Trude, I am Germany.' I found that too glib." Gertrud Jaspers to Hannah Arendt, April 17, 1946, in Arendt and Jaspers, *Correspondence*, 698.

89. Arendt to Gertrud Jaspers, May 30, 1946, in Arendt and Jaspers, *Correspondence*, 41.

90. See Friedrich Meinecke, *Die deutsche Katastrophe: Betrachtungen und Erinnerungen* (1946; reprint, Wiesbaden: Eberhardt Brockhaus, 1949). Both Fisher and Olick discuss Meinecke's concept of a *Kulturnation* based on *Goethegemeinden*. Fisher, "Germany's Youthful 'Catastrophe,'" chapter 3 in *Disciplining Germany*, 89–128, 92–94; Olick, *House of the Hangman*, 161–66.

91. Jaspers, *German Guilt*, 80. "Weil ich mich nicht entbrechen kann, in tiefer Seele kollektiv zu fühlen, ist mir, ist jedem das Deutschsein nicht Bestand, sondern Aufgabe. Das ist etwas ganz anderes als die Verabsolutierung des Volkes. Ich bin zuerst Mensch, ich bin im besonderen Friese, bin Professor, bin Deutscher, bin mit anderen Kollektiven nahe, bis zur Verschmelzung des Seelen, verbunden, näher oder ferner mit allen mir fühlbar

gewordenen Gruppen; ich kann mich in Augenblicken vermöge dieser Nähe fast als Jude fühlen oder als Holländer oder als Engländer. Darin aber ist die Gegebenheit des Deutschseins, das heißt wesentlich das Leben in der Muttersprache, so nachhaltig, dass ich mich auf eine rational nicht mehr fassliche, ja sogar zu widerlegende Weise mit verantwortlich fühle für das, was Deutsche tun und getan haben." Jaspers, *Schuldfrage*, 71–72.

92. Jaspers, *German Guilt*, 25, 48–50; *Schuldfrage*, 26, 45–46.

93. Jewish intellectual Ben Halpern was the first to note this, in an April 1948 review of Jaspers' book. Halpern's review, published in the respected New York Labor Zionist journal *Jewish Frontier*, is perhaps understandably more passionate and less charitable than Arendt was in offering a critique of Jaspers' text from a Jewish perspective. Halpern expresses his anger at what he sees as Jaspers' co-option of the Jewish category of the "Chosen People" for the disgraced Germans, when he addresses Jaspers' implicit idealization of the category of "the Chosen People" in the following scathing remarks: "It is a privileged delinquency which marks those who survived its [guilt's] ordeal with the brand of a Chosen People. The last words, of course, are not to be found explicitly in Jaspers (though his peroration hinges on a Biblical reference to the Jewish Exile); but what else can be the effect of construing German guilt as a special cosmic experience known only to Germans, which can be transmuted into a quasi-religious discipline accessible only to the brotherhood of charity of the German folk, and whose fine fabric is shattered by the irrelevant moral demands of outsiders?" Ben Halpern, "Guilty, but Not Answerable," *Jewish Frontier*, April 1948, 41–60, here 51.

94. Karl Jaspers most likely adopted the term from Max Weber, who used it to describe the Jewish social status as an outsider even when fully assimilated within a particular national society. In her 1944 essay "The Jew as Pariah," Hannah Arendt argues for a long implicit history of the concept and argues that it has become "a human type." In a footnote to her essay, Arendt gives a brief history of the word, tracing its path back from Max Weber's use of the word in his monograph *Ancient Judaism* (1921) to its origin in the Indian caste system. Hannah Arendt, "The Jew as Pariah," in *Reflexions on Literature and Culture*, ed. Susannah Young-Ah Gottlieb (Stanford: Stanford University Press, 2007), 69–90, 319n1. For an analysis of the advantages and the shortcomings of Weber's choice of the term *pariah* to describe the Jewish people, see Arnaldo Momigliano, "A Note on Max Weber's Definition of Judaism as a Pariah-Religion," *History and Theory* 19.3 (1980): 313–18.

95. Anson Rabinbach, *Shadow of Catastrophe*, 137–38, 148–50.

96. Jaspers, *German Guilt*, 36. "Die metaphysische Schuld hat zur Folge eine *Verwandlung des menschlichen Selbstbewußtseins vor Gott.*" Jaspers, *Schuldfrage*, 35.

97. Jaspers, *German Guilt*, 28. "Philosophie und Theologie sind berufen, die Tiefe der Schuldfrage zu erhellen." Jaspers, *Schuldfrage*, 30.

98. Jaspers, *German Guilt*, 11, 28. "Denn gerade in der Not kann das Unerläßlichste um so fühlbarer sein: in der eigenen Seele rein zu werden und das Rechte zu denken und zu tun, um aus echtem Ursprung von dem Nichts das Leben ergreifen zu können." Jaspers, *Schuldfrage*, 29.

99. Jaspers, *German Guilt*, 72, 122. The German phrases are "eine Umschmelzung unseres Wesens" and "ohne Durchhellung und Verwandlung unserer Seele." Jaspers, *Schuldfrage*, 65, 105.

100. In his critique of existence philosophy as a branch of existentialism, Adorno references Benjamin's notion of "aura" to describe the effect produced by this terminology: "Daß die Jargonworte, unabhängig vom Kontext wie vom begrifflichen Inhalt, klingen, wie wenn sie ein Höheres sagten, als was sie bedeuten, wäre mit dem Terminus Aura zu bezeichnen." ("The fact that the words of the jargon sound as if they said something higher than what they mean suggests the term 'aura.'"). Here Adorno refers to Benjamin's less optimistic interpretation of the role of aura in modernity. However, according to Adorno, these problematic quasi-theological words do not even make the grade of the auratic and are pronounced to be "Verfallsprodukte der Aura" (decaying byproducts of aura). Theodor W. Adorno, *Jargon der Eigentlichkeit*, in *Negativ Dialektik, Jargon der Eigentlichkeit*, vol. 6 of *Gesammelte Schriften*, ed. Rolf Tiedemann, with Gretel Adorno, Susan Buck-Morss, and Klaus Schultz (Frankfurt am Main: Suhrkamp, 2003), 415–526, here 419; Theodor W. Adorno, *The Jargon of Authenticity*, trans. Knut Tarnowski and Frederic Will (London: Routledge, 2003), 6

101. I thank Peter Fenves for this observation. For an analysis of Adorno's critique of Buber, see Micha Brumlik, "Adorno's Critique of Buber," in *New Perspectives on Buber*, ed. Thomas Zank (Tübingen: Mohr Siebeck, 2006), 247–54.

102. For an examination of Jaspers' idiosyncratic interpretations of Kant and Hegel in *Die Schuldfrage* and other postwar writings, see Chris Thornhill, "Republican Existence: Jaspers and Post-war Politics," in *Karl Jaspers: Politics and Metaphysics* (New York: Routledge, 2002), 168–207.

103. Heinrich Blücher, *Within Four Walls: The Correspondence of Heinrich Blücher and Hannah Arendt*, ed. Lotte Kohler, trans. Peter Constantine (New York: Harcourt Brace, 2000), 84, cited in Richard Wolin, *Frankfurt School Revisited*, 144.

104. Drawing on Elisabeth Young-Bruehl's biography on Hannah Arendt, Rabinbach explains that Hannah Arendt was irritated by the interwar Weberian nationalism and Jaspers' Protestantism in his *Schuldfrage* book. Elisabeth Young-Bruehl, *Hannah Arendt: For Love of the World* (New Haven: Yale University Press, 1982), 216; Rabinbach, *Shadow of Catastrophe*, 150.

105. Jaspers, "Philosophical Autobiography," 65; Jaspers, "Philosophische Autobiographie," 52.

106. Here I take out of context the well-known title of Giorgio Agamben's book *The Coming Community*, to underscore Jaspers' performative and future-directed use of the phrase to describe a transcendental ideal of sorts, to which one may aspire, but which can never be attained in identitarian terms. Agamben means quite the opposite here, and he certainly would not link the term to the concept of nationality, although I would argue that this connection, in and of itself, suggests a radical potentiality to throw the question of national belonging and statehood into question. Giorgio Agamben, *The Coming Community*, trans. Michael Hardt (Minneapolis: University of Minnesota Press, 1993).

107. Jaspers, *German Guilt*, 17.

108. Arendt to Jaspers, August 17, 1946, in *Correspondence*, 52–53.

109. Ibid., 54.

110. Jaspers to Arendt, October 19, 1946, in *Correspondence*, 62.

111. This line of critique is later developed most famously by Susan Sontag in her essay "Fascinating Fascism," where she examines how Nazism becomes symbolically

charged as a site of libidinal investment through imagined social transgression, proving that Jaspers' concerns were not ill founded. Susan Sontag, "Fascinating Fascism," *New York Review of Books*, February 6, 1974, reprinted in *Under the Sign of Saturn* (New York: Farrar, Straus and Giroux, 1980), 73–105.

112. Jaspers to Arendt, September 18, 1946, in *Correspondence*, 58.

113. Jaspers, *German Guilt*, 102. "Wir Deutsche besinnen uns alle, wenn auch in noch so verschiedener, ja entgegengesetzter Weise, auf unsere Schuld und Nichtschuld. Wir alle tun es, Nationalsozialisten und Gegner des Nationalsozialismus. Wenn ich 'wir' sage, so meine ich die Menschen, mit denen ich mich zunächst—durch Sprache Herkunft, Situation, Schicksal—solidarisch weiß. Ich will niemanden anklagen, wenn ich 'wir' sage. Wenn andere Deutsche sich schuldlos fühlen, so ist das ihre Sache, außer in den zwei Punkten der Strafe für Verbrechen derer, die sie getan haben, und der politischen Haftung aller für die Handlungen des Hitlerstaates." Jaspers, *Schuldfrage*, 89.

114. Jaspers, *German Guilt*, 7–9; *Schuldfrage*, 11–13.

115. Jaspers, *German Guilt*, 64–67; *Schuldfrage*, 58–60.

116. Jaspers to Arendt, March 12, 1946, in *Correspondence*, 34.

117. Jaspers to Arendt, September 18, 1946, in *Correspondence*, 58.

118. My translation. "Mit unvergeßlich einfacher Kühnheit ergriff er in der ersten großen Vorlesung nach dem Kriege—im Wintersemester 1945/46—den Gegenstand, der alle bedrängte, die Jungen wie die Alten. Wieder sprach der Titel zwar von der 'geistigen' Situation (genauer: von der geistigen Situation in Deutschland), aber unter diesem Titel wurde die Lage des okkupierten Landes erörtet, das Regiment der alliierten Militärregierung im Hinblick auf die Möglichkeiten der Forschung und der Universität, vor allem dann der Nationalsozialismus, der Anbruch des Zeitalters der Weltgeschichte, eine deutsche Selbstbesinnung. Ein Kernstück handelte von der Schuldfrage—dies allein ist publiziert." Dolf Sternberger, "Jaspers und der Staat," in *Karl Jaspers, Werk und Wirkung*, 134.

119. My translation. "Die alte Aula war voll bis in den letzten Winkel, nicht die leiseste Störung war zu verzeichnen, die Reinheit und Offenheit des Vortrages schuf eine unvergleichliche Autorität." Ibid.

120. For a short account sympathizing with Penham's reaction to the denazification attempts at Heidelberg University, see Rabinbach, *Shadow of Catastrophe*, 134–35. Penham is one of the most passionate and dramatic players to appear on the stage of German denazification. His zeal for his role in postwar Germany doubtless stemmed in part from his experiences as a German Jew and member of the French Resistance under National Socialism, coupled with his recruitment by the CIC after his emigration to the United States; this more than likely meant that he was exposed and vulnerable to intelligence about Nazi crimes and activities during World War II. For a more detailed account that convincingly and sensitively rehabilitates Penham, see Remy, *Heidelberg Myth*, 146–55, 161–76, 242–44.

121. Daniel Penham, "Report to 307th Counter-Intelligence Corps Detachment Headquarters Seventh United States Army," February 23, 1946, 7, box 8, Marshall Research Library, VA, cited in Clark, "Prophet without Honor," 54.

122. The timing of these events—at the end of winter 1946, during the deprivations of the so-called Hunger Winter—may have played a role in the students' disgruntlement.

123. Unless otherwise remarked on, references to Penham's memorandum to the CIC and the documents that followed in response to his missive are taken from the appendix ("Anhang: Dokumente") in Heß, Lehmann, and Sellin, *Heidelberg 1945*, 391–432, here 423.

124. Shepard Stone, "Report on the Mood of Germany: An Observer Finds Many of the People Unchanged, but a Few Who Seek the Road to Democracy," *New York Times*, January 26, 1947, 8, 49, 51–53.

125. Ibid., 8.

126. Ibid.

127. Ibid., 8, 49.

128. Shepard Stone, "Germany's Guilt-Complex: An Analysis and a Cure," *New York Times*, February 8, 1948, 3, 28, here 28.

129. Saul K. Padover, "The Failure of Reeducation of Germany," in *The Dilemma of Postwar Germany* (New York: H. W. Wilson, 1948), 180–92, here 190–91.

130. Clark, "Prophet without Honor," 211.

131. Alexander Mitscherlich to Karl Jaspers, January 7, 1946, Letter number 75.13118, Jaspers Estate, Deutsches Literaturarchiv, Marbach, cited in Clark, "Prophet without Honor," 211.

132. Ibid., 211–13.

133. Jaspers and his wife were prepared to commit suicide together should it be necessary, rather than submit to separation, humiliation, and certain death through deportation to a concentration camp. That this fear was no dramatic fantasy on their part is attested to by the fact that the Jaspers' deportation to Ravensbrück concentration camp was scheduled for April 1945; only the American occupation of Heidelberg intervened to save them. This fact is included in most accounts of Jaspers' life and work, including essays by Clark and Rabinbach and the intellectual biographies of Jaspers by Suzanne Kirkbright and Matthias Bormuth.

134. For an existential account of the National Socialist period and the immediate postwar period from the perspective of Gertrud Jaspers, see Kirkbright, *Karl Jaspers*, 190–93.

135. Karl Jaspers, "Philosophical Autobiography," 61. "Ich habe mit meiner Frau wohl innerlich diese Bedrohung des leiblichen Daseins, ohne sich wehren zu können, durch lange Jahre erfahren. Äußerlich sind wir ohne Schaden davongekommen. Der Abtransport war [. . .] für den 14. April 1945 vorgesehen. [. . .] Am 1. April wurde Heidelberg von den Amerikanern besetzt." Jaspers, "Philosophische Autobiographie," 49.

136. It may come as a surprise, considering Jaspers' reputation as a mandarin, that with approximately forty broadcasts to his name, most of which were recorded by Radio Basel, Jaspers ties with H. G. Gadamer for third place in terms of postwar intellectual contributions to the public sphere by way of radio and television appearances. First place goes, of course, to Max Horkheimer, who leads by a long stretch, with 194 appearances; Theodor W. Adorno is in second place, with 119; third place goes to Heidegger, with forty-six public talks and television appearances. "Die Massenmedien und die Frankfurter Schule," in Clemens Albrecht, Günter C. Behrmann, Michael Bock, Harald Homann, and Friedrich H. Tenbruck, *Die intellektuelle Gründung der Bundesrepublik: Eine Wirkungsgeschichte der Frankfurter Schule* (Frankfurt am Main: Campus, 1999), 202–46, here 228–29. In a brief but enthusiastic essay, Paul Meyer-

Gutzwiller, who oversaw Jaspers' contributions to Radio Basel, describes Jaspers' recognition of the increasing importance of developing technologies for transmitting one's "message" to a larger audience, as well as his ability to break down his philosophical ideas in the hope of making philosophy accessible to everyone. Meyer-Gutzwiller, "Karl Jaspers und der Rundfunk," 169–71.

137. My translations. The original reads, "für eine Jüdin sei es sehr schwer, hier zu leben"; "Gleichgültigkeit, mit der man dem Judenmassenmord und der Judenfrage überhaupt gegenüberstehe"; "Ruhe und Freiheit"; "einzige objective Verpflichtung"; "Im Dienste der Wahrheit an der abendländischen, übernationalen Idee der Universität deutscher Sprache zu wirken." Jaspers, "Von Heidelberg," in *Erinnerungen an Karl Jaspers [Gertrud Jaspers zum 95. Geburtstag am 26.2.1974]*, ed. Hans Saner and Klaus Piper (Munich: Piper, 1974), 178–79.

138. My translation. "Was uns forttrieb war klar: Das Ausbleiben der Konsequenzen des Massenmords an Juden—der radikale Abstand vom totalen Verbrecherstaat—meine Isolierung in der Universitätsbestrebung—die Feindseligkeit der Regierung—eine Überbeanspruchung durch vergebliche Bemühungen—eine Minderung der Kraft meines philosophischen Arbeitens." Ibid., 180.

139. Ibid., 166–67.

140. My translation. "Wenn ich Ihre Wirksamkeit als Schriftsteller der Zeit ernst nehme, dann muss ich sagen, dass mich Ihre Erklärung und das Schweigen zu den entscheidenen Punkten beleidigt. [. . .] Diese Missachtung Ihrer bisherigen, schicksalsmässig Ihnen zugewiesenen Umgebung, dass Sie sie nämlich nicht ernst genug nehmen, um sie wahrhaftig anzusprechen, sondern, dass Sie sie diplomatisch behandeln, und das heist taktisch, werden Ihnen viele Freunde in Deutschland nicht so rasch verzeihen." Alexander Mitscherlich to Karl Jaspers in Zurich, March 31, 1948, Briefe an Karl Jaspers von Alexander Mitscherlich, 1942–1952 (+1583), Letter number 75.13118, Jaspers Estate, Deutsches Literaturarchiv, Marbach.

141. There were, thankfully, exceptions to this, and in the period leading up to his decision, many people and institutions attempted to win Jaspers over in the hope that he would remain in Heidelberg. One such missive was a well-written, earnest, and balanced request written on January 8, 1948, on behalf of student signatories (more than 425 signatures were attached to the letter) and on the official paper of the "Allgemeiner Studentenausschuss der Universität Heidelberg," in box 11: Biographisches XIII, Weggang von Heidelberg, Jaspers Estate, Deutsches Literaturarchiv, Marbach.

142. My translation. "Der Philosoph der im Scheitern sich erfüllenden tragischen Existenz hat sich mittlerweile bereits eilig in die Schweiz aufgemacht und sich damit aus der Misere des deutschen Nachkriegs-Alltags davongemacht." H.N., "Jaspers," *Rheinischer Merkur*, no. 14, April 3, 1948. Emil Belzner, "Mit Schuldigem Respekt gegangen," *Rhein-Neckar-Zeitung* (n.d., n.p.), box 11: Biographisches XIII, Weggang von Heidelberg, Jaspers Estate, Deutsches Literaturarchiv, Marbach.

143. After an NDR (Norddeutscher Rundfunk) television appearance on the Panorama-Sendung on January 2, 1967, during which Jaspers criticized West Germany for electing former Nazi Party member Kurt Georg Kiesinger as chancellor, calling him a National Socialist, Jaspers was called "die deutsche Kassandra von Basel" in the press. Kurt Gehrmann, "Jaspers' Paukenschlag," *Neue-Rheinisch-Zeitung*, January 4, 1967, box 39: Politische Schriften I/Verschieden, Fernsehinterview "Panorama," Jas-

pers Estate, Deutsches Literatur Archiv, Marbach. In addition to critical press attention, Jaspers received a slew of vile, frequently anti-Semitic responses mainly sent from German addresses. For instance, on an anonymous postcard dated 1967 and with a Nuremberg postmark, the addresser writes, "Wie können Sie ehemaliger Naziaspirant, der wie kein anderer Heidelberger Professor die Hand zum Nazigruß hochriss, Ihr eigenes Nest so beschmutzen! Nun, ein Lump waren Sie immer schon u, bleiben es bis Sie verrecken!" (How dare you, a former aspiring Nazi, who raised his hand in the Nazi greeting like no other Heidelberg professor, foul your own nest in this way!). My translation. Box 39, Jaspers Estate, Deutsches Literaturarchiv, Marbach. The combination of historical misinformation, Nazi rhetoric, and the use of the formal "Sie" in addressing Jaspers form a particularly toxic cocktail.

144. The postcard was sent to Jaspers' home address at Plöck 60, Heidelberg. Box 11: Biographisches XIII, Weggang von Heidelberg, Jaspers Estate, Deutsches Literaturarchiv, Marbach.

145. Jaspers, "Von Heidelberg," 173.

146. The term *emotional refuge* is taken from Reddy, *Navigating Feeling.*

147. Jaspers, *German Guilt*, 33; *Schuldfrage*, 32.

148. Ahmed notes, "The word 'shame' comes from the Indo-European word for 'to cover,' which associates shame with other words such as 'hide,' 'custody,' 'house' and 'hut.'" Ahmed, *Cultural Politics of Emotion*, 101–21, here 104–5.

149. Ibid.

150. "Goethe-Preis für Karl Jaspers," *Abendpost*, August 28, 1947, 3.

151. My translation. "Die mit ihrer Unwiderstehlichkeit ihres sachlichen Gehalts, mit der fruchtbaren Milde des allen Möglichkeiten verstehenden Richters unser Schicksal an den rechten Platz rückt und uns zur Anerkennung unseres eigenen Seins zwingt." Ibid., 1.

152. Arendt, "Organized Guilt," 154.

153. Ibid., 154–55.

154. Johannes R. Becher, "Deutsches Bekenntnis," *Aufbau* 1 (1945): 649–50, cited in Helmut Peitsch, *Nachkriegsliteratur 1945–1989* (Göttingen: Vandenhoeck und Ruprecht, 2009), 77.

155. Peitsch, *Nachkriegsliteratur*, 76. For Aleida Assmann's differentiated and theoretically engaging account of shame and guilt (and trauma) in this immediate postwar period, see part 1 in Assmann and Frevert, *Geschichtsvergessenheit/Geschichtsversessenheit*, 17–147.

156. Ruth Benedict, *The Chrysanthemum and the Sword: Patterns of Japanese Culture* (Boston: Houghton Mifflin, 1946). See also Wolfgang Schivelbusch, *The Culture of Defeat: On National Trauma, Mourning, and Recovery*, trans. Jefferson Chase (New York: Metropolitan Books, 2003).

157. Peitsch touches on how all of these terms came up in another context during a discussion of guilt at the Berlin Authors' Congress (Berliner Schriftstellerverband) in 1947. Peitsch, *Nachkriegsliteratur*, 76.

158. Clark, "Prophet without Honor," 197; Wolin, "Karl Jaspers: The Paradoxes of Mandarin Humanism," in *Frankfurt School Revisited*, 144–45.

159. Karl Jaspers earns no fewer than a dozen much-deserved references in Fritz Ringer's seminal text on the complexities and ultimately politically dangerous elitism

of what might be called the professorial "academic class" in Germany prior to World War II. Fritz Ringer, *Decline of the German Mandarins: The German Academic Community, 1890–1933* (Cambridge, MA: Harvard University Press, 1969).

160. For a detailed account of Jaspers' involvement in the restructuring of Heidelberg University, see Klaus von Beyme, "Karl Jaspers—Vom philosophischen Außenseiter zum *Praeceptor Germaniae*," in Heß, Lehmann, and Sellin, *Heidelberg 1945*, 130–48. See also Clark, "Prophet without Honor," 203–9.

161. My translation. "Sie [die Anklageschrift] wird in diesen Tagen in der ganzen Welt eifrig gelesen, mit Erschrecken, mit Haß, mit Bitterkeit, mit Scham." Theodor Heuss, "Anklageschrift Nürnberg," *Rhein-Neckar-Zeitung* 1.15, October 24, 1945, 1–2, box 26: Schuldfrage; Briefe zu Undset; Zeitspanschnitte u.a., Jaspers Estate, Deutsches Literaturarchiv, Marbach.

162. My translation. "Es wäre gut, diese Geschichten würden bald aufgeräumt— dann wird die Luft in Deutschland wieder freier werden können. Ehe es soweit ist, müssen wir mit kühler Klarheit durch die Auseinandersetzung hindurch. Sentimentalität ist dabei nicht erlaubt." Ibid.

163. Jaspers to Arendt, March 12, 1946, in *Correspondence*, 34.

164. Jaspers to Arendt, September 18, 1946, in *Correspondence*, 58.

165. Ibid., 58–59.

166. Interview of October 28, 1964, "'What Remains? The Language Remains': A Conversation with Günter Gaus," in *Essays in Understanding, 1930–1954*, ed. Jerome Kohn (New York: Harcourt Brace, 1994), 12–13.

167. Jaspers to Arendt, August 19, 1950, in *Correspondence*, 154–55, cited in Remy, *Heidelberg Myth*, 222.

CHAPTER 2

The opening epigraphs are from Hannah Arendt, "The Aftermath of Nazi Rule," in *Essays in Understanding*, 266; and Hocking, *Experiment in Education*, 60.

1. Thomas H. Minshall, "The Problem of Germany," *International Affairs* 20.1 (1944): 3–18, here 9.

2. *OED Online*, http://www.oed.com/, accessed July 3, 2013.

3. See chapter 1, note 18, in this book.

4. The process of denazification quickly became a technical and political process, rather than a moral and just one. By the beginning of 1946, realizing the enormity of the task of denazification and wanting to give the process more credibility in the eyes of the German population, the US Office of Military Government (OMGUS) passed the Law for Liberation from National Socialism, officially handing over responsibility for the conduct of denazification hearings to the Germans under American supervision. This signaled a shift in the attitude toward the German population on the part of OMGUS, to a less punitive, rehabilitative ("soft") stance. Over twenty-two thousand German staff members und German lay judges went to work in what was known colloquially as the German *Spruchkammern*, which constituted a network of 525 "verdict courts," or, more literally translated, "slogan" chambers. In August 1946, the military governor of the American zone, Lucius Clay, issued an amnesty to all those born after January 1, 1919.

In addition to sheer logistical problems, such as where to store the masses of accumulated paper, the initial process of automatic arrest due to membership in the NSDAP meant that too many people were either excluded or suspended from the workforce pending their hearings. In fact, the number of indictable Nazis in the US zone comprised 27 percent of the adult population, which meant that it would be impossible to carry out denazification in an efficient and rapid manner. Further, many of the respondents were skilled wage earners in a depleted labor market, and by 1947, it became clear to Clay, in the face of the misery and hunger of the German population, that the priority of OMGUS should be ensuring that Germany had a functioning economy. (After the youth amnesty, there remained approximately three million people to be charged and a significant backlog of those currently indicted and awaiting their hearings.) Clay announced a second wave of amnesties at the end of 1946, this time based on categories of low income and disability. This reduced the number of Germans indicted by 2.5 million. The growing tension between the East and West zones created a situation in which the Americans needed a reconstructed and functional zone in quick order, to avoid losing Germany—and thus part of Western Europe—to the Soviet Union. Contemporary surveys revealed that German support for denazification, which originally had been surprisingly high, with 57 percent of the German population content with the process early in 1946, began to wane later in that year, coinciding with the introduction of the German-run *Spruchkammern*. In 1946, only 32 percent of Germans were content with the progress of denazification, and by 1949, only 17 percent thought that denazification was going well. Since 30 percent of Germans wanted OMGUS to take over the process of denazification again at the beginning of 1947, there appears to be a direct correlation between this and the shift from intimidation to laxity in the *Spruchkammern*, accompanied by a growing sense of the futility of this measure among the German population. In the final days of the denazification program, OMGUS was eager to have the process over and done with, particularly since they did not want the West German government to be placed in an embarrassing situation on the eve of its formation. However, due to circumstances such as the ongoing arrival of expellees and POWs, the denazification process continued until April 1952, some seven years after the war's end. In the final instance, according to Perry Biddiscombe, more than thirteen million Germans were registered, and by 1950, 958,000 had been tried; however, of those tried, twenty-five thousand or less were rated as "major offender" or "offender." More than twenty-three thousand people were banned from public office, over twenty-seven thousand people had their property confiscated, and thirty thousand received sentences of community work. See Julian Bach Jr., *America's Germany: An Account of the Occupation* (New York: Random House, 1946); Clay, *Decision in Germany*; Hocking, *Experiment in Education*; Saul K. Padover, *Experiment in Germany: The Story of an American Intelligence Officer* (New York: Duell, Sloan and Pearce, 1946); Harold Zink, *American Military Government in Germany* (New York: MacMillan, 1947); Uta Gerhardt, "A Hidden Agenda of Recovery: The Psychiatric Conceptualization of Re-education for Germany in the United States during World War II," *German History* 14.3 (1996): 297–324; Uta Gerhardt, *Soziologie der Stunde Null: Zur Gesellschaftskonzeption des amerikanischen Besatzungsregimes in Deutschland 1944–45/1946* (Frankfurt am Main: Suhrkamp, 2005); Perry Biddiscombe, *The Denazification of Germany: A History, 1945–1950* (Stroud, Gloucestershire: Tempus, 2007); Anna J. Merritt and Richard L.

Merritt, *Public Opinion in Occupied Germany: The OMGUS Surveys, 1945–1949* (Urbana: University of Illinois Press, 1970); Richard L. Merritt, *Democracy Imposed: U.S. Occupation Policy and the German Public, 1945–1949* (New Haven: Yale University Press, 1995); Olick, *In the House of the Hangman*; Tent, *Mission on the Rhine*.

5. For an analysis of the frequency of public discussions of guilt and persecution in postwar newspapers in Berlin, for example, see Ursula Heukenkamp, "Schuld und Verfolgung in den Berliner Zeitschriften der Nachkriegszeit," in *Der 8. Mai 1945 als historische Zäsur: Strukturen, Erfahrungen, Deutungen*, ed. Arnd Bauerkämper, Christoph Kleßmann, and Hans Misselwitz (Potsdam: Brandenburgische Landeszentrale für politische Bildung, 1995), 218–31.

6. For a brief history of the Allied book policy for Germany and their information control, see John B. Hench, *Books as Weapons: Propaganda, Publishing, and the Battle for Global Markets in the Era of World War II* (Ithaca: Cornell University Press, 2010), 230–33.

7. For a thorough and convincing argument refuting the absence of nationalism in postwar Germany, see Jörg Echternkamp, "'Verwirrung im Vaterländischen'? Nationalismus in der deutschen Nachkriegsgesellschaft, 1945–1960," in *Die Politik der Nation: Deutscher Nationalismus in Krieg und Krisen, 1760–1960*, ed. Jörg Echternkamp and Sven Oliver Müller (Munich: R. Oldenburg, 2002), 219–46.

8. Jost Hermand also notes that the strong expression of *ressentiment* against the US-Allied occupiers in von Salomon's book made it popular with the contemporary German readership. Jost Hermand, "Ernst von Salomons Romane 'Der Fragebogen' (1951) und 'Das Schicksal des A.D.' (1960)," in *Weiter schreiben—Wieder schreiben: Deutschsprachige Literatur der fünfziger Jahre; Festschrift für Günter Händtzschel*, ed. Günter Händtzschel, Adrian Hummel, and Sigrid Nieberle (Munich: Iudicium, 2004), 130–42, here 137–38.

9. Friedrich Nietzsche, *On the Genealogy of Morals*, in *Basic Writings of Nietzsche*, trans. and ed. Walter Kaufmann (New York: Modern Library, 2000), 563–64.

10. Friedrich Nietzsche, *Beyond Good and Evil*, in *Basic Writings*, especially 394–400.

11. Nietzsche, *Genealogy*, 510.

12. Ibid., 472.

13. Max Scheler, *Das Ressentiment im Aufbau der Moralen* (1912), trans. William W. Holdhelm as *Ressentiment*, ed. Lewis A. Coser (New York: Free Press of Glencoe, 1961).

14. Ibid., 47.

15. Ibid., 48.

16. Ibid., 51.

17. Ibid., 45, 50.

18. Ibid., 137.

19. Feminist theorists in the late twentieth and early twenty-first centuries have also critiqued the structures of neoliberal legal and social compensation as productive of a kind of Nietzschean *ressentiment* that ultimately threatens to reduce politics to acts of reparation. In short, these theorists demonstrate and critique the consequences of the ways in which "woundedness" has become a resource for identity politics. For a critique of how the logic of *ressentiment* found in neoliberal capitalist society has, in many

ways, clipped the wings of political imagination, see Wendy Brown, *States of Injury: Power and Freedom in Late Modernity* (Princeton: Princeton University Press, 1995). For a critique of *ressentiment* as a structure in feminism itself, see Janet E. Halley, *Split Decisions: How and Why to Take a Break from Feminism* (Princeton: Princeton University Press, 2006).

20. Scheler, *Ressentiment*, 122.

21. Ibid., 144.

22. Ibid., 45–50.

23. The edition I am referring to is a reprint from 2007, which continues to be published by Rowohlt in its rororo mass-market paperback line: Ernst von Salomon, *Der Fragebogen* (Hamburg: Rowohlt, 2007). The first edition of the text was published in 1951 and became an immediate best seller, going through many editions in the following ten years. The initial book version of *Der Fragebogen* was approximately eight hundred pages in length and cost DM 19.90, a tidy sum for a book in 1951.

24. The English language version I refer to is Ernst von Salomon, *The Answers of Ernst von Salomon to the 131 Questions in the Allied Military Government "Fragebogen,"* trans. Constantine Fitzgibbon (London: Putnam, 1954).

25. See Michael Wildt, *An Uncompromising Generation: The Nazi Leadership of the Reich Security Main Office*, trans. Tom Lampert (Madison: University of Wisconsin Press, 2009).

26. For analysis of Ernst von Salomon's writings in the Weimar period in relation to emotion, fascism, gender, the body, and violence, see Klaus Theweleit, *Male Fantasies*, vol. 1, *Women, Floods, Bodies, History*, trans. Stephen Conway (Minneapolis: University of Minnesota Press, 1987), and vol. 2, *Male Bodies: Psychoanalyzing the White Terror*, trans. Erica Carter and Chris Turner (Minneapolis: University of Minnesota Press, 1989). For a detailed political biography that is sympathetic to von Salomon, see Markus Josef Klein, *Ernst von Salomon: Eine politische Biographie mit einer vollständigen Bibliographie* (Limburg an der Lahn: San Casciano, 1994).

27. Ibid., 108.

28. For a romanticized fictional version of this historical movement, which was highly praised by Ernst von Salomon in his 1932 book *Die Stadt*, see Hans Fallada, *Bauern, Bonzen und Bomben* (Reinbek: Rowohlt, 1931), trans. Michael Hofmann as *A Small Circus* (London: Penguin, 2012). For a critique of Fallada's whitewashing of the *Landvolkbewegung*, see Ellis Shookman, "Making History in Hans Fallada's 'Bauern, Bonzen und Bomben': Schleswig-Holstein, Nazism, and the 'Landvolkbewegung,'" *German Studies Review* 13.3 (1990): 461–80.

29. Equating the US occupation with National Socialism seems to have been a prominent feature of postwar society. For example, see John Gimbel, *A German Community under American Occupation: Marburg, 1945–52* (Stanford: Stanford University Press, 1961), 177.

30. Ralf Heyer, *"Verfolgte Zeugen der Wahrheit": Das literarische Schaffen und das politische Wirken konservativen Autoren nach 1945 am Beispiel von Friedrich Georg Jünger, Ernst Jünger, Ernst von Salomon, Stefan Andres, und Reinhold Schneider* (Dresden: Thelem, 2008), 152–61, here 158.

31. Von Salomon, *Answers*, 233. "Überraschend aber war die Vehemenz, mit der Hitler die 'Rassenfrage' und mit ihr im engsten Zusammenhang die Bekämpfung des

Judentumes in den Mittelpunkt aller seiner Reden und Betrachtungen stellte." Von Salomon, *Fragebogen*, 335.

32. Von Salomon, *Answers*, 20–23; *Fragebogen*, 26–27.

33. Von Salomon, *Answers*, 22. "Heute jedenfalls sind meine Haare von einer so gut wie undefinierbaren, dunkelstaubigen Farbe, jedes einzelne zeigt eine gewisse Tendenz zum Grau und ich bemerke täglich mit Betrübnis, wie diese Tendenz immer mehr zum Siege schreitet, nicht ohne gleichzeitig, wie jeder Sieg, starke Anzeichen einer generellen Selbstauflösung der Substanz, also ein deutlich nihilistisches Gebaren aufzuweisen." Von Salomon, *Fragebogen*, 41.

34. Another example is von Salomon's response to the category "Gewicht" (weight), which receives the response "schwankend" (fluctuating), accompanied by a page-long description of the author's opinion on weight: "Es war mein Ehrgeiz, einmal im Leben ein Gewicht von 200 Pfund zu erreichen. Es ist mir nie gelungen. [. . .] Ich bin gerne dick. Ich habe nur in meinen behäbigen Zeiten bereitwillig Kredit gefunden, ich habe nie so behaglich gearbeitet wie im Gefühl auch körperlicher Fülle, und ich habe die Erfahrung gemacht, daß Frauen zu dicken Männern vorzugsweise zutraulich sind." Von Salomon, *Fragebogen*, 38–40.

35. Von Salomon, *Answers*, 290. "Ich hoffe, daß sich die Militärregierung ihrerseits des Vergnügens nicht enthalten kann, den einzigen Menschen in der ganzen Welt, der ihren Fragebogen wirklich ernst nimmt, unter Anklage zu stellen und zu bestrafen." Von Salomon, *Fragebogen*, 388. The negative form has been mistakenly omitted in the English translation, therefore I have amended the citation by including "[not]."

36. Von Salomon, *Answers*, 128. "Je mehr ich mich in diesen Fragebogen verstricke, desto öfter werde ich, ziemlich widerwillig, zu unangenehmen Geständnissen gezwungen." Von Salomon, *Fragebogen*, 208.

37. Von Salomon, *Answers*, 1–2. "Um von vornherein allen Ansprüchen zu genügen, die an mich auch in diesem Falle gestellt werden, möchte ich sogleich mitteilen, daß die Lektüre aller dieser Fragebogen stets die gleiche Wirkung hatte: sie löste in mir eine Reihe von Gefühlen aus, deren erstes und stärkstes das eines durchdringenden Unbehagens war. Wenn ich mich bemühe, dieses Gefühl genau zu bestimmen, so gelange ich dahin, es ehestens mit dem eines ertappten Schuljungen zu vergleichen, eines sehr jungen Menschen also, der erst zu Beginn seiner Erfahrungen mit jenen großen und drohenden Mächten steht, die sich ihm als Gesetz, Sitte, Ordnung und Moral darstellen. Er kann die Welt in ihrer Berechtigung, so zu sein, wie sie ist, noch nicht kennen, er hat ein gutes Gewissen, wenn er glaubt, mit ihr so weit in Einklang zu sein, und ein schlechtes, wenn dies nicht der Fall ist. Und er kann auch nicht wissen, daß sehr wohl einmal der Augenblick kommen wird, da er das berauschende Glück erfährt, diese Welt mit ihren Einrichtungen vor seinem eigenen Gewissen als schlecht zu empfinden, schlecht und von Grund auf neu zu gründen." Von Salomon, *Fragebogen*, 6.

38. Norbert Muhlen, "America and American Occupation in German Eyes," *Annals of the American Academy of Political and Social Science* 295 (1954): 52–61, here 56.

39. This citation refers, of course, to the title of Hannah Arendt's postwar collection of biographical essays on culturally and politically significant men and women, such as Lessing and Jaspers, and their response to their politico-cultural habitus, *Men in Dark Times* (1970). Needless to say, one would search in vain in that volume for an essay devoted to von Salomon.

40. Von Salomon, *Answers*, 2. "Nun bin ich infolge von Umständen, die in der Antwort auf die Frage 19 dieses Fragebogens behandelt werden müssen, in keiner Weise legitimiert, mich über Fragen des Gewissens gültig auszulassen. Nicht ich bin es, der es wünscht, dies zu tun. Aber wie soll ich die gesamte Einrichtung des Fragebogens anders auffassen als einen modernen Versuch, mich zu einer Gewissenserforschung zu bewegen?" Von Salomon, *Fragebogen*, 6.

41. Von Salomon, *Answers*, 2. "Denn nicht die katholische Kirche ist es, die in Fragen der Erforschung meines Gewissens an mich herangetreten ist, sondern eine Institution, weitaus weniger bewundenswürdig, die Alliierte Militärregierung. [. . .] Es waren Vertreter der Alliierten Militärregierung, Männer in schmucken Uniformen und mit vielen bunten Auszeichnungen, die mich eindringlich darauf aufmerksam machten, daß, die Frage nach dem Gewissen sich vor jedem Tun nicht zu stellen, eines Mannes unwürdig sei. Sie saßen vor mir, einer nach dem anderen, sympathische und gepflegte junge Leute, und sie sprachen schlicht und selbstverständlich von einer so großen Sache wie dem Gewissen, und ich bewunderte sie wegen ihrer apodiktischen Sicherheit und beneidete sie um die Geschlossenheit ihres Weltbildes." Von Salomon, *Fragebogen*, 6.

42. Von Salomon, *Answers*, 2. "Sie naht mir nicht wie der Geistliche dem armen Sünder in der von der Welt abgeschiedenen Zelle des Beichtstühles, sie sendet mir den Fragebogen ins Haus und beginnt sofort barschen Tones wie ein Untersuchungsrichter gegenüber dem Verbrecher mit einer Flut von 131 Fragen, sie fordern von mir kalt und knapp nichts weniger als die Wahrheit und droht gleich zweimal, am Anfang und am Ende des Fragebogens mit Strafen, deren Art und Ausmaß ich (siehe auch unter 'Bemerkungen') herzlich zu fürchten nicht umhin kann." Von Salomon, *Fragebogen*, 6.

43. Von Salomon, *Answers*, 3. "Angesichts des gesamten Tenors dieses Fragebogens und in Kenntnis der Tatsache, daß fast jeder Deutsche zumindest der westlichen Teile unseres Landes gehalten ist, ihn auszufüllen, muß ich geschärften Gewissens endlich die Befürchtung hegen, teilzuhaben an einem Akte, der unter seinen nicht kontrollierbaren Zuständen doch geeignet sein kann, einem Lande und einem Volke, dem ich unausweichlich angehöre, zu schaden im Auftrag fremder Mächte, die ihre Herrschaft ausüben lediglich durch die historische Tatsache des deutschen Zusammenbruchs und auf Grund einer Abmachung, die geschlossen wurde mit Männern, von denen ihre Partner von vornherein annahmen, daß sie Verbrecher seien." Von Salomon, *Fragebogen*, 7.

44. Grimm, the national conservative author of the notorious book *Volk ohne Raum* (1926), invited to the meeting poets and writers who had written and published about their own experiences on the battlefield in World War I; he hoped that he could rally them to defend a particular nationalist version of Germanness, informed by his own *Bildungsbürgertum*, over and against the brutishness and violence of the National Socialists. Von Salomon did not agree with this position, not least because of his self-proclaimed aversion to the upper middle class and what he saw as superannuated cultural values. Von Salomon, *Fragebogen*, 193–202.

45. Von Salomon, *Answers*, 118. "In meinem Herzen aber glühte nicht besonders viel mehr als eine unbändige Lust am Leben." Von Salomon, *Fragebogen*, 197.

46. Von Salomon, *Answers*, 101. "Ich, ich bin kein Bekenner, ich bin ein leidenschaftlich beteiligter Betrachter. So wurde ich kein Nationalsozialist." Von Salomon, *Fragebogen*, 178.

47. Von Salomon, *Answers*, 190. "Der deutsche Film war neutral. Er mußte es sein. Die Neutralität aufgeben, hieß sich selbst aufgeben." Von Salomon, *Fragebogen*, 293.

48. Von Salomon, *Answers*, 191. "Der deutsche Film war neutrales Ausland." Von Salomon, *Fragebogen*, 294.

49. For a book on film in the Third Reich that stages a definitive counterargument to von Salomon's claim, see Eric Rentschler, *The Ministry of Illusion: Nazi Cinema and Its Afterlife* (Cambridge, MA: Harvard University Press, 1996). By contrast, in a letter by von Salomon from 1940 to author Hans Grimm, von Salomon says exactly the opposite, specifying just how political and propagandistic the monopoly German film business UFA was under Nazi direction: "Minister Goebbels sagte einmal als Richtschnur für die Filmarbeit, Kunst sei Propaganda. Ich möchte diese Ansicht sogar zu meiner eigenen machen, mit dem Hinweis, dass gute Kunst bessere Propaganda ist. Der Film [. . .] ist ein Mittel der Massenbeherrschung und der Meinungsbildung." ("Minister Goebbels once stated as a guideline for work in film that art is propaganda. I actually would like to make this point of view my own, adding that good art is better propaganda. Film [. . .] is a medium for controlling the masses and for opinion making.") Ernst von Salomon to Hans Grimm, December 30, 1940. Grimm Estate. Deutsches Literaturarchiv, Marbach. Cited in David Oels, *Rowohlts Rotationsroutine: Markterfolge und Modernisierung eines Buchverlags vom Ende der Weimarer Republik bis in die fünfziger Jahre* (Essen: Klartext, 2013), 355–79, here 366.

50. Von Salomon, *Answers*, 191. "Der Film vertrage keine Tendenz." Von Salomon, *Fragebogen*, 293.

51. Von Salomon, *Answers*, 195. "Nach einem vorsichtigen Überschlag bedarf ich dazu, ohne Wesentliches auszulassen, der Muße und des Papiers für etwa tausend Seiten, die ich auf Anforderung natürlich jederzeit gern nachzureichen bereit bin. Aber vielleicht genügt es wirklich, in diesem Falle entgegen den Gepflogenheiten alliierter Militärgerichtshöfe die Beweislast eben jenen Herren von der Militärregierung zuzuschieben, die, mit dem Donnerkeil der strengen Gewissensforderung ausgestattet, getrost zu fragen vermögen: 'Was haben Sie in den neun Jahren von 1936 bis 1945 getan?' Dann, glaube ich, darf ich mich an meinen alten Meister Rowohlt erinnern, meinen Oberkörper hin und her wiegen wie ein Eisbär und mit satter, strahlender Miene beruhigt sagen: 'Ho, ho . . . mir kann nichts passieren! Ich war beim Film!'" Von Salomon, *Fragebogen*, 300.

52. Von Salomon, *Answers*, 524. "Nun, ich bin Filmautor geworden, da verdiente ich etwa dreimal so viel wie ein Gauleiter." Von Salomon, *Fragebogen*, 645.

53. Hocking, *Experiment in Education*, 65.

54. Ibid., 67.

55. Martin Lindner classifies the protagonists of von Salomon's fiction as heroes of "Neue Sachlichkeit" (New Objectivity), which might be difficult to prove in the case of *Der Fragebogen*. Although the book contains traces of that writing style's unflinching objectivity, its hero is, in many ways, both too absurd and too phlegmatic to be counted among von Salomon's earlier, more extreme and tortured protagonists. See Martin Lindner, *Leben in der Krise: Zeitromane der Neuen Sachlichkeit und die intellektuelle Mentalität der klassischen Moderne mit einer exemplarischen Analyse des Romanwerks von Arnolt Bronnen, Ernst Glaeser, Ernst von Salomon und Ernst Erich Noth* (Stuttgart: Metzler, 1994), 276–304. See also Richard Herzinger, "Eine extremistischer

Zuschauer; Ernst von Salomon: Konservativ-revolutionäre Literatur zwischen Tatrhetorik und Resignation," *Zeitschrift für Germanistik* 8.1 (1998): 83–96.

56. For example, see von Salomon, *Fragebogen*, 178, 182, 194, 212, 242.

57. Von Salomon, *Answers*, 482. "Es wurde eine Art Jux daraus. Ich zog Abend für Abend von Stube zu Stube und lieferte auf den Zuruf einer beliebigen Frage eine mündliche Anlage. [. . .] Es war spirituell gar nicht schwer meinen Verpflichtungen nachzukommen, ich erzählte einfach, was mir zu der betreffenden Frage in den Sinn kam, Billiges und Unbilliges, mich einfach auslaufen lassend." Von Salomon, *Fragebogen*, 595.

58. Von Salomon, *Answers*, 482. "Aber körperlich war es eine große Anstrengung. Seit einigen Tagen spürte ich Schmerzen in der Kehle, und wenn ich mich bemühte, etwas lauter zu reden, kam plötzlich nur heiße Luft. Wenn ich eine der wichtigeren Fragen beantwortet hatte, so kam ich unglaublich zerschlagen und ausgeleert in meine Baracke zurück, mein ganzer Körper war mit einem unangenehmen, kalten Schweiß bedeckt, und ich warf mich keuchend auf mein Bett." Von Salomon, *Fragebogen*, 595.

59. Rosenwein, *Emotional Communities*, 24–25.

60. Reddy, *Navigation of Feeling*, 129.

61. This account is significant because it is part of a larger tendency in non-Jewish German accounts about Jewish persecution by the Nazis. Of all anti-Semitic measures and punishments meted out by the National Socialist regime on Jewish Germans, including the more deadly bureaucratic persecutions, the Night of Broken Glass (Kristallnacht) seems to provide a German collective memory (screen memory?) of kinds and is prominent in the German postwar imagination. See, for example, Paul W. Massing, "Is Every German Guilty? A German Anti-Nazi Fighter Discusses Individual Responsibility," *Commentary* 3.5 (1947): 442–46, here 444–45.

62. Von Salomon, *Answers*, 220. "Wer hat Schuld an alledem?" Von Salomon, *Fragebogen*, 324.

63. Von Salomon, *Answers*, 221. "Was meinst du, wieviel Leute sitzen heute so wie du und ich im hintersten Zimmer bei heruntergelassenen Vorhängen und reden miteinander wie du und ich? Und was meinst du, wieviel Parteimitglieder sind dabei, das gleiche zu tun und zu reden wie du und ich, ehrliche, anständige Parteimitglieder? Das ist heute so ein Tag, der nie vorübergeht, der immer wiederkehrt, der meldet in der Geschichte immer wieder seinen Anspruch an, der trägt den Fluch mit sich, nie vergessen zu werden." Von Salomon, *Fragebogen*, 324–25.

64. Helmut Lethen, *Cool Conduct: The Culture of Distance in Weimar Germany*, trans. Don Reneau (Berkeley: University of California Press, 2002).

65. Assmann and Frevert, *Geschichtsvergessenheit/Geschichtsversessenheit*, 19–147, here 86–96.

66. Another example of this displaced logic of culpability can be found earlier on in von Salomon's text, when von Salomon and Hans Zehrer discuss who is responsible for the demise of the Weimar Republic and the rise of National Socialism: "Wer war eigentlich verantwortlich, wenn nicht jeder von uns? Der Reichspräsident und die Handvoll Männer um ihn herum? [. . .] Die Deutschen von 1932 erfuhren das Dämonium Nationalsozialismus, dessen Wesen der Zwang war, und dem sie sich unterwarfen." Von Salomon, *Fragebogen*, 186. Although von Salomon asks who is guilty, the question is rhetorical in nature and ultimately excludes him from the guilty collective of both those

in power at the time of the National Socialist takeover and the Germans of 1932, since he did not join or support the National Socialist Party. Note, too, his choice of words: National Socialism is equated with the demonic, placing it well beyond the capabilities of mere men to comprehend or halt.

67. Von Salomon, *Answers*, 280. "Wie konnte es kommen, daß alle schuld hatten, daß also niemand schuld hatte? Daß der Triumph des Willens unter seinem Zeichen jeden Willen verkümmern ließ?" Von Salomon, *Fragebogen*, 378.

68. Von Salomon, *Answers*, 281. "Ich weiß natürlich, was mit den Juden geschieht, wäre ich nicht Zeuge, es ist oft genug gesagt worden, was mit ihnen geschehen soll, die Synagogen zeigen, daß es nun wirklich geschieht. Das Entsetzliche ist, das niemand 'den Juden' helfen kann, weil jede Hilfe sie noch mehr gefährdet. Das Entsetzliche ist, daß wir uns selber nicht helfen können, daß viel mehr noch als den Juden uns geschieht." Von Salomon, *Fragebogen*, 379.

69. Von Salomon, *Answers*, 362. "Oh, wir hatten gut gelebt, kein Zweifel! Wir lebten ein bißchen verrückt, aber gut. Wir fraßen und soffen wie die Kapitalisten, aber da wir alles verfraßen und versoffen wie die Proletarier, kommt es auf eins hinaus." Von Salomon, *Fragebogen*, 459.

70. Von Salomon, *Answers*, 362. "Ich bekenne, daß ich kein einziges Mal dabei an die vielen Zeitgenossen dachte, die zur gleichen Zeit in den Konzentrationslagern saßen, so wenig wie die, die nun dort saßen, an mich dachten, als ich im Zuchthaus saß. Axel hob seinen Entlassungsschein aus dem KZ ebensogut auf wie ich meinen Entlassungsschein aus dem Zuchthaus. Man wußte ja nie, ob man diese Papierchen nicht noch einmal eifrig zücken mußte, um sich zu berühmen. Wenn wir sie betrachtet hatten, schmeckte es gleich darauf noch einmal so gut." Von Salomon, *Fragebogen*, 459.

71. Von Salomon, *Answers*, 268. "Vor der grausigen Alternative stehen, entweder dumm zu handeln oder feige." Von Salomon, *Fragebogen*, 368.

72. Von Salomon, *Answers*, 282. "Es mußte, es mußte eine dritte Lösung geben. Und wenn es keine gab,—was war besser: dumm oder feige zu handeln?" Von Salomon, *Fragebogen*, 380.

73. Von Salomon, *Answers*, 283. "Eine Art Gandhismus ohne Gandhi." Von Salomon, *Fragebogen*, 380.

74. Von Salomon, *Answers*, 436. "Was die Krieger vom Kriege erzählten, erweckte den Eindruck, es sei überall ungemein fröhlich zugegangen außer in Rußland, und die Zivilisten waren der Ansicht, der Nationalsozialismus habe doch auch viel Gutes mit sich gebracht, außer in ihrer Fachschaft. Alle miteinander, mich eingeschlossen, hielten das, was den Juden geschah und in den Konzentrationslagern, für eine große Schweinerei, und alle miteinander, mich eingeschlossen, beteuerten, daß sie davon zwar geahnt hätten, aber nicht gewußt, und daß sie nichts dagegen hätten machen können." Von Salomon, *Fragebogen*, 547.

75. Von Salomon, *Answers*, 436. "Es war nicht sehr interessant." Von Salomon, *Fragebogen*, 547.

76. Von Salomon, *Answers*, 500. "Die anderen unterhielten sich von Bett zu Bett, sie unterhielten sich lange und mühselig über den Begriff der 'Schuld.' Schließlich stellte sich heraus, daß alle miteinander eine 'Schuld' für sich ablehnten." Von Salomon, *Fragebogen*, 614.

77. Von Salomon, *Answers*, 517–18. "Ich hatte in diesem Lager über das entsetz-

liche Faktum der physischen Vernichtung des Judentums nicht ein einziges zynisches Wort gehört—außer von Amerikanern. In Nürnberg sammelten sich die Aktenstöße der Anklage; das Material sollte mich ebenso erdrücken wie diese Männer da und jeden im Lager. Ich mußte natürlich annehmen, daß eine ganze Reihe von diesen Männern von der Anklage persönlich getroffen werden mochte—es erschien mir logisch, daß sie der gleichen Willkür unterlagen wie die, welche sie einstmals ausgeübt haben mochten; das Recht ließ sich schließlich aus dem schnellen Prozeß des Volksgerichtshofes so wenig heraussublimieren wie aus den hunderttausend Aktenseiten von Nürnberg. Wichtig war nicht das Maß der Schuld, ihre Menge, sondern der Ort, wo sie Eingang in das Leben fand." Von Salomon, *Fragebogen*, 635.

78. For an analysis of the role of the "Jewish question" in von Salomon's work, including a critique of *Der Fragebogen*, see Ingo Piel, *Die Judenverfolgung in autobiographischer Literatur: Erinnerungstexte nichtjüdischer Deutscher nach 1945* (Frankfurt am Main: Peter Lang, 2001), 57–78.

79. Even postwar popular fiction drew on this trope of the returned and vengeful Jewish-German, as is portrayed by the self-destructive, vengeful US-Allied officer Felix Lessing in popular author Will Berthold's book *Die wilden Jahre* (Munich: Desch, 1964). For a historical account of these reactions, see John Gimbel, *A German Community under American Occupation: Marburg, 1945–52* (Stanford: Stanford University Press, 1961).

80. Von Salomon, *Answers*, 518. "Es mußte dies aber genau der Punkt sein, an welchem sich die Aufgabe mit dem Gewissen schnitt. Er wurde als solcher auch bei jedem Einzelnen empfunden. Auf welchem Wege auch immer der Einzelne zur Bewegung gestoßen war, das Judenproblem war als vorhanden gewußt worden. Aber praktisch lag es kaum in einem Falle im Bereiche der eigenen Aufgabe. Es griff nur ununterbrochen in die einzelnen Sektoren hinein. Für den Einzelnen ergab sich in solchen Fällen zu gegebenem Zeitpunkt die Frage der Abmessung, nämlich, in welchem Verhältnis die jeweils geforderte Maßnahme in ihrer—fast immer erkannten, aber nicht in ihrer Eigenschaft als Stufe eines weiterführenden Prozesses durchschauten— 'Unzulänglichkeit' zu der Durchführung der eigentlichen Aufgabe stand. Ich mußte dies annehmen; die Darstellung war aufrichtig. Aber gerade das hieß nichts anderes, als daß im Bereich jedes Einzelnen die schrecklichste Korruption eingeführt wurde, die vor dem Gewissen denkbar ist, die Korruption durch die Frage nach dem kleineren Übel." Von Salomon, *Fragebogen*, 635.

81. Nietzsche, *Genealogy*, 517.

82. Ibid., 554.

83. Von Salomon, *Answers*, 428. "Es ist uns gut gegangen, Ille, wir dürfen keine Ressentiments haben. Wir gehören zu den Wenigen, die keine Ressentiments haben dürfen. Gerade darum ist es unsere Pflicht, fortan das Vernünftige zu fordern, nichts als das Vernünftige!" Von Salomon, *Fragebogen*, 538.

84. Von Salomon, *Answers*, 429. "Und diese zwölf Jahre, sie haben mir meine Würde nehmen wollen! Was heißt denn leben, wenn nicht lieben? Ich wollte den Tag lieben und das Land, die Deutschen, unter denen ich lebte, und dich und mich! Und ich durfte es nicht. Ich mußte alles verachten lernen, den Tag und das Land, und die Deutschen und dich und mich! Wie konnte ich lieben und achten, wo ich nicht geliebt und geachtet wurde? Wo keine Würde ist, da ist Haß, ich wollte nicht hassen, und ich habe es lernen

müssen. Ich habe den Haß kennengelernt, am meisten den gegen mich,- am meisten haßte ich mich selbst. Ich wußte, daß ich in den Augen aller das geworden war, was im gleichen Augenblick alle für mich wurden." Von Salomon, *Fragebogen*, 539.

85. Von Salomon, *Answers*, 428. "Wir sollen es nicht vergessen; was uns die Phantasie nicht bewegte, soll das Gedächtnis tun." Von Salomon, *Fragebogen*, 539.

86. Nietzsche, *Genealogy*, 563.

87. Ibid., 572.

88. Ibid., 563.

89. Ibid.

90. Von Salomon, *Answers*, 423. "In der Tat, mein Zorn über die Amerikaner wuchs täglich. Es war mir klar, daß es ein Zorn allein aus dem Gefühl und nicht aus der Vernunft heraus war. Es war ein echt deutscher Zorn über verpaßte Gelegenheiten, über die Diskrepanz zwischen der Proklamation und dem tatsächlichen Handeln." Von Salomon, *Fragebogen*, 535.

91. Von Salomon, *Answers*, 424. "Zwischen der zum Prinzip erhobenen Ungerechtigkeit eines Staates und der Ungerechtigkeit der Einzelnen." Von Salomon, *Fragebogen*, 535.

92. Von Salomon, *Fragebogen*, 562; *Answers*, 453.

93. Von Salomon, *Answers*, 451–52. "Ich hatte gewissermaßen ein wildes Triumphgefühl, einmal, daß es gar nicht weh tat, schlagt ihr nur, halt, wo war Ursache, wo war Wirkung?—nein,—ich hatte das Triumphgefühl, weil ich es nicht war, der Unrecht tat, natürlich, das mußte es sein, dieser Offizier hatte eine solche Wut, ich nicht." Von Salomon, *Fragebogen*, 560.

94. Von Salomon, *Answers*, 452. "Es ist ein seelischer Schmerz, der den körperlichen taub macht, es ist nicht die Wut, es ist die Trauer. Halt, halt, dann ist das Triumphgefühl das Triumphgefühl des Leidens . . . darf ich mich so weit wagen, ich, gerade ich? Leiden ist wohl nicht produktiv, oder doch? [. . .] Leiden erhöht also?" Von Salomon, *Fragebogen*, 560–61.

95. Von Salomon, *Answers*, 461–62. "Wahrscheinlich verachteten sie uns darum so unmäßig, weil sie niemals zu begreifen vermochten, daß bei uns irgendeine ferne, fremde Vernunft am Werke war, die es mit einer Art von Wollust empfand, daß endlich, endlich einmal das Unrecht nicht auf unserer Seite war." Von Salomon, *Fragebogen*, 571.

96. Von Salomon, *Answers*, 467. "Neuankömmlinge hatten berichtet, daß das Lager in der Bevölkerung als 'Hunger- und Prügellager' berüchtigt sei. Es hatte sich also herumgesprochen, was uns mit einer gewissen Befriedigung erfüllte." Von Salomon, *Fragebogen*, 576. On the subject of whisper campaigns, see Biddiscombe, *Denazification*, 45.

97. Von Salomon, *Answers*, 118. "In meinem Herzen aber glühte nicht besonders viel mehr als eine unbändige Lust am Leben. Mir war jener psychologische Moment erst sehr viel später begegnet, nicht auf einem Schlachtfeld und jedenfalls nicht im Rahmen eines Gebildes, das man als Generation bezeichnen könnte, und vielleicht liegt es eben daran, daß ich zu den Vorgängen, die Hans Grimm so bewegend schilderte, in einem anderen Blickwinkel stand,—daß ich dem Akt der Zerstörung all der Werte, für die Hans Grimm so verzweifelt focht, Sitte, Würde, Anstand, und jenes sonderbare Ding, welches auch Hans Grimm das kostbare Gut der individuellen Freiheit nannte, nicht mit

dem eifervollen Zorn Hans Grimms, aber auch nicht mit der Gelassenheit der Frontsol-
daten zu begegnen vermochte, ja, daß ich diesen Akt der Zerstörung eher zu begrüßen
geneigt war, insoweit er sich auf die Möglichkeiten jener Gremien bezog, für die Hans
Grimm verantwortlich sprach, nicht weil ich etwa den Wert solcher Dinge wie Sitte,
Würde und Anstand und meinetwegen auch das kostbare Gut der individuellen Freiheit
nicht zu schätzen wußte, sondern weil ich vielmehr an der existentiellen Wirklichkeit
dieser Dinge zumindest als die Angelegenheiten dieser Welt bestimmende Kraft zu
zweifeln geneigt war,—mich dünkte es logischer, auch ihren Schein schwinden zu
sehen, als in ihrem Namen zu agieren, besser also, ein Vakuum zu schaffen, als eine alte
und, wie es sich erwiesen hatte, falsche Konstruktion." Von Salomon, *Fragebogen*, 197.

98. Von Salomon, *Answers*, 243–44. "Ich fürchte, Hitlers Behauptung, seine ideolo-
gische Konzeption sei die Konzeption der Demokratie, wird schwer zu widerlegen
sein." Von Salomon, *Fragebogen*, 345.

99. Von Salomon, *Answers*, 250; *Fragebogen*, 351.

100. For a brief overview of the role of Prussia in von Salomon's novels, see Franz
Futterknecht, "The Prussian Myth and Modern Nationalism in Ernst von Salomon's
Novels," *History of European Ideas* 16.4–6 (1993): 975–79.

101. Von Salomon, *Fragebogen*, 49; *Answers*, 26–29.

102. Von Salomon, *Answers*, 84. "Am 20. Juli 1944 ging nicht nur die preußische
Armee, es ging auch die Bildungswelt des neunzehnten Jahrhunderts zugrunde." Von
Salomon, *Fragebogen*, 151.

103. My translation. "Preußen [war] in seiner wahren Wesenheit fortan kein Begriff
mehr, es existierte nur noch das preußische Sein als Schein, der preußische Geist als
Gespenst, das preußische Wesen als Unwesen." Von Salomon, *Fragebogen*, 49. Fitzgibbon offers the grossly understated translation "[Prussia] had become merely the name
attached to a series of catch-phrases." Von Salomon, *Answers*, 30.

104. Von Salomon, *Answers*, 34. "Ich bin Preuße, und will ein Preuße sein." Von
Salomon, *Fragebogen*, 53.

105. Von Salomon claims, "When Ludin, as ambassador in Slovakia, received a message that the Slovak Jews, instead of being planted elsewhere as the Tiso government
had requested, were to be moved to extermination camps, he cried out: 'This is an un-
speakably foul blunder!' I knew Ludin well enough to believe him when he told me how
horrified he had been, yet I was nevertheless surprised." Von Salomon, *Answers*, 518. In
the documentary film about Hanns Ludin's life and its effect on his children and grand-
children, *Ein oder zwei Dinge, die ich von ihm weiß*, filmmaker Malte Ludin, the young-
est son of Hanns Ludin, exhibits documents regarding the deportation of the Slovak
Jews that had been signed by his father. It is unlikely that Hanns Ludin did not know of
the deportees' future; either he or von Salomon have thus indulged in poetic license in
this account. In his book about the history of the Rowohlt Verlag, the publishing house
responsible for von Salomon's *Fragebogen*, David Oels drives home von Salomon's
whitewashing of Nazi perpetrators when he cites from a letter to von Salomon from one
of the publishing house's readers, Kurt W. Marek (otherwise known under the pseud-
onym of C. W. Ceram, the renowned postwar nonfiction author and former Nazi propa-
gandist). Marek pleads with von Salomon, "Hier sollte wenigstens *einmal* ein echter
Nazi, ein KZ-Nazi auftreten. [. . .] Ihr Lager erscheint als eine Versammlung edler Menschen, unschuldiger Lämmer, weisser Täubchen." ("At least once, you need to allow

one true Nazi, a concentration-camp Nazi, to appear. [. . .] Your camp appears to consist of an assembly of noble human beings, guiltless lambs, little white doves.") Kurt W. Marek to Ernst von Salomon, October 2, 1950. Von Salomon Estate, Deutsches Literaturarchiv, Marbach, cited in Oels, 358.

106. Von Salomon, *Answers*, 518–21; *Fragebogen*, 657–62.

107. Von Salomon, *Answers*, 545–46. "Hanns Ludin, entsetzlich abgemagert in seinem viel zu weit gewordenen grauen Flanellanzug, bekam den Strick um den Hals gelegt. Der Henker drehte ihn langsam zusammen. Hanns Ludin litt zwanzig Minuten lang. Seine letzten Worte waren ein Gedenken an seine Frau und seinen Sohn Tille und der Ruf: Es lebe Deutschland!" Von Salomon, *Fragebogen*, 668.

108. In an early review of the book, Derek van Abbé describes the relationship between von Salomon and Ludin that is depicted in the text as one "between the Mephistophelian journalist and this mutely struggling twentieth-century Faust." He is struck by how von Salomon depicts Ludin as a "mild-mannered paragon of honesty" and "a pleasant Swabian, convinced even in internment of his role in bringing decency into public life." Derek van Abbé, "Germany's Twentieth-Century Twin Souls: Ernst von Salomon's *Der Fragebogen*," *German Life and Letters* 7.1 (1953): 137–43, here 143.

109. Nietzsche, *Genealogy*, 558–59.

110. Ibid., 560.

111. Armin Mohler cited by literary critic and translator Harry Zohn in *Books Abroad* 26.2 (Spring 1952): 166.

112. These publication figures are given in a letter of June 5, 1951, from Ernst Rowohlt (Hamburg) to Geheimrat Adolf v. Miller (Linz/Rhein). See also Rowohlt (Hamburg) to Graf von Moltke (Hamburg-Rissen), June 1, 1951. Both letters are in the folder titled Korrespondenzen des Rowohlt Verlags, von Salomon Estate, Deutsches Literaturarchiv, Marbach.

113. The figures are taken from a letter of March 12, 1953, from Ernst Rowohlt (Hamburg) to Alois Winbauer (Hamburg). In a recording of the *Kölner Mittwochgespräch*, Rowohlt declares that the first, 1951 edition of *Der Fragebogen* sold over 250,000 copies, with its second edition selling over 100,000 copies by the end of 1951. Korrespondenzen des Rowohlt Verlags, von Salomon Estate, Deutsches Literaturarchiv, Marbach.

114. Teresa Seruya, "Gedanken und Fragen beim Übersetzen von Ernst von Salomons *Der Fragebogen*," in *Konflikt-Grenze-Dialog: Kulturkontrastive und Interdisziplinäre Textzugänge*, ed. Jürgen Lehmann, Tilman Lang, Fred Lonker, and Thorsten Unger (Frankfurt am Main: Peter Lang, 1997), 227–37, here 229.

115. Van Abbé, "Twentieth-Century Twin Souls," 138.

116. Norbert Frei, *Vergangenheitspolitik: Die Anfänge der Bundesrepublik und die NS-Vergangenheit* (Munich: Deutscher Taschenbuch, 2003), 9–10.

117. Hans J. Morgenthau, "A Savage Hint of the New German Philosofy [sic]," *Chicago Daily Tribunal*, February 6, 1955, G2.

118. "Reviewed Works," *Journal of Modern History* 28.2 (June 1956): 196–213, 204.

119. "It Just Happened," *Time* 65.2 (January 10, 1955), 90.

120. Orville Prescott, "Books of the Times," *New York Times*, January 3, 1955, 25.

121. Harold Nicolson, "Evasive Action," *Observer*, April 11, 1954, 11.

122. E. Nelson Hayes, "This Will Anger You," *Daily Boston Globe*, January 2, 1955, A7.

123. Friedrich Luft, "Ein literarischer Remer: Zu Ernst von Salomons "Fragebogen," *Die Neue Zeitung*, no. 116, May 19, 1951, 10.

124. Süti and "W.S." to Ernst von Salomon, Berlin, August 18, 1951, Briefe, von Salomon Estate, Deutsches Literaturarchiv, Marbach.

125. M. Geuer to Ernst von Salomon, Stuttgart, November 10, 1951, Briefe, von Salomon Estate, Deutsches Literaturarchiv, Marbach.

126. "Solange die westlichen Besatzungsmächte nicht die in der Zeit des Waffenstillstandes (als während der 'friedlichen Besatzungszeit'") begangenen Untaten und Verbrechen wenigstens das so weit materiell möglich ist, wieder gut gemacht haben, werden wir jedes Zusammengehen mit dem Westen ablehnen. Das ist nicht Ressentiment sondern eine selbstverständliche Forderung internationalen Rechtes." Werner Dietz, Hamburg-Blankensee, to Ernst von Salomon, June 12, 1951, Briefe, von Salomon Estate, Deutsches Literaturarchiv, Marbach.

127. Constantin Graf Stamati, Detmold, to Ernst von Salomon, October 22, 1951, Briefe, von Salomon Estate, Deutsches Literaturarchiv, Marbach.

128. Beate Brass, Lindau/Bodensee, to Ernst von Salomon, July 27, 1951, Briefe, von Salomon Estate, Deutsches Literaturarchiv, Marbach.

129. For the only extant publication on these meetings, their consequences, and those who participated, see Wilfried Dörstel, Eberhard Illner, Renate Prieur, Rainer Steinberg, and Robert von Zahn, eds., *Freier Eintritt, Freie Fragen, Freie Antworten: Die Kölner Mittwochgespräche 1950–1956* (Cologne: Verlag der Mayerschen Buchhandlung, 1991). This publication consists of documents taken from the exhibition *Kölner Kulturleben nach 1945* (Cultural life in Cologne after 1945), which took place in Cologne in 1991, as well as a collection of essays on the "Wednesday conversations" by the five editors of the book.

130. Rainer Steinberg, "Kölns 'Kopfbahnhof': Die Mittwochgespräche 1950–1956," in Dörstel et al., *Freier Eintritt*, 13–15.

131. My translation. "Öffentlichkeit wurde gerade nach 1945 als wiedergewonnener Raum begriffen, um frei und ohne Angst vor Denunziation in den gesellschaftlichen Diskurs eingreifen zu können. Sie manifestierte sich zunächst—mehr oder weniger durch die britische Militärregierung kontrolliert—über Medien wie Rundfunk und Zeitung. Wenig später kamen Gesprächskreise sowie Diskussions- und Leseabende hinzu." Ibid., 16.

132. Ibid., 18.

133. On the dearth of interest in von Salomon's work and person, see Teresa Seruya, "Gedanken und Fragen beim Übersetzen von Ernst von Salomons 'Der Fragebogen,'" 229. See also Franz Futterknecht, "The Prussian Myth and Modern Nationalism in Ernst von Salomon's Novels," *History of European Ideas* 16.4–6 (1993): 975. Although there has been a slight but steady trickle of publications on von Salomon's work— particularly his earlier novels—most accounts approach him and his texts through a largely literary historical or openly historical approach.

134. Gerhard Ludwig cited in Steinberg, "Kölns 'Kopfbahnhof,'" 20.

135. This information was garnered from the recording of a radio broadcast on the

topic of the Kölner Mittwochgepräche and, in this instance, on von Salomon's appearance at the event in October 1951. "Der Streit der früheren Jahre: Der Fragebogen," Kölner Mittwochgespräche, Westdeutscher Rundfunk Köln, [Cologne], Germany, October 14, 1993. "Der Streit der früheren Jahre." This recording is part of a series of hourlong broadcasts on the Kölner Mittwochgespräche that explain the events and the historical and cultural context of the debate each author unleashed. Most valuably, each broadcast houses substantial amounts of the original broadcast—one can hear von Salomon's bellowing, as well as a quiet, querying voice from the public that has been identified as belonging to Heinrich Böll, who himself later presented on *Trümmerliteratur* (rubble literature) at the Mittwochgespräch. Unless otherwise stated, all references to the debate on von Salomon's book at the Kölner Mittwochgespräch are taken from the citations of the original recording included in the 1993 WDR broadcast "Der Streit der früheren Jahre."

136. The observation of the contribution of the events in Cologne to a broader public culture of discussion—the opening up of the public sphere—are taken from a contemporary newspaper account of the von Salomon event in Cologne in October 1951 and are cited in Steinberger's essay. About the treatment of the topics of guilt and responsibility on the evening of von Salomon's talk, Steinberger writes, "Die öffentliche Diskussion um Schuld und Verantwortung der Deutschen am Zweiten Weltkrieg erreichte an diesem Abend in Köln einen ihrer Höhepunkte: Nahezu die gesamte Presse der Bundesrepublik Deutschland ging auf dieses Ereignis ein." (The public discussion about guilt and the responsibility of the Germans for World War II reached a climax on this evening in Cologne; almost the entire national press of the Federal Republic of Germany responded to this event.) Steinberger, "Kölns 'Kopfbahnhof,'" 20–21.

137. That this was a common fear among readers of the book not invested in the "community of *ressentiment*" can be seen in many newspaper reviews of the book in Germany and the United States. For example, reviewer Rudolf Heberle praised the book as interesting, amusing, and "often touching," but he was concerned that the book's success was an indicator "that something is still foul in the state of Germany, that there must be an undercurrent of putchism, of militant nationalism, of political activism which has withstood the efforts at democratic re-education." Rudolf Heberle, review of *Der Fragebogen*, *German Quarterly* 30.1 (January 1957): 287.

138. Chantal Mouffe, *Agonistics: Thinking the World Politically* (London: Verso, 2013), 7.

CHAPTER 3

The opening epigraph is from Sigmund Freud, *Civilization and Its Discontents*, trans. Joan Riviere (New York: Martino, 2010), 142.

1. Margarete Mitscherlich, "Die (Un)Fähigkeit zu trauern in Ost- und Westdeutschland: Was Trauerarbeit heißen könnte," *Psyche* 47.2 (1993): 406–18.

2. While scholars frame and analyze the Mitscherlichs' argument in quite different ways, their text has had an impressive longevity as a point of reference in postwar culture. In sociology, see Olick, *House of the Hangman*. In history, see Dominick LaCapra, *Representing the Holocaust: History, Theory, Trauma* (Ithaca: Cornell University Press,

1996); Robert Moeller, *War Stories: The Search for a Usable Past in the Federal Republic of Germany* (Berkeley: University of California Press, 2001). In politics, see Gesine Schwan, *Politik und Schuld: Die zerstörerische Macht des Schweigens* (Frankfurt am Main: Fischer, 1997). All three recent biographies on Alexander Mitscherlich, which will be considered in more detail later in the chapter, also conclude that the Mitscherlichs' book has been underread and overcited.

3. Christian Schneider, "Die Unfähigkeit zu trauern: Von der Diagnose zur Parole," in *Psychoanalyse und Protest: Alexander Mitscherlich und die "Achtundsechziger,"* ed. Tobias Freimüller (Göttingen: Wallstein, 2008), 133–46.

4. For analyses of the excessively emotional reception of the mainstream American miniseries *Holocaust*, see *Im Kreuzfeuer: Der Fernsehfilm "Holocaust": Eine Nation ist betroffen*, ed. Peter Märthesheimer and Ivo Frenzel (Frankfurt am Main: Fischer, 1979); Andreas Huyssen, "The Politics of Identification: 'Holocaust' and West German Drama," in *After the Great Divide: Modernism, Mass Culture, Postmodernism* (Bloomington: Indiana University Press, 1986), 94–114; Anton Kaes, "1979: The American Television Series Holocaust Is Shown in West Germany," in *Yale Companion to Jewish Writing and Thought in German Culture, 1096–1996*, ed. Sander Gilman and Jack Zipes (New Haven: Yale University Press, 1997), 864.

5. See, particularly, Keilson's 1959 novel *Der Tod des Widersachers*, which was omitted from the postwar canon until its rediscovery through an English translation in 2010. For an analysis of the ethically unsettling ambivalence that structures the novel, see my article "Death of the Adversary: Enduring Ambivalence in Hans Keilson's Postwar Psychoanalytic Literature," in *"Die vergangene Zeit bleibt die erlittene Zeit": Untersuchungen zum Werk von Hans Keilson*, ed. Simone Schröder, Ulrike Weymann, and Andreas Martin Widmann (Würzburg: Königshausen und Neumann, 2013), 91–103.

6. For different and sometimes even conflicting accounts of the study of emotions in the field of history, see Norbert Elias, *The Civilizing Process: Sociogenetic and Psychogenetic Investigations*, trans. Edmund Jeffcott, ed. Eric Dunning, John Goudsblom, and Stephen Mennell (Oxford: Blackwell, 2000); Reddy, *Navigation of Feeling*; Rosenwein, *Emotional Communities*; Darcy Buerkle, "Caught in the Act: Norbert Elias, Emotion, and *The Ancient Law*," *Journal of Modern Jewish Studies* 8.1 (2009): 83–102. In the German-speaking context, see Ute Frevert, "Angst vor Gefühlen? Die Geschichtsmächtigkeit von Emotionen im 20. Jahrhundert," in *Perspektiven der Gesellschaftsgeschichte*, ed. Paul Nolte et al. (Munich: C. H. Beck, 2000); Assmann and Frevert, *Geschichtsvergessenheit/Geschichtsversessenheit*; Plamper, *Geschichte und Gefühl*.

7. For general overviews, see Melissa Gregg and Gregory J. Seigworth, eds., *The Affect Theory Reader* (Durham: Duke University Press, 2010); Helena Wulff, ed., *The Emotions: A Cultural Reader* (London: Bloomsbury Academic, 2008); Jennifer Harding and E. Deidre Pribram, eds., *Emotions: A Cultural Studies Reader* (New York: Routledge, 2009). For the American context, see Scott McLemee, "Getting Emotional," *Chronicle of Higher Education*, 21 February 2003, http://chronicle.com/ weekly/v49/i24/24a01401.htm. A useful overview in the German literary theoretical context is provided by Thomas Antz at http://www.literaturkritik.de/public/rezension.php?rez_id=10267&ausgabe=200612.

8. A subgenre of *Vergangenheitsbewältigung*, or memory studies research, "melancholic scholarship" in the field of German studies seems to be an international en-

deavor, with scholars emerging with book-length studies in this vein in North America, England, and Germany. For the American context, see Eric Santner, *Stranded Objects: Mourning, Memory, and Film in Postwar Germany* (Ithaca: Cornell University Press, 1990). For the English context, see Helmut Schmitz, *On Their Own Terms: The Legacy of National Socialism in Post-1990 German Fiction* (Birmingham: University of Birmingham Press, 2004). For the German context, see Günter Butzer, *Fehlende Trauer: Verfahren epischen Erinnerns in der deutschsprachigen Gegenwartsliteratur* (Munich: Wilhelm Fink, 1998). For examples of shorter contributions in this vein, see the essays (including my own "melancholic" contribution, "Of Death, Kitsch, and Melancholia") in *Germany and the Uncomfortable Past: Representations of National Socialism in Contemporary Germanic Literature*, ed. Helmut Schmitz (Aldershot: Ashgate, 2001); Ernestine Schlant, *The Language of Silence: West German Literature and the Holocaust* (New York: Routledge, 1999). For contributions of a more recent vintage, see Anne Fuchs, Mary Cosgrove, and Georg Grote, eds., *German Memory Contests: The Quest for Identity in Literature, Film, and Discourse since 1990* (Rochester: Camden House, 2006); Luisa Banki, "Mourning, Melancholia, and Morality: W. G. Sebald's German-Jewish Narratives," in *Panic and Mourning: The Cultural Work of Trauma*, ed. Daniela Agostinho, Elisa Antz, and Cátja Ferreira (Berlin: De Gruyter, 2012), 37–48. Perhaps the most recent incarnation of this scholarship, which couples the acknowledgment of the Mitscherlichs' thesis with the erroneous claim that there was a silence in postwar literature in regard to the German bombings, is W. G. Sebald's *Luftkrieg und Literatur: Mit einem Essay zu Alfred Andersch* (Munich: Carl Hanser, 1999). This lecture gave rise to a flurry of publications on analyses and representations of postwar German victimhood and German trauma resulting from wartime bombing; see particularly Vees-Gulani, *Trauma and Guilt*; Jörg Friedrich, *Der Brand: Deutschland im Bombenkrieg 1940–1945* (Berlin: List, 2004); Dagmar Barnouw, *The War in the Empty Air: Victims, Perpetrators, and Postwar Germans* (Bloomington: Indiana University Press, 2006); Bill Niven, ed., *Germans as Victims: Remembering the Past in Contemporary Germany* (New York: Palgrave MacMillan, 2006); Bill Niven, ed., *Memorialization in Germany since 1945* (New York: Palgrave MacMillan, 2010); Helmut Schmitz and Annette Seidel-Arpaci, eds., *Narratives of Trauma: Discourses of German Wartime Suffering in National and International Perspective* (Amsterdam: Rodopi, 2011).

    9. The term *useable past*, implying socially acceptable narratives of the past that may be redeemed from the debris of history, is taken from the title of historian Robert Moeller's book *War Stories: The Search for a Usable Past in the Federal Republic of Germany*.

    10. Wolfgang Schirmacher, "Der Seelenarzt der Deutschen: Zum 70. Geburtstag des Psychoanalytikers und Kulturphilosophen Alexander Mitscherlich," *Mannheimer Morgen*, no. 215, September 30, 1978, 30.

    11. "Verderblicher Einfluß," *Deutsche National-Zeitung*, no. 27, July 2, 1982, 8.

    12. Erhard Schreiber, "Alexander Mitscherlich: Ehe von Marx und Freud," *Rheinischer Merkur*, no. 27, July 2, 1982, 22.

    13. Wolfgang Bartsch, "Keine Vaterfigur: Alexander Mitscherlich 65 Jahre," *Frankfurter Rundschau*, no. 219, September 20, 1973, 17.

    14. E.G.L., "In den Fußstapfen von Sigmund Freud: Alexander Mitscherlich: Arzt, Lehrer, Zeitkritiker," *Allgemeine Jüdische Wochenzeitung*, no. 25, June 18, 1976, n.p.

15. "Wo Es war, soll Ich werden." The English version cited here is taken from James Strachey's translation of Freud's 1933 declaration in his *New Introductory Lectures on Psycho-Analysis*, in *The Standard Edition of the Complete Psychological Works of Sigmund Freud*, trans. James Strachey, vol. 22 (London: Hogarth, 1953), 1–182, here 80.

16. This is the title of a newspaper article written on the occasion of Alexander Mitscherlich's seventieth birthday: Wolfgang Ignée, "Wo Es war, sollen Wir sein: Zum siebzigsten Geburtstag des Analytikers Alexander Mitscherlich," *Stuttgarter Zeitung*, no. 217, September 20, 1978, 33.

17. The Mitscherlichs explain the process of struggle with propaganda, in which the individual's conscience is overmanned by the demands of an ego ideal, as follows: "Der psychologische Mechanismus, der einen Massenführer zum Sieg führt, ist dadurch gekennzeichnet, daß im Streit zwischen diesem alten Gewissen und dem fetischhaft geschmeichelten Ich-Ideal das Gewissen unterliegt. [. . .] Im Führer selbst bewirken die Massen, die ihm zujubeln, eine gewaltige Inflation seiner Machterlebnisse. Auch er kostet den Triumph des Zusammenfalls von Ich und Ich-Ideal aus. Für die Massenglieder ist der so idealisierte Führer das sichtbar existierende eigene Ich-Ideal; sie haben das Objekt 'Führer' an 'die Stelle des Ich-Ideals eingesetzt.'" In other words, the conscience is subdued or placed under the thrall of the ego ideal, in this case, that of Adolf Hitler, which, in turn, collapses into the ego, creating the narcissistic investment of the German population in their Führer and, in turn, in each member of the mass. As the citations indicate, the Mitscherlichs take this description of psychological processes directly from Freud's *Group Psychology and the Analysis of the Ego* (1921). Alexander Mitscherlich and Margarete Mitscherlich, *The Inability to Mourn: Principles of Collective Behavior*, trans. Beverley R. Placzek (New York: Grove, 1975), 72.

18. Mitscherlich and Mitscherlich, *Inability to Mourn*, 26–27.

19. As discussed in the introduction, Karl Jaspers documents in *Die Schuldfrage* how the Allied forces posted placards addressed to the German population depicting atrocities of the concentration camps in towns throughout Germany. See also Dagmar Barnouw, *Germany 1945: Views of War and Violence* (Bloomington: Indiana University Press, 1996); Brink, *Ikonen der Vernichtung*. See most recently Weckel, *Beschämende Bilder*.

20. Mitscherlich and Mitscherlich, *Inability to Mourn*, 19–20. "Was soll eigentlich ein Kollektiv tun, das schutzlos der Einsicht preisgegeben ist, daß in seinem Namen sechs Millionen Menschen aus keinem anderen Grund als aus dem der eigenen aggressiven Bedürfnisse getötet wurden? Es bliebe ihm kaum ein anderer Weg als der einer weiteren Verleugnung seiner Motive oder der *Rückzug in eine Depression*." Mitscherlich and Mitscherlich, *Unfähigkeit zu trauern*, 30.

21. Freud, *Civilization and Its Discontents*, 141–42. "Ich könnte nicht sagen, daß ein solcher Versuch zur Übertragung der Psychoanalyse auf die Kulturgemeinschaft unsinnig oder zur Unfruchtbarkeit verurteilt wäre. Aber man müßte sehr vorsichtig sein, nicht vergessen, daß es sich doch nur um Analogien handelt, und daß es nicht nur bei Menschen, sondern auch bei Begriffen gefährlich ist, sie aus der Sphäre zu reißen, in der sie entstanden und entwickelt worden sind. [. . .] Und was die therapeutische Verwendung der Einsicht betrifft, was hülfe die zutreffendste Analyse der sozialen Neurosen, da niemand die Autorität besitzt, der Masse die Therapie aufzudrängen? Trotz aller

dieser Erschwerungen darf man erwarten, daß jemand eines Tages das Wagnis einer solchen Pathologie der kulturellen Gemeinschaften unternehmen wird." Sigmund Freud, *Das Unbehagen in der Kultur* (1930), reprinted in *Gesammelte Werke*, ed. Anna Freud (Frankfurt am Main: Fischer, 1999), 504–5.

22. The first published critique of the Mitscherlichs' book was psychoanalyst Tilmann Moser's essay "Die Unfähigkeit zu trauern: Hält die Diagnose einer Überprüfung stand? Zur psychischen Verarbeitung des Holocaust in der Bundesrepublik," *Psyche* 46.5 (1992): 389–405. Moser critiqued the Mitscherlichs' slippage between psychoanalytic and moral registers, arguing that despite their plea for "Einfühlung" (empathy) in the population, barely a trace of this emotion is evinced in the Mitscherlichs' attitude toward their patients and the population to whom they extend their analysis. As Moser argues, this is a breach of the psychoanalytic contract between patient and analyst. Moser's critique is made more complicated, however, by the context of his argument, which was originally presented as a lecture at a conference at the Evangelischen Akademie Arnoldshain titled "Zur Gegenwart des Holocaust in Deutschland-West und Deutschland-Ost," with Jewish attendees whom Moser did not wish to offend should they understand his argument as apologetic. As a psychoanalyst, he is also well aware of the sway of affective familial loyalties on individuals: his father was a member of the SA and then a functionary of the NSDAP.

23. Mitscherlich and Mitscherlich, *Inability to Mourn*, 24. The Mitscherlichs use the word *Derealisation* in the German original. Mitscherlich and Mitscherlich, *Unfähigkeit zu trauern*, 35.

24. Mitscherlich and Mitscherlich, *Unfähigkeit zu trauern*, 40; *Inability to Mourn*, 28.

25. Mitscherlich and Mitscherlich, *Inability to Mourn*, 20. "Würden wir unsere nazistische Vergangenheit noch mit ungestörten Erinnerungen bewohnen, so würde es unserem Ich—auch wenn wir nur 'dabei'-gewesen wären, gehorsam, fatalistisch oder begeistert—schwerfallen, dieses Mitwirken mit der Art unseres Überlebens zu integrieren." Mitscherlich and Mitscherlich, *Unfähigkeit zu trauern*, 31.

26. The confusion of the pronoun *wir* in its multiple and often contradictory permutations in the book is taken up in psychoanalyst Gudrun Brockhaus' essay "*Die Unfähigkeit zu trauern* als Analyse und als Abwehr der NS-Erbschaft," *psychosozial* 31.4 (2008): 29–39; see especially 36–37. See also historian Alexander von Plato's critical meditation on his generation's problematic (non)identification with the Mitscherlichian "we," in "Waren 'wir' unfähig zu trauern? Vor 40 Jahren erschien *Die Unfähigkeit zu trauern* von Alexander und Margarete Mitscherlich; Ein persönlich-historiografischer Rückblick," *psychosozial* 31.4 (2008): 49–59.

27. Ben Witter, "Mit Professor Alexander Mitscherlich auf dem Philosophenweg: 'Die Dinge bekommen geheimnisvolle Zusammenhänge,'" *Die Zeit*, no. 20, May 17, 1968, n.p.

28. Timo Hoyer, *Im Getümmel der Welt: Alexander Mitscherlich—ein Porträt* (Stuttgart: Vandenhoeck und Ruprecht, 2008), 501–2.

29. Mitscherlich and Mitscherlich, *Inability to Mourn*, 25. "Wo Schuld entstanden ist, erwarten wir Reue und das Bedürfnis der Wiedergutmachung. Wo Verlust erlitten wurde, ist Trauer, wo das Ideal verletzt, das Gesicht verloren wurde, ist Scham die natürliche Konsequenz. Die Verleugnungsarbeit erstreckte sich gleichermaßen auf die

Anlässe für Schuld, Trauer und Scham." Mitscherlich and Mitscherlich, *Unfähigkeit zu trauern*, 36.

30. Mitscherlich and Mitscherlich, *Unfähigkeit zu trauern*, 80. Perhaps the Mitscherlichs intended the term to describe the affect aroused by political involvement.

31. In the postwar German context, see especially Weckel, *Beschämende Bilder*.

32. For an account of how shame can be made public and instrumentalized for purposes of regaining national pride in the Australian context, see Ahmed, *Cultural Politics of Emotion*, 101–21.

33. For an astute analysis of the uses of "mourning" at the point of transition from modernity to postmodernity, see Alessia Ricciardi, *The Ends of Mourning: Psychoanalysis, Literature, Film* (Stanford: Stanford University Press, 2003).

34. Mitscherlich and Mitscherlich, *Inability to Mourn*, 26. "Die Bundesrepublik ist nicht in Melancholie verfallen, das Kollektiv all derer, die einen 'idealen Führer' verloren hatten, den Repräsentanten eines gemeinsam geteilten Ich-Ideals, konnte der eigenen Entwertung dadurch entgehen, daß es alle affektiven Brücken zur unmittelbar hinter ihnen liegenden Vergangenheit abbrach. Dieser Rückzug der affektiven Besetzungsenergie, des Interesses, soll nicht als ein Entschluß, ein beabsichtigter Akt verstanden werden, sondern als ein unbewußt verlaufendes Geschehen, das nur wenig vom bewußten Ich mitgesteuert wird." Mitscherlich and Mitscherlich, *Unfähigkeit zu trauern*, 37–38.

35. Mitscherlich and Mitscherlich, *Inability to Mourn*, 9, 20. "Der ökonomische Gewinn dieses Vergessenkönnens, dieser Verfremdung der eigenen Vergangenheit, dieser Errichtung eines kollektiven Brührungstabus, ist nicht gering"; "Alle unsere Energie haben wir viel mehr mit einem Bewunderung und Neid erweckenden Unternehmungsgeist auf die Wiederherstellung des Zerstörten, auf Ausbau und Modernisierung unseres industriellen Potentials bis zur Kücheneinrichtung hin konzentriert." Mitscherlich and Mitscherlich, *Unfähigkeit zu trauern*, 31, 19.

36. Mitscherlich and Mitscherlich, *Inability to Mourn*, 38.

37. Ibid., 40.

38. Historian Frank Biess persuasively argues that up until the 1960s, politicians viewed strong emotions in the public arena with suspicion, cultivating instead "a style of sobriety" at odds with American models of sentimental and patriotic democracy. See "Feelings in the Aftermath," in Biess and Moeller, *Histories of the Aftermath*, 34.

39. In the section of their book titled "Die Unfähigkeit zu trauern—womit zusammenhängt: Eine deutsche Art zu lieben," the Mitscherlichs engage with three pieces of writing by Sigmund Freud: "Erinnern, Wiederholen, Durcharbeiten" (1914), "Trauer und Melancholie" ([1915] 1917), and *Massenpsychologie und Ich-Analyse* (1921). Mitscherlich and Mitscherlich, *Unfähigkeit zu trauern*, 13–85.

40. Mitscherlich and Mitscherlich, *Unfähigkeit zu trauern*, 39; *Inability to Mourn*, 27.

41. LaPlanche and Pontalis categorize the process as follows in their entry on disavowal: "first, what is involved here is the coexistence of two different forms of ego-defence and not a conflict between the ego and the id; secondly, one of these defences of the ego—the disavowal of perception—is directed towards *external reality*." J. Laplanche and J.-B. Pontalis, *The Language of Psychoanalysis*, trans. Donald Nicholson-Smith (New York: Norton, 1973), 118–20, here 119.

42. These categories are further blurred when the Mitscherlichs describe the defense mechanisms of the Federal Republic earlier on in their book as follows: "de facto ist unser Verhalten von unbewußt wirksam gewordenen Verleugnungen bestimmt" ("our behavior is determined de facto by effective unconscious disavowels"). Mitscherlich and Mitscherlich, *Unfähigkeit zu trauern*, 8.

43. Mitscherlich and Mitscherlich, *Inability to Mourn*, xxv. "Sozialen Immobilismus und Provinzialismus einerseits und der hartnäckig aufrechterhaltenen Abwehr von Erinnerungen, insbesondere der Sperrung gegen eine Gefühlsbeteiligung an den jetzt verleugneten Vorgängen der Vergangenheit." Mitscherlich and Mitscherlich, *Unfähigkeit zu trauern*, 9.

44. Mitscherlich and Mitscherlich, *Inability to Mourn*, xxvi; *Unfähigkeit zu trauern*, 10.

45. Mitscherlich and Mitscherlich, *Inability to Mourn*, 50. "Ohne eine wenn auch noch so verzögerte Schuldverarbeitung mußte die Trauerarbeit ausbleiben." Mitscherlich and Mitscherlich, *Unfähigkeit zu trauern*, 65.

46. Reddy, *Navigation of Feeling*, 106, 129–30.

47. Mitscherlich and Mitscherlich, *Inability to Mourn*, 68. "Die Affekte, die sie [die Psychoanalyse] erwecken mag, sollten aber auf die Autoren gerichtet werden und nicht auf das kostbarste Instrument der Menschenkenntnis, das wir besitzen, die Psychoanalyse." Mitscherlich and Mitscherlich, *Unfähigkeit zu trauern*, 84–85.

48. For an account of Alexander Mitscherlich's awareness of this problematic, especially at a time when most institutions were hostile toward the field, see Tobias Freimüller, "Kampf für die Psychoanalyse," in *Alexander Mitscherlich: Gesellschaftsdiagnosen und Psychoanalyse nach Hitler* (Göttingen: Wallstein, 2007), 177–205.

49. For a collection of recently published accounts of Alexander Mitscherlich's relationship to the 1968 generation in the Federal Republic of Germany, see Tobias Freimüller, ed., *Psychoanalyse und Protest: Alexander Mitscherlich und die "Achtundsechziger"* (Göttingen: Wallstein, 2008). See also "Psychoanalyse und Protest" and "Papiervater," in Freimüller, *Alexander Mitscherlich: Gesellschaftsdiagnosen und Psychoanalyse*, 361–76, 376–83; "Der Professor und die Protestbewegung," in Hoyer, *Im Getümmel der Welt*, 452–67.

50. For an account of *Die Unfähigkeit zu trauern* from its inception onward, see "Über 'Die Unfähigkeit zu trauern,'" in Hoyer, *Im Getümmel der Welt*, 491–515. As mentioned above, the Mitscherlichs' book has never gone out of print in Germany, and it has been translated into seven languages.

51. Tobias Freimüller categorizes the first critique of note as Hermann Lübbe's essay "Der Nationalsozialismus im politischen Bewußtsein der Gegenwart," *Historische Zeitschrift* 236 (1983): 579–99. However, in Lübbe's essay, Alexander Mitscherlich only rates a passing mention in a footnote, and his texts and ideas are not engaged with in any sustained fashion. Freimüller also discusses the postwar reception of the book, which was largely positive—or at least mostly agreed with the Mitscherlichs' concern for the future of democracy in the Bonn Republic. See Freimüller, "Die Unfähigkeit zu trauern: Von der Geschichte einer Diagnose," *psychosozial* 31.4 (2008): 21–27. The first English-language interventions of note were part of the proceedings of the symposium "Psychoanalysis and Power" held in 1994 at the New School for Social Research and published in *American Imago* 52.3 (1995): see there Karen Brecht, "In the Aftermath of Nazi Germany: Alexander Mitscherlich and Psychoanalysis—Legend and Legacy,"

291–312; Anson Rabinbach, "Response to Karen Brecht: 'In the Aftermath of Nazi Germany: Alexander Mitscherlich and Psychoanalysis—Legend and Legacy,'" 313–28.

52. Tilmann Moser, "Die Unfähigkeit zu trauern: Hält die Diagnose einer Überprüfung stand? Zur psychischen Verarbeitung des Holocaust in der Bundesrepublik," *Psyche* 46.5 (1992): 389–405. The article is a reworked version of an address Moser held at the Evangelischen Akademie Arnoldshain at the conference "Zur Gegenwart des Holocaust in Deutschland-West und Deutschland-Ost" on January 18, 1992. In 1993, an edition of *Psyche* titled "Psychoanalyse und Moral," including essays by Margarete Mitscherlich, Christian Schneider, and Dieter Rudolf Knoell, served as an extended response to (and a largely negative refutation of) Moser's essay. See *Psyche* 47 (1993). Moser responded, in turn, in a brief text published in the next issue of *Psyche*: "Nachwort zur Kritik an der 'Unfähigkeit zu trauern':Aus Anlaß einer Themen-Nummer der Zeitschrift 'Psyche,' August 1993," reprinted in Tilmann Moser, *Politik und seelischer Untergrund* (Frankfurt am Main: Suhrkamp, 1993), 198–203.

53. Christian Schneider notes the politically (and affectively) charged status of this text in the Federal Republic, when he terms it "einen sakrosankten Demokratietext der deutschen Nachkriegsgesellschaft." Schneider, "Die Unfähigkeit zu trauern: Von der Diagnose zur Parole," in Freimüller, *Psychoanalyse und Protest*, 133–46, 134.

54. Moser, "Die Unfähigkeit zu trauern," 390–91.

55. "Das liest sich eher wie ein Katalog von Beschimpfungen denn als ein Dokument des Verstehenwollens. [. . .] Einfühlung ist kaum zu erkennen." Ibid., 391.

56. Ibid., 393.

57. Ibid.

58. Ibid., 396.

59. Christian Schneider, "Jenseits der Schuld? Die Unfähigkeit zu trauern in der zweiten Generation," *Psyche* 47.2 (1993): 754–74; Margarete Mitscherlich, "Die (Un) Fähigkeit zu trauern in Ost- und Westdeutschland: Was Trauerarbeit heißen könnte," *Psyche* 47.2 (1993): 406–18.

60. "Und damit zugleich das Ticket, mit dem sich die damaligen moralischen Eliten von der Masse der Schuldigen abheben konnten." Christian Schneider, "Die Unfähigkeit zu trauern: Diagnose oder Parole?" *Mittelweg* 16.4 (2008): 79.

61. Schneider, "Jenseits der Schuld?," 760.

62. Schneider, "Die Unfähigkeit zu trauern: Von der Diagnose zur Parole," 133–37. For a recent book-length study of the same topic, see Ulrike Jureit and Christian Schneider, *Gefühlte Opfer: Illusionen der Vergangenheitsbewältigung* (Stuttgart: Klett-Cotta, 2010). Schneider's contribution forms the second half of the book and is entitled "Besichtigung eines ideologisierten Affekts: Trauer als zentrale Metapher deutscher Erinnerungspolitik" (*Gefühlte Opfer*, 107–253). Unless otherwise stated, citations of Schneider's argument are taken from "Die Unfähigkeit zu trauern: Von der Diagnose zur Parole."

63. Schneider, "Die Unfähigkeit zu trauern: Von der Diagnose zur Parole," 136.

64. Ibid., 137.

65. Many contemporary critics of the Mitscherlichs hedge the suspicion that their book remains, for the most part, superficially or entirely unread and that its enduring popularity is indebted to the imaginative political resonance evoked by the book's title and embodied by Alexander Mitscherlich's left-leaning reputation, encouraged partly

by his compilation with Fred Mielke of the documentation of the so-called Nuremberg doctors' trial (1946–47), published in 1949 as *Wissenschaft ohne Menschlichkeit*. The book was republished in 1960 with the new title *Medizin ohne Menschlichkeit*. Hans-Martin Lohmann, who wrote the first biography on Alexander Mitscherlich, claims, "Das Buch ist nie wirklich gelesen worden in Westdeutschland. Es ist vor allem der Titel bekannt geworden." Lohmann cited in Freimüller, *Psychoanalyse und Protest*, 153.

66. Schneider, "Die Unfähigkeit zu trauern: Von der Diagnose zur Parole," 134.

67. Schneider, "Die Unfähigkeit zu trauern: Diagnose oder Parole?," 70.

68. Alexander Mitscherlich, *Ein Leben für die Psychoanalyse: Anmerkungen zu meiner Zeit* (Frankfurt am Main: Suhrkamp, 1980).

69. Wolfgang Bartsch, "Keine Vaterfigur: Alexander Mitscherlich 65 Jahre," *Frankfurter Rundschau*, no. 219, September 20, 1972, 17.

70. Lohmann cited in Freimüller, *Alexander Mitscherlich: Gesellschaftsdiagnosen und Psychoanalyse*, 17. Until 2008, except for several publications concentrating on his contributions to psychosomatic medicine, his participation in the Nuremberg doctors' trial, and a volume celebrating his seventieth birthday (in 1978), the secondary literature on Alexander Mitscherlich and his intellectual legacy was limited largely to his own memoir and a single biography written by Hans-Martin Lohmann. Exceptions are the essays published by Karen Brecht ("In the Aftermath of Nazi Germany") and Anson Rabinbach ("Response to Karen Brecht").

71. The exception was Lohmann's slender, brief biography on Mitscherlich published in 1987, which largely perpetuated Mitscherlich's received public image. Hans-Martin Lohmann, *Alexander Mitscherlich: Mit Selbstzeugnissen und Bilddokumenten* (Reinbek: Rowohlt, 1987).

72. Martin Delhi, *Leben als Konflikt: Zur Biographie Alexander Mitscherlichs* (Göttingen: Wallstein, 2007); Freimüller, *Alexander Mitscherlich: Gesellschaftsdiagnosen und Psychoanalyse*; Hoyer, *Im Getümmel der Welt*. See Jason Crouthamel's review of Delhi's and Freimüller's biographies, "New Perspectives on the 'National Conscience' of the Federal Republic," H-German, H-Net Reviews, January 2010, accessed July 1, 2013, http://www.h-net.org/reviews/showrev.php?id=26228. See also Hans Martin-Lohmann, "Verstrickt in die Zeitläufe: 'Leben als Konflikt'; Martin Dehli entidealisiert Alexander Mitscherlich," *Frankfurter Rundschau*, no. 68, March 21, 2007, 13; Ludger Lütkehaus, "In Widersprüchen leben: Martin Dehli über den Psychoanalytiker Alexander Mitscherlich," *Neue Zürcher Zeitung*, no. 122, May 30, 2007, 26; Lorenz Jäger, "Wir, das Gericht: Ein Analytiker wird analysiert; Alexander Mitscherlichs Leben," *Frankfurter Allgemeine Zeitung*, no. 132, June 11, 2007, 39; Christof Goddemeier, "Leben in Brüchen: Turbulenz," *Freitag*, no. 5, February, 2008, 17; Ludger Lütkehaus, "Korrektur einer Biographie: Vor hundert Jahren wurde Alexander Mitscherlich geboren; Die Enkelgeneration wirft einen kritischen Blick auf den Psychoanalytiker," *Badische Zeitung*, no. 215, September 13, 2008, IV; Micha Brumlik, "'Der große Alexander,'" *Die Zeit*, no. 39, September 18, 2008, 53; Christof Goddemeier, "Spaß am Krach: Ein Aufstörer," *Freitag*, no. 38, September 19, 2008, 18; Caroline Fetscher, "Deutschland auf der Couch," *Der Tagesspiegel*, September 20, 2008, 25; Micha Brumlik, "Ein Mißverständnis: Alexander Mitscherlich und die antiautoritäre Studentenbewegung—Überlegungen zum 100," *Frankfurter Rundschau*, no.

221, September 20–21, 2008, 34–35; Christian Schneider, "Die Ein-Mann-Armee der deutschen Psychoanalyse: Timo Hoyer zeichnet ein biographisches Porträt des zerrissenen Multitalents Alexander Mitscherlich," *Süddeutsche Zeitung*, no. 220, September 20–21, 2008, 17; Katharina Rutschky, "Ein genialer Luftikus," *Die Welt*, no. 222, September 20, 2008, 7; Hans-Martin Lohmann, "Den letzten beißen die Hunde: 'Im Getümmel der Welt'; Timo Hoyer hat es mit der dritten Mitscherlich-Biographie in anderthalb Jahren nicht leicht," *Frankfurter Rundschau*, no. 240, October 14, 2008, 64.

73. The end of the Cold War and the death of the majority of witnesses who experienced the Third Reich as adults have certainly contributed to this new equanimity, despite what appear, at this point in time, as almost ritual public scandals addressing the history of National Socialism in Germany. One such debate took place in October 2010 surrounding the publication of the book *Das Amt*, on the involvement of the foreign office in facilitating the deportation and murder of European Jews. Interestingly, the incident garnered considerably less attention in a shorter time span than have similar debates in the past, including the Historikerstreit in 1986, the Goldhagen debate in 1996, the Walser-Bubis debate in 1998, and the scandal around the Wehrmacht Ausstellung in the late 1990s. This relatively short-lived "scandal" suggests a shift in generational opinion or perhaps even a form of medial saturation. See Eckart Conze, Norbert Frei, Peter Hayes, and Mosche Zimmermann, *Das Amt und die Vergangenheit: Deutsche Diplomaten im Dritten Reich und in der Bundesrepublik* (Munich: Blessing, 2010).

74. For a good overview of the main arguments of Dehli's and Freimüller's biographies, as well as an assessment of the achievements and weaknesses of the books, see Frank Biess, "Thinking after Hitler: The New Intellectual History of the Federal Republic of Germany," *History and Theory* 51.2 (2012): 221–45.

75. See Tobias Freimüller, "Verdrängung und Bewältigung: Alexander Mitscherlich und die NS-Vergangenheit," in *Psychoanalyse und Protest*, 118–32, here 120.

76. For detailed accounts of Mitscherlich's involvement in the Nuremberg doctors' trial and of the subsequent professional fallout this led to for Mitscherlich, see Martin Dehli, "Der Nürnberger Ärzteprozess," in *Leben als Konflikt*, 145–76; Freimüller, "Medizin ohne Menschlichkeit," in *Alexander Mitscherlich: Gesellschaftsdiagnosen und Psychoanalyse*, 97–33; Hoyer, "Berichterstatter des Bösen," in *Im Getümmel der Welt*, 376–429.

77. See Mitscherlich and Mitscherlich, *Unfähigkeit zu trauern*, 13–27, here 23.

78. Hans Krieger, "Das Spätwerk eines großen Moralisten: Erinnern sollst du, sollst erinnern; Alexander Mitscherlichs Psychoanalyse-Kurs für fortgeschrittene Anfänger," *Die Zeit*, no. 50, December 5, 1975, 42.

79. R. Hagen, "Alexander Mitscherlich: 'Die Demokratie in unserem Lande ins Spiel bringen'; Ein Mann mit vielen Feinden; Der Friedenspreisträger, porträtiert von R. Hagen," *Deutsches Allgemeines Sonntagsblatt*, October 12, 1969, 26.

80. Ben Witter, "Mit Professor Alexander Mitscherlich auf dem Philosophenweg: 'Die Dinge bekommen geheimnisvolle Zusammenhänge,'" *Die Zeit*, no. 20, May 17, 1968, n.p.

81. Ulrich Hoffmann, "Über einen kritischen Humanismus hinaus," *Süddeutsche Zeitung*, no. 258, November 6 1980, 61.

82. See, for example, Dehli's comment in the transcription of the conference discussions on Mitscherlich and the sixty-eighters in Freimüller, *Psychoanalyse und Protest*,

66. In the same volume, Paul Nolte argues that the postwar mission of West German sociology in political and moral terms was to overcome National Socialist categories. Ibid., 71.

83. Martin Dehli, "Vom 'Untergang des Abendlandes' zum 'Unbehagen in der Kultur': Spuren des Konservativen in Mitscherlichs Sozialpsychologie," in Freimüller, *Psychoanalyse und Protest*, 32–45.

84. Martin Dehli, "Alexander Mitscherlich in der Konservativen Revolution," in *Leben als Konflikt*, 35–86.

85. My translation. "Im Hause Jüngers verkehrten absonderliche Figuren, hauptsächlich rechtsgerichtete Verschwörernaturen, Überbleibsel aus den Baltikumkämpfen und ähnliche Gestalten, Schauwecker, Salomon, Roßbach und wie sie alle hießen." Mitscherlich, *Ein Leben*, 82.

86. Ibid., 59–80.

87. See Mitscherlich, *Ein Leben*, 82–100. See also Dehli, *Leben als Konflikt*, 56–67.

88. Dehli, *Leben als Konflikt*, 71–74.

89. Michael Wildt, *Generation des Unbedingten*, cited in Ulrike Jureit, "Geliehene Väter: Alexander Mitscherlich und das Bedürfnis nach generationeller Selbstverortung im 20. Jahrhundert," in Freimüller, *Psychoanalyse und Protest*, 158. Significantly, members of this generation listed by Jureit in her essay include Heinrich Himmler (1900), Theodor W. Adorno (1903), Sebastian Haffner (1907), Claus Schenk von Stauffenberg (1907), and Alexander Mitscherlich (1908), indicating a variety of political and ethical positions possible within what is traditionally viewed as a generational cohort.

90. See Dehli, "Vom 'Untergang des Abendlandes' zum 'Unbehagen in der Kultur'," 42–43.

91. In her essay, Jureit underscores how Mitscherlich downplays his relationship to these "geliehenen Vätern" by narrating the attachment as an oedipal drama, which she suggests is his attempt to cover over his earlier political identifications. Jureit in Freimüller, *Psychoanalyse und Protest*, 166–70. Similarly, Freimüller emphasizes the ongoing oscillation in Mitscherlich's work between the poles of conservative cultural critique and a call for radical liberalization in the Enlightenment tradition that aims at self-reflective autonomy. Ibid., 114–15. See also Paul Nolte, "Von der Gesellschaftsstruktur zur Seelenverfassung: Die Psychologisierung der Sozialdiagnose in den sechziger Jahren," in ibid., 70–94.

92. Alexander Mitscherlich was initially regarded as a role model by the generation of sixty-eighters as they went to war with their parents for tolerating or abetting the crimes of the Nazi dictatorship. For a reevaluation of Alexander Mitscherlich's role in the student unrest of 1968, see Freimüller, *Psychoanalyse und Protest*. In the same collection of essays, Hans-Martin Lohmann remarks on the support Mitscherlich received from the Allied Forces immediately after the war in Germany. Ibid., 24. For Mitscherlich's account of his own life, which supplies the basis for most twentieth-century scholarship on Mitscherlich, see his book *Ein Leben für die Psychoanalyse*.

93. See Freimüller, "Verdrängung und Bewältigung: Alexander Mitscherlich und die NS-Vergangenheit," in *Psychoanalyse und Protest*, 118–32, particularly 119–26.

94. Freimüller documents the newspaper article "Die Jugend von heute im Lichte der Psychotherapie," published in 1956, as one of the few contributions that refer to the

National Socialist past in Mitscherlich's writings from the 1950s. Ibid., 124–25. This reference is also clearly concerned with psychoanalysis. Further, Freimüller interprets Mitscherlich's silence on this topic throughout the 1950s as a sign of resignation toward a broader politico-social trend of focusing on the future rather than the past.

95. My translation. "Man muß dabei aber noch in Rechnung stellen, daß das Nachdenken für den einzelnen überhaupt sehr mühsam geworden ist, weil es sich in einer Lebensatmosphäre von Kummer und Kümmerlichkeit, von Hunger, Obdachlosigkeit, Unruhe, Mißgunst, Denunziation, von Enge, Freud- und Hoffnungslosigkeit abwickeln muß." Alexander Mitscherlich, "Die schwersten Stunden: Überschlag eines Jahres," *Die Fähre* 1 (1946): 131–38, reprinted in *Alexander Mitscherlich: Gesammelte Schriften*, vol. 6, ed. Klaus Menne (Frankfurt am Main: Suhrkamp, 1983), 79–87, here 83.

96. My translation. "Diesen wenigen Klarblickenden konnte es aber in diesem Jahr nicht verborgen bleiben, daß auch die Umwelt Deutschlands ein Opfer unkontrollierter Gefühle zu werden droht. Nirgendwo mehr wird ernsthaft zwischen Deutschen und Deutschen, zwischen Gläubigen an Diktatur und Gewalt und Gläubigen an sittliche Grundpflichten des Menschen, sozusagen zwischen bösen und 'weniger bösen' Deutschen unterschieden. Das Haßwort der Ächtung steht über allen gleich. Das hat zur Folge, daß, wie alles in unserem massenhaften Dasein, auch die Sittlichkeit von der Bürokratie her definiert wird. Dies ist die höhere Fragwürdigkeit des Fragebogens, die nicht mit einem Zweifel an die Notwendigkeit des Fragens überhaupt verwechselt werden darf. Aber auch jener, der einen reinen Fragebogen hat, gleicht verzweifelt einem Handlanger. Ein Beruf, der nicht nach dem Geschmack vieler ist, die sich lange und unter äußersten Opfern gegen den kollektiven Terror gewehrt haben: und die sich also in ihre gewohnt gewordene Vereinzelung zurückziehen." Ibid., 83–84.

97. My translation. "Leider muß man von der pessimistisch klingenden These ausgehen, daß die meisten Menschen unfähig sind, ihre politischen Anschauungen zu ändern. Sie lernen weder dazu noch vergessen sie etwas. Ihre politischen Thesen sind mit ihrer 'Ehre' verknüpft; hier könnte jede Diskussion ein Zeichen von Schlappheit sein." Alexander Mitscherlich, "Amnestie statt Umerziehung," *Frankfurter Hefte* 4.6 (1949): 508–9, reprinted in Menne, *Alexander Mitscherlich*, 138–39. See also Dehli, *Leben als Konflikt*, 124–44.

98. Mitscherlich, "Amnestie," 139.

99. Ibid. "Wir müssen also durch eine Amnestierung (die sich selbstverständlich nicht auf Verbrechen gegen die Menschlichkeit beziehen wird) den ehemaligen Nazis mit der Konsolidierung der deutschen Verhältnisse die Möglichkeit geben, in einem politischen fair play mitzumachen." The entire quote is emphasized by italics in the original.

100. To practice as a psychoanalyst, one usually has to have completed analytical training, replete with one's own analysis by a psychoanalyst.

101. See Brecht, "In the Aftermath of Nazi Germany," 292–302.

102. See Karola Brede in Freimüller, *Psychoanalyse und Protest*, 111.

103. R. Hagen, "Alexander Mitscherlich: 'Die Demokratie in unserem Lande ins Spiel bringen'"; Ein Mann mit vielen Feinden; Der Friedenspreisträger, porträtiert von R. Hagen," *Deutsches Allgemeines Sonntagsblatt*, October 12, 1969, 26.

104. See Martin Dehli, "Die Ein-Mann-Armee der Psychoanalyse: Alexander

Mitscherlich als Wissenschaftspolitiker," in *Leben als Konflikt*, 217–44. The title of a subsection in Hoyer's book captures the power relation between Adorno/Horkheimer and Mitscherlich by the time he moved to Frankfurt: "In der Frankfurter Schule: 'In Ihrer Nähe und mit Ihnen zusammen nachdenken zu dürfen.'" Hoyer, *Im Getümmel der Welt*, 316–28.

105. Brecht, "In the Aftermath of Nazi Germany," 300. In his memoir, Mitscherlich writes how Alan Gregg from the Rockefeller Foundation enabled Mitscherlich to take up a fellowship through his support of Mitscherlich's application, which Mitscherlich claims was due to his postwar status as "Nichtbetroffener" and "Verfolgter" according to Allied codes of denazification. The first category, Mitscherlich explains, was due to his complete lack of involvement in the Nazi regime; the second indicated that he had suffered to some extent at the hands of that regime. Mitscherlich, *Ein Leben*, 187–88.

106. Freudian psychoanalysis was received in a lukewarm or even hostile fashion by many practitioners of psychoanalysis in West Germany in the 1950s, not least because they found Freud's work to be too "rational," antimetaphysical, and anti-idealist. Freud's work was seen as overly pessimistic. It also had to compete against other popular schools of psychoanalytic thought, including the Binswangerian-inflected *Daseinsanalyse* and neoanalysts. See Anthony D. Kauders, "'Psychoanalysis Is Good, Synthesis Is Better': The German Reception of Freud, 1930 and 1956," *Journal of the History of the Behavioral Sciences* 47.4 (Fall 2011): 380–97, here 387–93.

107. Mitscherlich, *Ein Leben*, 187–216.

108. My translation. "Der Errichtung eines Institutes für Psychotherapie kann ich daher nur dann zustimmen, wenn es sich ausschließlich auf die Beratung und Behandlung nicht-psychiatrischer Zustände beschränken und keinesfalls psychogene Zustände (missverständlicher Weise vielfach 'Neurosen' genannt) annehmen würde. Auch müsste seine Bezeichnung anders lauten und dürfte die Silbe 'psych' in keiner Verbindung führen." Excerpt from a statement appended to a letter from Kurt Schneider to Karl Jaspers (with a copy sent to Alexander Mitscherlich), May 6, 1946, Briefe an Karl Jaspers von Alexander Mitscherlich, 1942–1952 (+1583), Letter number 75.13118, Jaspers Estate, Deutsches Literaturarchiv, Marbach.

109. Brecht, "In the Aftermath of Nazi Germany," 300–302.

110. For a brief version of the history of the Sigmund Freud Institute and a detailed overview of its current activities, see http://www.sfi-frankfurt.de/home.html (accessed on June 29, 2011).

111. Nolte, "Von der Gesellschaftsstruktur zur Seelenverfassung," 71–76.

112. Ibid., 70, 76–84.

113. Alexander Mitscherlich, *Auf dem Weg zur vaterlosen Gesellschaft: Ideen zur Sozialpsychologie* (Munich: Piper, 1963). For an account of the book's argument, see Hans-Joachim Busch, "Demokratie und Bildung in der 'vaterlosen Gesellschaft': Alexander Mitscherlich als politischer Psychologe," in *Unterwegs in der vaterlosen Gesellschaft: Zur Sozialpsychologie Alexander Mitscherlichs*, ed. Robert Heim and Emilio Modena (Giessen: Psychosozial-Verlag, 2008), 49–67.

114. Nolte, "Von der Gesellschaftsstruktur zur Seelenverfassung," 92.

115. For an account of the positive reception of Mitscherlich by the sixty-eighters, especially in light of his and Margarete Mitscherlich's critique of West German society's disavowal of the National Socialist past, see Freimüller, "Verdrängung und Bewäl-

tigung," 118–32. On Mitscherlich's ultimate rejection of the student movement as "narcissistic" and "infantile," see Anthony D. Kauders, "Drives in Dispute: The West German Student Movement, Psychoanalysis, and the Search for a New Emotional Order, 1967–1971," *Central European History* 44 (2011): 711–31, here 727–30.

116. For a detailed reconstruction of the process from the original lecture in 1963 up to the publication of the book by Piper in 1967, see Timo Hoyer, "Ein Bestseller ensteht: Zur Entstehungsgeschichte von *Die Unfähigkeit zu trauern*," *psychosozial* 31.4 (2008): 13–19.

117. Hoyer, *Im Getümmel der Welt*, 14. In a recent article, Gary Baker argues that Alexander Mitscherlich's focus on empathy, and how a lack thereof can damage a collective, originated with the case of Egon Schultz. Schulz was a criminal turned psychopathic murderer; in 1946, the district court of Heidelberg sought Mitscherlich's advice on Schulz's puzzling psychological profile. Baker argues that the understanding of empathy that provided the basis for many of Mitscherlich's best known publications, including *The Inability to Mourn*, originated with this case history. Gary L. Baker, "The Case of Egon Schultz and the Origin of Alexander Mitscherlich's Empathy Concept," *German Studies Review* 35 (2012): 55–72.

118. Hoyer, *Im Getümmel der Welt*, 15.

119. Ibid., 17.

120. With examples drawn from the Mitscherlich archive of the correspondence between the author and the editors, Hoyer describes how Walter Hinderer not only argued for a less informal or journalistic formulation of many passages but also required a more precise usage of psychoanalytical terminology, at times even reformulating the theoretical basis of some of Mitscherlich's formulations. Hoyer, *Im Getümmel der Welt*, 17.

121. This formulation is attributed to Hans Rössner, coeditor of the book at Piper publishing house. Ibid., 503.

122. Ibid., 18–19.

123. The figures are cited in Freimüller, "Die Unfähigkeit zu trauern: Von der Geschichte einer Diagnose," *psychosozial* 31.4 (2008): 21. See also Hoyer, *Im Getümmel der Welt*, 19.

124. The book's success was commented on by Gert Kalow in the *Frankfurter Allgemeine Zeitung* on the occasion of Mitscherlich's sixtieth birthday: "Dieses eminent politische Buch hat—siehe die Bestsellerliste—eine erstaunlich breite Öffentlichkeit gefunden" (This eminently political book has—take a look at the best-seller list—reached an astoundingly broad public). Gert Kalow, "Der Auszug aus dem Elfenbeinturm: Alexander Mitscherlich zum 60. Geburtstag," *Frankfurter Allgemeine Zeitung*, no. 219, September 20, 1968, 32.

125. For two notable exceptions to this tendency, perhaps partly due to their East German subject matter, see Julia Hell, *Post-Fascist Fantasies: Psychoanalysis, History, and the Literature of East Germany* (Durham: Duke University Press, 1997); Anke Pinkert, *Film and Memory in East Germany* (Bloomington: Indiana University Press, 2008). For an approach that attempts to gain a hearing particularly for the figure of the postwar German perpetrator and bystander and that, in turn, engenders its own moral position, see Barnouw's *Germany 1945* and *The War in the Empty Air*. For a recent publication that analyzes precisely this process of moralizing in terms of "shame," see Weckel, *Beschämende Bilder*.

126. Sigmund Freud, *Totem and Taboo*, trans. James Strachey (New York: Norton, 1962.) 18–74. See especially chapter 2, "Taboo and Emotional Ambivalence."

127. Freud, *Totem and Taboo*, 30. "Infolge der stattgehabten Verdrängung, die mit einem Vergessen—Amnesie—verbunden ist, bleibt die Motivierung des bewußt gewordenen Verbotes unbekannt und müssen alle Versuche scheitern, es intellektuell zu zersetzen, da diese den Punkt nicht finden, an dem sie angreifen könnten. Das Verbot verdankt seine Stärke—seinen Zwangscharakter—gerade der Beziehung zu seinem unbewußten Gegenpart, der im Verborgenen ungedämpften Lust, also einer inneren Notwendigkeit, in welche die bewußte Einsicht fehlt." Sigmund Freud, *Totem und Tabu: Einige Übereinstimmungen im Seelenleben der Wilden und der Neurotiker* (1913), reprinted in *Gesammelte Werke*, vol. 9 (Frankfurt am Main: Fischer, 1999), 40.

128. Freud, *Totem and Taboo*, 30. "Die Trieblust verschiebt sich beständig, um der Absperrung, in der sie sich befindet, zu entgehen, und sucht Surrogate für das Verbotene—Ersatzobjekte und Ersatzhandlungen—zu gewinnen. Darum wandert auch das Verbot und dehnt sich auf die neuen Ziele der verpönten Regung aus. Jeden neuen Vorstoß der verdrängten Libido beantwortet das Verbot mit einer neuen Verschärfung. Die gegenseitige Hemmung der beiden ringenden Mächte erzeugt ein Bedürfnis nach Abfuhr, nach Verringerung der herrschenden Spannung, in welchem man die Motivierung der Zwangshandlungen erkennen darf." Freud, *Totem und Tabu*, 40–41.

129. Freud, *Totem and Taboo*, 30. "Diese sind bei der Neurose deutlich Kompromißaktionen, in der einen Ansicht Bezeugungen von Reue, Bemühungen zur Sühne u. dgl., in der anderen aber gleichzeitig Ersatzhandlungen, welche den Trieb für das Verbotene entschädigen." Freud, *Totem und Tabu*, 41.

130. This residual sense of remorse is expressed in even stronger terms as guilt felt by the primal sons who, in Darwin's theory of the "primal horde," murder and devour their violent primal father who keeps all women to himself, resulting in a strong sense of guilt. This guilt, in turn, effects the establishment of the taboos of totemism—the prohibition against murder and incest, which are internalized in the postpatriarchal society, even in the absence of the father. Of course, this also provides a prehistoric model for Freud's own theories of the Oedipus complex. See Freud, "The Return of Totemism in Childhood," in *Totem and Taboo*, 100–161.

131. Freud, *Totem and Taboo*, 66. "Wo früher der befriedigte Haß und die schmerzhafte Zärtlichkeit miteinander gerungen haben, da erhebt sich heute wie eine Narbenbildung die Pietät und fordert das: *De mortuis nil nisi bene*. Nur die Neurotiker trüben noch die Trauer um den Verlust eines ihrer Teuren durch Anfälle von Zwangsvorwürfen, welche in der Psychoanalyse die alte ambivalente Gefühlseinstellung als ihr Geheimnis verraten." Freud, *Totem und Tabu*, 83.

132. Freud, *Totem and Taboo*, 68. "Gewissen ist die innere Wahrnehmung von der Verwerfung bestimmter in uns bestehender Wunschregungen; der Ton liegt aber darauf, daß diese Verwerfung sich auf nichts anderes zu berufen braucht, daß sie ihrer selbst gewiß ist. Noch deutlicher wird dies beim Schuldbewußtsein, der Wahrnehmung der inneren Verurteilung solcher Akte, durch die wir bestimmte Wunschregungen vollzogen haben." Freud, *Totem und Tabu*, 85.

133. Ibid.

134. Freud, *Totem and Taboo*, 69. "Dazu wollen wir erinnern, daß auch beim Schuld-

bewußtsein etwas unbekannt und unbewußt ist, nämlich die Motivierung der Verwerfung." Freud, *Totem und Tabu*, 86.

135. Freud, *Totem and Taboo*, 73. "Diese Abweichung führt sich in letzter Auflösung darauf zurück, daß die Neurosen asoziale Bildungen sind; sie suchen mit privaten Mitteln zu leisten, was in der Gesellschaft durch kollektive Arbeit entstand." Freud, *Totem und Tabu*, 91. The word *asoziale* in the German original is mistranslated "social" in the English translation.

136. Mitscherlich and Mitscherlich, *Inability to Mourn*, 79. "Einsicht ist eine Funktion des Ichs, das auch seine Bindung an das Triebverlangen periodisch—reflektierend, prüfend—lockern kann. Das Ich ist dann in der Lage, die mitmenschliche Realität und sich selbst ohne die groben Färbungen und Einstellungen wahrzunehmen, die ihnen unsere Affekte verleihen." Mitscherlich and Mitscherlich, *Unfähigkeit zu trauern*, 97.

137. Mitscherlich and Mitscherlich, *Inability to Mourn*, 176. "Je leidenschaftlicher dieser einzelne durch denkende Anteilnahme beteiligt ist, desto weniger ist er emotionell, durch Ansprechen seiner primärprozeßhaften Phantasien, manipulierbar." Mitscherlich and Mitscherlich, *Unfähigkeit zu trauern*, 211.

138. Mitscherlich and Mitscherlich, *Inability to Mourn*, 242. "Die Ordnung des kritisch denkenden Ichs, ob sie nun durch das Individuum oder durch die Gesellschaft vertreten wird, ist unstabil; sie wird durch Lernprozesse gegen emotionale Orientierungen (Triebhunger, Angst etwa) erworben und kann leicht wieder von diesen außer Kurs gesetzt werden; das zeigt sich in der Faszination, welche die mythisierend wirren Lehren des Nationalsozialismus auf Millionen ausübten." Mitscherlich and Mitscherlich, *Unfähigkeit zu trauern*, 284.

139. Mitscherlich and Mitscherlich, *Inability to Mourn*, 93. "Ausschaltung der kritischen Ich-Leistungen." Mitscherlich and Mitscherlich, *Unfähigkeit zu trauern*, 114.

140. See Foucault on the "incitement to discourse" that results in response to perceived repression and that is mistaken for an expression of freedom in the face of adversity. This underscores the potential productivity of the act of prohibition that may perversely encourage rather than prevent that on which a prohibition is enacted. Michel Foucault, *History of Sexuality*, vol. 1, *An Introduction*, trans. Robert Hurley (London: Penguin, 1978).

CONCLUSION

The opening epigraphs are from Max Horkheimer and Theodor W. Adorno, *Dialectic of Enlightenment: Philosophical Fragments*, ed. Gunzelin Schmid Noerr, trans. Edmund Jephcott (Stanford: Stanford University Press, 2002), 165; and Theodor W. Adorno, *Guilt and Defense: On the Legacies of National Socialism in Postwar Germany*, ed., trans., and intro. by Jeffrey K. Olick and Andrew J. Perrin (Cambridge, MA: Harvard University Press, 2010), 96. The quote in the title, "A Stroll through the Battleground of Murdered Concepts," comes from *Guilt and Defense*, 86.

1. Benedict Anderson. *Imagined Communities: Reflections on the Origin and Spread of Nationalism* (London: Verson, 1991), 1–7.

2. An Anglo-American account of *ressentiment* in the context of moral philosophy

interprets the affect in the context of forgiveness, mainly in a transnational context. For a brief overview of this interpretative framework from Joseph Butler over Adam Smith to John Rawls in the context of West Germany, see Melanie Steiner-Sherwood, "Jean Améry and Wolfgang Hildesheimer: Ressentiments, Melancholia, and the West German Public Sphere in the 1960s and 1970s" (PhD diss. Cornell University, 2011). Steiner-Sherwood is interested in the role of *ressentiments* and melancholia in the postwar West German public sphere of the 1960s and 1970s. Specifically, her dissertation offers an interesting analysis of the role of melancholia in the work of Jewish-German writer Wolfgang Hildesheimer and *ressentiments* in the context of Jewish-German essayist Jean Amery.

3. "Die gemeinsame Ebene solcher Äußerungen ist das Ressentiment. Und wer steht heute in Deutschland über dieser Ebene? Wer ist erhaben über die eigene Leidensgeschichte, über die Mißgunst gegen alle, denen es besser geht oder einmal besser gegangen ist? In der ersten Zeit nach 1945 herrschte das Ressentiment der "Antifaschisten." [. . .] Wir haben heute Gegenressentiment unter den "Nazis" gegen die "Anti-faschisten" und die Besatzungsmächte, unter den Soldaten gegen die Widerstandskämpfer, unter den Vertriebenen gegen die Einheimischen, unter der jüngeren Generation gegen die ältere." Ernst Friedlaender, "Es gibt Wichtigeres als Hedler," *Die Zeit* 8.5, February 23, 1950, cover page, box 33/1: Zeitungsausschnitte: Zeitungsausschnitte zu Deutschland 1947–1950, Jaspers Estate, Deutsches Literaturarchiv, Marbach.

4. Ibid. "Wir müssen endlich versuchen, vom Kollektivurteil und vom Ressentiment loszukommen. [. . .] das Ressentiment des echten Widerstandskämpfers gegen alle, die nicht mit ihm gemeinsame Sachen machten, und das des Normaldeutschen, der in vielen Fällen PG, in noch weit mehr Fällen Soldat war, gegen den Widerstand."

5. r.h., "Ernst von Salomons *Fragebogen*, Rowohlt, DM 19.80," *Die Gegenwart*, May 1, 1951, 20–21. "Die Lektüre des literarischen 'Fragebogens' [. . .] löst eine Reihe von Gefühlen aus [. . .] Offenbar glaubt er, mit seinem Fragebogen der Volksmeinung am ehesten zu genügen, aber er hat nicht nur die Fragen der Amerikaner, er hat mit seinen Ressentiments und mit seinen Überheblichkeiten sein literarisches Experiment selbst ad absurdum geführt. [. . .] Es genügt aber nicht." The following responses to von Salomon's book are also included in Jaspers' collection of newspaper clippings: Christian E. Lewalter, "Lufthieben gegen einen Unpolitischen: Ernst v. Salomons 'Fragebogen,' seine Gegner und seine falschen Freunde," *Die Zeit*, June 21, 1951, 4; O.Z., "Auch ein 'Fragebogen,'" *National-Zeitung*, July 3, 1951, 2. Box 33/1: Zeitungsausschnitte: Zeitungsausschnitte zu Deutschland 1947–1950, Jaspers Estate, Deutsches Literaturarchiv, Marbach.

6. Dolf Sternberger, Gerhard Storz, and Wilhelm E. Süskind, *Aus dem Wörterbuch des Unmenschen* (Hamburg: Claassen, 1968).

7. Sternberger, "Vorbemerkung 1967," in ibid., 11–15. The forewords of both the 1945 and 1957 editions are also included in the same volume.

8. Ibid., 168.

9. Ibid., 169.

10. Ibid., 171.

11. Sternberger underscores the important moral impetus that Germans attached to *ressentiment*, when, in response to the English and French definitions of the term,

which define *ressentiment* as an affective response to an actual—and not imagined—experience of injustice or insult, he writes, "Denn wenn ein 'Ressentiment' durch erfahrenes Unrecht begründet, also berechtigt, wenn es gar gerecht und edel wäre (und gleichwohl diesen Namen trüge)—wo bliebe dann noch moralischer Raum, seine Abwesenheit als Tugend zu rühmen!" ("For, if a *ressentiment* were grounded in an experience of injustice, and therefore justifiable; if it were completely just and noble [and nevertheless went by this name]—then what further moral ground would exist for extolling its absence as a virtue!") All translations of Sternberger's text are my own. Ibid., 171–72.

12. "Dem 'Ressentiment' hingegen kann man sein Recht durchaus streitig machen, es hat—nach seiner deutschen Bedeutung—kein Recht, weil es keine Gründe hat. Keine Gründe, sondern nur Abgründe." Ibid., 171–72. The wordplay in the original German unfortunately does not translate into English.

13. Ibid.

14. Another example given by Sternberger concerns affective responses to "die Hitlersche 'Endlösung'" ("the Hitlerian final solution"). Ibid., 171.

15. "Der 'falsche' Wortgebrauch entspringt am Ende aus dem Bedürfnis, die Gründe wegzuwischen, sie vergessen zu machen, selber zu vergessen, und sei es auch auf Kosten derer, welche Gründe haben." Ibid., 172.

16. Hanns Braun, "Die Studenten und die nationalen Ressentiments," *Die Wandlung* 5 (1949): 387–94.

17. Ibid., 388–89.

18. Ibid., 392. "Aus nichts hat das nationale Ressentiment bei uns so viel Kraft gesogen wie aus dem Gegensatz zwischen dem moralischen Anspruch der Sieger, der sich in Gerichten und einer großen Zahl diffamierender Verfahren ausdrückte, und den Erfahrungen der Praxis, die auf die uralte Erkenntnis hinausliefen: daß wir Menschen allesamt keine Engel sind, und somit wenig Anlaß besteht, sich über den 'Andren' zu erheben. Welche Folgerung aber hat man bei uns weithin aus dieser richtigstellenden Erkenntnis gezogen? Sie können's an jeder Ecke hören. In allen Variationen meint sie immer das eine: weil die anderen gesagt haben, sie seien besser als wir, und weil sich herausgestellt hat, daß sie das nicht sind, darum war das, was sie uns zur Last legen, auch nicht weiter arg, sondern eben das, was 'sie alle tun,' das Normale, Gewöhnliche schlechthin."

19. Marc Ferro, *Resentment in History*, trans. Steven Rendall (Cambridge: Polity, 2010).

20. Jeffrey K. Olick, *The Politics of Regret: On Collective Memory and Historical Responsibility* (New York: Routledge, 2007), here 153–73. For a reading of Germany (after Nazism) in terms of transitional justice, see Neil J. Kritz, ed., *Transitional Justice: How Emerging Democracies Reckon with Former Regimes*, vol. 2 (Washington, DC: United States Institute of Peace, 1995), 1–69.

21. Roger D. Petersen, *Understanding Ethnic Violence: Fear, Hatred, and Resentment in Twentieth-Century Eastern Europe* (Cambridge: Cambridge University Press, 2002), here 40–61.

22. Ibid., 127–32. Political theorist Wendy Brown argues convincingly that in contemporary litigious, neoliberal society, this would take the shape of an identity con-

structed out of "woundedness," and politics would be reduced to revenge, at worst, or redress, at best. See Brown, *States of Injury*. For a critique of feminist practices wedded to the victim status, see Halley, *Split Decisions*.

23. Jean Améry, "Ressentiments," in *Jenseits von Schuld und Sühne: Bewältigungsversuche eines Überwältigten* (Munich: Szczesny, 1966), 101–30, trans. Sidney Rosenfeld and Stella P. Rosenfeld as "Resentments" in *At the Mind's Limits: Contemplations by a Survivor on Auschwitz and Its Realities* (Bloomington: Indiana University Press, 1980), 62–81.

24. Améry specifically names British publicist Victor Gollancz and Austrian philosopher Martin Buber in this respect. He also expresses his distaste for the fervent desire for reform expressed by "those so-called re-educators from America, England, or France." Jean Améry, "Resentments," 65.

25. Ibid., 63.

26. For an extensive and sensitive reading of Améry's essay, see Thomas Brudholm, *Resentment's Virtue: Jean Améry and the Refusal to Forgive* (Philadelphia: Temple University Press, 2008), 70–103. See also Melanie Steiner Sherwood, "Jean Améry and Wolfgang Hildesheimer."

27. Améry, "Resentments," 67.

28. Ibid.

29. Aleida Assmann, "Two Forms of Resentment: Jean Améry, Martin Walser, and German Memorial Culture," *New German Critique* (2003): 123–33, here 124.

30. Améry, "Resentments," 69–72.

31. Ibid., 69.

32. Ibid., 78.

33. Ibid., 80.

34. Horkheimer and Adorno, *Dialectic of Enlightenment*, 140. "Die Wut entlädt sich auf den, der auffällt ohne Schutz. Und wie die Opfer untereinander auswechselbar sind, je nach der Konstellation: Vagabunden, Juden, Protestanten, Katholiken, kann jedes von ihnen anstelle der Mörder treten, in derselben blinden Lust des Totschlags, sobald es als die Norm sich mächtig fühlt." Max Horkheimer and Theodor W. Adorno, *Dialektik der Aufklärung: Philosophische Fragmente*, vol. 3 of *Gesammelte Schriften*, ed. Rolf Tiedemann, with Gretel Adorno, Susan Buck-Morss, and Klaus Schultz (Frankfurt am Main: Suhrkamp, 1981), 195.

35. Horkheimer and Adorno, *Dialectic of Enlightenment*, 154. "Der Antisemitismus beruht auf falscher Projektion. Sie ist das Widerspiel zur echten Mimesis, der verdrängten zutiefst verwandt, ja vielleicht der pathetische Charakterzug, in dem diese sich niederschlägt. Wenn Mimesis sich der Umwelt ähnlich macht, so macht falsche Projektion die Umwelt sich ähnlich. Wird für jene das Außen zum Modell, dem das Innen sich anschmiegt, das Fremde zum Vertrauten, so versetzt diese das sprungbereite Innen ins Äußere und prägt noch das Vertrauteste als Feind. Regungen, die vom Subjekt als dessen eigene nicht durchgelassen werden und ihm doch eigen sind, werden dem Objekt zugeschrieben: dem prospektiven Opfer. [. . .] Stets hat der blind Mordlustige im Opfer den Verfolger gesehen, von dem er verzweifelt sich zur Notwehr treiben ließ, und die mächtigsten Reiche haben den schwächsten Nachbarn als unerträgliche Bedrohung empfunden, ehe sie über ihn herfielen." Horkheimer and Adorno, *Dialektik der Aufklärung*, 211–12.

36. Horkheimer and Adorno, *Dialectic of Enlightenment*, 156. "Anstatt der Stimme des Gewissens hört es Stimmen; anstatt in sich zu gehen, um das Protokoll der eigenen Machtgier aufzunehmen, schreibt es die Protokolle der Weisen von Zion den andern zu." Horkheimer and Adorno, *Dialektik der Aufklärung*, 214–15. The reference to the "Protocols of the Elders of Zion," a document fraudulently attributed to Jewish authorship, which outlines a plan for Jewish world domination through control of the global economic market, is a particularly relevant concretization of Horkheimer and Adorno's discussion of the projective behavior of the anti-Semite. Published in Russia in 1903, then translated and disseminated internationally throughout the early twentieth century, this anti-Semitic document was declared authentic by Hitler and became mandatory school reading during the Third Reich.

37. Horkheimer and Adorno, *Dialectic of Enlightenment*, 172. "Nicht erst das antisemitische Ticket ist antisemitisch, sondern die Ticketmentalität überhaupt. Jene Wut auf die Differenz, die ihr teleologisch innewohnt, steht als Ressentiment der beherrschten Subjekte der Naturbeherrschung auf dem Sprung gegen die natürliche Minderheit, auch wo sie fürs erste die soziale bedrohen." Horkheimer and Adorno, *Dialektik der Aufklärung*, 233.

38. This return is well documented and has been much discussed, particularly in the slew of biographies published on Adorno on the occasion of the centenary of his birth, in 2003. See, for example, Detlev Claussen, *Theodor W. Adorno: One Last Genius*, trans. Rodney Livingston (Cambridge: Cambridge University Press, 2008). See also the locus classicus of the Frankfurt School: Rolf Wiggershaus, *The Frankfurt School: Its History, Theories, and Political Significance*, trans. Michael Robertson (Cambridge: Cambridge University Press, 1994). For a fascinating collection of essays on the Frankfurt School and its return to Germany, see Monica Boll and Raphael Gross, eds., *Die Frankfurter Schule und Frankfurt: Eine Rückkehr nach Deutschland* (Göttingen: Wallstein, 2009). See also Olick and Perrin, "Guilt and Defense: Theodor Adorno and the Legacies of National Socialism in German Society," in Adorno, *Guilt and Defense*, 3–42.

39. Theodor W. Adorno, *Minima Moralia: Reflections from Damaged Life*, trans. E. F. N. Jephcott (London: Verso, 2006), 39; Theodor W. Adorno, *Minima Moralia: Reflexionen aus dem beschädigten Leben*, *Gesammelte Schriften*, vol. 4, ed. Rolf Tiedemann, with Gretel Adorno, Susan Buck-Morss, and Klaus Schultz (Frankfurt am Main: Suhrkamp, 1984), 43.

40. For an exploration of Adorno's investment in a politics and a pedagogy of emotion in the postwar West German public sphere, see my article "Adorno on the Airwaves: Feeling Reason, Educating Emotions," *German Politics and Society* 32.1 (Spring 2014): 43–59.

41. Theodor W. Adorno, "Was bedeutet: Aufarbeitung der Vergangenheit?," in *Erziehung zur Mündigkeit: Vorträge und Gespräche mit Hellmut Becker 1959–1969*, ed. Gerd Kadelbach (Frankfurt am Main: Suhrkamp, 1970), 10–29; Theodor W. Adorno, "What Does Coming to Terms with the Past Mean?," in *Bitburg in Moral and Political Perspective*, trans. Timothy Bahti and Geoffrey H. Hartman, ed. Geoffrey Hartman (Bloomington: Indiana University Press, 1986), 114–29.

42. Theodor W. Adorno, "Introduction to the Lecture 'The Meaning of Working through the Past,'" appendix 2 in *Critical Models: Interventions and Catchwords*, trans.

Henry W. Pickford (New York: Columbia University Press, 1998), 307, cited in Olick and Perrin, "Guilt and Defense," 7–8.

43. Adorno, "What Does Coming to Terms with the Past Mean?," 115. "Es soll alles vergessen und vergeben sein." Adorno, "Was bedeutet: Aufarbeitung der Vergangenheit?," 10.

44. Adorno, "What Does Coming to Terms with the Past Mean?," 115. "Von den Parteigängern derer praktiziert, die es begannen." Adorno, "Was bedeutet: Aufarbeitung der Vergangenheit?," 10.

45. Adorno, "What Does Coming to Terms with the Past Mean?," 11. "Im Hause des Henkers soll man nicht vom Strick reden; sonst hat man Ressentiment." Adorno, "Was bedeutet: Aufarbeitung der Vergangenheit?," 10.

46. Adorno, "What Does Coming to Terms with the Past Mean?," 116. "So etwas, tröstet sich das schlaffe Bewußtsein, könne doch nicht geschehen sein, wenn die Opfer nicht iregendwelche Veranlassung gegeben hätten, und dies vage 'irgendwelche' mag dann nach Belieben fortwuchern." Adorno, "Was bedeutet: Aufarbeitung der Vergangenheit?," 12.

47. Adorno, "What Does Coming to Terms with the Past Mean?," 116. "Unbestreitbar gibt es im Verhältnis zur Vergangenheit viel Neurotisches: Gesten der Verteidigung dort, wo man nicht angegriffen ist; heftige Affekte an Stellen, die sie real kaum rechtfertigen; Mangel an Affekt gegenüber dem Ernstesten; nicht selten auch einfach Verdrängung des Gewußten oder halb Gewußten." Adorno, "Was bedeutet: Aufarbeitung der Vergangenheit?," 11.

48. Olick and Perrin, "Guilt and Defense," 3–42.

49. Institute for Social Research, *Gruppenexperiment: Ein Studienbericht*, ed. Friedrich Pollock, with a foreword by Franz Böhm (Frankfurt am Main: Europäische Verlagsanstalt, 1955).

50. Friedrich Pollock, Theodor W. Adorno, et al., *Group Experiment and Other Writings: The Frankfurt School on Public Opinion in Postwar Germany*, trans. and ed. Andrew J. Perrin and Jeffrey K. Olick (Cambridge, MA: Harvard University Press, 2011). A second and related publication by these authors offers a collection of documents by Adorno including his contribution to the group study, the study's negative reception by Austrian social psychologist Peter R. Hofstätter, Adorno's disappointed and pointed response to this review, and Adorno's radio broadcast on "Aufarbeitung der Vergangenheit" discussed above. Adorno, *Guilt and Defense*. My own account of the context and history of these texts is indebted to Olick and Perrin's introduction to that text and to the other writings in the volume.

51. Although more detailed analysis would be needed to explore the topic adequately, it is interesting to note the continuity in sociological methods used by the members of the Institute for Social Research for their studies of prejudice in the United States and in West Germany from the 1940s to the 1960s.

52. David Jenemann, *Adorno in America* (Minneapolis: University of Minnesota Press, 2007). See also Clemens Albrecht, Günter C. Behrmann, Michael Bock, Harald Homann, and Friedrich H. Tenbruck, *Die intellektuelle Gründung der Bundesrepublik: Eine Wirkungsgeschichte der Frankfurter Schule* (Frankfurt am Main: Campus, 1999).

53. Theodor W. Adorno, Else Frenkel-Brunswick, Daniel J. Levinson, and R. Nevitt Sanford, *The Authoritarian Personality* (New York: Harper, 1950).

54. Franz Böhm cited in Olick and Perrin, "Guilt and Defense," 20–21. Olick and Perrin point out the parallel between this binary and that of manifest versus latent personality in *The Authoritarian Personality.* Ibid., 17. The postwar German population not only held back with its opinions; sometimes it also actively mimicked official political public discourse in response to surveys conducted by the US Office of Military Government, as documented by Frank Stern in *Im Anfang war Auschwitz: Antisemitismus und Philosemitismus im deutschen Nachkreig* (Gerlingen: Bleicher, 1991), 65–110.

55. David Jenemann discusses Adorno and Horkheimer's attempts to have an experimental test film made in Hollywood during the early to middle 1940s. Tentatively titled *Below the Surface,* the project is first mentioned in 1941 in "Research Project in Anti-Semitism." After many failed attempts to get the project off the ground, it was apparently abandoned in 1946. Among other conceptual aims, the film was intended to act as a stimulus for indirect research of prejudice (specifically anti-Semitism). In a film treatment, most likely written by Adorno and Horkheimer, we find the following description for potential screenwriters about the principles of composition for what they call a test film: "Audience reactions are significant only if they are expressed spontaneously, involuntarily. The purpose of this test film must therefore be veiled. The interest of the audience must be diverted from the test proper and concentrated upon something else." In other words, the film was to be framed in such a way that the audience's attention is not immediately and solely drawn to the anti-Semitic encounter in the film that is intended to provide the indirect stimulus for audience reaction. For instance, one version of the script suggested distracting the audience by embedding the episode in a love story between a "handsome soldier on leave" and a "pretty nurse." Horkheimer's desire to simulate the environment of unencumbered discussion in a railway car in *Group Experiment* could be seen as a parallel strategy of indirect research. David Jenemann, *Adorno in America,* 128–47. I thank Johannes von Moltke for drawing my attention to the episode of the test film.

56. Olick and Perrin, "Guilt and Defense," 21–23.

57. Ibid., 23.

58. "Final Version of the Basic Stimulus (Colburn Letter)," in Adorno, *Guilt and Defense,* 45–47, here 45.

59. Ibid.

60. Ibid., 46.

61. Ibid.

62. Ibid.

63. Adorno, *Guilt and Defense,* 104–5.

64. Olick and Perrin, "Guilt and Defense," 24.

65. Adorno, *Guilt and Defense,* 53.

66. Ibid., 114.

67. Ibid.

68. Ibid., 181–82.

69. Ibid. 83–87. The term *Nestbeschmutzer* would seem to warrant its own entry in Dolf Sternberger's *Wörterbuch des Unmenschen,* considering the regularity of its use to describe returned émigrés, critics of Germany's Nazi past, and so forth in the postwar decades. For example, in the context of the revenant nationalism after the denazification program was aborted, Cornelia Rauh-Kühne states, "Daran trug indes nicht die Entnazi-

fizierung Schuld, sondern über die politische Zensur von 1945 zurückziehende Erfahrungen und mentale Dispositionen, die sich erst seit etwa 1948 wieder ungeniert ent-
falten konnten: übersteigertes nationales Geltungsstreben—nun vor allem auf
wirtschaftlichem Gebiet ausgelebt—, die immer noch wirkende 'Volksgemeinschafts-
ideologie,' die diejenigen zu Nestbeschmutzern stempelte, die sich dem allgemeinen
Trend des Verdrängens widersetzen, die in Deutschland traditionell geübte Pflege ide-
ologischer Feindbilder." Rauh-Kühne, "Die Entnazifizierung," 70.

70. Peter R. Hofstätter, "Zum Gruppenexperiment von Friedrich Pollock: Eine kri-
tische Würdigung," *Kölner Zeitschrift für Soziologie und Sozialpsychologie* 9 (1957):
97–104, translated and reproduced in full in Adorno, *Guilt and Defense*, 189–96.

71. Ibid., 191–92.

72. Ibid., 196.

73. Ibid., 195–96.

74. Ibid., 195.

75. Ibid.

76. Theodor W. Adorno. "Replik zu Peter R. Hofstätter's Kritik des Gruppenexperi-
ments," *Kölner Zeitschrift für Soziologie und Sozialpsychologie* 9 (1957): 105–17,
translated and reproduced in full in Adorno, *Guilt and Defense*, 197–209.

77. Ibid., 198.

78. Ibid., 205, 207–8.

79. Ibid., 208.

80. This essay was first delivered as a paper, in the same context in which Adorno
had delivered his 1959 paper on working through the past—namely, at a conference for
educators organized by the German Coordinating Council of the Societies for Christian-
Jewish Cooperation in Wiesbaden in 1962. Theodor W. Adorno, "Bekämpfung des Antisemitismus heute," *Das Argument* 29.6 (1964): 88–104. It appears in Theodor W.
Adorno, *Gesammelte Schriften*, vol. 20.1, ed. Rolf Tiedemann, with Gretel Adorno,
Susan Buck-Morss, and Klaus Schultz (Frankfurt am Main: Suhrkamp, 1997), 360–83.

81. Indeed, in the essay "Bekämpfung des Antisemitismus heute," Adorno repeats
almost verbatim from *Dialektik der Aufklärung*: "Sie dürfen nicht annehmen, der Antisemitismus sei ein isoliertes und spezifisches Phänomen. Sondern er ist, wie Horkheimer und ich das seinerzeit in der 'Dialektik der Aufklärung' ausgedrückt haben, der
Teil eines 'Tickets,' eine Planke in einer Platform. Überall dort, wo man eine bestimmte
Art des militanten und exzessiven Nationalismus predigt, wird der Antisemitismus gleichsam automatisch mitgeliefert." Adorno, "Bekämpfung," 361.

82. Adorno credits the term *secondary anti-Semitism* to his colleague Peter Schönbach. The term is revived later on in the twentieth century to describe a form of anti-
Semitism caused by resentment over perceived ill-treatment of Germany as a response
to the Holocaust.

83. "Wirksam ist hier ein Projektionsmechanismus: daß die, welche die Verfolger
waren und es potentiell heute noch sind, sich aufspielen, als wären sie die Verfolgten."
Adorno, "Bekämpfung," 368. Adorno also says of the reversal of positions, "[S]ich als
Verfolgte darzustellen; sich zu gebärden, als wäre durch die öffentliche Meinung, die
Äußerungen des Antisemitismus heute unmöglich macht, der Antisemit eigentlich der,
gegen den der Stachel der Gesellschaft sich richtet, während im allgemeinen die Anti-
semiten doch die sind, die den Stachel der Gesellschaft am grausamsten und am erfol-

greichsten handhaben." Ibid., 363. The structural similarity of *ressentiment* and the logic of anti-Semitism is unmistakable here. Again, a dialectical reversal takes place, with the persecutor perversely perceiving his or her role as that of the victim.

84. Ibid., 381.

85. Adorno also writes, "Wirksame Abwehr des Antisemitismus ist von einer wirksamen des Nationalismus in jeglicher Gestalt untrennbar." Ibid.

86. Martin Walser, "Erfahrungen beim Verfassen einer Sonntagsrede," in *Die Walser-Bubis-Debatte: Eine Dokumentation*, ed. Frank Schirrmacher (Frankfurt am Main: Suhrkamp, 1999), 7–17.

87. For discussion of the role of political emotion in the debates, see A. Dirk Moses, *German Intellectuals and the Nazi Past* (Cambridge: Cambridge University Press, 2007), 254–62. For a comparison of the role of resentment for Walser and Améry, see Assmann, "Two Forms of Resentment."

88. Thilo Sarrazin, *Deutschland schafft sich ab: Wie wir unser Land aufs Spiel setzen* (Munich: Deutsche Verlags-Anstalt, 2010).

Index

Adenauer era, 19, 133, 178n58, 179n60, 186n22

Adorno, Theodor W., 137, 147, 186n22, 197n136, 224n89; on authoritarian personality, 15, 160, 235n54; critique of existentialism, 48; *Dialektik der Aufklärung* (Horkheimer and Adorno), 156–58, 163, 166; on existential philosophy, 190n51; *Group Experiment*, 160–65, 234n50; *Guilt and Defense*, 147, 162; *Minima Moralia*, 48; "Was bedeutet: Aufarbeitung der Vergangenheit?" ("What Does Coming to Terms with the Past Mean?"), 158–59, 178n55; "Zur Bekämpfung des Antisemitismus heute," 165

affect: and critical thought, 8; deconstructive approaches to, 175n40; excess of, 72; in postwar West German culture, 1–10, 115; responding to affect (emotional reflexivity), 4, 47, 115, 127; use of term, 11–17. *See also* emotion

affect theory, 13–14

"after Auschwitz," 148, 158, 186n22

Agamben, Giorgio, *The Coming Community*, 195n106

agonistic politics, 111

Agrarromantik, 75

Ahmed, Sara, 61, 182n77

Allied occupation: as agents of aggression, 82; anti-Semitism in, 94; atrocity campaign as anti-Nazi propaganda, 2–4, 9–10, 118, 133, 164, 169n2, 217n19; conflated with National Socialism, 152, 203n29; democratization, 15, 27, 53–55, 67–70, 130; denazification, 2–4, 9, 16, 26–29, 33, 37, 47, 53–55, 68–69, 184n17, 200n4; emotions of Allied soldiers, 68; and German political climate, 26; Mitscherlich's privileged status, 129–30, 132; punitive intentions of, 27, 33, 36–37; questionnaire on Nazi involvement (*Fragebogen*), 21, 28, 74, 77–78, 133; rape of German women by occupation soldiers, 179n60; reactions of Germans to, 30–31, 53–55, 68–70, 94, 105, 191n60; reeducation, 2–4, 6, 9, 16, 26–30, 33, 37, 47, 53–55, 69–70, 134, 142, 184n17; reports on student emotions in *Schuldfrage* lectures, 52–55

"America and American Occupation in German Eyes" (Muhlen), 79–80

Améry, Jean, 154–56, 232n24

amnesty, 134–35, 200n4

Ancient Judaism (Weber), 194n94

Anderson, Benedict, 147

anger, 55, 62, 98–99, 115–16

"Anklageschrift Nürnberg" (Heuss), 63–64

The Answers of Ernst von Salomon. See Der Fragebogen

anti-Americanism, 86, 94, 98, 166

anti-fascism, 114, 126, 148

anti-Semitism, 47, 56–58, 75–76, 199n143; attacks on Jewish synagogues and cemeteries, 159; emotional intersubjectivity of, 157–58; Night of Broken Glass (*Reichskristallnacht*), 89–90; and *ressentiment*, 72, 94, 150–51, 156–66; secondary, 167, 236n82. *See also* Jews

anxiety, 10, 20, 143

apathy, 7, 9, 55, 76, 130

Arendt, Hannah: affective attachment to Germany, 65; banality of evil, 50; on complicity, 36–37; correspondence with Karl Jaspers, 20, 23, 26, 28, 35–37, 47, 51–52, 60, 64–65, 188n39, 190n58; hyperbole, 36, 39; on Jaspers' German cultural identity, 45; on Jaspers' philosophy, 34–35; on lack of emotion in postwar Germany, 6, 72, 145; *Men in Dark Times*, 204n39; "Organized Guilt and Universal Responsibility," 25, 35–37, 39, 62, 89, 90, 95; "The Jew as Pariah," 194n94; on wartime and postwar Germany, 29, 49–50, 67

assimilation, 172n12

Assmann, Aleida, 63, 90, 155, 170n6, 182n7

atonement, 10, 44, 49, 155

Aufarbeitung, 159

Auf dem Weg zur vaterlosen Gesellschaft (*Society without the Father*, Mitscherlich), 137

Aus dem Wörterbuch des Unmenschen (From the Lexicon of the Inhuman, Sternberger), 149, 235n69

The Authoritarian Personality (Adorno et al.), 160, 235n54

autobiographies: nationalist sentiment in, 22. See also *Der Fragebogen* (von Salomon); nationalism

Baker, Gary, 227n117

Balint, Michael, 136

Ball, Karyn, 177n54

banality of evil, 50

Becher, Johannes R., 62–63

Benedict, Ruth, 63

Benjamin, Walter, 195n100

Berkeley group study, 160

Berlant, Lauren, 181n76

Berlin Republic, 129

Berlin *Widerstandskreis* (circle of resisters), 131

Berthold, Will, *Die wilden Jahre*, 209n79

Beyond Good and Evil (Nietzsche), 71

Biddiscombe, Perry, 201n4

Biess, Frank, 188n42, 219n38

Bildung, 28, 80, 183n11

bitterness, 63

Blücher, Heinrich, 47, 48–49

Böhm, Franz, 160, 162

Böll, Heinrich, 108, 136

Bourdieu, Pierre, 15, 174n29, 176n45, 192n76

Braun, Hanns, 88; "Die Studenten und die nationalen Ressentiments," 152–53

Brecht, Karen, 222n70

Brink, Cornelia, 2

Brown, Wendy, 231n22

Buber, Martin, 48, 232n24

Bubis, Ignatz, 167

Butler, Judith, 175n38, 180n61

Catholic Church, 81

Ceram, C. W., 211n105

change, 10, 21–22, 27, 50, 59, 125, 134

Chicago Daily Tribune, 104

Christianity, 72, 81

cinema: Deutsche Film-Aktiengesellschaft (DEFA), 18; UFA (film production company), 83–84, 206n49. See also Hollywood

Clark, Mark, 52–53, 55

Clay, Lucius D., 32–33, 184n17, 200n4

cognitive psychology, 12, 88, 174nn27–29

cognitive science, 10, 12, 153, 173n26

"Colburn Letter," 161–63

coldness (*Gefühlskälte*), 5, 8, 33, 39. See also emotional rigidity

Cold War, 55, 69, 149

collective guilt, 26–30, 36, 43, 95, 161, 185n20, 186n26; and "inability to mourn," 127; Jaspers' critique of concept, 40–41; and nationalism, 70

collective memory, 170n6, 207n61

collective "we," 117

The Coming Community (Agamben), 195n106

"coming to terms with the past." See *Vergangenheitsbewältigung*

"common man," 35

communication (*Miteinanderreden*), 34–35, 39, 42–44, 48

complicity: Arendt's concept of, 36–37; disavowal of, 151; Jaspers' concept of,

40–42, 44; and "lesser of two evils,"
95; and shame, 61; US knowledge of
Nazi atrocities, 163; von Salomon's
disavowal of, 89–95
compromise actions, 141
concentration camps, 91–93, 99,
197n133, 217n19; German responses
to photographs of, 2–4, 9–10, 96, 118,
133, 164
conscience, 32, 80–81, 142–43; bad conscience, 95, 103
conservative revolutionaries, 20, 74–76,
116, 129, 131, 134
Cosgrove, Mary, 180n62
Counter Intelligence Corps (CIC), 52–53,
85
criminal guilt, 25, 31–32, 36–37
critical self-reflection. *See* self-reflection
Crum, Earl, 53
culpability, 30, 49, 51, 99, 119, 165,
207n66; individual, 44, 90, 96–97,
102. *See also* guilt
cultural pessimism, 132, 134–35
Curtius, Robert, 30
Cvetkovich, Ann, 170n7
cynicism, 7, 76–78, 85, 92, 97, 103, 105,
107, 109–10

Dagerman, Stig, *Germany in Autumn*,
7–9
Daily Boston Globe, 104
Darwin, Charles, 228n130
Das Amt (Conze, Frei, Hayes, and Zimmermann), 223n73
Das Landvolk, 75
*Das Ressentiment im Aufbau der Mo-
ralen* (Scheler), 72–73
Decline of the West (Spengler), 131
DEFA. *See* Deutsche Film-
Aktiengesellschaft
defense mechanisms, 10, 72, 103,
130, 151, 157–59, 162–63, 173n25,
220n42
defensiveness, 162–63, 166–67
Dehli, Martin, 131–32
demilitarization, 182n6, 190n60
democratization: emotional regimes and
norms, 106–7, 111, 123–24, 130, 134–
35, 167; Jaspers' approach to, 183n11;
Mitscherlich on, 116; and public de-

bate, 110–11; and *ressentiment*, 22–24,
69–70, 73, 110–11; role of Hollywood
films in, 6; US-Allied efforts, 15, 27,
53–55, 67–70, 130; von Salomon on,
100
denazification, 2–4, 9, 16, 26–29, 33, 37,
47, 53–55, 68–69, 184n17, 200n4; of
Heidelberg University, 28, 47, 56;
Mitscherlich on, 133; US-Allied questionnaire, 21, 28, 74, 77–78, 133 (see
also *Der Fragebogen*); von Salomon's
perspective on, 69, 74, 77–87
depression, 57, 118
Der Fragebogen (von Salomon): anti-
Americanism, 86, 94, 98; arrest and
incarceration by Allied forces, 76, 85–
86, 92, 98–99, 157; as autobiography,
4, 74; on conscience, 80–81; cynicism
of, 76–78, 85, 92, 97, 103, 105, 107,
109–10; on democracy, 100; form of,
76–77; on guilt, 81, 88–103, 109; hyperbole in, 78, 83, 86, 95, 98, 101; international reviews, emotions in, 104–
5; at Kölner Mittwochgespräche, 20,
107–11; manic tone, 97–98; on martyrdom of National Socialists, 102–3;
narrative voice and affect, 76–86; nationalism, 22, 75, 82; and National Socialism, 75–76, 80, 83–85, 207n66; nihilism in, 76–78, 80, 83, 92, 99–102,
106; on persecution of Jews, 89–96; on
political engagement in Nazi Germany,
83–85; popularity of, 103–4, 203n23;
reception and reviews, 20–23, 103–11,
149, 166; "Remarks" section, 85–86;
ressentiment, 23, 70, 86, 88–103, 154–
55, 162–63; community of, 105–7,
109–11; schoolboy analogy, 79–80;
shame in, 89–90; shirking responsibility, 79, 84; title of English version, 73–
74; on US-Allied denazification and
reeducation, 69, 74, 77–87; victimhood, 80, 82, 85, 88–103, 162; West
German reception of, 105–7. *See also*
von Salomon, Ernst
Derrida, Jacques, 110
"Der Wilde" (Seume), 59
despair, 62, 126
Deutsche Film-Aktiengesellschaft
(DEFA) film, 18

Dialektik der Aufklärung (*Dialectic of Enlightenment*, Horkheimer and Adorno), 156–58, 163, 165–66
dialogue, 42–43
Die Fähre, 133
Die freudlose Gesellschaft (1981), 167
Die neue Zeitung, 105
Die Schuldfrage (*The Question of German Guilt*, Jaspers), 1, 4, 17, 19–20, 25–27, 37–56; affective atmosphere in Germany, 33–34, 37–39; Cartesian view of emotion and reason, 38; categories of guilt, 25, 30–32; on collective guilt, 40–41; complicity (*Mitschuld*), 40–42, 44; as depolitical, 49–50; existence philosophy and guilt, 38–39; existential guilt, 44–45; German national identity, 39–41, 45–47; phatic communion, 42, 43; and *ressentiment*, 148–49; students at 1945/46 lectures, 26, 28, 30–32, 50–56; tone and rhetoric, 43; on US-Allied reeducation campaign, 215n8; written responses, 55–56. *See also* Jaspers, Karl
"Die Schuld und die Schulden" (Kästner), 185n20
"Die schwerste Stunde" (The darkest hour, Mitscherlich), 133
"Die Studenten und die nationalen Ressentiments" (Braun), 152–53
die Tat (the act/deed), 74–75
Die Unfähigkeit zu trauern. See *The Inability to Mourn* (Alexander and Margarete Mitscherlich)
"Die Unfähigkeit zu trauern" ("The inability to mourn," Moser), 125–27, 218n22
"Die Unfähigkeit zu trauern" (lecture, Mitscherlich), 138
Die Wandlung, 28–29, 35, 37, 149
Die wilden Jahre (Berthold), 209n79
Die Zeit, 120, 148
difference, 92, 110–11, 158
Diktat der Menschenverachtung (*Doctors of Infamy*, Mitscherlich), 132
Dirks, Walter, 64; "The Path to Freedom," 25
disavowal of guilt, 3, 23, 89–95, 151, 163; as morally reprehensible behavior, 122–23

discourse, 174n29, 229n140; common, 192n76
doubt, 20, 62

East Germany. *See* German Democratic Republic
economic miracle (*Wirtschaftswunder*), 23, 118, 120–22
Ehre (honor), 134
Ein Leben für die Psychoanalyse (A life for psychoanalysis, Mitscherlich), 135
Ekman, Paul, 176n41
elitism, 199n159
emotion: "after Freud," 10–17; binary of reason versus, 10, 38, 144–45; moral valence, 120–21; performative aspect of, 16–17. *See also* affect; politics of emotion
emotional ambivalence, 116, 140–43
emotional asceticism, 155
emotional communities, 16, 88, 174n29, 192n76
emotional counterregime, 26, 69
emotional habitus, 15, 27, 29
emotional inabilities, 5, 23, 139. *See also* "inability to mourn"
emotional intersubjectivity, 4, 20, 27, 47, 61, 115, 133, 145, 147, 167; of anti-Semitism, 157–58; dynamic aspect of, 10; of *ressentiment*, 157–58
emotional norms, 2, 13–20, 23–24, 27, 60, 69, 192n76; democratic, 106–7, 123–24; mourning as ideal, 23–24, 114–16, 120–22; and taboos, 139; in terms of morality, 133, 143
emotional reflexivity (affect responding to affect), 4, 47, 115, 127
emotional refuge, 15
emotional regimes, 15–16, 147, 167–68; of democratic guilt, 69–70; of democratic sentiment, 111, 123–24, 130, 135, 167; of National Socialism, 134; privileging reason over emotion, 145; psychoanalysis, 136; of US-Allied reeducation, 26, 134
emotional rigidity (*Gefühlsstarre*), 5, 122–23, 139, 145. *See also* coldness
emotional scripts, 17
emotional states, analysis of context and form, 16

emotional subjectivity, 174n28
emotional suffering, 88, 156
emotionlessness, 6–9, 17, 122, 141, 160
emotion studies: debates on binaries, 173n26; "the emotional turn," 10–17, 115
emotives, 17; defined, 12–13, 177n53
empathy, 24; in Freudian psychoanalysis, 119; lack of, in *Inability to Mourn*, 125–26; with Nazi victims, 113; West German lack of, 122, 130
Erfüllungspolitik (politics of appeasement), 74, 75
Erikson, E. H., 136
ethics, 44, 49–50
evil: banality of, 50; "lesser of two evils," 95
existence philosophy (*Existenzphilosophie*), 20, 28–31, 33–35, 37–38, 47–50, 184n14, 195n100
existentialism, 48, 63
existential spirituality, 47
"Experiences When Writing a Soap-Box Oratory" (Walser), 166–67

"fantasy of normalcy," 24, 181n76
fascism, 15, 26, 48, 156, 163, 165–66, 180n60; F-scale, 160
Faust (Goethe), 58–59
Fay, Jennifer, 6
fear, 39, 55, 96–97
Federal Republic of Germany: 1949 founding of, 69; economic reconstruction of, 23
Fehrenbach, Heide, 180n60
female subjectivity, 179n60
feminist theory, 202n19
Ferro, Marc, *Resentment in History*, 153
Fisher, Jaimey, 184n14
Fitzgibbon, Constantine, 82, 83
food availability, 32–33, 188n35, 188n37, 188n39
forgetting of guilt, 17
forgiveness, 230n2
Foucault, Michel, 192n76, 229n140
Fragebogen. See *Der Fragebogen* (von Salomon)
Frankfurter Hefte, 134
Frankfurter Rundschau, 128

Frankfurt School, 135, 137, 158, 160. *See also* Institute for Social Research
Frei, Norbert, 5, 27, 104
Freikorps (volunteer paramilitary organizations), 74, 76
Freimüller, Tobias, 220n51, 224n91, 224n94
"Fremdwörter," 190n51
Freud, Sigmund: *Civilization and Its Discontents*, 118–19, 131; cultural pessimism, 132; on melancholia, 118; on pathology of civilized communities, 113, 119; on taboo, 116, 139–43; *Totem and Taboo*, 116
Freudian psychoanalysis, 10–12, 24; empathic environment in, 119; return to Germany, 117, 125, 129, 136–37, 144; use in *Group Experiment*, 160
Friedlaender, Ernst, 148
frozen affect, 5–6. *See also* coldness; emotional rigidity
F-scale (fascism scale), 160
Fuchs, Anne, 181n62

Gadamer, H. G., 197n136
Gegengefühle (counterfeelings), 88
gender studies, 18
The Genealogy of Morals (Nietzsche), 70–71
"Generation des Unbedingten" (unconditional generation), 74, 132
genocide, 50; Jewish, 92, 109–10, 180n62. *See also* Nazi atrocities
German Democratic Republic (East Germany), 18, 56, 113, 126
Germanness. *See* national identity
"German question." See *Die Schuldfrage*
"German Reactions to Nazi Atrocities" (Janowitz), 9
Germans' emotional state and affective responses, 1–10, 19–24, 63–65; appropriateness or inappropriateness of, 8–10, 23–24, 25, 114–24, 126–27, 130, 145, 160; community of *ressentiment*, 105–11; effect of hardship and suffering on, 6–7, 32–33; emotionlessness, 6–9, 17, 122, 141, 160; in *Group Experiment* (1955), 160–65; guilt paradigm, 17; "inability to mourn" paradigm, 17–18, 115; Jaspers' depiction

Germans' emotional state and affective
responses (*continued*)
of, 33–34, 37–44; negativity in response to defeat, 40–41; as recalcitrant
or malicious, 119; as stagnant, 23; unconscious forces and, 141–42. See also
ressentiment; *specific emotions*
"German soul," 49
Germany: boundaries under Morgenthau
plan, 190n60; defeat as social crisis,
14; as guilt culture, 63; hardship and
suffering in postwar era, 6–7, 32–33,
55, 126, 152, 184n17, 188n35, 201n4;
in state of exception, 13, 134, 141;
unification, 129; zero hour, 13–14
Germany Abolishes Itself (Sarrazin),
167
Germany in Autumn (Dagerman), 7–9
Globke, Hans, 178n58
Goebbels, Joseph, 191n60
Goethe, Johann Wolfgang von, 45; *Faust*,
58–59
Goldhagen debate, 223n73
Gollancz, Victor, 232n24
"good Germans," 25, 45, 47, 60, 89
Görlitz, Walter, 108
Gotthelft, Ille, 83, 85, 89, 91, 95–98;
Jewish identity, 96
Gould, Deborah, 15, 27
Grass, Günter, 180n62
Green, André, 11–12
Green, Graham, 173n16
Gregg, Alan, 226n105
grief, 6, 16, 27, 98–99
Grimm, Hans, 83, 86, 99–100; *Volk ohne
Raum*, 205n44
Group Experiment (1955), 160–65,
234n50
Gruppe 47, antifascist works by, 114
Gruppenexperiment (*Group Experiment*,
1955), 160–65, 234n50
guilt, 9–10, 19–20, 24, 40–45; Arendt's
arguments on, 35–37; in artifacts of
Nazi past, 114; consciousness of, 143;
criminal, 25, 31–32, 36–37; disavowal
of, 3, 23, 89–95, 122–23, 151, 163;
emotional regimes of, 69–70; forgetting of, 17; individual, 43; Jaspers'
categories of, 25, 30–32, 81, 94; juridical, 94; moral, 25, 32, 37, 43; political,

25, 31–32, 37, 191n71; in postwar
West Germany, 118, 120–23; rational
approach to, 26–27; rejection of, 166;
relationship between shame and, 62–
63, 89–90, 141–42, 170n6; and religion, 81; semantics of, 81; sociological analysis of, 160–63; survivor's
guilt, 29, 44; voicing, 27–31. *See also*
collective guilt; defense mechanisms;
Die Schuldfrage; metaphysical guilt;
ressentiment
Guilt and Defense (Adorno), 147, 162
guilt culture, Germany as, 63
guilt paradigm, 5, 17

Habermas, Jürgen, 35
habitus, 15, 174n29, 176n45, 192n76
Haffner, Sebastian, 224n89
Hake, Sabine, 180n60
Halpern, Ben, 194n93
Hartshorne, Edward Y., 28
hatred, 63, 96, 103
Heberle, Rudolf, 214n137
Heidegger, Martin, 48, 187n28, 190n51
Heidelberg University: denazification
and rebuilding of, 28, 47, 56; Depart-
ment for Psychosomatic Medicine,
136. See also *Die Schuldfrage*
Heimann, Paula, 136
Heimatfilme, genre of, 180n60
Hermand, Jost, 202n8
Hermlin, Stephan, 33
Heuss, Theodor, "Anklageschrift Nürn-
berg," 63–64
Heyer, Ralf, 76
Hildesheimer, Wolfgang, 180n62
Himmler, Heinrich, 224n89
Hinderer, Walter, 138
Historikerstreit, 223n73
Hitler, Adolf, 37, 92, 100–101, 105, 131,
233n36; as unmourned object, 113,
117–18
Hocking, William Ernest, 7–8, 67, 85
Hofstätter, Peter R., 164–65, 234n50
Hollywood: experimental film project on
anti-Semitism, 161; films used in de-
mocratization, 6
Holocaust. *See* Jewish genocide; Nazi
atrocities; Nazi past
Holocaust (television series), 114

honor/pride-disgrace ("Ehre/Stolz-
Schande") dichotomy, 63
Horkheimer, Max, 137, 147, 186n22,
197n136; *Dialektik der Aufklärung*
(Horkheimer and Adorno), 156–58,
166; *Group Experiment*, 161, 163
Hoyer, Timo, 138
Huber, Franz Josef, 187n26
humanism, 73, 100; cosmopolitan, 49,
59; existential, 45; and guilt, 44; universalizing, 62
humiliation, 153–54
hunger, 7, 32–33, 188n35, 188n37,
201n4
Hunger Winter (1946/47), 188n39,
196n122

identity politics, 153, 202n19
Ignée, Wolfgang, 117
imaginary community, 147, 163
immigrants of Turkish and Arabic backgrounds, 167
impotence, sense of, 153–54
"inability to mourn," 72, 126, 147, 167;
as lack of empathy with victims of National Socialism, 113; paradigm, 16–
18, 115; as slogan, 128, 138. See also
Inability to Mourn
The Inability to Mourn (Alexander and
Margarete Mitscherlich), 4–5, 16, 23–
24; anger in, 115–16; critiques of,
125–28; disappointment in, 115–16,
126; and emotional regime proper for
democracy, 123–24, 130; first-person
plural *wir* (we), 119–20; on guilt, 118,
120–23; Hitler as unmourned object,
113, 117–18; on inappropriate emotional comportment, 117–24, 130; lack
of empathy in, 125–26; "misreadings"
of, 113; moralizing tone, 124–28, 139,
143–45; politico-historical context of,
116–17, 129–39; *politische Affekte*
(political affects), 120; popularity of,
114, 124–25, 138–39, 221n65; psychological inaccuracies in, 116; resonance of title phrase, 138; *ressentiment*, 139, 144–45; on taboo, 139–43;
on unconscious processes, 122–23. *See
also* Mitscherlich, Alexander;
Mitscherlich, Margarete

indifference, 9, 50, 55
Institute for Social Research (Frankfurt),
136, 156–66, 186n22, 234n51. *See
also* Frankfurt School
Institut und Ausbildungszentrum für Psychoanalyse und Psychosomatik (Institute and Training Center for Psychoanalysis and Psychosomatics), 137
interiority, 97
International Military Tribunal, 94. *See
also* Nuremberg trials
irrationality, 33, 98, 189n42

Jackson, Robert H., 31
Janowitz, Morris, 169n2; "German Reactions to Nazi Atrocities," 9
Japan, as shame culture, 63
Jaspers, Gertrud, Jewish identity of, 45,
56–57, 61, 186n23
Jaspers, Karl: animosity toward, 58–59,
63, 65, 199n143; approach to democracy, 183n11; cognition/feeling binary,
60, 144; concept of communication
(*Miteinanderreden*), 34–35, 39, 42–44,
48–49; correspondence with Hannah
Arendt, 20, 23, 26, 28, 35–37, 47, 51–
52, 60, 64–65, 188n39, 190n58; *Die
Idee der Universität*, 183n9; emigration to Switzerland, 56–60, 63, 65;
emotional comportment, 26–28, 52–
53, 60–62, 65, 152; German national
identity, 39–40, 45, 65; guilt of passivity, 29; and Heidelberg University,
136; humanist understanding of guilt,
44–45; Mitscherlich's opinion of, 129;
Nazi persecution of Gertrud and Karl,
56–57, 197n133; in Nazi years,
186n23; as *Nestbeschmutzer*, 163;
newspaper clippings about Germany,
148, 178n58; "Philosophical Autobiography," 56; on psychoanalysis, 138;
radio and television appearances,
197n136, 198n143; rationality, 26, 33–
34, 42–43, 50, 52–53, 60–62, 64–65;
shame, 60–65; theological terminology, 192n79; transparency, 34–35. *See
also Die Schuldfrage*
Jenemann, David, 235n55
"The Jew as Pariah" (Arendt), 194n94
Jewish Frontier, 194n93

Jewish genocide, 92, 109–10, 180n62
Jews: blamed for Germany's "misfor-
tune," 167, 173n22; as "chosen people," 72, 194n93; deportation of Slovakian Jews, 102; discrimination against,
72; German responses to persecution
of, 9–10, 93–96; Gertrud Jaspers identity as, 45, 56–57, 61, 186n23; Holocaust survivors, 114; Ille Gotthelft's
identity as, 96; Nazi persecution of, 9,
56–57, 89–93, 93–96, 207n61; outsider
status of, 46; and *ressentiment*, 72,
150–51. *See also* anti-Semitism; genocide; victims of National Socialism
Joint Chiefs of Staff Directive 1067 (US),
27, 33, 182n6
Journal of Modern History, 104
Jung, C. G., 185n20
Jünger, Ernst, 74–75, 86, 110, 131
Jureit, Ulrike, 224n89, 224n91
juridical guilt, 94
justice, 36, 94, 106; transitional, 153. *See
also* Nuremberg trials

Kalow, Gert, 227n124
Kant, Immanuel, 34, 127
Kapczynski, Jennifer, 29
Kaschnitz, Marie-Luise, 29
Kaster, Robert, 173n26, 177n52
Kästner, Erich, "Die Schuld und die
Schulden," 185n20
Kauders, Anthony D., 177n54
Keilson, Hans, 114
Kiesinger, Kurt Georg, 198n143
Kneip, Jakob, 107–8
Kollektivschuld, 27. *See also* collective
guilt
Kölner Mittwochgespräch (open public
forums), 20, 107–11
Korn, Salomon, 166–67
Kristallnacht (Night of Broken Glass),
89–90

Lacan, Jacques, 12
Lampl-de Groot, Jeanne, 136
Landvolkbewegung (farmers' move-
ment), 75–76
LaPlanche, J., 219n41
Lazarsfeld, Paul, 160
Lessing, Felix, 209n79

Lessing, Gotthold Ephraim, 34
Lethen, Helmut, 89
Leys, Ruth, 14, 173n26
liberation, 174n28
Linder, Martin, 206n55
Lippoldsberger *Dichtertreffen* (writers'
meeting), 83, 99
Lohmann, Hans-Martin, 128, 222n65,
222n71, 224n92
Lorre, Peter, 107
loss, category of, 18
Lowenfeld, Henry, 137
Löwenthal, Leo, 5–6
Lübbe, Hermann, 220n51
Ludin, Hanns, 86, 102–3, 211n105
Ludin, Malte, 211n105
Ludwig, Gerhard, 107–9
Luft, Friedrich, 105

malaise, 21
Mann, Thomas, 29, 45, 46
Marcuse, Herbert, 136, 137
Marek, Kurt W., 211n105
Massumi, Brian, 13–14, 176n45; *Para-
bles for the Virtual*, 14
Mayer, Hans. *See* Améry, Jean
Meinecke, Friedrich, 45
melancholia, 18, 118, 121, 126, 180n61
melancholic scholarship, 18, 115–16,
147, 215n8
memory contests, 181n62
memory studies, 170n6, 215n8
Men in Dark Times (Arendt), 204n39
metaphysical guilt, 25, 30, 32, 37, 44–45,
47–49, 190n52; and shame, 60, 62
Meyer-Gutzwiller, Paul, 35, 190n51,
197n136
Mielke, Fred, 222n65
militarism, 74
Minima Moralia (Adorno), 48
Minshall, T. H., 21; "The Problem of
Germany," 67–68
Mitgefühl (compassion), 121
Mitscherlich, Alexander: *Auf dem Weg
zur vaterlosen Gesellschaft* (*Society
without the Father*), 137; authorship of
The Inability to Mourn, 120; biographies of, 116, 128–29, 135; critique of
denazification and *Fragebogen* (questionnaire), 133; "A Defense against

Mourning" (lecture), 137; "Die schwerste Stunde" (The darkest hour), 133; "Die Unfähigkeit zu trauern" (lecture), 138; *Diktat der Menschenverachtung* (*Doctors of Infamy*), 132; *Ein Leben für die Psychoanalyse* (A life for psychoanalysis), 135; and Freudian psychoanalysis, 116–17; intellectual development, 130–37; on Jaspers' emigration, 57–58; on Jaspers' lectures, 55; as *Nestbeschmutzer*, 163; Peace Prize of German Book Trade, 128, 135; persecuted by Nazi regime, 129, 131, 226n105; political orientation, 130–37; postwar West German public persona, 116; psychoanalysis, involvement with, 135–37. See also *The Inability to Mourn*

Mitscherlich, Margarete, 113, 120, 126, 137–38. See also *The Inability to Mourn*

Moeller, Robert, 17

Mohler, Armin, 103

moral attribution, logic of, 159

moral guilt, 25, 32, 37, 43

morality, 71, 133

moralizing, 167

moral renewal, 28–29

moral time, 155

Morgenthau, Hans J., 104

Morgenthau, Henry, Jr., 190n60

Morgenthau Plan, 36–37, 189n39, 190n60

Moser, Tilmann, "Die Unfähigkeit zu trauern" ("The inability to mourn"), 125–27, 218n22

Moses, Dirk, 166

Mouffe, Chantal, 111

mourning, 18, 180n62; and emotional ambivalence, 142; as ideal normative emotional comportment, 23–24, 114–16, 120–22

Muhlen, Norbert, "America and American Occupation in German Eyes," 79–80

Münchener Merkur, 138

narcissism, 22, 117–19

narrative processes, 17

national identity, 40–41, 45–47, 113, 195n106, 205n44; and *ressentiment*, 150–52; stereotyping, 123

nationalism, 41, 45–47, 49, 63, 69–70, 98, 99–103; displacement of guilt with honor, 163; and racism, 167; and *ressentiment*, 152–53; and von Salomon, 22, 75, 82

national pride, 103, 152. *See also* nationalism

National Socialism (Nazism): affect channeled for propaganda purposes, 122; ideology, 33; indoctrination and propaganda, 47, 48, 51; NSDAP party members, 68, 84, 89–90, 102–3, 218n22; persecution of Alexander Mitscherlich, 129, 131, 226n105; persecution of Gertrud and Karl Jaspers, 56–57, 186n23, 197n133; rise of, 207n66; as rupture of communication, 39; SS officers incarcerated by US military, 86; whisper campaigns, 36–37, 99

National Socialist People's Court, 94

Nazi atrocities, 2–4, 9–10, 50, 89, 93–94; international responses to, 63–64; in medical profession, 130; US complicity with, 163. *See also* anti-Semitism; concentration camps; genocide; victims of National Socialism

Nazi past: amnesty for middle class, 134–35; approaches to, 5, 21–22, 113–14, 158–59, 177n54; denial of emotional participation in, 127; derealization of, 121–23; former officers returned to positions of power, 178n58, 198n143; former soldiers, 33, 44, 50–51, 152; German responses to persecution of Jews, 9–10, 93–96; public scandals related to, 223n73; as site of fascination, 50, 180n60, 195n111. *See also Vergangenheitsbewältigung* (coming to terms with the past)

negativity, 111

Negt, Oskar, 126

neoliberal capitalist society, 202n19

Nestbeschmutzer (bird who befouls his own nest), 130, 163, 235n69

neuroses, 139–43

New Objectivity, 89, 206n55

New York Times, 104
Nicolson, Harold, 104
Niekisch, Ernst, 129, 131
Nietzsche, Friedrich, 23; *Beyond Good and Evil*, 71; *The Genealogy of Morals*, 70–71; on punishment, 95; on *ressentiment*, 69–73, 86, 88, 96, 99, 103, 148, 150; on taboo, 145
Night of Broken Glass (*Reichskristallnacht*), 89–90
nonpublic opinion, 160, 162, 166
normative emotions. *See* emotional norms
normativity, 14–16, 19, 24, 181n76
NSDAP. *See* National Socialism (Nazism)
Nuremberg trials, 31, 63–64, 93–94; doctors' trial, 130, 132, 136

Observer, 104
Oels, David, 211n105
Olick, Jeffrey, 29, 153, 234n50, 235n54
OMGUS. *See* US Office of Military Government
Oppenheimer, Siegfried, 52
Organisation Consul (ultranationalist group), 74, 75
"Organized Guilt and Universal Responsibility" (Arendt), 25, 35–37, 39, 62, 89, 90, 95

Padover, Saul K., 54–55
Parables for the Virtual (Massumi), 14
paralysis, 39
pariah people (*Pariavolk*), 46, 194n94
passivity, 29, 90, 92, 95, 100, 102
"The Path to Freedom" (Dirks), 25
Peace Prize of German Book Trade, 128, 135, 166
Peitsch, Helmut, 63, 199n157
Penham, Daniel F., 52–53
Perrin, Andrew J., 234n50, 235n54
Petersen, Roger, 153
phatic communion, 42, 43
philosophy, 31
Pinkert, Anke, 18
Piper (publisher), 138
Plaas, Hartmut, 83
political guilt, 25, 31–32, 37, 191n71

politics of emotion, 14, 19–24, 38–39, 102, 111, 120–21, 130, 148, 168; as ethical challenge, 154–56
Pontalis, J.-B., 219n41
poststructuralism, 174n28
poverty, 32–33
power structures, reversal of, 153–54, 157–58
Prescott, Orville, 104
primal horde, 228n130
Princeton Radio Project, 160
"The Problem of Germany" (Minshall), 67–68
prohibitions, 140–45; productivity fueled by rebellion against, 145, 229n140
projection, 157–59, 162–63
"Protocols of the Elders of Zion," 233n36
Prussian nationalism, 74, 80, 89–90, 100–101
Psyche, 113, 125, 126
psychoanalysis, 174n29
public debate, 110–11. *See also* democratization
public opinion studies, 160–65
public sphere, 35, 101, 107–11, 164, 214n136
purification (*Reinigung*), 32, 38, 42, 47

Querido publishing house, 156
questionnaire, denazification. *See* denazification; *Der Fragebogen* (von Salomon)
The Question of German Guilt. See Die Schuldfrage

Rabinbach, Anson, 46, 187n28, 195n104, 222n70
Radio Basel, 35, 197n136
rage (*Wut*), 24, 33, 59, 126, 151, 157–58
rape, 179n60
Rathenau, Walther, 75
rationality, 20, 26, 33–34; as approach to guilt, 26–27; Jaspers', 26, 33–34, 42–43, 50, 52–53, 60–62, 64–65
Rauh-Kühne, Cornelia, 235n69
reading for emotion, 4–5, 10, 19, 22–24, 115, 143, 145, 148, 167–68; "feeling differently," 69–70, 111

reason versus emotion, binary of, 10, 38, 144–45
reconstruction (*Wiederaufbau*), 122. *See also* economic miracle (*Wirtschaftswunder*)
Reddy, William, 10, 12, 14, 26, 88, 123, 177n53, 182n3
reeducation: Jaspers on, 215n8; US-Allied occupation campaign of, 2–4, 6, 9, 16, 26–30, 33, 37, 47, 53–55, 69–70, 134, 142, 184n17; von Salomon on, 69, 74, 77–87
regret, 114
Reich, Wilhelm, 137
Reichskristallnacht (Night of Broken Glass), 89–90
Remer, Otto-Ernst, 105
remorse, 8, 120, 127, 139, 141–42, 173n25, 228n130
Remy, Steven, 28
reparation, 190n60, 202n19
repentance, 8
"Report on the Mood of Germany" (Stone), 53–55
repression, 17, 70, 122–23, 140, 143, 166, 177n54, 181n62, 229n140
Resentment in History (Ferro), 153
responsibility, 9, 163, 185n20; individual, 32, 91; and political statement addressed to victims, 49–50; von Salomon's shirking of, 79, 84
ressentiment: affective structure of, 70–73, 148–50; afterlife in postwar Germany, 166–68; and anti-Semitism, 72, 94, 150–51, 156–66; characteristic qualities of, 153–54; community of, 105–11, 168; defensive displacement, 154–55; definitions of, 149–51; and democratization, 22–24, 69–70, 73, 110–11; in *Der Fragebogen* (von Salomon), 23, 70, 86, 88–103, 105–7, 109–11, 154–55, 162–63; English and French definitions, 229n2, 230n11; historical contexts, 153; Jewish, 72, 150–51; motility of, 162; and national identity, 150–52; negative emotions and, 43; Nietzsche on, 69–73, 86, 88, 96, 99, 103, 148, 150; as perverted guilt, 69; reverse logic of, 165; toward Allied victors, 15–16, 22–24, 69; to-ward Jaspers, 26; and victims of National Socialism, 151–55, 159
restitution, 190n60
revenge, 38, 42–43, 71–73, 86, 103, 232n22
reversal of power structures, 153–54, 157–58
Rheinische Merkur, 58
Riefenstahl, Leni, *Triumph of the Will*, 90
Ringer, Fritz, 199n159
Rockefeller Institute, 136
Roehm, Ernst, 86
Rosenwein, Barbara, 10, 16, 88, 177n52, 192n76
Rote Kapelle resistance network, 83
Rowohlt, Ernst, 23, 75–76, 84, 110, 212n113
Rowohlt Verlag (publishing house), 73, 75, 211n105
rue, 7–8, 114, 126, 141–42

Salon Salinger, 86
Sarrazin, Theo, *Germany Abolishes Itself*, 167
Schallück, Paul, 108
Schaper, Edzard, 108
Scheler, Max, *Das Ressentiment im Aufbau der Moralen*, 72–73
Schmid, Carlo, 108
Schmidt, Hannes, 107
Schneider, Christian, 114, 126–28, 221n55
Schneider, Kurt, 136
Schönbach, Peter, 236n82
Schücking, Nikolaus, 107
Schuldfrage. See Die Schuldfrage (The Question of German Guilt, Jaspers)
Schultz, Egon, 227n117
Schulz, Hermann, 138
Schulze-Boysen, Harro, 83
Sebald, W. G., 180n62
Sedgwick, Eve Kosofsky, 175n40
self-reflection, 71, 80–81, 91, 173n25; critical, 10, 145, 158
self-reflexivity, 7, 59, 87, 117
sentimentality, 6, 62, 64, 182n76
Seume, Johann Gottfried, "Der Wilde," 59
sexuality studies, 18

shame, 20, 39, 60–65, 175n40; and complicity, 61; of Germany by Allied forces, 82; and guilt, 89–90; latent, 27; national, 152, 166; over persecution of Jews, 9–10; in postwar West Germany, 120–21, 126; relationship between guilt and, 62–63, 89–90, 141–42, 170n6; in response to atrocity images, 3, 10; structure of concealment and exposure, 61

shamelessness, 173n25

shock, 2–3, 63

Sigmund Freud Institute, 125, 126, 137

Simmel, Georg, 11

sixty-eight generation (1968), 132; student unrest in, 137, 224n92

Slovak Republic, 102

social crisis, and emotional norms, 14

sociology, 137, 160, 234n51

Sontag, Susan, 195n111

sorrow, 55, 88, 142

Spann, Othmar, 83

Spengler, Oswald, *The Decline of the West*, 131

Spruchkammern ("verdict courts"), 200n4

stagnation, 59

starvation, 32–33, 36, 99, 184n17, 188n35, 188n37

state of exception, 13

Stayer, Morrison, 33

Steiner-Sherwood, Melanie, 230n2

Sternberger, Dolf, 20, 28, 35, 52, 149–51, 154–55; *Aus dem Wörterbuch des Unmenschen* (From the Lexicon of the Inhuman), 149, 235n69

Stone, Shepard, "Report on the Mood of Germany," 53–55

Strachey, James, 11

Strasser, Otto, 106

students: at 1945/46 *Schuldfrage* lectures, 26, 28, 30–32, 50–56; emotional state of, 33–34; returned soldiers as, 33, 44, 50–51; unrest in 1968 generation, 137, 224n92

Stuttgarter Zeitung, 117

subjectivity, 174n28, 175n38; and political ideologies, 15; and social structures, 11

suicide, 33, 197n133

survivor guilt, 29, 44

Syberberg, Hans Jürgen, 167

taboo, 24, 116, 139–43, 145

terror, atomizing effects of, 5–6

Time, 104

Tomkins, Silvan S., 14, 176n41

totemism, 228n130

transitional justice, 153

trauma paradigm, 18

Treaty of Versailles, 75

Trevor-Roper, Hugh R., 21–22

Triumph of the Will (Riefenstahl), 90

truth (*Wahrheit*), 33–34, 38, 42

Turkish immigrants, 167

UFA (film production company), 83–84, 206n49

unconscious, 11, 121–22, 126–27, 150–51, 153, 157; desires and wishes, 139–45. *See also* taboo

Undset, Sigrid, 30

Unfähigkeit (inability), 118

Unfähigkeit zu trauern. See *The Inability to Mourn* (Alexander and Margarete Mitscherlich)

United States: incarceration of SS officers, 86; Joint Chiefs of Staff Directive 1067, 27, 33, 182n6; knowledge of Nazi atrocities, 163. *See also* Allied occupation; anti-Americanism

universalizing humanism, 62

University of Basel, 56–60

US-Allied occupation, German documents quarantined by, 21

US Office of Military Government (OMGUS): Law for Liberation from National Socialism, 200n4; surveys, 235n54

van Abbé, Derek, 104, 212n108

Vergangenheitsbewältigung (coming to terms with the past), 4–5, 17, 115–16, 158–59, 164, 215n8

victims of National Socialism, 29, 50, 106, 165; empathy with, 113; and *ressentiment*, 151–55, 159

victim status, appropriation of: appropriation of, 23, 71, 106, 167; as defense mechanism against unconscious guilt,

72, 157–59; identification with, 126; by von Salomon, 80, 82, 85, 88–103, 162. See also *ressentiment*

Volk ohne Raum (Grimm), 205n44

Vom Unglück und Glück in der Kunst in Deutschland nach dem letzten Kriege (Syberberg), 167

von Moltke, Johannes, 180n60, 235n55

von Salomon, Bruno, 75–76

von Salomon, Ernst: conservative political views, 74–76, 86, 99–101, 131; incarceration in Weimar era, 75, 92; militaristic books by, 75; scholarship on, 213n133. See also *Der Fragebogen*

von Stauffenberg, Claus Schenk, 224n89

von Weizsäcker, Viktor, 129

Walser, Martin, "Experiences When Writing a Soap-Box Oratory," 166–67

Walser-Bubis debate, 223n73

"Was bedeutet: Aufarbeitung der Vergangenheit?" ("What Does Coming to Terms with the Past Mean?," Adorno), 158–59, 178n55

Weber, Alfred, 29

Weber, Marianne, 32

Weber, Max, *Ancient Judaism*, 194n94

Weckel, Ulrike, 3, 10, 170n6, 173n25

Wehrmacht Ausstellung, 223n73

Weimar Republic, 74–75, 89, 100, 131, 132, 207n66

whisper campaigns, 36–37, 99

Wiederaufbau (reconstruction), 122. See also *Wirtschaftswunder* (economic miracle)

Wiedergutmachung (compensation), 29, 106, 155

Wildt, Michael, 74, 132

Winckler, Josef, 108

Wirtschaftswunder (economic miracle), 23, 118, 120–22

Wissenschaftspolitiker (politician on behalf of research), 135

Wolin, Richard, 186n23

woundedness, 153, 202n19

xenophobia, 167

Young-Bruehl, Elisabeth, 195n104

Zehrer, Hans, 83, 86, 207n66

Zeitdokumente, 4

Zeitgeist, 106

zero hour, 13–14

Zinn, Georg August, 137

"Zur Bekämpfung des Antisemitismus heute" (Adorno), 165

Printed and bound by CPI Group (UK) Ltd, Croydon, CR0 4YY

11/12/2024

14610122-0002